Contents

List of Illustrations

Preface

NO MILITARY STRATEGIST has ever been so quoted, and misquoted, as Carl von Clausewitz. His most famous *dicta* have been adopted by statesmen, including Lenin and Mao Tse-tung, as their own creations. Today in America the neo-Clausewitzians attempt to link his strategical thoughts to the terrifying theories of nuclear warfare. Yet while Clausewitz's *On War* is so well-known and has had such a profound effect upon military strategy throughout the world, until now his life has been allowed to remain obscure for most English-speakers, despite the vital inter-relationship between his experiences and his thoughts. This biography therefore attempts to describe his experiences, opinions and character, in such a way that the eventual appearance and content of *On War* may perhaps be better explained and understood. In the hope that readers will include those still unfamiliar with *On War*, a knowledge of Clausewitz's works is not taken too much or granted. Instead I have sought to offer as complete an account as possible of Clausewitz's writing, military career, and even his domestic life—although a major difficulty with the latter is the dearth of source material.

Without the help of my good friend Dr. Frederick Bechtle, this would have been almost impossible. The bombed and battered South Vietnamese jungles around Da Nang hardly seem appropriate for the start of a friendship which would lead to a biography of Clausewitz—and yet, perhaps, there is a certain relevance. Without Dr. Bechtle's rapid and generous acquisition of German source material for me, this account of his fellow-countryman's life would, at the least, have taken far longer.

Ever since Michael Howard was my first college tutor, I have numbered myself among his strongest admirers, both of his writing and his teaching, and I welcomed with extreme gratitude his consent to honour *Clausewitz* with his words. While working upon the manuscript I was conscious that he would eventually read it, and this feeling could only have been beneficial.

I owe my wife Betty a special debt of gratitude for her invaluable help. She managed far more than the typing and the encouragement which suffering wives often have to provide. Her translation of French material, her research for the maps, her critical examination of the manuscript and her subsequent suggestions—all these really invest her with a share of the authorship. Indispensable assistance also came from Ezra Jurmann, who gave so much help with German translation, and in such a short space of time. I apologize to him for my bullying demands and for recreating memories of school-lessons he would have preferred kept forgotten. My thanks also to Miss Linda Cicalese for her magnificent effort in obtaining illustrations, to Stella Robinson for her maps, to Yuri Dianov of the Russian Embassy in London, to the staff at the German Embassy in London and at the London Library, and to the Librarian at the Institute for Strategic Studies, London.

FOREWORD

Michael Howard

IT IS USUALLY said of Clausewitz, as of many other sages, that he is much quoted and little read. He has also been much abused and misused even by the few who have read him. He has been seen as a "militarist"; his famous epigram on war as a continuation of policy by other means being cited as a cynical justification of war. He has been condemned as the apostle of mass slaughter, the theorist whose influence was chiefly responsible for the dreadful holocaust on the Western Front in the Great War. Like Machiavelli before him he became a bogeyman in a European and American cultural myth; a myth which influenced international relations at least to the extent of fathering the Kellogg Pact of 1928, whereby the great powers solemnly foreswore war "as an instrument of policy" a mere decade before engaging in the greatest conflict in the history of mankind.

Since the Second World War the balance has been very largely redressed. Universities now recognise Clausewitz as a serious political as well as a military thinker, and he has his place in most courses on international relations. Several excellent abridgements of *On War* are now available, as well as studies of his writings by British, German and American scholars. His teaching indeed has been the point of departure for a whole generation of American thinkers, termed not inappositely by one of their critics "Neo-Clausewitzians," who have pioneered the serious study of the control of force in the nuclear age. One of them, Dr. Henry Kissinger, is at the moment of writing the Special Adviser of International Security to the President of the United States. Although Clausewitz is still for many hard-core liberals a profoundly suspect figure—and his contemporary disciples are still more suspect—his thinking today enjoys a degree of influence such as it has not possessed since the heyday of the Prussian General Staff in the latter years of the nineteenth century.

But Clausewitz as a man remains almost completely unknown. The description of him as "a Prussian General" conjures up for most people so stereotyped and disagreeable an image that Clausewitz's portrait usually comes as a pleasant surprise. The high forehead; the large, intelligent, rather mournful eyes; the sensitive and faintly humorous mouth: this might be a poet or composer of the early Romantic period rather than a man who had first put on uniform at the age of twelve and who served as a professional soldier from beginning to end of the Revolutionary Wars of 1792–1815. He was in no way a typical Junker: few of the men responsible for the reform of the Prussian Army and the salvation of the Prussian State were—least of all the great Scharnhorst whom Clausewitz served with such dedication. These were men who saved the Prussian monarchy in spite of itself; and as happens only too often in such cases, the monarchy once saved relegated them to positions of impotent obscurity.

Clausewitz, like his contemporaries in this most formative period of German history, has had his German biographers, though he has yet to receive the scholarly study devoted to his better-known colleagues Scharnhorst, Gneisenau, Boyen and Yorck. But as yet there has appeared no serious biography in English, and for this reason alone Roger Parkinson's book breaks important new ground. If it did nothing else, it makes available to the English-speaking reader a great deal of new information about Clausewitz's background, personality and intellectual development; and unless we understand the circumstances of his life we are likely radically to misinterpret his teaching. But even for those who have no interest in his writings, the life of a man who first smelled powder before his 'teens, who was swept up in the rout of Jena in 1806 and then helped to negotiate Prussia's change of allegiance, and who finally took part in the three years of battle which reached its climax at Waterloo—such a life is worth the writing; and Mr. Parkinson deserves our gratitude for undertaking it.

Military biographies can be insufferably dull, and a depressingly high proportion of them are. This is not one of them. Mr. Parkinson shows a sensitive understanding of Clausewitz's personality and a thorough grasp of the background, political and military, against which he moved. He obtrudes neither his comments nor his opinions, but allows the tremendous drama of the times to unfold at its own speed. Quite how tremendous that drama was, it is very easy for us to forget; and it is good to be reminded that Europe has been through earlier upheavals which have unleashed new forces, swept away old landmarks, and compelled men to reconsider their basic political and social loyalties, even before our own troubled century.

There is one aspect of this book which should be of particular value to the British, if not to the American reader; and that is the full and vivid account it gives of the Wars of Liberation in Germany in 1813–1814. British military historians, with a very few honourable exceptions, tend to concentrate exclusively on the activities of the British Army during the Napoleonic Wars, which as a result consist for them all too often simply of the Peninsular campaigns and the Battle of Waterloo—and a very restricted view of Waterloo at that. But the climax of those wars was reached in military campaigns fought by Continental armies numbering hundreds of thousands in a huge theatre extending from Moscow to the Rhine. The British did no more than pin down and defeat a segment of the French Army in Spain before arriving to assist in administering the *coup de grace* at the very end; rather like the Americans in France in 1918. Mr. Parkinson's account of the succession of merciless battles from Borodino to Waterloo, of the ghastly bloodshed they involved on an unprecedented scale, rubs our insular noses in the full horror and grandeur of the Continental experience; one which was to dominate the European consciousness until it was eclipsed, a hundred years later, by yet more terrible events. This was part of the European experience which the British never shared. It is all the more important that we should understand it.

All Souls College, Oxford.

ONE

Apprentice of War

"The propositions of this book, with
their arch of inherent necessity, are
supported either by experience or by
the conception of War itself."
(Introduction to *On War*.)

I

IN THE LATE summer of 1792 a soldier and his youngest son passed through
the iron gates of the army garrison at Potsdam, a thriving country town
lying twenty miles from Berlin, the capital of Prussia. The soldier was
retired, his right hand shattered while fighting for Frederick the Great; his
twelve-year-old son was about to begin his thirty-nine years of military
service for the Fatherland which would lead him into battles still honoured
by European regiments today. And from his experiences, from war and from
study, would emerge his writing: over twenty-five years later, Major-
General Carl von Clausewitz began to draft *On War*, the most influential
work of military strategy of all time, and the most dangerous when
misunderstood.

Times were turbulent for Prussia. This embryo of modern Germany was
still locked in rivalry with Austria for the leadership of the Holy Roman
Empire, the loose collection of German states which was in danger of
disintegration. Above all, Europe was threatened by new forces and new
emotions, generated by the French Revolution which had erupted three
years before. Only a few weeks after the young Clausewitz had joined his
regiment at Potsdam, Prussia was to pit her outdated forces against the
armies of the French revolutionaries. She was to be allowed to emerge
unscathed. Yet warfare was changing, changing in a way unrecognized by
most Prussian leaders until it was too late. War with France broke out again
in 1806; Prussian soldiers marched shoulder to shoulder in rigid, archaic
formations upon the battlefields of Jena and Auerstädt to meet the seasoned,
flexible, and all-enveloping swarms of Napoleon's men. Even General von
Yorck, commander of Prussia's most mobile troops, went to the fight heavily
laden with three trunks, two crates, two baskets, two bedrolls and a
bedstead complete with mattress and bedding. The Prussian army believed

itself still to be the glorious weapon of Frederick the Great. But "Old Fritz" had been in his grave for twenty years, and his method of warfare had died with him.

The result of Jena and Auerstädt was total and humiliating downfall for Prussia's once-great army. Few countries have ever suffered a more crushing defeat. But a handful of men, including Carl von Clausewitz, now reformed and transformed the Prussian army while it was still pinned under Napoleon's heel. Revolutionized, it returned to the battlefield in 1813, 1814 and assisted the British in the overthrow of Bonaparte in the Waterloo campaign of 1815. In those few years of turmoil the Prussian army had embarked upon a road where the French army's peaked cap, the *képi*, would soon be replaced by the Prussian spiked helmet, the *pickelhaube*, as the most revered and feared symbol of European military might.

Carl von Clausewitz survived the most bloody battles of the Napoleonic struggle. He witnessed those massive changes which swept over the making of war during Europe's years of conflict; and he helped Prussia adapt to those changes in a way which would later make the name of Germany synonymous with militarism and the nation-in-arms. He also wrote a book which was to have a profound influence upon Generals and Statesmen in the nineteenth century, who believed it contained an infallible formula for victory: the use of huge armies hurled at "the decisive point." Military leaders were to be "intoxicated with the blood-red wine of Clausewitzian growth."[1] Colonel F. N. Maude, introducing the first English translation of his work in 1918, wrote: "It is to the spread of Clausewitz's ideas that the present state of more or less immediate readiness for war of all European armies is due."

The life of Carl von Clausewitz is the story of a Prussian soldier, who suffered in Prussia's disgrace of 1806; who, disgusted with his country's outmoded policies and leadership, served with Russia in the horrors of the 1812 campaign; and who returned for the final war against Napoleon in the towns and villages of Germany and Belgium. It is also the story of a book, the story of how one soldier used his experiences at Auerstädt and Borodino, the Berezina and Gross-Görschen, Ligny and Wavre, and blended them with his studies and observations to create the most powerful study of strategy of modern times, *Vom Kriege (On War)*. Yet Clausewitz the man was very different to Clausewitz the author. The author was called the "Apostle of Violence" and the "Mahdi of Mass" for declarations like these: "Let us not hear of Generals who conquer without bloodshed;" "The destruction of the enemy is the foundation-stone of all actions in war." As an author, Clausewitz was assertive, positive and entirely sure of himself.

But in private life Clausewitz was shy, nervous and insecure. Throughout his life he needed someone older to lean upon. First there was Gerhard Scharnhorst, the Hanoverian soldier who led the reorganization and reform of the Prussian army after the 1806 catastrophe. Then there was his

Above left *Carl von Clausewitz*
Above right *Marie von Clausewitz*
Right *King Friedrich Wilhelm II of Prussia*
(1744–97)

colleague August Gneisenau, Chief of Staff to Field-Marshal Lebrecht von Blücher in the Waterloo campaign. Clausewitz was a "quill-scribbler" and "ink-splasher," when such men were derided in the proud Prussian army, although he was also a brave soldier. He himself said: "I would rather have won fame at the front of a company of soldiers, with sword in hand."[2] "My life is a trackless existence," he wrote, when aged only twenty-seven. Twenty years later he was to believe he had been a failure. Carl von Clausewitz never fully belonged either to the dashing, duelling officer corps, or to the intellectual's world of philosophy and scholarship. He tried to combine elements of both and was left an outsider. He had to be a part of the great Prussian officer society, where the first qualification was to be a nobleman. As Frederick the Great had said: "The breed of the old Prussian nobility is so fine that it deserves to be preserved." Yet Clausewitz's own nobility was of such a weak and obscure origin that it was suspected to be fictitious. His nobility was not confirmed by the Prussian King (Friedrich Wilhelm III) until four years before Clausewitz died in 1831.

Lauded by the Germans after his death, Clausewitz was sometimes scorned and often ignored by fellow Prussians during his life. While he was writing his *Hinterlassene Werke*, the first three volumes of which were *On War*, he was believed to be closeted away, a secret alcoholic. Yet the man was indeed the author. This withdrawn and sensitive soldier wrote the words which one day helped to lead mass armies into a strategy of slaughter. *On War* is a unique work in the library of military strategy. Yet Carl von Clausewitz was a man who stood apart in the Prussian officer corps, not because of his brilliance, he simply did not belong.

II

In 1792, Carl von Clausewitz was accepted by the Thirty-Fourth Infantry Regiment (Prince Ferdinand) at Potsdam, and enrolled as an officer cadet. He was twelve years old. One reason for this early start to his military career was his father's lack of money, which made it difficult to keep him at home. Carl was lonely, but happy with his thoughts of the future. Twenty-nine years later he re-visited Potsdam as a Major-General, and wrote to his wife Marie: "I am well used to the fact that Potsdam always reminds me slightly of all kinds of serious and sad thoughts. It was always so. And it is natural enough, since I always feel strange and lonely here. I have returned to the house where I stayed with my father when he brought me for the start of twenty-nine years with the regiments. Not least, I have the highest feeling of gratitude for all the happiness which Fate has given me since that time."[3] So Clausewitz, a slightly-built, reddish-haired, good-looking young boy, entered the world of swaggering Prussian noblemen with their battle memories and endless talk of glorious campaigns in the Seven Years' War.

Indeed, the Prussian army thought very highly of itself, and arrogance

Facing page *A ball in Berlin in 1790*

was a prime characteristic of the officer corps. Duelling continued to be common, despite the issue of a civil code in 1785, which threatened heavy penalties for those who duelled, and which placed cases of alleged personal insult before a civilian tribunal of honour.[4] The Prussian army would have nothing to do with this. The regiments considered they should hold their own tribunals. The officer corps believed it had the right to expel undesirables, a category which included any gentleman who refused to defend his honour. The maimings and deaths from duelling continued, an integral part of the semi-independence of the aristocratic officer class.

This *élite* group, of which the young Carl was soon to be a full member, was extremely inward-looking. It was disliked by the mass of the Prussian population, from whom it was separated by class and conduct. "The army was no more that finely disciplined phalanx bequeathed by Friedrich II, but was corrupted by the example of its sovereign," wrote an anonymous observer in Berlin to a friend in London. "Discipline was totally relaxed. There was no subordination; the officers in general were a scandal to their profession. They thought of nothing but feasting, drinking, wenching, gambling, and all the vices which attend debauchery and intrigue."[5] There is no evidence that the Regiment Prince Ferdinand differed from other army units. It certainly believed rigidly that only noblemen could be officers. At the head of the army stood the King, Friedrich Wilhelm II, a pale successor to his father, Frederick the Great, and on the verge of being ruined by his dissipation. "He totally neglected all business in the Cabinet," complained the anonymous correspondent. "His sole enjoyment was dally-ing with an opera dancer, who did all she could to make his time pass agreeably. His favourite procuress, Mrs. Rietz, he had raised to the rank of Countess of Lictenau . . . She so studied his taste, that she always previously initiated the fresh victims of his love in those mysteries she knew to be the most gratifying."[6]

The Clausewitz family's claim to nobility rested upon an ancestor in the dim Silesian past, Ernst Friedrich Baron von Clausewitz. The *von*, denoting nobility, had been dropped according to later members of the family when the Baron's descendants had entered the religious and teaching professions. This claim that one's forbear had relinquished the *von* prefix, in order to preach or teach, was used by many other would-be noblemen. It was used for example by Baron von Steuben, who had sailed to the Thirteen Colonies to help the Americans fight for their independence from the British in 1777, and by General von Yorck, the future commander of the Prussian army in the 1812 campaign. Nevertheless, the Clausewitz nobility did not have the firmest of foundations. Members of the family did not possess country estates and did not form part of the senior country aristocracy. They were little more than *Nominaladel*, noble in name only. It was barely sufficient for entry into the officer corps.

Only during Carl's father's lifetime had the Clausewitz family started to select military service as a career for its sons. Carl's great-great-grandfather had fled into Saxony at the time of the Thirty Years' War (1618–48). His son, Johann Carl Clausewitz, at that time without the *von*, was born in 1663. He became a schoolmaster in Wittenburg in 1691. The same year he was appointed priest at Gross-Wideritzsch near Leipzig, where he married his predecessor's daughter, Johanna. The only child of this marriage was Benedictus Clausewitz, whose surname was sometimes spelt without the "e." After 1703 Benedictus, Carl's grandfather, attended classes at Leipzig, where his fine brain soon began to show its capabilities. He studied Latin, Greek, Hebrew, and then went on to Leipzig University in 1708, where he studied Syrian, Arabic, French, Italian and English. In 1723 Benedictus took over his father's old position at Gross-Wideritzsch, staying there until 1732. In 1738 he became Professor of Theology at Halle University. He wrote eleven important theological treatises, nine in Latin and two in German.

While he was the incumbent at Gross-Wideritzsch he had married Christine Marie. They had nine children, one daughter and eight sons, but the daughter and three sons were stillborn. The five remaining boys went into a variety of professions; none of them chose the army. Carl's grandfather's first marriage had a tragic ending. In 1737 at Merseburg, while giving birth to a son, who was stillborn, his wife died. Benedictus' old mother, who was present, was so shocked that she too died. So his wife, son and mother were buried in the same vault. Not long afterwards, just before he made his academic reputation at Halle, Benedictus married Fredericka Juliana Kirsten, the eldest daughter of a church official. Three sons were born from this marriage; two of them died in infancy. The survivor was Friedrich Gabriel, Carl's father.

So far the Clausewitz family had never considered the army as a career. But Friedrich, born in Halle on 13th February, 1740, was only nine years old when Carl's grandfather died, and he chose the profession of his mother's second husband, a Major in the Regiment Eichenau. The *von* was adopted, and from then on the name Clausewitz would be closely linked with the Prussian, and later the German, army. Only one of Friedrich's four sons, Gustav, did not go into the army, starting instead by studying theology and then taking a career in public administration. And of Carl's nephews, nine out of the ten joined the army. Friedrich fought in the Seven Years' War (1756–63) as a Lieutenant in the Regiment Nassau-Ufingen, but had to leave military service after his right hand had been crippled by a battle wound. He was provided with a civilian post as Royal tax collector in Burg in 1767, with a salary of three hundred thalers a year, not a high sum. He married Fredericka Schmidt, daughter of a civil servant, and they had four sons and two daughters, all born in Burg: Gustav, Friedrich, Wilhelm, Charlotte, Carl and Johanna. Carl was born on 1st June, 1780.

The change from academic to military streams was nowhere more striking

than in Carl's small, scantily furnished childhood home at Burg, not far
from Magdeburg. His father, a sociable man who disliked his employment
as a tax collector, still had many friends in the army; he had been only
twenty-seven when obliged to retire from it. Often these former colleagues
came to the house to talk over old times and discuss the latest military
topics. It was in this atmosphere of soldier's tales that Carl grew up. His
education at the local school was deficient; by the time he was twelve he
only had "the rudiments of Latin." This alone marks the difference between
his upbringing and those of previous generations of Clausewitz children.
Instead of table-talk on religious and academic subjects, he listened to
discussions and gossip about manoeuvres, about the personal merits of this
or that officer. Carl, who throughout his life preferred to listen rather than
talk, absorbed it all.

It was hardly surprising that the three Clausewitz brothers took up the
army as a career. Friedrich, or Fritz, the second son, born in 1771, was the
first to join. The eldest, Wilhelm, followed in 1787, and finally Carl, in
1792, an added reason in his case being the poor state of the family finances,
as the father was finding it increasingly difficult to manage on his three
hundred thalers a year. After Friedrich's death in 1802 Carl's mother was to
find life an even harder struggle, existing on a basic pension of fifty thalers,
in addition to whatever her sons could give her. Nor were the sons free from
money worries. Carl's sister Johanna died unmarried, while Charlotte
married an army Captain, who was also a Count. The three brothers were
very different to one another. Fritz was a "soldier's soldier," hardheaded,
an excellent leader of men, and uneducated except in practical military arts.
Wilhelm, like Carl, took it upon himself to increase his general education
and attended university lectures at Breslau. But he was also an excellent
field commander, much respected by his men, and a courageous fighter.
Owing to his obvious intelligence he was engaged in staff work for some
periods of his career; and he disliked it. He always wanted to rejoin his
troops and the line units.

Carl on the other hand was chiefly engaged in staff work throughout his
career—although not without regrets that this occupation, while still expos-
ing him to the dangers of battle, meant less chance of glory gained leading a
line regiment. "Of all the noble feelings which fill the human heart in the
exciting tumult of battle, none, we must admit, are so powerful and
constant as the soul's thirst for honour and renown," wrote Clausewitz in *On
War*.[7] Carl was the opposite of Fritz, and Wilhelm stood halfway between
the two. Yet all three were to rise to the high rank of General: Carl and
Wilhelm to Major-General and Fritz to Lieutenant-General. All three were
to fight in the major campaigns of those hectic years, at one point on
different sides; and all three were to prove themselves in combat.

So Carl, as a twelve-year-old cadet, had two advantages when he joined
his regiment that morning in 1792 at Potsdam. First, there was the presence

in the regiment of his elder brother Wilhelm, who had begun his military career five years before at the age of fourteen, and who was now a Second-Lieutenant. Second, there was his upbringing. But for the moment, Carl was not a fully-fledged member of the regiment's officer corps. Following the standard practice he became a kind of special non-commissioned officer, a *Fahnenjunker*, or flag officer, roughly equivalent to a corporal. It was his duty to carry the small regimental standard during marches. In this way he was to serve his apprenticeship in war.

Nor would Carl's first experience of battle be long in coming. The French Revolution had been watched with delight by many Germans until it turned sour; and a defensive alliance against France was signed by Austria and Prussia in February, 1792. On 20th April the French legislature replied by voting for a declaration of war against Austria. This was the start of twenty-three years of almost unbroken warfare in Europe, in which Carl von Clausewitz and his two officer brothers were to be fully involved. Initially, the war aroused little enthusiasm in Prussia. But in July, 1792, just before Carl arrived at Potsdam, the allied army finally started out from Koblenz on its march for Paris, led by the Duke of Brunswick. After suffering disease, demoralization, and the cannonade at Valmy on 20th September, it turned back to retire behind the Rhine.

The French followed with an army under General Custine. One city after another was taken in the vulnerable area of small German principalities along the River Rhine. Speyer fell on 30th September, Worms on 4th October, and a French detachment even occupied Frankfurt for five weeks. But the surrender of Mainz was the biggest prestige gain for the French. As the historian Thomas Carlyle put it, Custine's troops were "not uninvited."[8] Men and women in the city flocked to sign the Red Book provided for citizens to mark their allegiance to the Revolution. A Tree of Liberty was planted. Some who could have gone stayed for the excitement. "Fancy, if I could tell my grandchildren that I lived through a seige!" wrote Caroline Michaelis, a guest of the German scholar Georg Forester who had come out openly in support of the French. Caroline soon succumbed to the advances of a French officer and was packed off with a baby in disgrace.[9] The task of driving the French from Mainz was given to a Prusso-Austrian army, again led by the Duke of Brunswick. Attached to the army was the infantry Regiment Prince Ferdinand, one of whose battalions included Wilhelm and Carl von Clausewitz. The regiment marched out from Potsdam in early 1793. At the same time Prussia and Austria issued an appeal to German patriotism. "The Fatherland is in danger. The constitution, religion, property, tranquillity—all are menaced by near ruin. The bloody projects of the French are unveiled."[10]

So Clausewitz went to his first war. According to a French biographer: "When passing through villages the inhabitants would stare in amazement at the sight of the small boy bent under the weight of the colours."[11]

III

Germans were looking upon the French Revolution with increasing disfavour. The horrors of the Jacobin Terror were rapidly over-shadowing the
glory of France. In March, 1793, the German Empire as a whole finally
declared war on this nightmare, so enabling Saxon, Palatinate and Hessian
troops to join the Brunswick army for the seige of Mainz. At the city, a
French force of 23,000 had been gathered under the intelligent command of
General D'Oyré. Before the German army arrived fortifications had been
built, and existing ones strengthened, in the city itself, at the bridgehead at
Castel, and on the Rhine islands, especially those of Petersau and the
Ingelheimer. The town of Weissenau was also in French hands.

The allied force began to arrive in late March. The seige opened on 1st
April but for the first two weeks events were quiet. The Prusso-Austrian
army took up positions on the right bank of the Rhine, with its headquarters
at Gustavsburg, the rat-infested and dilapidated fort built by King Gustavus
Adolphus of Sweden. The Prussians were deployed along the River Main
towards Kostheim, threatening Weissenau and Castel. The Regiment Prince
Ferdinand and the other infantry units were fully occupied digging ditches
and throwing up earthworks. Gradually the whole countryside was covered
and scarred with the apparatus and debris of war. Goethe, who was present,
told the author Nicholas Vogt: "My friends can be thankful not to witness
the misery in this part of the world and in unhappy Mainz."[12]

On 14th April, hostilities began on the two sides of the river. Both
besieged and besiegers sent out raiding parties, which clashed in short but
bloody skirmishes. Carl was based at the regimental headquarters, still a
Fahnenjunker. As part of his duties he had to visit the sick and wounded in the
crude field hospitals, after which he made a report to the *Fahnrich*, or flag
officer, then to the duty Lieutenant and finally to the duty Captain. He was
sent scurrying through the communication trenches carrying messages,
engrossed by it all. If the sight of the wounded affected him during his visits
to the casualty stations, Carl made no mention of it in his writings. On the
contrary, he was enthralled by the noise, the smoke and confusion, the
glimpses of the enemy not far away in their own positions. Like most soldiers
who come under fire for the first time, he was excited by the danger and
convinced that he himself would not be hit.

In *On War* he described the feelings of a novice in battle, and the sights
and the awareness of personal danger, all of which he experienced before
the French at Mainz. "Usually before we have learned what danger really
is, we form an idea of it which is rather attractive than repulsive," wrote
Clausewitz. "Let us go with the novice to the battlefield. As we approach,
the thunder of the cannon becoming plainer and plainer is soon followed by
the howling of shot. Balls begin to strike the ground close to us, before and

behind. We hurry to the hill where the General and his Staff stand. Here the close striking of the cannon balls and the bursting of shells is so frequent that the seriousness of life makes itself visible through the youthful picture of imagination. Suddenly someone known to us falls—a shell strikes among the crowd and causes some involuntary movements. We begin to feel we are no longer perfectly at ease and calm. Even the bravest is at least to some degree worried." Clausewitz continued: "Grape rattles on the roofs of the houses and in the fields. Cannon balls howl over us, and plough the air in all directions, and soon there is a frequent whistling of musket balls. A step farther towards the troops, to that sturdy infantry which for hours has maintained its firmness under heavy fire. Here the air is filled with the hissing of balls which announce their proximity by a short sharp noise as they pass within an inch of the ear, the head, or the breast. To add to all this, compassion fills the pounding heart with pity at the sight of the maimed and fallen."[13]

On 18th June the allied guns which were massed on the right bank of the Rhine opened up with a large-scale bombardment of the city. The effect was terrible. It was the first time Clausewitz had seen and heard cannon fired in anger. He was to know this experience many times again, and be subjected to it himself. But never again did he see the army in which he served deliberately set out to destroy a city. The thundering guns, screaming shells, violent explosions, were all branded upon his memory. Fire swept through the wooden houses of Mainz, and flames leapt up to the thick black cloud which hung over the streets. "Every heart was burdened with sadness," wrote Goethe in his book *The Siege of Mainz*. "Every moment one was filled with anxiety for one's dearest friends, and one forgot to think of one's own safety. As if enchanted by the threatened confusion, one rushed to the danger points and let the cannon balls fly over one's head and burst by one's side. For the gravely wounded one wished speedy release. And the dead one had no wish to recall to life."[14] But to the schoolboy Clausewitz, it was a magnificent spectacle. "I stayed while Mainz was being burned to the ground in the fire we had started," he wrote later. "I added my childish shout to the triumphant cheers of the soldiers."[15] But despite the cannonade the tenacious French garrison still refused to surrender.

Carl's twenty-year-old brother Wilhelm distinguished himself during the siege, showing that bravery and coolness which marked him as an excellent field commander. One French sortie surprised the Prussian outpost where he was on duty, and for a while it seemed as if his position would be overrun. But with characteristic calmness, Wilhelm helped to reorganize the men, and the Prussians were able to throw back the French. His action was brought to the notice of King Friedrich Wilhelm who was attending the siege, and young Wilhelm was taken to see him. As a reward the King granted Wilhelm's two sisters, Johanna and Charlotte, the expectancy of rents from property at Neuenberg and Marienborn. But the ladies found it difficult to collect the money. Not until thirty years later did Wilhelm, by then a Major-General serving at the War Ministry, manage to secure an annual pension of two hundred thalers for the surviving sister, Johanna.

On 20th July, 1793, with the siege still in progress, Carl von Clausewitz was promoted to full officer rank, becoming an ensign or *Fahnrich*. He no longer had to carry the flag, but served and fought on horseback like every officer, and wore the same uniform as the others; since the days of Friedrich Wilhelm I all Prussian army officers from *Fahnrich* to Field-Marshal wore the same tunic, except that generals also wore distinctive braid and plumage.

Two days after Carl's promotion, with rising prices threatening a famine, no fodder for the horses and no medicine for the sick and wounded, the fortress of Mainz at last surrendered. According to the surrender terms signed at the Marienborn camp, the French general and defending army received a free pass with full pardon in recognition of their courage; issued on condition they agreed not to serve against the allies for one year. Karl Freiherr von Stein, the future Prussian Minister, constitutional reformer and friend of Clausewitz, described the events in a letter to Frau von Berg. "I came back to Mainz to witness the surrender of the town and the departure of the garrison," he said. "The expression of licence, stolid insolence, immorality, on the faces of the garrison as they marched out was insufferable; and there was not one face among them which one could easily look at. The town itself showed many outward signs of devastation. The insides of the houses were almost universally ruined, and a disgusting degradation seemed to me stamped on the faces of most of the women."[16] Stein was biased. He admitted another time that he "hated the French as much as a Christian can hate." So, for most of his life, did Clausewitz.

But Goethe also described the scene, in terms not too dissimilar: "Escorted by the Prussian horse came first the French garrison. Nothing could look stranger than this latter: a column of Marseillese, slight, swarthy, multi-coloured, in patched clothes, came tripping on, as if King Edwin had opened Dwarf Hill and sent out his nimble host of dwarfs." Goethe continued: "Next followed regular troops, serious, sullen, not as if downcast or ashamed. But the most remarkable appearance, which struck everyone, was that of the *chasseurs* coming out mounted. They had advanced quite silent to where we stood, when their band struck up the *Marseillaise*. This revolutionary *Te Deum* has in itself something mournful and bodeful, however briskly played; but now they gave it in altogether slow time, proportionate to the creeping step they rode at. It was piercing and fearful, and a most sombre thing, as these cavaliers, long, lean men, of a certain age, with mien suitable to the music, came pacing on. Singly, you might have likened them to Don Quixote. *En masse* they were highly dignified."[17] This was Clausewitz's introduction to the men he would consider as his enemy for most of his life.

He went into Mainz to see the destruction that the allied army had caused. Whole streets were filled with rubble and charred timbers, still smoking. There was a stench of sickness and death. Goethe also explored the city and described its terrible condition. "What centuries had constructed was now in ruins and ashes," he wrote. Mobs ran loose, looting the houses of those who had supported the enemy. French losses at Mainz were estimated to be over 5,000 dead, wounded and missing. Allied casualties were high for a besieging force—over 3,000. But the Prusso-Austrian army was still intact, despite signs of dissension among its leaders. Here was an excellent opportunity to strike west, deep into the heart of France herself. The chief obstacle in the way of a successful allied offensive into Alsace seemed more geographical than military: the high and difficult Vosges mountains. The Regiment Prince Ferdinand marched west with the rest of the victorious army. But things were far from satisfactory. Brunswick's force suffered from Prusso-Austrian political arguments, and from lack of mutual confidence among the commanders from the two countries. A large-scale offensive was not therefore carried out. Long periods were spent in the mountains, where the allied soldiers felt extremely vulnerable to enemy ambushes. Clausewitz wrote in *On War*: "When a column, winding like a serpent, toils its way through narrow ravines up to the top of a mountain, and passes over it at a snail's pace, artillery and train-drivers with oaths and shouts flogging their over-driven cattle through the narrow rugged roads, each broken wagon having to be got out of the way with indescribable trouble, whilst all behind are detained, cursing and swearing, then everyone thinks to himself, 'Now if the enemy should appear with only a few hundred men, he might rout us all.' "[18]

It was a frustrating period for the young Clausewitz. He learned a lesson which was to be underlined time and again throughout his life: without the correct political basis, an army can never be fully effective, no matter how great the military potential might be. He also wrote in *On War*: "Prussia had neither anything to conquer nor to defend in Alsace—she continued the war with a feeling of very little interest."[19] In December, 1793, lack of proper Prusso-Austrian co-operation enabled Hoche to push the allies from the Palatinate position, and Brunswick's army began the withdrawal to the east bank of the Rhine; there were still no large-scale engagements. The last six months had been exhausting and disappointing for Clausewitz, and he wanted the campaign to be done with. Fourteen years later he described his feelings as the troops, weary and dirty, had crossed the last ridge of the Vosges and had seen the Fatherland before them. "Nothing is more impressive than the moment when you suddenly leave the mountains and see in front of you the green plain, magnificently revealed in all its richness. We had passed six months in the mountains, very wooded, rough, poor and gloomy. Finally, after a hard march, we found ourselves at the last ridge and there before us and far below was the glorious valley of the Rhine, from Landau to Worms." Clausewitz added: "In that moment I felt that life, until then serious and sombre, had become kind again . . . it was not just the spectacle, but also the circumstances."[20]

Meanwhile, events were swinging back into France's favour, both politically and militarily. Trouble threatened in Prussia's territory of Poland, far to the north-east. In spring, 1794, a general revolt erupted. The lower nobility, townspeople and clergy rose against their Prussian overlords, and troops quickly had to be moved to the area. As a consequence, Prussian participation in the Rhine campaign had to be reduced. The Regiment Prince Ferdinand was ordered into cantonments in Westphalia, where it would act as a reserve, and the long march north began for the Clausewitz brothers. While Carl was slowly winding his way up the picturesque Rhine valley, Prussian forces in Poland were showing ominous deficiencies, faults which would be largely ignored with disastrous results twelve years later. The Prussian army was by no means as mighty as it considered itself to be. Her commanders were not as skilled as their limited successes against the French had encouraged them to believe, and there were serious defects in the military administrative structure. French forces had meanwhile pushed to their country's "natural frontiers": the Pyrenees, the Alps, and the Rhine. In Paris, this was seen as far enough. The politicians were ready to talk peace.

As the military operations dwindled, Carl von Clausewitz went on leave. Typically he spent the time digesting the lessons he had learned. "I lived for three to four months alone with a farmer's family," he wrote later. "I was taken away in one fell swoop from war to the peace of rustic life." And, while staying with this family, in the county of Taklenberg, Clausewitz "looked for the first time into my soul."[21] The fourteen-year-old boy, the newly blooded soldier, had serious thoughts about his future. He began to read more books, riding to get them from nearby Osnabruck, and he soon realized how sketchy his schooling had been. As he also wrote some years later: "I went on my first campaign at the age of twelve after a very mediocre education . . . my teacher was experience. Before, I had had the shelter of a careful upbringing."[22] The books from Osnabruck lifted him from the restricted mental environment in which he had previously lived. "By sheer chance I obtained some political and religious tracts and other books about the perfectibility of man. There, with one stroke, the vanity of the young soldier became a great philosophical ambition. I was then, at that time and moment, so close to inspiration as the nature of the spirit will allow. If this glow had been maintained better in me and had been used better, I might have become a much more worthwhile person than I am."[23] Already, the young Clausewitz was developing thoughts and ambitions untypical of those held in the Prussian officer corps. But for the moment they did him no good.

On 5th March, 1795, still only in his fifteenth year, Carl was promoted to Second-Lieutenant. Meanwhile his King was losing interest in his army and abandoning himself to the pleasures of Berlin's female society. Fearing that a continuation of hostilities might threaten the security of Prussia and chances of further gains in Poland, Friedrich Wilhelm was willing to discuss peace terms with the French. Besides, the war had never been a popular one in Berlin. So, one month after Carl's promotion, the Peace of Basle was signed. It was a heavy blow to the tottering remains of the Holy Roman Empire. The separate treaty between Prussia and France, with war to be kept away from Prussian territory, meant a deepening of the fissure between north and south Germany. Deep resentment was felt against Prussia who seemed determined to stand aside while the rest of Europe suffered. An anti-Prussian attitude began which she would have cause to regret in just over a decade, when allies were urgently needed. With peace, the Regiment Prince Ferdinand went to Neu-Ruppin, an insignificant garrison town. Clausewitz's inspiration, which the books at Osnabruck had given him, rapidly faded. "Soon, forced into a small garrison, surrounded by prosaic people and events, my existence was no better than that of my friends. In other words I was still a very common human being, with perhaps the only difference being a little more inclination to think, read, and with a little more military ambition." Clausewitz added: "This was all that remained of my former impetus. However, even this was more of a hindrance than it was healthy, as long as there was no means of satisfying it."[24]

Peace had made better schooling even more necessary: with the ending of hostilities Carl could no longer hope to gain promotion through abilities displayed in the field. He enrolled at the local school to learn mathematics, history and French. Not surprisingly, he was attracted to the history of Frederick the Great. Frederick's exploits, and his works, were just the food for young Carl's eager mind. But to improve this mind, he still had to rely upon his own efforts. The local school was unsatisfactory and the teaching poor. Carl stayed at Neu-Ruppin, bored with the military inactivity, reading all the books he could find, while in 1796 the young French General Napoleon Bonaparte conquered north and central Italy and advanced into Carinthia and Styria. A preliminary peace was signed between Austria and the French at Leoben, followed by the Peace of Campo Formio in October, 1797, on terms distinctly unfavourable to the Austrians.

The same year, Friedrich Wilhelm II of Prussia died of an excess of sensuality, according to his many critics. "Still his whole mind was only bent on procuring himself the means of indulging his lascivious appetites," wrote a Berlin commentator. "Nature, which had been lavish in his favour, had long been exhausted; and the provocatives of art had been so liberally employed, that they now refused their wonted effect, until at length every nerve was thus robbed of its elasticity, and the whole system overthrown. Though formed by nature to last, perhaps, for a century, yet he fell a dreadful sacrifice to his own excesses."[25] His son, the twenty-seven year old Friedrich Wilhelm III, now took his seat on the Prussian throne. He was to rule for forty-three years; and he was to cause Carl von Clausewitz much anger and misery.

The new King was basically good-natured and mild. He was also timid and lacking in imagination, and totally unsuited to rule in the crises which were soon to overtake his kingdom. He had been neglected by his father and brought up mainly by his tutor. The young boy had retired further into himself. Then he had been placed under the care of Count von Brühl, father of Marie von Brühl, the future Frau von Clausewitz. Brühl "possessed every accomplishment that could adorn the man, or the courtier;"[26] and he was, said Stein, "honourable, honest, benevolent, and amiable; the social talents and accomplishments of a man of the world, he possessed in the most favourable degree."[27] But he came too late to help Friedrich Wilhelm's development. The boy's shyness increased. The Prince attended the campaigns on the Rhine and in Poland, and he conducted himself with courage. He even commanded the siege of Landau in person, but again his nervousness and hesitancy showed themselves—he lacked sufficient confidence to exploit any advantages his troops might gain. The one redeeming feature of the young King's life was his vivacious and pretty Queen, Louise. "The delicacy of her mind, the gentleness of her character, added to the loveliness of her person, unite all the charms of her sex, and render their mutual love a happy example to their whole kingdom."[28] Clausewitz, who admired the Queen—she too hated the French—said Friedrich Wilhelm had "that Nordic, cold, sense of doubt." This pessimism made the King reluctant to attempt important military innovations. He was more interested in his army than his father had been in his later years, but concerned himself with details of uniform rather than fundamental reforms.

Clausewitz became one of his strongest critics. One of the reasons for his condemnation of the King was Friedrich Wilhelm's later refusal to alter the Prussian tactics and strategy which so fully occupied Clausewitz's time now at Neu-Ruppin. He was depressed with the regular, dull routine of the garrison, which revolved round the endless drills and barrack-square manoeuvres. These manoeuvres laid heavy stress upon close-order and precision. Laid down by the Prussian tactics of the day, these procedures were meant to be easily transposed to the field of battle, with soldiers trained to advance in stiff straight lines, elbow to elbow, as if still on parade. This was the whole basis of the Prussian method of fighting war, and Clausewitz drilled it and drilled it until he was sick of it. Already he was finding fault with this tactical system—and already the French were developing methods which would make it outdated.

While the war with the allies had been continuing Lazare Carnot, the

French War Minister, had recruited new military talents, such as Lazare Hoche, Charles Pichegru, Jean Baptiste Jourdan and Napoleon Bonaparte, and had laid the foundations for the victorious French mass armies of the future which were to teach Prussia such a bloody lesson. By the spring of 1794 this French citizen-soldier army had reached a massive strength of 800,000 men. The *levée en masse*—mass conscription—was in marked contrast to the current European practice of hiring mercenaries. Making use of the skirmisher or *tirailleur*, the new system was based upon new flexible tactics which involved open-order manoeuvres.

So, while the Prussians continued to stress the importance of inflexible linear formations, the French were partially abandoning the idea. Unlike the *tirailleur*, the Prussian infantryman was not expected to show independent judgement, not even to the extent of aiming his weapon. The most important points were considered to be the volume and rate of fire, not its accuracy. The massive, rolling, regular volleys from the steadily advancing rigid Prussian lines were thought to be all-powerful. Actually to aim the weapons would slow down this rate of fire and make the volley ragged. Prussian soldiers were therefore ordered to point their muskets waist-high. Claiming that men usually fired too high anyway in the heat and panic of battle, some officers ordered their troops to fire in the general direction of the enemy's feet. This was the type of drill Clausewitz was engaged with at Neu-Ruppin. It needed long hours of practice. And, under Frederick the Great, the Prussian armies which had used this method had indeed done so with deadly effect.

Few could equal the Prussian speed in the intricate loading drill, involving up to twenty-two separate actions to load and fire a round. In the time of Frederick the Great, the line troops managed—at their best—to fire three rounds per minute. It mattered little if some of the Prussian troops shot wild in their haste, or if some of the weapons misfired. Nor did it matter if the Prussian muskets were almost impossible to fire accurately anyway. Thus, by 1782 the *Infanteriegewehr* infantry weapon was extremely difficult to hold on a target because of its imbalance and weight.[29] Moreover, the precise Prussian drill called for strict discipline, which was best obtained through mercenaries. So, by 1804, the Prussian army at full strength was almost half composed of foreign troops;[30] and, by 1806 according to Clausewitz, the men were armed with the worst musket in Europe, unsuited for anything except rapid firing.[31] The effects of the new French troops, equipped with the *fusil* musket and new tactics, were not generally noticeable before the Peace of Basle. Clausewitz continued to perform intricate drills on the square at Neu-Ruppin, with the endless orders of "Load-Advance-Fire-Load-Advance."

Clausewitz continued to be dejected. The more he read, the more he became aware of his lack of education. Self-tuition was soon clearly insufficient. The answer would be entry to The Institution for the Young Officers in Berlin, one of the military schools founded by Frederick the Great in 1763. There, Carl would receive formal education in science, tactics and strategy. In the autumn of 1801, he managed to pass the entrance examination, which was not of a high standard. Clausewitz took leave of his regiment and travelled to the Prussian capital to begin the initial two-year course. But his depression soon returned. With his meagre education, Clausewitz rapidly found difficulty even in following the lectures and in keeping up with the other officer students. Once again he was an outsider. At Neu-Ruppin this had been so because he wanted to educate himself and not be limited to routine garrison activities; in Berlin it was again, this time because his education was lacking, as was his money. He could not afford to take part in all the student activities, even if he had wished to do so. Clausewitz felt painfully misplaced and lonely. He was even on the verge of leaving the army in despair.[32]

Then began his friendship with a man who was also shy and reserved, Gerhard von Scharnhorst. This relatively unknown Hanoverian, twenty-five years older than Carl, was to become his closest companion, and probably the greatest influence upon him. To Clausewitz he was "the father and mother and friend of my soul."[33] Without Scharnhorst, Clausewitz might well have left the army in 1802. Although he stayed, it is unlikely that *On War* could ever have been written in the way it was without the influence of the older man. Scharnhorst was to provide the young officer with encouragement, patronage and opportunity—all of which he very much needed—in a relationship which was both fatherly and comradely. Above all, Scharnhorst was someone to lean upon. Nor was the relationship one-sided. Scharnhorst was heard to say on numerous occasions that apart from his children no human being on earth had been so close to him, and no-one had understood him as well as Clausewitz.[34] Scharnhorst was soon to be involved at the very centre of Prussia's great military debate. At his side would be Carl.

TWO

Scharnhorst

"In these feints, parades, half and
quarter thrusts of former Wars, they
find the aim of all theory, the
supremacy of mind over matter, and
modern Wars appear to them mere
savage fisticuffs."
(*On War*, bk. iii, ch. xvi.)

SCHARNHORST'S CLAIM TO nobility was even weaker than that of his pupil and friend and he had to endure many a slight because of his common background. He was born at Bordenau, not far from Hanover, in 1755, the son of a soldier. His father had risen to the rank of Quartermaster, but, seeing little chance of further promotion because of his low birth, had left the army. The Kingdom of Hanover at that time had an even stronger caste system than the Kingdom of Prussia. Scharnhorst's father wished to marry a girl in his village who belonged four ranks higher up the local hierarchy. Permission was refused until the matter was forced in the traditional manner by the birth of a baby.

Gerhard was the Scharnhorsts' second child. He decided to join the army after meeting an acquaintance of his father, Count Lippe-Bückeburg, then one of the most distinguished soldiers and military writers in Germany, and an extremely forward thinker in some strategical subjects.[1] In 1773 Gerhard entered the military school founded by the Count at Wilhelmstein and stayed with his patron until the Count's death in 1777. He then entered Hanoverian military service, joining a unit to which a regimental school had recently been attached, and he began to distinguish himself as a lecturer on military subjects. He moved to Hanover itself in 1782, as an ensign in the artillery, and began to write a number of technical books, including *An Officer's Handbook* and *A History of the Siege of Gibraltar*. He married Clara Scmalz in 1785, whom he met when her brother, Dr. Theodor Scmalz, was writing a life of Count Lippe-Bückeburg.

Three years later Scharnhorst was editing the *New Military Journal*. Then came the French Revolution and his first practical experience of war. King George III of England and Hanover ordered his Hanoverian army to join the British operation in the Netherlands in March, 1793. Scharnhorst distinguished himself with his bravery and skill, rising to the rank of Major, and Assistant Quartermaster-General. By 1801 he had become Quarter-master-General, and was offered a post in the Prussian army by the Duke of Brunswick. At first he refused. Then, probably feeling that his lack of noble birth would deny him further promotion in Hanover, especially in the cavalry, he agreed. He was commissioned as Lieutenant-Colonel in the Third Cavalry Regiment based in Berlin. At the same time, Scharnhorst was offered a post at the military school, to superintend the artillery department under the nominal command of the Director, Lieutenant-General von Geusau. He took up the appointment, and in the following year, 1802, King Friedrich Wilhelm III granted him noble status.

The explanation of the extremely close friendship which was to develop between Scharnhorst and Clausewitz lies in the similarity between the two men. Like Clausewitz, Scharnhorst was often misunderstood and underesti-mated. "He seemed," said Clausewitz, "to the people of the outside world, and even to the intelligent part of it, a dull *savant* and pedant, while military men took him for an irresolute, unpractical, unsoldierly book writer."[2] Shy, unassuming, like a quiet scholar—but brave in battle—he lived apart from the military society of which he was a member. So too did Clausewitz. Scharnhorst was a good deal older than Clausewitz, and was already many of the things Clausewitz wished to be. Clausewitz was unlike his "General" in some ways. He was more impetuous, more emotional when pushed too far, more sensitive. He needed protection and encouragement. Recognizing in Clausewitz the ability and potential which no-one else quite saw, Scharnhorst believed he could help him. So, because of their similarities, and also because of their dissimilarities—especially in age—a partnership of master and pupil, leader and disciple, man and assistant, was formed. It would last throughout the next crucial decade of Prussia's history.

Meanwhile, Scharnhorst believed—like Clausewitz—that there could not be an intelligently officered army, nor any great development in military skill, unless military literature and education was soundly based. In 1804 Scharnhorst was to propose to the King that the Berlin war school should be elevated to the status of War Academy; this was done immediately, and Scharnhorst was appointed its Director. The Academy closed with the war of 1806, but was reconstituted in 1810. Improvements in army education were long overdue; a very low educational standard prevailed throughout the officer corps, as it had done for many years. An observer in the time of Friedrich Wilhelm I had noted: "A general was not regarded as unedu-cated, even though he could barely write down his own name. Whoever could do more was styled a pedant, inksplasher and scribbler."[3] Over sixty years later, in 1802, very little improvement had been made. The situation was made worse by the entry of *Junker* sons into the officer corps at an extremely early age. Even Frederick the Great described these officers' sons as "snatched from their mothers' breasts," but he did little about it.[4]

Closely guided by Scharnhorst, Clausewitz was rapidly expanding his own slim education. At the school, he studied tactics and strategy, the effects of field artillery, military history, mathematics, engineering, and the work of the General Staff. But he went much further than this. He eagerly attended the philosophical lectures of Professor Kiesewetter at the College of Medicine. The Professor, nicknamed by Berlin society "the national philosopher," explained the work of Kant. These lectures and Clausewitz's study of the Professor's writings and of Kant himself, have been held responsible for the logical methods and dialectic sharpness in Clausewitz's own work.[5] Especially at this time, Clausewitz was forever attempting to reason out the thoughts in his impressionable mind. It was not always an easy task. He had great enthusiasms, and always would have, following these with a serious and almost obsessive passion, flinging himself after them in a way which could be extremely tiresome for others. He tried to exercise strict discipline upon himself, saying "I have always tried to adopt a rational view, broad and practical, of the life and beliefs of others." But he sometimes failed.

While attending the war school Clausewitz worked his way with evident enjoyment through the writings of political philosophers—Dupan on the French Revolution, Voltaire, Montesquieu, and above all Machiavelli. "No reading is more necessary than the writing of Machiavelli," he said. "Those who pretend to be revolted by his principles are nothing but dandies who take humanist airs."[6] Upon his bedside table lay works on travel and on people, both of which always fascinated him. For lighter reading he had Laurence Sterne's *Tristram Shandy*, one of his favourites.[7] Clausewitz was happy at the school. He now felt he belonged. Although he still kept much to himself he did form at least one strong friendship with an officer of his own age, Carl Ludwig Heinrich von Tiedemann. This friendship continued as the two officers moved along remarkably parallel paths, until it was abruptly and sadly ended a decade later.

Scharnhorst considered Clausewitz and Tiedemann to be his best students. "They were distinguished in talent, judgement and industry, and by their altogether exceptional knowledge," he said. In an early assessment of Clausewitz he commented: "The character of Lieutenant von Clausewitz is distinguished by being modest and pleasant. Moreover he possesses a thorough knowledge of mathematics and military scholarship."[8] Clausewitz, his tutor added, could rapidly digest a large and complex topic, and then give a sound opinion on it: he had "an unusually rare judgement of the whole."[9] All this marked Clausewitz as excellent staff officer material. It also led to him being placed by Scharnhorst at the top of his class. The effect of this distinction upon the young man, who only a few months before had thought himself well below the school's standard, was long-lasting. He wrote to his *fiancée* in 1807 that two events in his life had made him so happy as to make him forget everything else for the time being. One, naturally, was meeting her; and the other "was the mark which was conferred upon me when I was placed at the top of forty young men who had all attributes of intellect and hard-earned military knowledge." Clausewitz continued: "I would never have believed this preference could have happened to me, that I could come out before the others in intellectual qualities, but he (Scharnhorst) convinced me he had thought me the most able in the school, and when I believed myself capable of this, I went ahead with confidence."[10]

Clausewitz did not confine himself to the study of past and present military theory. He also took part in the important discussion over strategical and tactical reform. Again with Scharnhorst's help, he became a member of the Military Society (*Militärische Gesellschaft*) founded by Scharnhorst in 1802 and which, starting with a group of nine, rose to a membership of 188 by 1805, when it broke up with the general mobilization. The society, which functioned like a club, held discussions and presentations which were attended by officers of all ranks, by two royal Princes, and by influential civilians such as Baron Stein who were interested in military subjects. The club was of considerable importance. For the three years of its existence it was a meeting point for new ideas from some of the most active military minds in Berlin at that time. As an unknown junior officer, Clausewitz was very fortunate to be a part of it. Notably, the club debated fundamental changes to the whole structure of Prussian tactics, including the prospects of moving away from the Frederickian rigid lines of attack and the stress on massive volleys, towards a greater use of light troops and flexible tactics as the French had adopted.

So far the issue had only been relevant to Clausewitz on the tactical level, through his experiences on the Neu-Ruppin parade ground. Now he realized the full and far-reaching significance of any change. If any alteration to the Prussian tactics were carried out, it would amount to nothing less than a revolution in the Prussian army, and one which would have an impact far beyond the tactics employed on the battlefield and even beyond the army itself. Rigid linear tactics meant that as far as possible all should be planned before the engagement with the enemy. There had to be precise execution, to enable the precise Prussian lines to deploy exactly to pattern. The approach march to the battlefield had to be as carefully planned as the battle itself, so that the army could arrive in the form required. Once set in motion, the intricate manoeuvre machinery could not change gear without the risk of disastrous confusion. Tactics therefore influenced the wider realm of strategy. Ideally, there should be an element of inevitability about the whole affair, with well-drilled regiments arriving after a complicated and well-planned approach, then moving forward at the required pace in the required direction, each component well-ordered and linked with the others, and the whole advancing, engaging, and defeating the enemy with minimum confusion and interruption. It was, Clausewitz wrote when condemning this system in *On War*, "a kind of algebraic action."[11]

Making war in this fashion was artificial and often extremely inflexible. But it worked, at least under Frederick the Great, and at least until the French *tirailleurs* swarmed across the European battlefields.

Until the French threw grit into the complex military machine, the decisive factor in battle was the concentrated weight of metal fired. Thus at the battle of Crefeld in 1758 the first Prussian volley slaughtered 75 per cent of the enemy front line.[12] At the Battle of Prague on 6th May, 1757, Frederick the Great's soldiers themselves came out the worst in one of these mass executions: the Prussian battalions were ripped to pieces, and in one shattering volley several units lost over 50 per cent of their men—over 350 troops out of 700. But even before the French tactical changes, a number of disadvantages and adverse implications could be seen in the Prussian method. Drill had to be as near perfect as possible; in turn, discipline had to be harsh. There was always a fear of confusion, of the unexpected, which might throw the tight formations into a rabble of panicked men. Because of this inflexibility, the lines of battle had to be organized before the battle opened, rather than after fighting had started, one side could more easily be manoeuvred into defeat: if the opposing army had stolen the advantage of the approach march, and was organized for battle before the other, then the battle was lost before it had begun. And in fact, battles sometimes were counted as defeats even though they never actually took place. This added to the artificiality, and gave disproportionate importance to manoeuvre. As a result, it was difficult to snatch the sudden opportunity; and it was hard to follow up a victory once it had been gained. Beaten enemy forces could not be easily routed, because the exact Prussian formations could not pursue them quickly enough without losing cohesion themselves. Armies were often allowed to regroup and fight another day.

Virtually the only flexibility came from the small number of Prussian light infantry troops, designed for secondary use in patrols and ambushes. But instead of having ordinary infantrymen trained in these tasks as well as in linear drill, the light troops were provided by a few units hired for the campaign, and by the *Jäger*. The latter, organized by Frederick the Great soon after he ascended the throne, were originally formed from foresters and huntsmen. But by 1806 this regiment only numbered about 2,000 men. In addition, Friedrich Wilhelm II had agreed, in 1787, to ten sharpshooters—*Schützen*—for each line company. But ten per company only amounted to about forty in a battalion of 700. More important was the formation, also in 1787, of twenty fusilier battalions, which were used in two ranks instead of the more common three, and were therefore easier to deploy into extended order for skirmishing.

Generally, however, Prussia stayed apart from the main shifts in emphasis in military tactics during the last years of the eighteenth century. These changes covered the merging of irregular light infantry troops with the line regiments, the increasing use of open order and aimed fire—as opposed to tight formations firing unaimed volleys—and the application of light infantry tactics to the battle. All were important elements in the transition of the old form of war to the new, which was itself to form the foundation of Clausewitz's *On War*. It was in the context of these changes that the book was written.

Gradually other European armies were training infantrymen who could either fight in the line or as skirmishers, acting individually or in small detached units. The French were the first to experiment. Even before the Seven Years' War, the French soldier and strategist Maurice de Saxe considered it feasible to have up to one-tenth of a standard infantry battalion fighting as skirmishers. And in the last decade before the Revolution there were twelve battalions of *chasseurs à pied* (light foot soldiers) in the French army, also termed *tirailleurs en grande bande*, or massed skirmishers. These troops were ready for use and expansion when the French Revolution let loose new sources of energy. But the Prussian leaders refused to follow the French example; nor was this example easily recognized for what it was.

Moreover, after the Peace of Basle, Prussia was a bystander to events in south Germany and Italy, which was yet another reason why her leaders failed to see that military reforms were urgently needed. There was no test of war. It was believed that the army was still that of Frederick the Great; General Rüchel said on parade at Potsdam: "His Majesty's army can produce *several* generals equal to M. de Bonaparte."[13] There was no way of showing the opposite until it was too late. Prussia could even have looked abroad for valuable hints: to the American War of Independence (1775–83). Again the opportunity was missed, as it was by other European nations. When the young Gneisenau, who had spent some months in the British army fighting the colonists, applied to join the Prussian army, the King said: "People who come back from America imagine they know all there is to know about war, and yet have to start learning all over again in Europe."[14]

One of the main drawbacks to change was the problem of timing. Alterations would mean a transitional period in which the Prussian army would be confused, less effective, and vulnerable. But the implications spread even further. If skirmishing and open order tactics were to be adopted on a large scale, training would have to be quite different. Men would have to be allowed greater initiative; and this meant greater freedom. Discipline would consequently be affected. Mercenaries, liable to desert, would be unsafe, and more nationals would have to be recruited; but it would be difficult, dangerous and a contradiction to give those peasants who enjoyed little liberty at home, wider freedom in the army. A change to open order battle tactics meant nothing less than a modification of the whole Prussian social system, of the existing and accepted relationship between officer and man, soldier and citizen, master and servant, and even between soldier and sovereign, all of which were basic to the structure of the Prussian state. Yet it was becoming apparent to a number of Prussians that important alterations were long overdue. And these thinkers met and talked throughout the medium of Scharnhorst's *Militärische Gesellschaft*.

Scharnhorst himself had given his opinions of French *tirailleur* tactics a number of years before. In his *Basic Reason for the French Success*, written when he was still in Hanoverian service, he had said: "The physical agility and excellent intelligence of the ordinary man allows the French *tirailleurs* to profit from all the advantages offered by the terrain and overall situation, while the phlegmatic Germans, Bohemians and Dutch deploy on open ground and do nothing but what their officer tells them to do."[15]

The use of light troops and the integration of open and close order tactics formed an increasingly high proportion of the subjects discussed in the *Militärische Gesellschaft*, and articles on these topics appeared in the privately circulated proceedings of the club, the *Denkwürdingkeiten der Militärischen Gesellschaft*. One such article was written by Hermann von Boyen, the future War Minister, and won a competition organized by the club in 1804 which asked the question: "Should line infantry be taught the light service and how to fight *à la débande* (in open order)?" Boyen suggested that the third rank of the line battalion should be trained to fight in this way. This idea had already been put forward by Scharnhorst in his lectures at the Berlin war school, attended by Clausewitz and Tiedemann, and he had recommended the suggestion to Friedrich Wilhelm in a memorandum of 1800 or 1801.[16] Several units had experimented with the system; but once again it was on an insufficient scale.

Other Prussians advocated even more radical changes; among them Henrich Dietrich von Bülow, a retired Lieutenant and the brother of the successful general. He wrote a succession of volatile books between 1799 and 1806, savagely attacking all aspects of Frederick the Great's army, and even "Old Fritz" himself. Bülow believed close order tactics were "servile." Skirmishing "restores to the individual his courage, his effectiveness, his intelligence, in a word his human dignity." But even Bülow still retained the geometric framework of close order strategy, with his "points of domination" and "angles of approach."[17] This, then, was the debate to which the young Clausewitz listened and in which he took part; a debate which on the surface was concerned with technical military matters, but which in reality was concerned with the very basis of Prussian existence, and with the fundamental difference between the old and new forms of war.

Clausewitz, the disciple of Scharnhorst, agreed with the views of his teacher during those Military Society discussions. His first article appeared at this time, a critique of Bülow's scientific laws of strategy, printed in the journal *Neue Bellona* edited by Heinrich Philip von Porbeck. In this article, Clausewitz strongly disagreed with the retired Lieutenant's combination of geometric analysis and almost romantic notions of skirmishing. But he agreed with Bülow upon the advantages of large armies operating in open formations. He believed that the *élite* professional force fighting in strict close order was to some extent outdated, but he nevertheless believed it could not entirely be abolished. Instead, the two systems should be merged. But Clausewitz, as always, listened more than he talked. He absorbed the to-and-fro of the debate. And he was to make use of it in *On War*. Yet in those years the debate could achieve little. As Clausewitz said, the thinkers and advocates of radical change were unable to make more than a slight scratch upon the "rare conceit" of Prussia's monarchy and military class.[18] Clausewitz was an especially harsh critic of the King. And although Friedrich Wilhelm scrapped certain nonsensical regulations, such as loosening screws on musket-butts to make a better noise during parades, he still supported the existing ideas of complex linear drill. "I don't understand why the most beautiful troops shouldn't also be the best," said the King.[19] In a very short time understanding would be forced upon him by the points of French bayonets.

Meanwhile, Clausewitz now entered the heady atmosphere of Friedrich Wilhelm's elegant court. In 1803, on Scharnhorst's recommendation, Carl was made *aide-de-camp* to Prince August of Prussia, soon to be his friend, commanding officer—and fellow prisoner of war.

THREE

The Plaything of Princes

"But war's a game which, were their
subjects wise, Kings would not play
at."
(William Cowper, *The Task*.)

MADAME GERMAINE DE STÄEL, who visited Berlin for the first time during the
same months as Clausewitz entered the proud Berlin court society, said:
"The two classes of society—the scholars and the courtiers—are completely
divorced from each other. As a result, the scholars do not cultivate
conversation and mundane society is absolutely incapable of thought." She
added, in another letter home: "The thinkers are soaring in the empyrean;
on earth you find only grenadiers." Madame de Stäel, a French lady who
disliked Berlin, observed that the thinkers themselves accepted the social
rigidity without question. In their thoughts and conversation they were more
radical than their counterparts in France; on earth they bowed to rank, title
and authority.[1]

Clausewitz could only be out of place in this society. He was helped
through the friendship which developed with Prince August. The Prince,
younger brother of Prince Louis Ferdinand, cousin of the King, and son of
Frederick the Great's youngest brother, Prince August Ferdinand, was about
the same age as Carl. The two were different in character: August was
sociable and an excellent conversationalist. But apart from Tiedemann the
Prince became the closest friend Clausewitz had of his own generation. As
aide to the Prince, Clausewitz had to escort him on numerous public and
semi-private occasions, attending balls and banquets, army manoeuvres and
ceremonial functions at the glittering court. Apart from being an entirely
new life for Clausewitz, it was one he could scarcely afford. He was without
a private income and as always he was short of money. But for the moment
Clausewitz was absorbed by his surroundings. Gerhard von Scharnhorst was
a frequent visitor to the court and the two men maintained close contact.
Clausewitz was also befriended by Princess Louise, sister of August and
Louis Ferdinand, who had married the Elector Anton von Radzivill in
1796, and who had a small circle within the court of those whose company
she preferred. Belonging to this group, although initially on the fringe,
Clausewitz was able to make contact with many of the most influential men

of his time, including Baron von Stein, Chancellor Hardenberg, the leading politician Neibuhr, and later Gneisenau. Scharnhorst was also part of the intimate circle. Clausewitz took up his appointment at the court in spring 1803, but his appointment was not formally confirmed until 26th June, 1804. At the same time he was promoted to full Lieutenant.

Affairs on the international level were a main topic of conversation at the Berlin court. In May, 1803, the Peace of Amiens was ended and France and Britain once more declared war. Napoleon assembled a large army at Boulogne and planned an invasion of England, but owing to Britain's naval superiority, the operation was postponed. The British Prime Minister, William Pitt, was to succeed in forging a new continental alliance with Russia, Sweden and Austria, aimed not at intervening in French internal affairs, but at pushing France back over the Rhine and out of Holland, Switzerland and Italy.

Closeted with his Cabinet Ministers in Berlin, Friedrich Wilhelm III was determined to keep out of it all. Clausewitz and many other Prussian officers, young and old, were disappointed and furious. They wanted Prussia's neutral policy scrapped.

But Clausewitz had something else to occupy his mind. For once it had nothing to do with war. In December, or late November, 1803, at a dinner given by Prince Ferdinand, August's father, Carl met Marie. Countess Marie von Brühl came from an excellent family, far higher up the social ladder than Clausewitz's line. She was the granddaughter of the famous government minister, Count Heinrich von Brühl, who gave his name to an elegant Dresden terrace of luxury houses. The name Brühl was long connected with Dresden high society. Heinrich's second son, Count Carl Adolf von Brühl, had married the daughter of the English Consul in Petersburg, Sophie Gomm. Marie was their first child, born on 3rd June, 1779, in Warsaw.

Marie spent the first five years of her life in Saxony, alternately at Pegau and Dresden, but her parents moved to Berlin in January, 1787, when her father was appointed military tutor to the Crown Prince, the future King Friedrich Wilhelm III. Life in the palace and in Berlin was, she said, "the entry into a new world,"[2] as it would be later for Carl. The family usually spent each spring in Potsdam and the summer in fashionable Charlottenburg, although Marie's father was often away for long periods escorting the Crown Prince or the King. Marie was presented to the court on 1st January, 1798. Her two closest friends were Margaret Brown, daughter of the King's British physician, and Countess Louise von Voss. When the Brown family returned to England in 1802 Marie went to stay with Countess Louise in the country at Gross-Giewitz in Mecklenburg, apparently for the good of her health. But in July that year she had to return to Berlin when her father suddenly died. A sad year followed, and although she began to appear at court again the following autumn, Marie was still in mourning. On one of these infrequent court visits she first met Carl. "To this sad day is joined the beginning of my greatest happiness," she wrote. "I shall always remember it."³ But the first meeting was not entirely auspicious. Carl noticed her at the banquet and had himself introduced, yet conversation was brief. Marie felt it improper to talk too long with a strange man when she was still in mourning.

Nevertheless, Marie was interested in this good-looking, quiet officer. She met him again a few days later when Prince August and his *aide* came to visit the Queen. In the meantime, Graf Carl von Brühl, Marie's cousin, had had a conversation with Clausewitz and had reported back to Marie that he appeared to be a most distinguished young man and extraordinarily capable. They saw each other more frequently in court circles and friendship between them grew. But Carl, typically, remained withdrawn. The more impulsive Marie had to make the pace, or at least be patient until Carl overcame his shyness. "There were weekly balls and I saw Clausewitz several times. Once he didn't come until very late and I couldn't stop myself looking impatiently at the door . . . another time Fraulein Dreiberg found him in the antechamber and asked him to come in. I stood next to the door and when I found him in front of me, so unexpectedly, my surprise and my excitement in seeing him were so great that for a moment I could not speak . . . It was rather more serious than I had believed before."⁴

So the friendship ripened. If it was not courtship, then it was only because the reserved Carl had not made it one. Marie continued to jot down her thoughts during the spring and summer of 1804. "I came back at the end of July from Giewitz and I saw Clausewitz on 3rd August during the King's dinner at Charlottenberg. I lived with my mother in Charlottenberg and I went with the ladies of the court often to the Commentator Theatre. The wish to see Clausewitz, which grew every day, was mostly the reason. And this wish also made me very unhappy when I wasn't invited to Prince Ferdinand's golden wedding celebrations . . . I spent the time with the unpleasant feeling that Clausewitz was very near me and yet I was unable to see him."⁵ Marie was worried lest she might appear too forward to her shy suitor. "The last time Clausewitz accompanied me down the palace staircase and on a walk not far from Charlottenberg he must have thought me very cold and unfriendly on the outside, but that wasn't how I felt inside."

But success was near. "We met again in the palace and spoke to one another leaning against a marble table, then we stepped towards the window to look at the troops. I had put my hands on the window, Clausewitz his too, and by coincidence they touched for a moment . . ." Clausewitz was indeed becoming bolder. Excitedly, Marie wrote: "The evening I was at Bellevue, with Prince Radzivill sitting next to me, Clausewitz not very far away, Clausewitz came across and helped me put on my shawl."

Meanwhile, as Clausewitz was awkwardly plucking up courage to be the suitor, events were quickening on the international level. In May, 1805, Napoleon assumed the Italian crown and, as a result, Austria committed herself to the alliance with Britain. But Prussia, pressed by both Napoleon and Czar Alexander I to state her position, remained neutral. Friedrich Wilhelm refused the French Alliance, yet also refused to join the coalition against her. In early October, 1805, French troops passing on their way from Hanover to the Danube marched through the Prussian Ansbach. The court at Berlin was incensed by this direct challenge to Prussian sovereignty. Prussia had stood silent while insult after insult had been tossed at her, including the capture by French troops of Sir George Rumbold, the English *chargé d'affaires*, from Hamburg the previous year, and sporadic frontier violations. But even Friedrich Wilhelm could not ignore the challenge of Ansbach. He sent an emissary, Count Haugwitz, to Napoleon's headquarters threatening that if the French Emperor refused a treaty on the basis of that between Austria and France signed at Luneville in 1801, Prussia would join the coalition against him. Then, at last, Friedrich Wilhelm mobilized his army. But he had delayed too long.

While Haugwitz was still on his way, Napoleon took the initiative in southern Germany. In one of his most brilliant campaigns he slashed the Austrian army's communications and forced the incompetent General Mack to capitulate at Ulm on 20th October, 1805. Vienna was occupied on 13th November. The Czar waited neither for the skilled Austrian Commander, Archduke Carl, to return to Italy, nor for possible Prussian intervention, but immediately engaged the French. His army suffered crushing defeat on the field of Austerlitz on 2nd December, 1805. The coalition was shattered. If Prussia were to act, she would now have to do so alone.

As a result of the mobilization Clausewitz travelled with August to the regiment that the Prince was to command. The imminence of his departure prodded Clausewitz into action with Marie. Nominated a Captain in November, he at last found sufficient courage to declare himself. It had taken him almost exactly two years to find the necessary confidence. Now, on 3rd December, the day after Austerlitz and the day on which he was about to leave Berlin, he and Marie stood together waiting to be served in a fashionable fur shop. "The other customers were coming and going," wrote Marie afterwards, "but we remained standing unobserved in a corner of the shop. I said I hoped he wouldn't forget his friends when he went away. Perhaps it was more the way I said it than what I said, because then he took my hand and he kissed it and said, very moved: 'Someone who has seen you once will never forget you.'

"His expression and the tone of his voice when he said those words touched me down to the depth of my heart, and will always be remembered. We would have fallen into each other's arms had we been alone, and we would then have had one beautiful memory more. Even so, this moment belongs to the most beautiful and important of our lives, because we understood each other at last and the union of our hearts was silently made. Never, never, will I forget what I felt that day. Even a day before, a load of hundredweights seemed to lie on my soul. When I was alone for a moment I immediately sank into deep, depressed thoughts. As if with magic this one moment had changed pain to happiness. I didn't think of the future. I didn't think of the past. Everything was lost in the bliss of seeing myself so loved and to have shown my beloved my love."[6]

Clausewitz was away for two months. Prussia remained neutral. Haugwitz, who had arrived at Napoleon's headquarters on the eve of Austerlitz, never presented the demands put forward by Friedrich Wilhelm. On the contrary, two weeks later the Count had to sign a humiliating Franco-Prussian alliance at Schönbrunn. The remnants of the Russian and Austrian armies were then sent scurrying away by the victorious French forces; Czar Alexander retired back into Russia and Austria was compelled to sign the Peace of Pressburg. News of the Treaty of Schönbrunn was received with shock and amazement in Berlin. The Treaty allowed Napoleon to make sweeping territorial changes in Southern Germany and granted him the Franconian principalities and Cleves. In return, Prussia would receive Hanover; but should Prussia attempt to take it, England would inevitably open hostilities against her, which was exactly what Napoleon wanted. The Treaty was a complete violation of Friedrich Wilhelm's attempt to remain uncommitted. In Berlin, ratification of the Treaty was refused unless modifications were made. Friedrich sent Haugwitz to Paris to make the necessary alterations. Unwisely, he also demobilized his army.

So, in February, Carl came back to Berlin and to Marie. To begin with she did not hide her feelings: "To see him again made me feel so very, very happy. The danger had banned all fearful and proud caution from my heart. And I felt completely what Clausewitz meant to me. With the greatest love and most complete surrender, I took him into my arms."[7] But the surrender was not quite complete. Marie soon had regrets over displaying her feelings so openly and more to the point, her mother disapproved: an unknown captain was considered by this prim Englishwoman to be quite unsuitable as a husband for her daughter. Frau von Brühl was a person of strict principles and had become increasingly narrow-minded in the secluded life she had led since her husband's death. Her two main interests were her daughter and discussing international affairs; and she had an intense dislike of the French. According to a contemporary, she "lived in the passion of politics and hatred of the French."[8] Marie would never think of acting in defiance of her mother's will. Much to Clausewitz's surprise, she was determined to be more cautious with him and keep herself under tight control. Carl withdrew into himself again.

Clausewitz had other matters to occupy his mind in addition to Marie. Friedrich Wilhelm was continuing to make mistake after mistake in his handling of foreign relations. With the Prussian army re-established on a peace footing, partly owing to financial reasons, the way was left clear for Napoleon to increase his demands. When he reached Paris to ask for modifications to the Schönbrunn Treaty, Haugwitz was presented instead with far less favourable terms. Prussia was without allies. In England, Pitt had died and the war party was therefore weakened; Russia and Austria were still recovering from defeat. Prussia could do nothing but pay the higher price demanded. On 15th February, Haugwitz had to sign the Treaty of Paris under threat of immediate war, and as a result Prussia was bound to even greater dependence upon French policy. Prussia's neutrality was completely finished and Friedrich seemed to be condemned to a servile partnership with Napoleon.

Scharnhorst and the other would-be army reformers—including Clause-witz—were horrified. The atmosphere at court grew tense. Some of the more volatile officers became increasingly noisy in their protests, encouraged by the handsome, fearless and reckless Prince Louis Ferdinand, Prince August's elder brother. Louis Ferdinand was described by Clausewitz as "loving danger as he loved life."[9] He was the idol of the soldiers and the younger members of the officer corps. One night the windows of Haugwitz's house were shattered by stones thrown by a jeering crowd of anti-reformers but as Prince Louis was suspected to be behind the demonstration no official action was taken.[10] Baron Stein, a friend of the Prince, had already nagged at him for his unruly behaviour: "What makes you, Sir, disregard so many other moral considerations, offend against so many other principles?"[11] The princely young hot-blood was to deal his beloved Prussia a blow almost as great as Napoleon's in only a few months time.

Meanwhile, only one faint flicker of hope seemed to remain. Relations between Prussia and Russia had been improved considerably as the result of a visit to Petersburg by the Duke of Brunswick, and the prospects of alliance between the two countries was increased. It soon became clear that Napoleon had no intention of treating Prussia as an equal; nor did he make any effort to avoid alienating her. On 12th July the French Emperor announced his proposals to remodel the Holy Roman Empire into the Rhenish Confederation, which was to form part of his federative system. On 1st August, sixteen German states declared their secession from the Empire, and five days later Emperor Francis laid down his crown. When the crown was offered to Napoleon he contemptuously refused it.

Napoleon allowed Prussia to believe that she should lead a North German Confederation, a project which was discussed with vigour in Berlin. But the French Emperor was intent upon achieving favourable negotiations with the Czar, who had not yet signed a treaty with France after the Russian defeat. He also wanted to negotiate with England and, as an inducement to the London politicians, hinted that he would hand Hanover back to England. Lord Yarmouth, England's negotiator in Paris, allowed this to be leaked to the Prussians. At the same time, the disposition of French troops suggested that France was preparing further plans against Prussia. In Berlin, Friedrich Wilhelm came under mounting attacks for his abject policy. Even Haugwitz, who supported the idea of a French alliance had become alarmed. Haugwitz had heard reports that Napoleon was working underground in Dresden and Cassel against the North German Confederation. Even he now advised the Prussian King to mobilize his army. One whisper followed another in the Prussian court. Clausewitz and everyone else near the King waited anxiously for news of what would happen. This was a painful time, especially for those like Clausewitz who prayed for a chance to fight the French and revive the fallen spirit of Prussian honour.

Finally, King Friedrich Wilhelm III ordered Prussian mobilization. It was the most disastrous decision of his reign. An ultimatum was presented to Napoleon, whose chief demand was the withdrawal of French troops from Prussian frontiers. All officers were ordered to rejoin their regiments. Carl went to say good-bye to Marie. It was an emotional farewell. All Marie's feminine caution vanished; and when her reserve melted, so did Carl's. Soon after he had left for the Grenadier battalion which Prince August would command, he poured out his feelings in a most un-Clausewitzian fashion. "I was not to see you any more. It would have been good to have seen you for just another time, to see you my beloved Marie and press you to my heart! The future looks forbidding to me. I cannot and will not show you what I feel deep inside, but I do not think I despair for lack of courage. God will save me from that as long as there is a spark of life in me. This peace of mind, which I am able to have through humility, I will give up for ever if I cannot live freely and honourably as a citizen of a free and honoured state, and to enjoy in your arms the golden fruit of peace. So may it flee my breast for ever.

"Enough of this gloomy talk. Let me be happy and full of hope. If this happiness which now smiles upon me shows itself true, I will happily return to you. Oh Marie, what a moment of joy that meeting will be! Until then I have the thought that you are mine, that I may call you my Marie, as you yourself have done, that you think of me full of love—all these blissful pictures of this pure and beautiful love shall make up for the bitter parting. Now farewell my beloved Marie. I must make an end. Your picture lives in my heart."[12]

Napoleon Bonaparte was even less likely to fear Prussia's attempt at an ultimatum now, than a few weeks before. The Czar was delaying final ratification of a treaty drawn up in Paris on 20th July, which would have broken the understanding between Russia and England. Napoleon suspected that the Czar's hesitation was linked with the Prussian mobilization, and that an agreement existed between the Russian and Prussian leaders which England would join. Prussia must therefore be crushed before the union could be made. The Emperor wrote to General Alexander

Berthier on 5th September: "Send officers of the engineers to make good reconnaissance at all risk on the outlets of the roads from Hamburg to Berlin."[13] Prussia's ultimatum was countered by a demand for the demobilization of her army. In reply, Friedrich Wilhelm, with fresh but ill-founded bravado, issued a war manifesto on 9th October. Many Prussians were confident of the outcome of the war with France: relations with Russia were good and military help might come from that quarter, as well as from England and perhaps Austria; Prussia had also enjoyed eleven years of peace while other countries had exhausted themselves in war; during this time the Prussian army had continued its precise drill and was now polished and prepared for battle—or so it seemed as the troops marched confidently away to war.

Despite his vision of the "foreboding future," Clausewitz was happy. He was off to fight and greatly excited by the prospect. "I saw men passing one by one, their weapons sparkling through the green branches of the forest. And even when they could no longer be seen their arms still glinted through the mist which rose above the hollow of the valley, enveloping the marching army."[14] When he reached Rozbach, Clausewitz wrote that Prussia should follow the example of Frederick the Great, who was "resolved wholly to lose or wholly to win, like a gambler who risks his last penny."[15] Although he was concerned about signs of disunity in the High Command, and wished more army reforms had been carried out, the young Captain put on a great air of confidence. Others lacked even this youthful optimism.

Heinrich von Bülow spoke out with a sombre prophetic voice. Friedrich Wilhelm, he said, had missed his chance. "He who from horror of war lets his army, that is his capital, lie idle in garrison service where it rusts and bastardizes and sinks into a spiritless militia, and who believes that you can make the enemy turn and run at the first chance with tailors, apothecaries, or periwig-makers—he must look on while more adventurous speculators earn wealth and power and honour, and must grow impoverished and paralyzed while he pines in inaction." Bülow was arrested and his trial began with a medical examination to determine whether or not he was insane.[16]

The efforts of the reformers had resulted in some slight changes in the Prussian rigid tactical system, including the sending out of a few skirmishers and the introduction of a more humane army discipline. In addition, the General Staff was reorganized in 1803. Previously only a subsidiary body, this small section had been moved away from merely making maps and working out routes for supplies and approach marches, towards a study of strategic and operational planning. Moreover, the Prussian commander, Prince Hohenlohe had issued new instructions to infantry regiments in Lower Silesia on 30th March, 1803. Influenced by the theories of Scharnhorst and Bülow, Hohenlohe ordered the third rank of all infantry formations to be trained in open as well as close order. Colonel von Yorck also improved his *Jäger* troops.[17]

But nearly all Prussian reforms before 1806 were "belated, partial and ineffective."[18] Other commanding generals refused to follow Hohenlohe's lead. Yorck's *Jäger* were only few in number; Scharnhorst's appeal for a national militia fighting in conjunction with trained soldiers had failed to receive support; Scharnhorst, Boyen, Clausewitz, and the few other reformers, remained very much a minority. Nearly all officers and government departments remained unconvinced of the need for more improvements, or of the prospects of introducing more at that time. These military and governmental establishments were themselves ill-organized and clumsy. At the summit, of course, stood the King. All subordinate bodies were seen as mere extensions of his will. Frederick the Great had created an extremely centralized structure, revolving around himself as the state's personification. Yet even he had needed helpers and a steady process of bureaucratization had gone on.

By 1800 there were five main army agencies: the Inspector-Generals; the Military Department of the General Directory; the influential group of royal adjutants (*Generaladjutantur*) headed by the Expediting Adjutant-General with power to advise the King directly; the governors of the garrisons; and finally the *Oberkriegskollegium*, a committee formed in 1787 of the various department heads responsible for supply, personnel, mobilization and day-to-day administration. Among them was confusion, rivalry, competition for power; if Frederick the Great had been able to keep control, Friedrich Wilhelm III certainly could not; he had received the legacy of power without the ability, or inclination, to shoulder the burden. "It was not, in truth, a time for so humane, so gentle a Monarch to guide this unwieldy and disordered machine of government."[19] Instead of quietly being used to strengthen the army, free of outside pressure, peace had, in Bülow's words, made the armed forces rusty. "As a patriot I sigh," said Gneisenau. "In time of peace we have neglected much, occupied ourselves with frivolities, flattered the people's love of shows and neglected war, which is a very serious matter."[20] On 18th December, 1805, Scharnhorst had advised his son against soldiering. "You will not serve the French, and the other armies are for the most part in such a condition that little honour for the future is to be gained in them. As to the Prussian army, it is animated by the best spirit. With courage and ability nothing is wanting. But it will not, it cannot, in the condition in which it is, or into which it will come, do anything great or decisive."[21]

Recruitment of the local population, decreased by Frederick the Great, had been reduced still further by his successors, who had placed greater reliance upon mercenaries to man the Prussian forces.[22] Moreover, in order to reduce military spending, Frederick the Great had also shortened the annual manoeuvre period, during which the army was supposed to be at full strength. Again, Friedrich Wilhelm II and III had continued the process. They had limited the royal manoeuvres to as few as four weeks a year, training new conscripts during their first year of service for only ten weeks and granting extensive furloughs.[23] Many of Prussia's highest ranking officers had been junior officers during the Seven Years' War. "They combined a veneration for the methods of Frederick the Great with a stubborn reluctance to admit that the practices of war may change."[24] Moreover, they were now too old: by 1806, of the 142 Generals four were over eighty years of age, thirteen were over seventy and sixty-two over sixty, while 25 per cent of the regimental and battalion commanders were also over sixty.[25]

This was the army with which Prussia intended to beat Napoleon's seasoned soldiers. Even the Prussian mobilization was disorderly and incomplete. Clausewitz wrote that 150,000 men might have been available. But the whole of the army was not called to arms simultaneously, and such large detachments were held back in Poland and Silesia that he estimated the actual Prussian strength in the Thüringian area at not more than 110,000. Scharnhorst put it even lower, at 96,840 on the morning of the Battle of Jena. The French, on the other hand, mustered 160,000.[26] The Prussians moved slowly, heavily encumbered with baggage. Colonel von Yorck in command of the *Jägers* had his trunks, crates, baskets, bedrolls and a bedstead with him.[27] Discerning officers had good reason to be apprehensive. The Prussians were out-numbered, outdated, too slow-moving.

Yet Clausewitz was still enjoying himself. He enjoyed military life on the eve of battle, and enjoyed being in love with the beautiful countess whom he had had to leave behind. Now she sent him her ring to wear in battle. He wrote to her from Merseburg, using the familiar "thou" for the first time, in a letter which showed his great delight in the prospect of battle, and of danger: "Coming from headquarters, I found the letter from my beloved Marie. I thank you. I thank you with deepest tenderness for the letter and this ring which is for me so full of beautiful significance. I was as happy with it as a child, and now I wear it. Here I may permit myself this great joy; in Berlin I shall only be able to look at it, as often as possible. From my soul, I beg you to let me wear it on the day when glories and dangers surround us. If you ever get it back, dear Marie, you will be proud, perhaps, to know that in the wildest violence of the struggle, where the glory and freedom of the Fatherland and our own honour drive us with full sail over volcanic dangers, always ready to die, that some look of sadness and quiet joy fell upon this ring."[28]

FOUR

Auerstädt

"Woe to the cabinet which . . . meets
with an adversary who like the rude
elements knows no other law than
that of his intrinsic force."
(*On War*, bk. iii., ch. xvi.)

FROM THE FIRST the Prussian commanders were caught off-balance. They were never able to recover. "We went to sleep on the laurels of Frederick the Great," said Queen Louise. Prussia's brutal awakening shocked the whole of Europe. "The indecision and embarrassment of the Prussians in 1806," wrote Clausewitz in *On War*, "proceeded from antiquated, pitiful, impracticable views and measures being mixed up with some lucid ideas and a true feeling of the immense importance of the moment."[1]

The Prussian army was divided into three field corps. The first, about 20,000 strong, was commanded by the Duke of Brunswick. The second under Rüchel and Blücher totalled about 30,000 men, and the third, about 50,000 men, was led by Friedrich Louis, Prince of Hohenlohe. Clausewitz's grenadier battalion, commanded by Prince August, initially belonged to the latter Corps, but was soon detached to Kalkreuth's Corps in Brunswick's main army. Clausewitz thoroughly opposed this division of Prussian strength, with its consequent confusion of authority. He wrote in *On War*: "There is nothing more unmanageable than an Army divided into three parts, except it be one divided into only two, in which case the chief command must be almost neutralized."[2] The situation was made even worse by the King's decision to travel with the Duke of Brunswick. Personal initiative by the three commanders was restrained, without any firm overall control replacing it.

In Friedrich Wilhelm's party went his group of experts, the *Oberkriegskollegium*, and the Chief of Staff, Colonel Phull, whom Clausewitz had encountered when the Colonel had lectured at the War School and whom he would meet again in Russia; and the King's confidential adviser, the aged General von Möllendorf. "Three Field-Marshals and two General Quartermasters are with the army," wrote Clausewitz to Marie, "where there should only be one Field-Marshal and one Quartermaster."[3] On 13th September, Hohenlohe proceeded to Dresden, and increased his strength by the addition of two Saxon divisions, each 10,000 strong. But not until 25th September, when Hohenlohe was still at Dresden, was the first council of war held between the Prussian commanders. The commanders could not agree among themselves what to do. One plan after another was put forward and argued out of existence, with Christian von Massenbach, Hohenlohe's Chief of Staff, being especially obstructive. Scharnhorst was Brunswick's Chief-of-Staff. According to Clausewitz in a letter to Marie on 29th September from Merseburg: "I have never met a man more suitable for his position. But much will be lost from the effectiveness of his talent, with so many hindrances, and the paralysis of incessant friction between opposing opinions."[4] Scharnhorst wrote in despair on 7th October: "What we ought to do I know right well. What we *shall* do, God only knows."[5]

Nearly twenty years later Clausewitz launched the harshest attack of all upon the Prussian leadership in his *Nachrichten über Preussen in seiner grossen Katastrophe*. Here, he suggested in considerable detail the ideas he felt should have been adopted. The work provides an excellent example of his common sense, and of his ability to blend together an accurate knowledge of tactics, strategy, the prevailing circumstances, and the nature of the ground.

At the beginning of October, the Prussian units were deployed to the north and north-east of the difficult, wooded, countryside around the Thüringian Wald. "We are now advancing slowly and the day after tomorrow we will go from here to the area around Naumburg on the Saale," Clausewitz told Marie in his letter from Merseburg on 29th September. "Our enemy, the overbearing Emperor, is expected in Mainz. By the end of the next four weeks the main events will probably have taken place."[6] "The question was," Clausewitz wrote in his *Nachrichten*, "by which roads to move against the enemy? Should one leave the Thüringian Forest on the right and advance by Hof and its vicinity, on Bamburg?—leave it on the left and move along the Frankfurt road?—cross the forest and strike at Würzburg?—or separate and move in two, if not in three, columns in all three directions?" He believed that the main points to be considered in choosing one of these four alternatives were, firstly, "to keep together as much as possible, because concentration on the battlefield was the principal point," and secondly, "to strike an important part of the enemy's force and destroy it—a victory over an inconsiderable part of his Army would only give him time to concentrate." Bearing in mind the first point, he added, the idea of marching in more than one direction should be scrapped. The second factor eliminated a move on Frankfurt, since only Augereau's Corps was situated there.

"There remained only the choice between the advance across the Thüringian Forest, or by Hof on Beireuth. If Magdeburg and Wittenberg were taken as the principal line of retreat, then our communication lines would be best covered by the former. If Dresden were chosen for the retreat, then the latter was preferable. Undoubtedly, Magdeburg and Wittenberg were

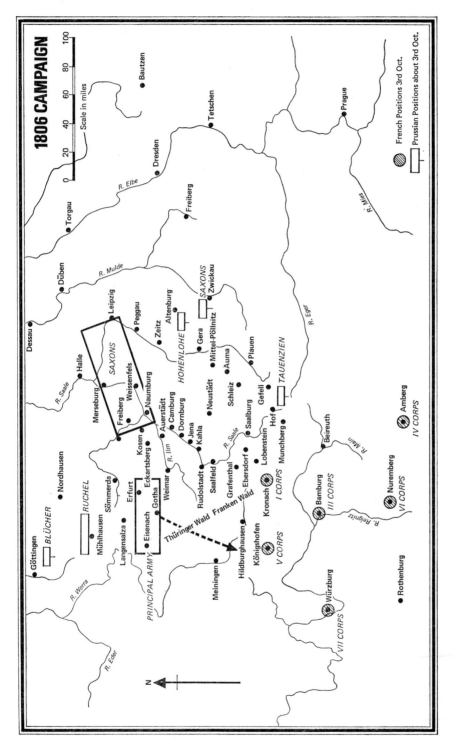

1806 CAMPAIGN

Scale in miles

0 20 40 60 80 100

French Positions 3rd Oct.

Prussian Positions about 3rd Oct.

N

BLÜCHER

RÜCHEL

PRINCIPAL ARMY

Thüringer Wald   Franken Wald

SAXONS

SAXONS

HOHENLOHE

TAUENZIEN

I CORPS

III CORPS

IV CORPS

V CORPS

VI CORPS

VII CORPS

Göttingen
Nordhausen
Mühlhausen
Sömmerda
Langensalza
Eisenach
Meiningen
Erfurt
Eckartsberg
Gotha
Weimar
Hildburghausen
Königshofen
Rothenburg
Würzburg
Kronach
Bamburg
Nuremberg
Amberg
Beireuth
Hof
Munchberg
Lobenstein
Ebersdorf
Grafenthal
Saalfeld
Rudolstadt
Kahla
Jena
Dornburg
Camburg
Auerstädt
Kosen
Freiberg
Weissenfels
Naumburg
Merseburg
Halle
Dessau
Düben
Leipzig
Peggau
Zeitz
Altenburg
Gera
Mittel-Pöllnitz
Zwickau
Neustädt
Schleiz
Plauen
Auma
Gefell
Saalburg
Neustädt
Torgau
Freiberg
Dresden
Tetschen
Bautzen
Prague

R. Werra
R. Eder
R. Saale
R. Ilm
R. Saale
R. Regnitz
R. Main
R. Eger
R. Mulde
R. Saale
R. Elbe
R. Mies

4—C

the best points, since they covered Berlin more directly, and the Elbe between these towns formed a greater obstacle than it did about Dresden, whilst Silesia, with its many fortresses and sheltered positions behind the Bohemian mountains, could safely be left to take care of itself. "These considerations should have resulted in choosing the advance through Thüringia. Besides, on these lines one was more in the centre of events and could meet a turning movement against the right better than from the line Hof to Beireuth." Clausewitz added: "Lastly, an offensive through the forest district was more likely to disconcert the enemy, since owing to the lack of roads, this was the last direction likely to be selected."

Initially, the Duke of Brunswick wished to move along these lines. Clausewitz wrote: "In accordance with these ideas, the Duke proposed to move ten divisions in six columns through the mountains to Meiningen and Hildburghausen, after which they were to advance to the attack, while one division watched the country around Beireuth, and three divisions— Rüchel's command—remained facing Augereau towards Frankfurt." Clausewitz believed Brunswick's plan to be "simple, natural, and founded on sound common-sense." But it "threw Hohenlohe and Massenbach into a perfect frenzy of rage." He continued: "They had already submitted their plans of campaign to the King, in accordance with which the Prince's command was to be increased to six divisions and was to picket the passes and defiles of Saalfeld, Saalburg, Hof and Adorf, while the main army was to move along the main road to Eisenach and Vach, and so, in continuation of its offensive, was to turn the Thüringian Forest with two great masses, like 'wing bastions,' and, while 10,000 held this area, General von Rüchel was to carry out an 'active defensive action' on the right flank."

Describing these schemes as the "confused ideas emanating from Massenbach's inflamed brain," Clausewitz went on to attack the formalistic, empty and dangerous attitude to strategy which created them, an attitude belonging to the past days of complex geometric operations and not to the present age of mass conflicts. It was, he believed, an example of the failure to realize the changes which had come about in the conduct of war. "Some day, and let us hope soon," he wrote in *Nachrichten*, "the conviction will prevail that the great movements and combinations of War must always be very simple, not only because complicated ones are difficult to carry out, but because they usually involve useless roundabout movements which do not lead directly to the purpose. Then people will see this pedantry of the General Staff in all its nakedness, by which governments and nations have been tormented for more than a century. Then too people will marvel how it was possible for their ancestors to be so deceived by hollow phrases and false similes, like 'wing bastions' and 'active defensive' in such important matters, where only the clearest and most precise expressions should be used." Drawing upon his 1806 experiences, Clausewitz was to underline this message in *On War*, in which he noted that such phrases and similes were often "nothing but hollow shells without any kernel."

Meanwhile, Clausewitz continued in *Nachrichten* that the Prince of Hohenlohe and Massenbach, who were "completely beside themselves" upon hearing of the Duke of Brunswick's proposals, attempted to bring about a *fait accompli* which would make him cross over to the right bank of the Saale. This crossing, which they wanted but the Duke did not, would have been acceptable as a defensive measure, Clausewitz maintained, but it contradicted the Duke's scheme for an offensive, and only increased the confusion at headquarters.

Brunswick was forced to call a war council on 5th October. This was preceded by a preliminary meeting on 4th October and attended in the King's absence by the Duke, his Chief-of-Staff Scharnhorst, Phull, Massenbach, Kleist and Müffling. Arguments continued all day on the 4th, and confusion still reigned when the full Council met on the morning of the 5th. Massenbach repeatedly insisted at the Council that the Saale should be crossed. The arguments continued. "Scharnhorst, weary of this continuous disagreement," wrote Clausewitz, "and seeing the dangers which it presented if it carried on, submitted: 'In war it isn't so much what one does that matters, but that whatever action is agreed upon should be carried out with unity and energy.' " This observation later became a well-known saying in the German army.[7] Scharnhorst therefore proposed that in the absence of agreement, and since further talk would waste more valuable time, they should adopt Prince Hohenlohe's plan, including the "wing bastions." But even this could not be agreed. Massenbach put forward another idea. This also came to nothing, and the meeting broke for lunch.

When the discussions began again in the afternoon it was at last agreed "to continue the movements already in progress until the 8th, which was appointed a day of rest for the troops, and meanwhile to send out reconnaissance from all three Armies." Even this attempt to find out what was happening, which should have been done long before, and which continued night and day, met with opposition from the King. In the end, according to Clausewitz, only Captain Müffling was sent, towards the Upper Saale. His information would be in by the 8th, and then, if still advisable, the original movement through the Thüringian Forest could be started the following day. By this time the Duke of Brunswick was disillusioned and demoralized and acting, said Clausewitz, "like a man who feels he is not up to his work and can no longer master his cares and anxieties, and ends by entangling himself completely whilst seeking alternatives where none exist."

Yet despite all the bumbling, despite the biased arguments and the time-wasting, all of which had gone on while Napoleon was steadily organizing his forces, Prussia might still perform adequately. "The position of the Prussian army on 6th October was neither involved nor even dangerous," wrote Clausewitz. "If it was no longer possible to count on a strategic surprise, the only thing to be done was to fall back frankly on the advantages of the defensive and make the most of them. This either meant waiting for the enemy's advance through Saxony in order to attack him oneself, or selecting a strong position he would have to attack, or, finally, if he appeared too strong, to retreat step by step into the interior in order to collect reinforcements."

Since the decision whether to attack, defend or retreat depended upon circumstances yet to be discovered by Müffling's reconnaissance, nothing more could be done for the moment except wait, "as we actually did, at the centre of the area of operations and to reconnoitre a suitable position for a decisive battle." Clausewitz held that as long as the Prussians were unsure whether the enemy was coming by Eisenach, or the Thüringian Forest, or by Hof, the army should take up positions on the left bank of the Saale. But if it was learned that the weight of the enemy attack was coming from the south, the position could only be considered as a strong flanking operation. "If, therefore, we renounced the offensive, the decision to be taken on 6th October was quite simple: to leave Tauentzien at Hof as an observation corps, with orders to withdraw towards Naumburg without allowing himself to be drawn into a serious engagement; to occupy the passages of the Saale from Saalburg to Jena, and to place Hohenlohe behind Jena; Rüchel and the main Army should be around Erfurt, with outposts towards the Thüringian Forest and Eisenach." The measures eventually adopted were not far different from those which Clausewitz outlined. "And we might," he continued, "in spite of everything, have looked forward to the battle of 14th October without much anxiety." Clausewitz wrote to Marie at the time: "If I were to forecast a result, there is still the probability we will be the victors in the next great battle."[8]

But other factors came into play. These were listed by Clausewitz in *Nachrichten*: the actions of Tauentzien, the actions of Prince Louis Ferdinand, the panic, the hesitation, the lack of confidence. "Had it been possible to forecast the lack of skill shown in action, the indecision and lack of council of our leaders, the great degree of insubordination, the confusion and the contradiction which events actually disclosed, then the only rational course to have pursued would have been to take up a position square across the Leipzig road so as at least to have retained the possibility of running away." But the Prussians did not run away—yet.

Clausewitz wrote his *Nachrichten* after many years of puzzling out why the Prussians went so disastrously wrong. At the time of the fighting, he had different views. For example he believed that the Prussians should advance rather than withdraw. On 12th October, when he was near Weimar, he drafted a plan of attack purely for his own interest. In this he argued that the Prussians should march with the main force to the Saale, cross the river, and cut off Napoleon at the Franken Wald.[9] It was an over-bold idea, too much so for the standard of leadership in the Prussian army. At that time

Clausewitz was still optimistic. He had written to Marie on 26th September, after he had joined General Friedrich von Kalkreuth's Corps in the main army: "It is getting serious now, and I myself do not doubt anymore that there will be battle. I admit I feel somewhat deceived in my ideas about our Cabinet. Matters are rather better than I was inclined to believe earlier on. What results we will therefore have to expect I will not try to imagine. If one considers all the intelligence we get, brought by those who have recently been in France and have gone through the French theatre of war, it would seem that Fate offers us at this moment a revenge, which will cover all faces in France with a pale horror, and will topple the arrogant Emperor into a precipice, where his bones will dissolve to nothing."[10]

Meanwhile "the arrogant Emperor" was mystified by the Prussian moves, or lack of them. On 10th September he had written to Berthier, who was in command of the Grand Army: "The movements of the Prussians continue to be most extraordinary. They want to be taught a lesson." The Grand Army was then still at Munich, and Napoleon had still not decided on the ultimate direction for his forces to take into Prussia. It depended on what the Prussian army would do—just as, in turn, the Prussians were waiting to see what Napoleon would do before they deployed. But on 18th September Napoleon learned that the Prussians had entered Saxony five days before, and he considered this a declaration of war. He sent Berthier instructions for the general dispositions for the assembly of the Grand Army, and soon afterwards the French began to move forward, crossing the Saxony frontier on 8th October.

At last the campaign had begun; and now it was to accelerate rapidly. Tauentzien's Saxon division, lying south of Hohenlohe's main army, was attacked by Bernadotte's advance troops on 9th October, and was driven back with heavy losses. Already, events were going wrong for the Prussians; as Clausewitz had said, Tauentzien should have withdrawn in order to avoid a serious engagement. To support Tauentzien, Hohenlohe ordered a general advance across the River Saale, but then he cancelled it. The French continued to move forward.

On the morning of 10th October, French skirmishers clashed with Prussian troops who were manning the outposts near Rudolstadt, where Hohenlohe's vanguard commanded by Prince Louis Ferdinand was situated. Prince August's fiery brother had been ordered not to engage the enemy before the arrival of the main force, but he could not resist the temptation to attack the French. He had been waiting impatiently for too many months for this opportunity. "The ardent character of Prince Louis," wrote a contemporary, "for want of a proper channel, had taken an unhappy course. And the bottle became one of his favourite enjoyments. In this he appears to have indulged himself to such an excess, that his nerves began to suffer."[11] Fortified by his bottle and his hatred of the French, Prince Louis Ferdinand moved his troops from their defensive positions and threw them against the enemy. But the

French were only using skirmishers to cover the main body of Lannes' Corps, and the Prince found himself heavily outnumbered on the road to Saalfeld. His 6,000 men were cut off. The *tirailleurs* swarmed in. The Prussians were routed. Yelling "Death or Victory," Prince Louis himself was hacked down by a Sergeant and a "common French hussar;" his body was stripped and his uniform carried away in triumph.[12] Not only had Hohenlohe's vanguard been shattered, but the tired and terrified fugitives who staggered back to the Prince's main positions spread panic and consternation. Louis Ferdinand, the hero of the troops, had been rated one of Prussia's best younger commanders: now he was dead. Once the fear had begun it ran unchecked. The Prussian soldiers, unused to war, were ill-equipped to brave the setbacks which often came with it. There could not have been a worse start to the fighting. In view of the French advance not far up the road, Hohenlohe fell back to Kahla.

King Friedrich Wilhelm and Brunswick, fearing that their communications would be disrupted, decided to collect the whole army together at Weimar. But Napoleon had already anticipated this move. As he had hoped, the Prussians were falling back upon their communications, with Hohenlohe withdrawing to Jena after Kahla. Clausewitz wrote to Marie on 11th October: "Now is the crucial point of time. And everyone agrees it will certainly be a hard struggle."[13] On the 12th he added: "The day after tomorrow . . . there will be a great battle, for which the entire Army is longing. I myself look forward to this day with joy as I would to my own wedding day."[14]

With the initiative slipping from their grasp, the Prussians were acting more under pressure of events than as part of an overall plan. Upon hearing the news that the French forward troops had reached Naumburg, Friedrich Wilhelm held a war council on 13th October. He decided to retreat to the Elbe River by way of Auerstädt, Freiberg and Merseburg, collecting the Duke of Würtemberg's 15,000 reserves at Halle on the way. Hohenlohe was ordered to provide a flank force to the main army while the latter moved from Auerstädt; he and Rüchel were then to form the rearguard. To accomplish this movement, Hohenlohe had to march to Capellendorf, a village on the Weimar-Jena road, and then, supported by Rüchel, march in the direction of Weimar. The armies began to move that same day, 13th October. Hohenlohe was then visited by Massenbach, who informed him the King had ruled out any general engagement between his army and the enemy. Hohenlohe was to remain on the defensive. But in avoiding a clash with the enemy, Hohenlohe neglected to move forward and occupy in strength the Landgrafenberg, a plateau overlooking Jena. This was to be a disastrous mistake.

With a number of intelligence reports in his hands, Napoleon had already decided that the Prussians would try to withdraw to Halle and then to Magdeburg. He therefore ordered his First and Second Corps and most of his cavalry to take the right bank of the Saale, while he himself led the Grand Army to force a crossing of the Saale between Kahla and Jena before advancing upon Weimar-Erfurt. In this way, he calculated that the detached corps commanded by Marshal Louis Davout would either hit the Prussian left flank, or move behind the enemy to sever their communications. "At length the veil is torn," Napoleon wrote to Marshal Joachim Murat on 13th October. "The enemy begins his retreat on Magdeburg." Bonaparte then set out with the Grand Army in the direction of Jena. That evening, when his troops skirmished with Prussian outposts in the vicinity of Jena, the Emperor believed he was opposed by the main Prussian army; he prepared to do battle. But Napoleon was wrong. He was about to engage Hohenlohe, not the main enemy force. The Royal Prussian army had marched up the Weimar-Naumburg road that day, and as Napoleon's troops positioned themselves before Hohenlohe at Jena, King Frederick Wilhelm and his units bivouacked at Auerstädt, which lay fourteen miles away to the north.

This main Prussian force totalled 40,000 infantry, comprising fifty-two battalions organized into five divisions. There were 10,000 cavalrymen in eighty squadrons, and 230 guns. Prince August's grenadier battalion formed part of one of Kalkreuth's two reserve divisions. During the evening orders were issued. Next day, one Prussian division preceded by a cavalry squadron was to advance up the road to the bridge at Kosen, where the defile would then be masked. The rest of the army would move to Hassenhausen, branch north by the Freiberg road, cross the river Unstrut, and camp for the night at Freiberg and Laucha. The Prussians knew that the enemy was at Naumburg, yet on 13th October Brunswick had only sent a few cavalry patrols forward, instead of a force sufficiently strong to clear the territory ahead. The patrols skirmished with Davout's advance posts near Taugwitz, so warning the French of the Prussian approach. Davout immediately rode forward from Naumburg and reinforced the Kosen bridge with an additional French battalion.

Prince Jean-Baptiste Bernadotte also had his headquarters at Naumburg, with orders to march on Apolda by way of Dornburg. During the night of 13th October, Davout urged him to advance with him by way of Kosen to engage the Prussians. Bernadotte, possibly because of jealousy, insisted upon following his original orders. Despite Bernadotte's refusal to co-operate, Davout did not hesitate to advance against the Prussians, even though he believed their strength to be about 70,000 (he had less than 30,000). Early on 14th October his troops moved forward in the darkness.

Dawn came, cold, with a thick fog lying on the ground. At 8 a.m. Davout's three divisions deployed on to the plain surrounding Hassenhausen, the gun carriages creaking, cavalry harnesses jingling, shadowy figures moving in the mist. The Prussians were also advancing, making for Kosen. And in the murky half-light 600 Prussian cavalry led by Blücher

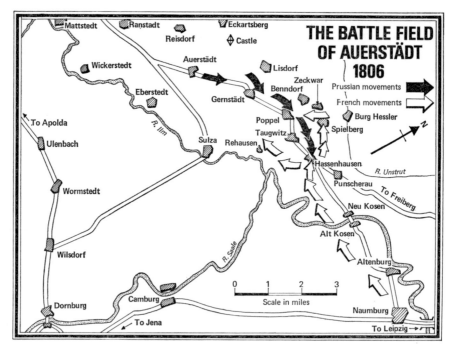

stumbled upon the leading French troops. In the shouting, firing, cursing and confusion, neither side knew what had happened. But the French recovered first. Under cover of the fog, Davout rapidly organized his leading division, commanded by General Gudin. On the Prussian side General Schmettau's division had been advancing behind Blücher's cavalry, and with Schmettau rode the King and the Duke of Brunswick. Friedrich Wilhelm, Brunswick and old Field Marshal Möllendorf now began to argue about what should be done, wasting still more vital time. With typical overcaution, Brunswick wished to wait until the next Prussian division, led by Wartensleben, moved up. Möllendorf wanted to attack at once, and Friedrich Wilhelm finally ordered Schmettau to prepare his troops for the assault. Then the fog lifted and swirled away. Before them the Prussians saw Gudin's division, ready for battle. Clausewitz was among Kalkreuth's troops farther down the road at Gernstädt. Muffled by the mist, noise of firing had floated down from the front, then the order to halt had reached back down the line.

It was decided to throw 2,500 cavalry, led by Blücher, against the French right flank. But Gudin anticipated the move and sent more men running over to strengthen his forces on that side. The Prussian front line heard the French officers shouting their orders, and saw the enemy shuffling into regimental and battalions squares, ready to face the cavalry. Blücher's troopers formed for the charge. Then they thundered across the flat ground at the French. The French muskets rattled out, horses and men were sent screaming to the ground, and Blücher ordered the bugles to be sounded for the cavalry to retire. Three more times they charged, three times they were repulsed. Then, at 9.0 a.m., Davout's second division under General Friant came up, and the French commander regrouped his forces into better positions. Gudin's division was drawn in round Hassenhausen, and Friant was placed on the right between this village and Spielberg.

Hassenhausen was the pivot for the battle, and Schmettau's men were ordered into the attack. The French crouching behind the walls and hiding in the houses drove them back again. Anxiously Brunswick called for more reinforcements, but Wartensleben's division and troops under the Prince of Orange were delayed by baggage wagons which were blocking the road. The vehicles were dragged aside into the ditches and the Prussian troops rushed past toward the fighting. The battle noise increased. Black gun smoke billowed into the sky to mingle with the fading mist. But the French still held the village. Then Schmettau himself was mortally wounded, and soon afterwards the Duke of Brunswick, leading a regiment of grenadiers against the village, fell screaming, shot through both eyes. His blood-stained body was carried off the field, and he died at Ottensen near Hamburg, on 10th November.

Further back, Clausewitz and Prince August still waited tensely by their horses for orders to move. From farther up the road came the thunder of the guns and the thick clouds of rolling smoke. There was no way of knowing what was happening; reports from the front were muddled and contradictory. In fact the whole of the Prussian command was falling into confusion. The Prussians were virtually leaderless after Brunswick had fallen; Friedrich Wilhelm had neither named Brunswick's successor nor taken over himself. Moreover, as relations between Brunswick and his Chief-of-Staff Scharnhorst had not been close enough, Scharnhorst had stayed out of the Duke's way, and was at another part of the battlefield when his commander was mortally wounded. With Brunswick's staff dispersed, immediate action was delayed. Discipline and order within the Prussian ranks now began to suffer. Here was another result of the lack of experience of the confusion of war, the "fog of war" as Clausewitz called it.

In an increasingly desperate attempt to force out the French from Hassenhausen, two brigades from Orange's division went forward, one under Lützow to support Wartensleben's left, the other under Prince Henry to the left of Schmettau's division. But on the French side, Friant was pushing Schmettau's troops back towards Zeckwar. Morand's division also arrived, and Davout ordered it to be deployed to the south of Hassenhausen. Gradually the Prussian line was being forced to give way. In an effort to halt Morand, King Friedrich Wilhelm threw forward the whole of his cavalry under his son, Prince Wilhelm. But Morand rapidly formed his men into squares, and charge after charge failed to break through. Exhausted, disorganized and demoralized, the Prussian cavalry withdrew to Sulza and Auerstädt. Relentlessly Morand's breakthrough continued, and the French now began to advance upon Rehausen.

As Morand was pushing forward on the left, Friant was pressing his advance on the right. His troops gained Spielberg, then struck south to attack the village of Poppel. This village, situated on the main road, was crucial to the struggle. If the French seized and held it, Prussian forces farther forward around Hassenhausen would be cut off and the retreat of the shattered remnants of the Schmettau, Orange and Wartensleben units would be blocked. Poppel, the gateway for the Prussian withdrawal, therefore had to be kept open. Some battalions from Kalkreuth's reserve were ordered forward to hold the village. Included in this reinforcement was Prince August's grenadier battalion. At last the Prince and Clausewitz mounted their horses.

But while the Prussian troops were moving the mile up the road to Poppel, the French succeeded in taking the village. Isolated Prussian survivors ran out from the houses, and the French took up defensive positions. Prince August received orders to send his 700 men into an immediate attack, before the enemy could strengthen their defences. Men from the Rheinbaben battalion and the Knebel Lancers were to join the assault.[15] Clausewitz led the third line of his battalion as the Prussians moved forward, steadily walking towards the waiting French.[16] The military regulations laid down that Prussian infantrymen should advance to the attack at a steady pace, 108 paces to the minute, and the troops should march with "shouldered arms" for as long as possible. In practice, the lines began to waver up to 2,000 yards from the enemy, when ricochet fire from the grape shot, the equivalent to modern shrapnel, began to be felt. Two hundred paces was considered to be the limit of effective musket fire, but at extreme elevation the musket would carry 1,200 paces. As today, therefore, the last 200 yards were deadly. It was only then that the men were officially allowed to break ranks and run screaming at the enemy positions. This was the pattern of the attack which Clausewitz now took part in: the men retained good order but suffered severe casualties, especially in the last hundred paces. Nevertheless, Clausewitz's battalion managed to reach the shelter of the orchard trees and the walls around the outlying houses. The men collapsed to the ground, panting, and looked back to see the bodies of their comrades who had been struck down by the powerful French fire. Crouching behind the walls the Prussians regrouped, then went forward again. Bloody hand to hand fighting followed. For a few critical minutes it seemed as if Prince August's battalion and the other Prussian units might be repulsed. Then the French began to withdraw and the noise in the village of Poppel subsided. August deployed his men among the houses. The men re-primed their weapons and waited for a French counter-attack.

The Prussian position was still desperate. Gudin held Hassenhausen in the face of repeated Prussian attacks; Morand and Friant were strengthening their positions to the north and south of Poppel; the Prussians in the U-shaped area between were still in acute danger of being enveloped. The Prussians fearfully hurried back along the road through the village, the officers yelling at the men to move faster, wagon wheels screeching as the heavy baggage vehicles were hauled back to safety.

The French counter-attack on Poppel now began. Clausewitz and the other Prussians saw the lines of French horses and men moving down the slopes towards them, heard the French officers shouting out their commands. Prussian guns were wheeled and pushed into position. For a moment there was silence, then the guns blazed into life in an attempt to batter the solid French phalanx. But still the enemy came on. A black, sulphur-laden fog swirled over the village once again. The Prussian advance positions clashed with the French, steel sabres and swords ringing against the bayonets. Gradually the French infiltrated into the village and the Prussians were forced to pull back, from wall to wall, house to house, and then out into the open ground, anxiously looking behind to see whether the French would pursue their advance.

But for the moment the French were satisfied. Prince August's unit was still in reasonable order as it moved back again towards Gernstädt. There the battalion reformed. The French wings continued to push forward on either side of the road. The village of Lisdorf fell to Friant's troops. The main Prussian divisions withdrew still further; and shortly after midday Gudin's main force advanced past Taugwitz towards Gernstädt.

Kalkreuth's reserves were still in the village, and were rejoined by Prince August's battalion. The Prussians could see the French approaching. Blücher and Kalkreuth both urged Friedrich Wilhelm to launch the reserves and the cavalry against the enemy, but the King, believing that Hohenlohe's and Rüchel's forces around Jena were still intact, decided to withdraw and join them. Once the armies had been merged, he said, the battle could be re-opened the following day. And yet by heading south west away from Berlin, instead of manoeuvring north, Friedrich Wilhelm simply moved farther inside the French embrace. Meanwhile, Kalkreuth's battalions with Prince August's among them covered the retreat. But the French pressed no farther than Eckartsberg. Davout's troops were in need of rest, and his cavalry were too few to drive on ahead. So, still in moderately good order, the Prussian army marched back to Mattstedt. Here in the dusk the Prussians could see camp fires near Apolda, twinkling on the dark skyline. The Prussians believed that they belonged to Hohenlohe's forces; the armies would soon be merged. A welcome rest would follow, the French would be engaged, and there would be every prospect of victory.

But groups of men soon began to filter in from the darkness, bleeding, weary, fear-stricken and battle-shocked. More and more of them began to arrive. They sobbed out the terrible news. Hohenlohe's army had been shattered and routed on the hills around Jena; it had ceased to exist as a coherent fighting force. The camp fires not far away belonged to the victorious French army commanded by Napoleon Bonaparte. Immediate panic filled the Prussians, and the withdrawal was now a retreat. For any commander, the task of keeping his forces organized under such conditions would be a monumental one; for Friedrich Wilhelm it was impossible. As his army continued to retreat during the night, the Prussian King twice changed direction and exhausted and scattered his weary forces even more. During this time Clausewitz heard the full horror of what had happened at Jena. When his scouts had told him of enemy activity nearby on 13th October, Hohenlohe had been under a misapprehension. He believed that he was only opposed by the enemy flank guard and that the main French force was hurrying along the road to Dresden.

At dawn on 14th October fog covered the fields near Jena. Even so, French and Prussian outposts on the Landgrafenberg plateau above Jena were so close that the glow of burning torches could be seen through the mist. Hohenlohe had not placed many men on this important area of high ground; the few he had were alarmed when the nearby French began to call "*Vive l'Empereur!*" Why should Napoleon be with these troops when they merely constituted a flank guard? Bonaparte too was under a misapprehension. He believed that the Prussians would accept battle on the Landgrafenberg plateau, the natural position for Hohenlohe to take up. He also thought he was still facing the main Prussian army. He therefore decided on the evening of 13th October to assault the plateau with the whole of Lannes' corps and the Imperial Guard; the attack would take place the following morning, while two corps struck at the Prussian flank. During the night of 13th October a rough track leading from Jena to the plateau was widened by French engineers. Napoleon helped with lantern in hand. French guns began to move along the track early in the morning.

At six o'clock Napoleon gave the order to attack. Under cover of the fog, Marshal Louis Gabriel Suchet's division on the right advanced on Closewitz village, and on the left Gazen attacked Cospeda hamlet. By 8.30 both had been taken, and Lützeroda too. This was all part of Napoleon's plan to thrust up from the Saale valley north west on to the heights. In addition, on Suchet's right, Soult's leading division left Lobstedt village and pushed up to Zwätena wood, and on Gazan's left Augereau's leading troops moved towards the Fohberg. So, by the time that the fog began to lift at around nine o'clock Napoleon had gained enough space in which to deploy his army across the plateau. He ordered a halt to allow his troops to regroup and form into line, but Marshal Michael Ney, impatient, pushed on.

Hohenlohe had at last realized that he was fighting more than a subsidiary of the French main force. He left three Saxon brigades on the vital Weimar road, told them to hold it at all costs, and sent forward most of his

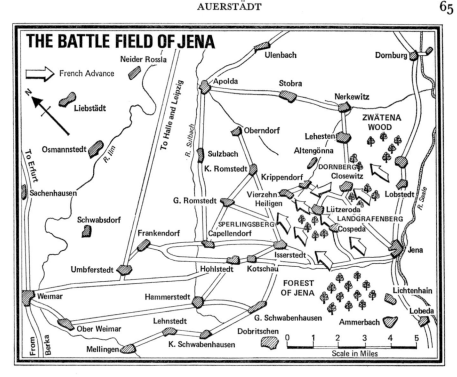

THE BATTLE FIELD OF JENA

French Advance

N

To Halle and Leipzig

R. Sulbach

R. Ilm

To Erfurt

From Berka

Neider Rossla

Liebstädt

Osmannstedt

Sachenhausen

Schwabsdorf

Umbferstedt

Weimar

Ober Weimar

Mellingen

Ulenbach

Apolda

Stobra

Oberndorf

Sulzbach

K. Romstedt

G. Romstedt

Frankendorf

Krippendorf

Vierzehn Heiligen

SPERLINGSBERG

Capellendorf

Hohlstedt

Kotschau

Isserstedt

Hammerstedt

Lehnstedt

K. Schwabenhausen

Dobritschen

G. Schwabenhausen

Dornburg

Nerkewitz

ZWÄTENA WOOD

Lehesten

Altengönna

DORNBERG

Closewitz

Lützeroda

LANDGRAFENBERG

Cospeda

Lobstedt

R. Saale

Jena

FOREST OF JENA

Lichtenhain

Lobeda

Ammerbach

Scale in Miles

0 1 2 3 4 5

infantry under General Grawert to retake the villages on the slopes. Tauentzien's troops, who had been pushed from the villages by the French, were sent to the rear to regroup. To support the advance, Hohenlohe brought up General Dyherr's Saxon divisions and the Prussian commander sent off an urgent appeal for help from Rüchel. The mist lifted, clinging to the trees on the slopes for a few minutes longer, then finally dispersed at ten o'clock.

Hohenlohe's forty-five squadrons of cavalry approached the village of Vierzehn Heiligen and split into two wings to charge the skirmishers sent forward by Suchet and Gazan. Then French forces under Ney, who had moved on ahead despite Napoleon's orders to halt, became heavily engaged by the Prussian troopers and were forced to form protective squares. Napoleon heard the heavy firing around the village and learned that Ney's troops were being attacked. He thought these men were in the rear. Immediately he sent Betrand ahead with two cavalry regiments and ordered Lannes, on Ney's right, to advance. Lannes took Vierzehn Heiligen, then came face to face with Grawert's lines on the northern side of the village. The Prussians used their well-tried tactics of massive volleys and rigid advance, and Lannes' men were sent scurrying back to the cover of the houses and orchards in the village. From these positions they opened heavy fire upon the vulnerable Prussian close-order lines.

Then came a striking example of Prussian unwillingness to adopt the new, more flexible tactics so strongly urged by Scharnhorst and other army reformers. Grawert's soldiers were in the open, standing in their tight formations; the French were scattered among the trees and behind the walls. Yet Hohenlohe insisted upon keeping Grawert's men where they were, exposed and unprotected, until help came from Rüchel; no-one knew when this would be. Nor would he agree to an advance to try to take the village. "It was one of the most extraordinary and pitiful incidents in military history," wrote the military historian Colonel F. N. Maude. "This line of magnificent infantry, some 20,000 strong, stood out in the open for two whole hours whilst exposed to the merciless case shot and skirmishing fire of the French, who behind the garden walls offered no mark at all for their return fire. In places the fronts of the companies were only marked by the individual files still loading and firing, whilst all their comrades lay dead and dying around them."[17] This one, terrible episode was a tragic vindication of all the *Militärische Gesellschaft* had asked for in the way of more flexible methods of making war.

These brave Prussians stood firm under the enemy fire, and were bloodily slaughtered. On other parts of the battlefield, men panicked under fire, and were quickly reduced to a rabble. As a dry official report put it: "The impossibility of countering the devastating fire of the enemy *tirailleurs* robbed the men of their composure."[18] There were other failings—of weapons, even of clothing, as one Prussian reported: "Even if called upon, what more could a poor half-starved Prussian soldier do than *creep*, whose every limb is so laced and confined that he could never maintain the necessary hurrying stride of up-hill attack. Besides, his musket is of little service, as it carries scarcely thirty yards, whilst the French *tirailleur* hits his object at twice that range. When they experienced this, it made the Prussian soldiers shy."[19]

While Grawert's men were being senselessly sacrificed, Lannes' and Ney's troops penetrated Isserstedt wood and isolated the Saxons who were holding the Weimar road. Hohenlohe was forced to bring Dyherr's brigade from the rear to plug the gap. By 10 p.m. Hohenlohe had no reserves left, apart from Tauentzien's decimated division. He could only hope for rapid relief from Rüchel.

With 54,000 troops engaged, Napoleon still had some 42,000 in general reserve. Early in the afternoon, when he calculated that the critical moment had arrived, Bonaparte ordered the final offensive. Nothing could stop the force of the French assault as it forced its way forward. Skirmishers darted from cover to cover, and soldiers of the line advanced solidly behind them, both pressing the Prussians down the slopes into the valley of the Sulbach. With his men faltering and falling all around him, Hohenlohe had to order a withdrawal to Gross and Klein Romstedt. But by now his troops were so exhausted and demoralized they were in total disorder, with the exception of one Saxon division which desperately formed a square where Hohenlohe himself sought safety. Hordes of panicking soldiers were taken prisoner by the French; complete batteries were seized; abandoned weapons and equipment were strewn across the countryside.

One last chance remained, if complete defeat was to be avoided. If Rüchel were to arrive and take up a protective position on the Sulbach between Capellendorf and Hammerstedt, Hohenlohe hoped that the Prussians might be able to retire behind his lines, and make an orderly withdrawal when night fell. But Massenbach, whom Hohenlohe had sent to Rüchel for help, had ordered the other Prussian commander to march on Capellendorf and attack the French on Hohenlohe's right. Although six miles from the village, Rüchel's advance had been so slow that he did not arrive until two o'clock in the afternoon. He marched through the village and deployed his men at the foot of the Sperlingsberg, a ridge lying northwest of Isserstedt.

Almost at once French light batteries opened up with case shot from the slopes above him, and the Prussians were attacked by hundreds of *tirailleurs*. Within fifteen minutes Rüchel's troops, enveloped by the enemy, suffered 50 per cent casualties. A further fifteen minutes later the Prussian lines collapsed. The troops were driven back towards Weimar, harassed and cut by French cavalry. Rüchel was fatally wounded. Hohenlohe, therefore, could not rally his troops, and had to fall farther back over the river Ilm to Sachenhausen and Liebstädt. Only the Saxons on the Weimar road still held out against all odds, until they were either killed or captured.

By four o'clock the battle was over. The French pursuit began. Murat's cavalry rode forward to Weimar, capturing thousands of Prussians. That night Lannes advanced to Umbferstedt, Augereau and Ney to Weimar, Soult to Schwabsdorf. Napoleon returned with his Imperial Guard to Jena, convinced that he had thrashed the main Prussian army. He heard the news of Auerstädt from Captain Torbiant, a member of Davout's staff. "Your Marshal must have seen double," the Emperor told the Captain. In one bloody day each one of Prussia's three armies had been dispersed. Over 25,000 prisoners had been taken, together with 200 guns and sixty regimental standards. French casualties were unknown; but Gudin's division at Auerstädt lost 41 per cent of its strength, one of the highest losses ever recorded for victorious troops in battle.[20]

But for the Prussians, the full horrors of the campaign had still a long way to run. Owing to the defeats, the Weimar road was blocked during the night of 14th October, and Friedrich Wilhelm ordered his army to turn northward on the Sömmerda route. More and more fugitives began to catch up with the army as it withdrew. Confusion and chaos grew worse, and Friedrich Wilhelm's frail control over his forces was broken. Unit after unit wavered, and then broke formation to disperse across the open countryside, believing that the French were at their heels. Men mutinied against their officers; officers deserted their men. Broken baggage wagons littered the roads. Houses were looted for food. Men fell exhausted by the roadside and in the fields. Shocked, unnerved, demoralized, the shattered Prussian forces had utterly collapsed. Even so, the main French pursuit did not begin until the morning of 15th October. Murat, Soult, Ney and Bernadotte set out with all possible speed to follow, encircle and eliminate the Prussian fragments. Napoleon, accompanied by Davout, Augereau, Lannes and the Guard, took the main road to Berlin.

Clausewitz had gained a profound experience of full-scale retreat, an experience which he was to use in *On War*: "The weak remains of battalions already in disorder are cut down by cavalry, exhausted men strew the ground, disabled guns and broken *caissons* are abandoned. Others in the bad state of the roads cannot be removed quickly enough, and are captured by the enemy's troops; during the night numbers lose their way, and fall defenceless into the enemy's hands, and thus the victory mostly gains bodily substance after it is already decided. Here would be a paradox, if it did not solve itself in the following manner." He continued: "The loss in physical force is not the only one which the two sides suffer in the course of the combat; the moral forces also are shaken, broken and go to ruin. It is not only the loss in men, horses and guns, but in order, courage, confidence, cohesion and plan, which come into consideration when it is a question whether the fight can be still continued or not."[21] Many in the Prussian army behaved appallingly. "Below no confidence, above no force of will or ability," Gneisenau reported to the King. "Each man wants only to save himself and his own comfort, so that to the man of honour nothing is left but to envy those who fall in the field of battle."[22] Prince August and Clausewitz were in the midst of the rout. In their case, it was to continue for two unrelieved weeks, during which they were harried and hounded from one brief stop to another as they tried to keep some kind of order in the dwindling battalion; seeking food, sleep and rest, and some army unit to which they could attach their weary men. They knew little of what was happening to their country.

On 27th October, Napoleon entered Berlin, in triumph. Friedrich Wilhelm III was meanwhile fleeing to the north-east corner of his kingdom, his army units and fortressses collapsing around him often without a fight. Napoleon began to set peace talks in progress. But Friedrich Wilhelm received a dispatch from Petersburg informing him that if he stood by the Prusso-Russian alliance, the Czar would come to his aid with 140,000 men. Friedrich continued to hope that his kingdom would be saved; a final treaty with France was not to be signed for another eight months.

About the same time that Napoleon rode into the Prussian capital, Clausewitz's part in the campaign was reaching an unhappy conclusion. Prince August's grenadier battalion had been reduced to 240 men out of its original 700. The rest had either been killed in the struggle for Poppel, or

Top "*The Corsican Carcase-Butcher's Reckoning Day*" (*London,
1803*). *The Anglo-French Peace of Amiens had ended in the spring
of 1803*
Left *A French infantryman* (*private*)
Right *A Prussian military band on parade*

Top *Napoleon at Jena, with Murat on the left and Berthier in the centre*
Bottom *Panoramic view of the Battle of Jena, 14th October, 1806*

had since collapsed and been left behind. But as the depleted unit continued its retreat from Schönermark, Prince August joined up with remnants of the Rheinbaben battalion, with which he had co-operated during the battle. Together, they made a total of about 600 men, all of them weak with exhaustion and lack of food. The Prince then tried to make his way to Prenslau down the Neu-Ruppin road, following other Prussian forces, in the hope that some regrouping could take place inside the town. There was terrible chaos on the road, as battalions mixed with other units and threatened a complete breakdown of organization and cohesion. Confusion grew even worse as the retreat continued during the hours of darkness. French cavalry were known to be near and possibly outflanking the staggering Prussian soldiers.

Then came the morning of 28th October. Clausewitz gave a detailed account of the later events.[23] As Prince August and Clausewitz passed through the village of Güstow at dawn, about a mile from Prenslau, they heard that the rearguard was to assemble at the town in a last-minute bid to stop the French. "At that moment some hundreds of wagons, which had been between us and the rest of the troops during the night, moved quickly out of the way, so we had a considerable gap in front of us. We carried on towards Prenslau as rapidly as possible." Not far behind, stragglers were being cut down or shot by the cavalry and the fast-moving *tirailleurs* who were moving freely over the countryside.

A horseman came clattering up the road from Prenslau: it was Count Stolberg, sent by Prince August's divisional commander General Hirschfeld with still more orders for the battalion to hurry, or risk being cut off before it reached the town. "Prince August ordered me to go with Count Stolberg to Prenslau," wrote Clausewitz, "to see what the situation was." So Clausewitz rode on, leaving the half-dead battalion to struggle up the road. Then, just outside Prenslau, as the battalion in front was hurrying into the safety of the city, he saw French cavalrymen massing on the slopes to the side of the road. "Count Stolberg said, 'We haven't any time to lose. Come with us—the others are all cut off.' I replied, 'You go your way, I'll go mine. You catch up with your regiment. I'll wait for August.' " Clausewitz was left by the side of the road, watching the French cavalry near by. "I waited some time, and saw the fight which a company of the Dohna grenadier regiment and dragoons from the Pritwitz regiment had with the enemy cavalry. They routed the enemy over the road we marched along."

For the moment the way was clear again, but it would not be so for long. At the entrance to Prenslau were "cavalry and infantry, friend and enemy, everyone in total confusion." Then Clausewitz's road toward Prenslau was totally blocked again. It was too late for August's battalion to reach the town. Clausewitz quickly mounted his horse and rode back to the Prince, who was approaching with his men. "I told him what I had seen, and we discussed what we should do. Since we didn't think we could expect much

5—C

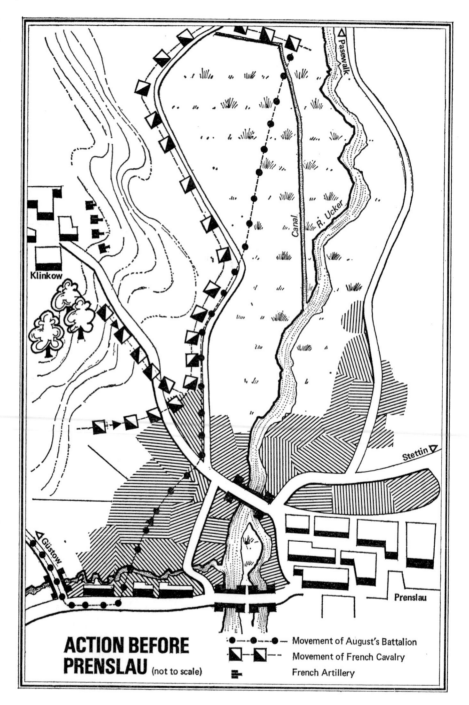

ACTION BEFORE PRENSLAU (not to scale)

● ● ● ● ● Movement of August's Battalion

◣ ◣ Movement of French Cavalry

▬ French Artillery

more from our men, and since we still believed it impossible for an infantry unit to escape when chased by enemy cavalry, we decided it best to move off the road to the left, so we could slip away, unnoticed because of the confusion in front of Prenslau."

Prince August believed that his battalion was the last on the road, with only the enemy behind. But then some of his soldiers began to cheer, and a Prussian cavalry unit was seen coming towards them. With these troopers, recognized as being from the Quitsov regiment, Prince August and his men would be in a much stronger position to withstand a French attack. "But while we were still on the road, enemy guns positioned on the other side of the little brook that comes from Boitsenburg, opened fire. And with these few shots the Quitsov regiment scattered, like peas when you throw a handful on the ground." Prince August's battalion rapidly found cover, leaving the road, wading through a small brook and scrambling "through a cabbage and garden field," where the men were formed into a square in anticipation of a French attack. For the moment no attack came.

Since it could no longer hope for refuge in Prenslau, the tired battalion had to find some other sanctuary. The frightened men were re-formed into a column and Prince August led them off in the direction of Ellingen, with the river Ucker flowing a thousand paces to one side. "Prince August berated Colonel Kospoth, commander of the Quitsov regiment, about the behaviour of his troopers, but he himself was highly incensed about it, and took great trouble to collect them again by blowing the bugle for the recall. He managed to get about a hundred together, in other words about a squadron, while the rest were soon lost to our sight." Clausewitz added: "Prince August now tried to persuade Colonel Kospoth to stay with him, which he promised to do. But nothing came of it."

The battalion marched on for half an hour more, hoping that their move from the road into the fields had gone unnoticed by the French. But then horsemen were seen on the left, across the slope of a low hill. There appeared to be 300 to 400 of them, or three or four squadrons. "At first we thought they were the Quitsov men who had fled in that direction. But when we saw, immediately afterward, an even larger number forming behind us, we recognized that it was the enemy."

The battalion had no choice but to stand and fight. Seven officers and 400 exhausted infantrymen faced over 1,000 French troopers. "The Prince encouraged us to put up an honourable fight. And he ordered the privates and officers to remain calm and not panic; and above all he told the privates not to fire under any circumstances before the order had been given. Our men were physically and mentally exhausted. The French cavalry were, thanks to their uninterrupted successes, bold and flushed with confidence. The strength facing us was so unequal that our situation was indeed extremely critical." Instead of firing as the French charged, when the shots would be inaccurate owing to the long range, Prince August and Clausewitz decided not to give the order until the very last moment. The charging French would be surprised that the enemy had not begun firing, and would begin to fear the effect of the fire when it eventually did break at short range. They might hesitate, slow down, and present better targets.

The French cavalry trotted down the slopes, joined the horsemen coming up from behind, and prepared to charge. "The battalion performed. 'Halt! Prepare Arms!' And the officers repeatedly shouted to the men to hold their fire."[24] The charge began. The thick line of horsemen drummed down the hill towards the small Prussian square, which adamantly refused to open fire. "It was seen they awaited with disquiet the moment when they would suffer our volley. And when at a hundred paces they did not receive the fire, they held back their horses more and more, until they went from a gallop into a trot, from trot to jog. It was at that moment, about thirty paces away, the volley was fired."

The result, at point blank range, was deadly. Horses and riders fell in a tangled *mêlée* of wounded and dead, and panic-stricken men struggled to free themselves from below their slaughtered animals. "The rest took cover behind the necks of their horses, turned tail, and fled. Now we had gained everything with our men. They seemed to be very astonished about our success with this manoeuvre which they had practised so often on the barrack square, but which they had only, until now, thought of as a kind of joke. Then an enemy dragoon whose horse had been killed just in front of the square crawled out from under his dead horse and fled in panic. The contrast of this frightened retreat with the wild appearance of those helmeted and horsed dragoons made such an impression on the men that all of them started laughing." Momentarily the tension passed. Leaving the dying Frenchmen, the small Prussian unit continued its desperate march. But not for long. The French cavalry regrouped and reappeared not far away, just out of musket range. Again the remnants of the Prussian battalion formed a square. Again the men stood silent, some shivering with fear as the officers ordered them not to fire. "Hold, hold, hold, steady!" Nearer came the charging horses. The French dragoons raised their sabres, ready to slash them down upon the Prussians' heads. And then came the same shattering volley, the same terrible screams, the same French retreat. The Prussians cheered, slapping one another on the backs, excited, and some hysterical.

The Prussians pressed on again, hoping to find a way across the river where the French would be unable to follow, only to find the muddy track before them blocked by two French squadrons. Other French troops hovered nearby. "We therefore stopped again, took the few sharp-shooters whom we still had, and let them fire with single shots into the thickly clustered squadrons. This had an immediate effect. They scattered in all directions and the road was clear." Five more times within the next thirty minutes the battalion had to withstand French cavalry charges, made,

Clausewitz found out later, by General Beaumont's division. The holding-fire tactic continued to work, and the French had no artillery with which to smash the Prussian square. But the Prussians suffered casualties nonetheless, from pistol shots, musket fire, and from sheer physical exhaustion.

Then a messenger arrived from a nearby village, attracted by the sound of the musket fire. He told Prince August that there was no ford across the river for another four miles, and that no crossing could be made without a ford because of the muddy banks, which would trap the troops and render them an easy target. Prince August and Clausewitz had another hurried consultation. If they carried on as they were, the ammunition which was already running low would be gone, even if the men did not give up first. They decided to strike across country to reach Pasewalk. The bad terrain with its bogs and ditches was likely to be hard going for the men, but it would be harder still for the French horses. The messenger, a local farmer, warned them against the idea, but the Prince gave the order and the battalion turned off the track. For a while, all went well. Enemy cavalry followed along the higher, drier, ground to one side, but they were fewer in number than before. The Prussians watched some of them leaving, dismounting and leading their horses away. The going became harder. Ditch followed ditch, with each so deep the men sank up to their armpits. About a hundred of the Prussians, bogged in the mud, were so tired they were unable to haul themselves out, and had to be left to their fate, feebly struggling in the slime. All the horses, including Clausewitz's, had been turned loose, except the Prince's: his, a beautiful English stallion, had belonged to his brother Louis Ferdinand, who had been "chopped up," in Clausewitz's words, at Saalfeld. His blood still stained the saddle. Finally, even this horse bolted as the Prince was leading it by the bridle. August would no longer be able to escape if all was lost, as he had planned to do "by virtue of his noble descent."

To make matters worse, the Prussians now heard the squealing of wheels to their left, and there upon the slope of the hill, they saw French horse-artillery being dragged into position. The battalion would be an easy target as it struggled slowly through the bogs. Moments later, grey smoke billowed from the guns and cannon balls whistled towards them. One thing saved them from terrible casualties: the French were using ordinary cannon balls instead of grape shot, and as these thudded into the soft earth, the mud stopped them from rolling red-hot among the men. The battalion came to a wide canal and only managed to cross it with great difficulty. Many of the men were collapsing, crawling forward a few yards more, and then lying motionless. On the other side of the canal came the finish. The ground was drained, and harder, "and this meant the enemy cavalry could approach us, however slowly, in great numbers. As we reached this drier ground we called to the men to form themselves in a square." But despite the efforts of the officers, the square remained unformed. The men were half-dead, and in any case their weapons were useless. "The soldiers had used their muskets as supports in order to get over the ditches. Most of them had been up to their armpits in water and consequently the ammunition in their pockets was completely wet through." The French cavalry rode closer. There was nothing the Prussians could do. Cautiously the enemy surrounded the battalion. Many of August's men threw their weapons away, others just slumped to the ground. Prince August and Clausewitz stood waiting. Only about a hundred of the Prussian unit remained. All were taken prisoner, including August and his aide. As they stood waiting to be taken away, even more weary now that it was all over, their sodden clothes, covered with slime from the swamps, clung to their skin.

General Beaumont, the French divisional commander, rode up almost at once and spoke in a courteous fashion to the Prince. He ordered August's bag, decorations and watch, which had been taken away from him by the French troopers, to be returned to him, and his horse to be found. General Beaumont also told the Prince and Clausewitz that Prenslau had fallen. Ironically, it was to Prenslau which they had tried so hard to reach earlier, that the Prince and his aide were now to be taken. Later, Clausewitz learned the full details of what had happened to the Prussian forces. Having struggled from Jena with an army of 12,000 men still in some semblance of fighting order, and with Blücher anxiously awaiting reinforcements, Hohenlohe had capitulated between Prenslau and Stettin. He had ordered his troops to lay down their arms on the advice of his Chief-of-Staff, Massenbach. At least Prince August was spared the disgrace of that capitulation. But for the rest of his life he was taunted that he had let himself be taken simply because he had fallen into a swamp.

As they were escorted away from the canal, August and Clausewitz saw some of their stragglers running for safety behind them. Others, still stuck fast in the mud, were bravely but vainly firing at the French who were trying to capture them. General Beaumont told Prince August that he should order these men to stop shooting: they were technically prisoners since their commander had been taken. "The Prince gave the noble reply: 'These people are happier than myself. They are no longer under my orders, and I can only be happy if they defend themselves as brave soldiers.' " A few of them managed to escape to Stettin by floating down river on a board, but most were either captured or killed, picked off one by one by the French.

August and Clausewitz were escorted to Prenslau, where they were told they would be sent to Berlin, guarded by a staff officer. So without rest, without even time to wash, the two prisoners took the road to the Prussian capital, riding throughout the night and the following morning and arriving in Berlin at midday. People in the streets stared curiously at the two dishevelled noblemen. Napoleon said that he wished to see the Prince. "We were taken immediately to the palace where we found the Imperial Staff collected together in the rooms of the deposed King. The Prince was taken to see the Emperor immediately, while I had to remain, dishevelled as I was, among all the glittering, almost disdainfully elegant, uniforms of the Imperial *aide-de-camps*." Clausewitz stood, ignored, his clothes filthy and stinking of the long retreat, in the same room where he had talked, laughed and danced with Marie, a room now filled with French officers, the victorious staff of the conquering Bonaparte. He stared at their heavily braided jackets, their fashionable tight white trousers, gleaming black boots and his contempt increased. Prince August stepped out, Napoleon's questions finished. August told Clausewitz that they were both to be detained as prisoners-of-war in Berlin.

For an officer, the status of prisoner-of-war was often not especially uncomfortable. Usually, nothing suffered except personal honour. A certain chivalry still existed, and sometimes officers were even paid salaries by their captors during the period of "internment." During the 1812 campaign for example, there was much grumbling among captured German officers, then serving for the French, that the Russians were not paying them enough; this was considered discourteous, and contrary to the rules of war.[25] Normally a prisoner spent his time on parole, with his quarters or lodgings provided for him. If the conquering army was in occupation of the prisoner's homeland, he would be allowed to move about freely, perhaps even living at home. He would merely have to give his word that he would not take up arms against his victors. So it was for Clausewitz and August. The Prince was allowed to return home to his royal parents. Clausewitz, who spent some of his time in Berlin and some weeks in Neu-Ruppin, saw for himself something of the humiliation which was heaped upon Prussia and her capital.

When the first shock of Jena was received in Berlin, the city commandant Count Schulenburg hastened to calm the people. In fact, he was in greater need of calm than they. "The King has lost a battle," proclaimed an official notice that Schulenburg had posted in the streets. "The first duty of the citizen is now to be quiet. This duty I charge the inhabitants of Berlin to perform. The King and his brothers live."[26] Henriette Hertz, the wife of a leading Berlin citizen, made a typically acid comment upon the announcement. "How laconic! And yet part of it is superfluous. For who in Berlin thought of disturbing his quiet? The announcement was read, but few countenances showed any expression of fear, most no expression at all." When Count Schulenburg himself fled from the city, Henriette declared: "The people thus charged to be quiet were so childishly disposed to quiet, that when the General, the preacher of quietism, rode out of town a few days after at the head of a few troops that had remained behind, they crowded round him entreating that they might not be forsaken. 'Surely, I leave my children with you,' was the warrior's reply. The people looked at each other with a bewildered air. Scarcely anyone knew who these children were. Some saw in the words a symbol or mystery, some palladium hitherto unknown. But the 'children' had a literal existence: they were simply

Princess Hatzfeld and her husband."[27] Many other leading Berlin citizens behaved, according to Hermann von Boyen, as if they had been deprived of their manliness.[28]

When Napoleon made his triumphal entry into Berlin, French troops flooded the capital. City society received the officers well. Although Berliners were "accustomed to put off the Prussian troops with the meanest lodgings and accommodation, they were now, by command, obliged to indulge the new uniform with their newest rooms, and the best of everything the house afforded."[29]

Clausewitz had only one consolation: Marie, with whom he had been joyfully and tearfully reunited. He wished to forget everything else: the sight of foreign troops in the streets, and, even worse, the need to associate with French officers during those functions where he still acted as August's *aide*. Small talk never came very easily to him in any case. His dislike of the French grew daily, no matter how much courtesy his victors may have shown him. During those weeks, Clausewitz's duties as the Prince's *aide* were gradually allowed to lessen, possibly because of the personal embarrassment which Carl was suffering.

Meanwhile, despite the disgraceful conduct of most of the Prussian commanding officers, and despite the widespread losses of fortresses such as Erfurt, Hameln, Spandau, Küstrin and Stettin, a small group of Prussians valiantly pursued the fight. Reports were reaching Berlin of the struggle waged by Scharnhorst and Blücher, and Clausewitz felt added frustration at his incapacity to fight alongside the man he most deeply admired. In September Blücher assumed command of the remains of Prussia's army, about 22,000 men, and appointed Scharnhorst as his Chief-of-Staff. The two men tried to draw as many French forces as possible away from the advance upon Mecklenburg and East Prussia. They decided that, if necessary, they would even enter neutral territory, to save their own force for a counter-attack, perhaps after Russia joined the struggle. But the French always kept close behind them. On 1st October the Prussian rearguard fought a delaying action against Bernadotte's troops. During this action Colonel Yorck, who had been engaged neither at Jena nor at Auerstädt—his *Jäger* force had been posted too far away—was slightly wounded. The main Prussian body managed to slip away, and Blücher marched for the walled town of Lübeck. Here he hoped to be able to regroup, protected by the river which encircled the town. Afterwards he planned "to entrust his fate to a decisive battle."[30]

Late on 5th October Blücher's force reached Lübeck. But the Prussians were denied the rest they so badly needed. Early next morning French light cavalry attacked the Prussian forward positions and by midday enemy infantry columns had arrived. They attacked at once and broke through the town walls. In the street fighting Colonel Yorck was wounded twice more, and taken prisoner. Blücher and Scharnhorst escaped with only 9,000 men.

On 7th October they had no choice but to surrender. Final Prussian resistance of any significance had been crushed. In a report to King Friedrich Wilhelm, Blücher praised Yorck and Scharnhorst, adding that Scharnhorst's "ceaseless activity, firm determination, and intelligent advice" contributed to "a great part of the successful progress of my retreat."[31] Writing a bitter letter a few days later, Scharnhorst believed that "on the whole no-one mattered in the corps but Blücher, myself, and Colonel Yorck."[32]

In the north-east corner of Prussia, sheltering first at Königsberg and then at Ortelsburg, King Friedrich Wilhelm laid plans for the continuation, and widening, of the war. Napoleon had similar plans. In November, Bonaparte issued orders for the levy of a Prussian regiment of four battalions for French service, under the command of the Prince of Isenburg. The Prince published a proclamation on 18th November, which was read by Clausewitz with deep disgust: "Hasten my bold warriors, to march under the glorious banners of the great Napoleon! Partake with him in Victory and Immortal Fame! The rendezvous is at Leipzig."[33] Napoleon was also planning an even more ambitious scheme: the Continental System. On 21st November he issued from Berlin a proclamation excluding all British trade, and all British citizens, from the Continent. This was a programme of economic warfare, but to make it a success, he would need Russian support. Both Napoleon and Friedrich Wilhelm, therefore, tried to make an alliance with the Czar, which was seen by the Prussian King as the only hope that his kingdom might be restored.

Friedrich Wilhelm also worked to build a framework of government for the small territory he still had under his rule. On 29th November, Baron von Stein was formally invited by the King to be Minister of State for the Interior. But Beyme, who was disliked by Stein, still remained chief adviser, and Stein on his part believed that the Cabinet system with its favourites and over-influential members would only continue. Nor did Friedrich Wilhelm seem to want Stein for his own merits, but only as a second choice while Haugwitz was incapacitated by gout. Stein was not prepared to accept the office on these terms, and declined the offer. Friedrich Wilhelm sent back a virulent reply. "I have been forced, to my great regret, to admit that unfortunately I was not mistaken in you at the beginning, but that you are to be regarded as a refractory, insolent, obstinate and disobedient official, who, proud of his genius and talents, far from regarding the good of the State, guided purely by caprice, acts from passion and from personal hatred and rancour . . ."[34]

A similar display of peevishness by the King would one day be turned upon Clausewitz.

Friedrich Wilhelm also vented his anger upon his army, with more reason, and certainly in more civil terms. On 1st December he issued the following proclamation from Ortelsburg: "His Majesty is far from attributing to his gallant army any share of those dreadful calamities and disappointments which have persecuted both himself and his country. On the contrary, he has perceived with the greatest satisfaction that many, from the highest to the lowest, have distinguished themselves by their courage, perseverance, and true sense of honour. But there are also others, and to their shame be it spoken, who have been guilty of most atrocious conduct, which proclaims so loudly their own ignominy, as not to require further examination. It is of so flagrant a nature that it cannot be passed over in silence, but must, as an example to others, be punished in the most severe and public manner . . . His Majesty in consequence orders . . . Major Prusechoeck to be dishonourably discharged for unnecessarily giving up his charge at Erfuth . . . Lieutenant-Commander Romberg, Governor and Commander of Stettin, and Major-General Knobelsdorff, shall be both broke; Major-General Rouch, Vice-Commander, dishonourably dismissed; Major Harenberg, 'Ingenieur de la Place,' broke . . ." And so it continued. Many of those listed were distinguished soldiers, including General Kleist, Governor of Magdeburg, and Du Trossel, both of whom were dishonourably dismissed. The proclamation issued a severe warning about future army conduct. "Every soldier, who, in flight, throws away his arms shall be shot . . . Natural born subjects who may have entered into the service of the enemy, and be taken in battle, shall, without mercy, be shot."[35]

Meanwhile Clausewitz, still a prisoner-of-war, was at Neu-Ruppin. He gave careful thought to his recent experiences. Typically, he projected them into a wider appreciation of military tactics. "Because of our small fight," he wrote, "I became convinced that infantry can be strong against cavalry . . . that it is in the nature of the troopers to hunt, not to get killed. Generally one tends to believe that the enemy's cavalry, just at the moment when they turn tail, could carry on without any danger. But this is a wrong supposition. The fire of infantry, in whatever form it may be given—with us a volley fired by the whole battalion, and this form in such serious cases is the only one which can be done—does not stop so quickly that the enemy's cavalry, if it carries on riding would not be fired at more and more, and finally, they would receive it point blank—and it is these point blank shots which everyone fears." Clausewitz continued: "In all cases where we saw with certainty that the infantry squares collapsed, we can take it with certainty that the infantry was no longer in good order and was already beginning to give way before the courageous cavalry had time to turn back; or perhaps they fired too early, say between one hundred and two hundred paces, so that when the cavalry came nearer they received little or no fire from the square."[36]

Clausewitz also drafted three letters on the campaign, which appeared next year in *The Minerva*, a journal published in Hamburg between 1792 and 1808. The Prussian retreat from Auerstädt need not, he said, have been a disaster. Both French and Prussian armies were exhausted after long marches. But whereas the French stragglers were able to regroup, the Prussian soldiers were lost.

Nevertheless, Clausewitz continued, Prussia had still had a number of chances, which had been thrown away by the commanders. Before the retreat, some troops might have been gathered and sent directly to Magdeburg. It might have been possible, with better leadership, to have made a stand at Prenslau. Again, some troops, at least, ought to have reached Stettin and retrieved some Prussian honour by fighting there. But Hohenlohe's courage had expired. The more the Prussian commander had avoided combat, the more he dreaded having to engage in it. The more a man fixed his eyes upon an approaching danger, the greater was his fear of it. Blücher at least provided a fine example of heroism, Clausewitz added. But some said he had been wrong to sacrifice the lives of his men when everything seemed so hopeless. This attitude was "mean." Besides, Blücher had tied up important enemy strength for several days, and his actions had boosted Prussia's fallen morale. "I will always consider the name of Blücher as one of those who, at the moment of extreme peril, restored the courage of the nation." Clausewitz concluded: "Accordingly, we need to redouble our courage to support the nation and carry the burden of the misfortune and disgrace of this time. Let me cry out to all Germans: 'Honour yourselves—don't despair of your destiny!' "[37]

The letters, emotional and deeply influenced by the shock of events, were in places factually inaccurate. He said, for example, that Davout had engaged with 50,000 men at Auerstädt, whereas the figure of 27,000 was nearer the mark. Clausewitz admitted that he lacked relevant information. Later he drafted a document titled *Memoirs of 1806*, in which his judgement of Jena was so critical that his family refused permission to publish the manuscript.[38]

Clausewitz continued to study the reasons for the disaster for the rest of his life. In about 1825, he wrote a detailed account of events in *Nachrichten*. He admitted then he had been wrong in his 1806 plan of war drafted at Weimar; the Prussian army had acted correctly in refusing the perilous crossing of the Saale, and in not attacking Napoleon on the right of the river. Here the land, which was rough and wooded, would have been very unfavourable for the deployment of the rigid, formalized Prussian lines. But Jena should not have been yielded up, he wrote. Hohenlohe should have pulled back to rejoin the main army and delay Napoleon's march along the river Saale. Kalkreuth's reserve corps should have been fully engaged at Auerstädt, he added (in the *Minerva* letters Clausewitz had been less sure about this difficult point). He was to be even more convinced in *On War* that these reserves should have been thrown in, saying that the Prussians "neglected to use the reserve of 18,000, under General Kalkreuth, to restore the battle which, under these circumstances, would have been impossible to lose."[39] By the time he wrote *Nachrichten* Clausewitz's judgement of the 1806 campaign was slightly less severe than it was at the time. But in this same document, he offered some extremely harsh comments on the Government of Prussia, both before and during the 1806 disaster. He gave perceptive descriptions of the principal Prussian politicians and military leaders.

Meanwhile, in December 1806, Clausewitz was faced with another personal upheaval. The Governor of Berlin, General Clarke, informed Prince August that he was to be sent away from the capital and out of Germany itself. He was to serve his time as a prisoner-of-war in France. Clausewitz, as his *aide-de-camp*, would accompany him. The two young men were told to leave Berlin by the end of the month.

FIVE

Prisoner of War

"With psychological and
philosophical sophistries no theory,
no General should meddle."
(*On War*, bk. ii, ch. ii.)

CLAUSEWITZ SAID GOODBYE to his sad Countess and left with Prince August on 30th December, 1806, for the journey into France and "captivity." The Prince and his *aide* rode through the Harz county and over the mountains to Frankfurt, thence along to Mainz, up the Moselle valley to Metz and south to Nancy, where they had been instructed to report. They arrived on 18th January, 1807. But towards the end of February Prince August received fresh orders to leave Nancy: he must choose between Senlis, Beauvais, Meaur and Soissons. He decided upon Soissons and on 1st March the two officers began their second journey. They rode *via* Rheims, where they admired the great cathedral, and on to the plain of Picardy and to their lodgings at Soissons.

During their stay in Soissons, Clausewitz worried constantly over the reasons for Prussia's disaster, setting down on paper his ideas for a Prussian come-back. He began to draft an operational plan for Austria if she were ever to take part in the war against France.[1] He believed that Napoleon's greatest strength was the lethargy and fatalism of the defeated peoples. He proposed that Napoleon should be attacked from all of Austria's frontiers. Later, however, he rejected this idea, in favour of concentrating the forces in order to gain one great decisive advantage. Victory was possible, he argued, providing the attack was made with the proper mixture of boldness, speed and caution, a combination which Frederick the Great had been able to achieve many years before.

The stay in Soissons and Clausewitz's writing were interrupted by a fortnight's visit to Paris. Here, in Napoleon's capital, Clausewitz behaved like any tourist, visiting museums and galleries, while the gay Prince August typically played the gallant and devoted most of his time to the *salons* and *boudoirs*, earning himself the title of Prince Don Juan.[2] But Clausewitz found it impossible to be happy. He could not put Prussia's humiliation out of his mind. His letters to Marie, which were often extremely emotional, sharply reflected his misery. "What an inexhaustible spring of pain and sadness lies in thinking about the past," he wrote on 28th January.[3] Even Paris failed to cheer his spirits and on 2nd April he wrote from the capital: "There is no joy in me . . . it annoys me when I see the greatest happiness suddenly crash down as if hit by lightning."[4]

Clausewitz had a brief hope that he might return home sooner than expected. He had read in the *Gazette de l'Empire* that Blücher and Tauentzien had been exchanged for French prisoners-of-war, and "one reads that Prince August will also be exchanged." He doubted if this would happen, "but it does give us a glimmer of hope and I should like to meet the person who would not give himself up to some joy for at least a few days."[5] But nothing happened. On 25th June Clausewitz commented: "My life is a trackless existence."[6] He gave much thought to his own situation and the nature of his odd personality: "I have grown up to my twenty-seventh year with a piecemeal development, and because of this the result is a very incomplete and imperfect development." Two sentiments were to haunt him for the rest of his life, and cause him a good deal of misery: "It is not enough to be on the right road, it is also very important to have arrived, and in the period of time which we have on earth, to travel slowly is often the same as not travelling at all . . . apart from this, I am one of those people who are always concerned about the future, and that is why I am seldom happy in the present."[7]

Clausewitz said on 3rd July: "I have seen nothing in our brief campaign which was not bad and pitiable." His dearest wish was to return home and fight again; he pictured in his imagination Marie wishing him goodbye as he departed once more for battle: "One of the most beautiful of these pictures for me is to see myself sinking down at Marie's feet to be bid a happy farewell from her. Why should this farewell not be happy? What can happen to me? A beautiful death, honourable wounds . . . one of these must be mine, and even if it hurts the hearts of my friends and brings forth tears, are these not worthwhile tears, and is it not a sweet pain, closely linked with a better existence?"[8]

Important events were taking place in the international arena. Even before Clausewitz had been sent away from Berlin, Napoleon had left the Prussian capital for Posen on his way to thrash the Russians, Prussia's last hope of salvation. On 8th February, 1807, in a blinding snowstorm, French armies attacked the two Russian armies at Prüssisch-Eylau. A Prussian Corps led by Gerhard von Scharnhorst also fought against Napoleon, and Clausewitz's older friend increased his now fast rising reputation as a soldier. The battle was bloody, but not decisive. On 26th April Russia and Prussia signed a military pact, the Convention of Bartenstein. They were now supported by Britain who undertook to pay Friedrich Wilhelm a subsidy of £1 million and to send 20,000 troops to Stralsund to reinforce King Gustav IV's 16,000-strong Swedish force. Many observers expected little from the Convention or from Friedrich Wilhelm's actions. Stein wrote:

"I can expect nothing from the ingredients of the Court of Memel (the King's latest headquarters). It is a soulless, meaningless combination, capable of nothing but corrupt fermentation." Clausewitz agreed. Even before the final signature of the convention, he wrote: "The theatre has now been constructed, the players have assembled, in a few days the curtain will rise. God, what a spectacle for us!"[9]

Having failed in pitched battle, the first time he had done so, Napoleon now laid siege to Danzig. The important seaport capitulated. On 14th June a Russian army under General Levin Bennigsen was routed by the French at Friedland. Much to Clausewitz's disgust, the Czar not only asked for peace, but proposed an alliance with Napoleon. On 25th June the French and Russian emperors discussed terms on a raft moored in the river Neimen. Friedrich Wilhelm awaited their decision, standing impatiently on the river bank in the pouring rain. Czar Alexander agreed to a return to the League of Armed Neutrality signed by his father Paul I in 1780, and the Baltic Sea was once more closed to English shipping. On 7th July the peace treaty between France and Russia was formally concluded. Friedrich Wilhelm was effectively isolated. Two days later he signed the Treaty of Tilsit with Napoleon. Prussia was deprived of all her territory west of the Elbe, of the Polish provinces she had annexed in 1793, of the southern part of west Prussia acquired in 1772. She was obliged to agree to join in common cause with France and Russia against England. On 12th July a new convention was signed: the French undertook to evacuate Prussia east of the river Elbe if a large and unspecified indemnity were paid.

Prussia's humiliation and Napoleon's triumph seemed complete. At a farewell dinner, Queen Louise of Prussia raged bitterly against Alexander for his treacherous conduct, and then burst into tears. Her husband issued a sad farewell address to his lost provinces: "That which centuries and worthy forefathers, that which treaties, love and confidence once bound together, must now be severed. Fate commands that the father should part from his children; no fate, no power can tear your memory from the hearts of me and mine."[10]

But at least Clausewitz and Prince August could now go home. First they had to wait for their passports to be documented. In the meantime Clausewitz continued his writing, this time in partnership with August, who proved himself an able military thinker as well as a persuasive lover. On 15th July, immediately after the peace had been signed, Friedrich Wilhelm ordered Scharnhorst and one of his royal adjutants, Count Friedrich Karl von Lottum, to draw up a demobilization plan. On the same day, this team was reconstituted as a five-man Military Reorganisation Commission. Although he had recently been offered an excellent position in the English army, as Director of an Artillery school,[11] Scharnhorst agreed to be chairman, and the group was commanded by a Cabinet Order of 25th July to investigate and adjudge the army's conduct in the war.

The Commission was to receive reform proposals from a great many people. One of the earliest was the memorandum compiled by Prince August and Clausewitz while they were still at Soissons. Entitled *Vorschläge zur Verbesserung der preussischen Militair-Verfassung*, dated 13th June, 1807, it was submitted in the Prince's name. Nevertheless, Clausewitz had a large share in its production, although he opposed sending it to the Commission as he felt it might be considered presumptuous.[12] As usual, Clausewitz was belittling himself. Not only was the memorandum received with interest by Scharnhorst, but it may even have influenced Friedrich Wilhelm's "Guidelines" which he issued for the Reorganisation Commission.[13] This document from the King, *Richtlinien für die Reorganisation der Armee*,[14] contained nineteen paragraphs. The first five of these concerned the officer corps, and the study of its conduct during the war; punishments were to be meted out to those who had failed in their duty. The *Richtlinien* also raised the possibility of admitting more non-noble officers, and went on to discuss the reorganization of the infantry and cavalry, including the training of the third ranks of infantry battalions for light service.

According to the memorandum drafted by Prince August and Clausewitz, the lost war had been characterized by the extreme tardiness of Prussian movements, and by the imperfect co-ordination of infantry, cavalry and artillery. Branches of the services should therefore be regrouped into permanent divisions—as Scharnhorst had already suggested—and the troops themselves made more mobile. Cumbersome equipment should be ruthlessly scrapped and field supply systems made more flexible. Tactical matters, too, had to be reconsidered. Closer co-operation was needed between the line and the light troops. Sharpshooters had not been used to full effect in the war; in fact in his Guidelines the King proposed to abolish these company *Schützen* completely.

The memorandum selected three main areas for reform, which were to be the main preoccupations of the Military Reorganisation Commission. They were: universal conscription, the admission of the *bourgeoisie* to the officer corps, and the relaxation of the harsh system of discipline in the Prussian Army. "It is every citizen's duty to defend the state," wrote August and Carl. "This principle, admitted as it is theoretically, is subject in most states to large exceptions, owing to the privileges of certain classes and occupations. In modern times it has only been accepted in France and Italy since the Revolution swept those privileges away. It is not to be denied that the State acquires a great military power when this principle is raised to a law and every soldier made eligible to the higher ranks." It was essential to make every soldier eligible for high promotion. The memorandum said: "Indeed it is very doubtful whether it would be possible without this to introduce conscription, since the disaffection it would cause would balance the advantages it would bring . . . and that citizens as well as nobles may be actuated by principles of honour is strikingly shown by the example of the

Top *Prussia's humiliation: Napoleon victoriously enters Berlin*
Bottom *Napoleon passing through the Brandenburg Gate*

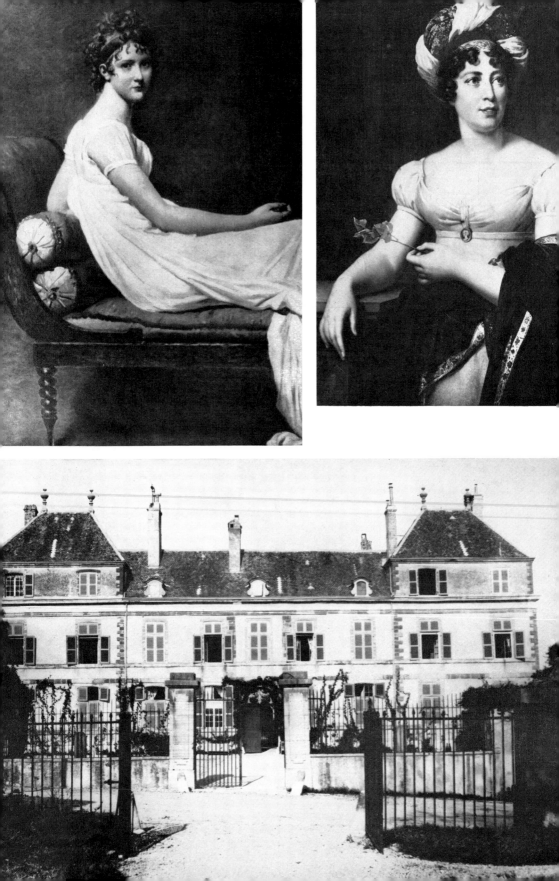

present French officers." Military discipline should be made more humane, argued August and Clausewitz, and should be equated with the principle of honour. "Nothing runs counter to this so much as corporal punishment and the unfortunately still widespread custom of forcing men to serve in the army. Both must be abolished if military service is to agree with the principles according to which the soldier should act."[15]

Clausewitz was soon diverted from his studies and contemplations again. The effervescent Prince August wished to see more of society outside Prussia while he had the opportunity. The two of them set out for Switzerland, arriving at Geneva on 5th August and making an excursion on the 11th to see the glaciers in Savoy. Afterwards they were invited to stay at Ouchy, near Lausanne, and then at Coppet, exile homes of the famous, and notorious, Madame de Staël. The next few weeks promised to be among the most fascinating of Clausewitz's life.

Madame Germaine de Staël, described to George Washington as "a wonderful wit and above prejudices of every kind" and described by Napoleon as "that hussy Staël," was then aged forty-one; she was the most intriguing woman in Europe, and was approaching the peak of her incredible career. This novelist, propagandist, schemer, wit and seducer, was taking on Napoleon, whom she had once wooed, single-handed. Germaine was the proud daughter of Jacques Necker, the financier and Controller-General who had helped precipitate the French Revolution by his stupidity and blindness. Germaine had been brought up with no playmates, but was on familiar terms with such great men as Diderot, D'Alembert, Edward Gibbon and Buffon. While still a child, Voltaire and Jean-Jacques Rousseau had been her acquaintances. Her mother had planned to marry Germaine to the twenty-three-year-old ex-Chancellor of the British Exchequer, William Pitt, but had been obliged to settle for a Swedish diplomat, Eric Magnus Staël von Holstein. Her husband shared Germaine's passion for infidelity. The crippled Talleyrand was probably her first lover, and Louis Vicomte de Narbonne her second, before she fell in love with the son of one of his mistresses. She persuaded the King Louis XVI to appoint Narbonne Minister of War. During the French Terror, Germaine acted as a kind of female "Scarlet Pimpernel."

She had a love-hate feeling for Napoleon. It was her friend Barras who, wishing to be rid of his mistress Josephine, had passed her on to the young General Bonaparte. Germaine had tried to win Napoleon for herself, and the future Emperor had first reacted coldly, and then with panic when she persisted. Rejected by Napoleon, and disliking his autocratic policies, Germaine turned viciously and completely against him. Her writings were powerful propaganda, her intrigues were infuriating; and on the last day of 1806 Napoleon instructed his police chief "not to let that bitch of a Madame de Staël approach Paris." In her own words, she had come to Coppet in Switzerland "like a wounded pigeon." But she continued her verbal bombardment

Facing page *Interlude at Coppet*. Top left *Juliette Récamier*, top right *Germaine de Staël, and* bottom *a view of Coppet itself* of Napoleon, demanding to return to her beloved Paris, screaming out for pity at the way she had been treated. Napoleon replied: "She's much to be pitied indeed! Except for Paris all Europe is her prison."[16]

During the weeks at Coppet, the quiet Clausewitz gained the favour of this volatile woman. "She likes me very much," he wrote to Marie on 5th October. "I don't quite know why."[17] While Prince August busily flirted with the other ladies, Madame de Staël made a point of drawing conversation from the withdrawn *aide-de-camp*, an art in which she specially excelled. Her most remarkable talent was to inspire and help other people formulate and express their opinions. The effect was almost one of seduction—and in fact sometimes was; but not with Clausewitz. She was always attracted by shy, retiring, handsome young men, and later married one. Germaine was already used to what she put down as the withdrawn nature of the German race. On her first visit to Clausewitz's homeland three years before, she had noted that people locked away their thoughts and feelings "like objects never to be used, not even on Sundays."

Life at Coppet revolved about two suns: Germaine, "flaming, explosive, commanding," and Juliette Récamier, "cool, distant and beckoning."[18] With her loud voice, plump figure, bare, ruddy arms and bosom, turbans and bird feathers, Germaine spent a good deal of time with her incongruous companion, Clausewitz, each using their newly acquired knowledge of the other's language. Juliette, on the other hand, contrived to spend all of her days and many of her nights with Prince "Don Juan" August of Prussia. Juliette's list of lovers was longer than that of Germaine, whom she completely outshone in physical if not mental attributes. The daughter of a lawyer and married at fifteen, she was sentimental, frivolous, irresistible to many men, including Germaine's lap-dog Benjamin Constant, who cried: "She has played with my happiness, my career, my life. May she be cursed!" Others who fell in love with Juliette included Chateaubriand, Germaine's son Auguste, and above all Prince August of Prussia. Later, a finer soldier than the Prince was also smitten for a while, the Duke of Wellington.

Juliette infuriated her lovers, not least because while she played with passion she was terrified of surrendering to it. It was widely rumoured that she was physically incapable of losing her virginity. Nor did she, until 1818. August was immediately captivated by her dark curls and dark eyes. Taking advantage of the glorious last summer-lit days, the Prince and Juliette spent their time riding alone across the fields, exploring the vineyards of the nearby countryside, or rowing on Lake Geneva, while Clausewitz talked and walked with Germaine, or with another member of the Madame de Staël entourage, August Wilhelm Schlegel.

Germaine had met Schlegel on her visit to Germany. "I have met here a man who in literary matters is better informed and more ingenious than almost any other person I know."[19] By then Schlegel had already translated sixteen of Shakespeare's plays, his most famous work. He returned from Germany officially as tutor to Germaine's children, and was to be one of her camp followers for the rest of her life, writing notes to her even if she were in the next room. One read: "Do not abuse your power; you might easily make me miserable, while I would be defenceless against you. Above all, I beseech you, do not ever banish from your presence your slave."[20] But Clausewitz believed that Germaine was as much under Schlegel's influence as *vice-versa*. "She really is completely a follower of Schlegel and has at least all the good contained in his views," he wrote to Marie.[21] This small, rather ugly Hanoverian of thirty-eight, was vain and quarrelsome, but he had a lucid and precise mind. "Schlegel every now and again reads to me from his works and gives me great pleasure . . . Nothing do I love more in Wilhelm Schlegel than his warm patriotism. He is such an original German." Clausewitz added: "Madame de Staël calls us 'the two Germans,' something we are both very proud about, and we always sit next to each other at table."[22]

Life at Coppet was fascinating and busy, if a little insane, full of wild talk and wild activity. Napoleon was later to say: "Her house at Coppet became a veritable arsenal against me. One went there to win one's spurs."[23] At the time of Clausewitz's visit, Germaine's lakeside chateau at Geneva was enjoying its heyday. For the guests, everything was erratic and nothing was formal. No-one knew where to find anyone else. The doors were always left wide open, and people wandered about anywhere. "Wherever a conversation developed," said one visitor, the Comtesse de Boigne, "one set up camp and stayed for hours or for days, without being interrupted by any of the normal routines of life. Talking seemed to be everybody's chief business."[24] Breakfast was eaten up to eleven o'clock, dinner was served at five o'clock, and was followed by walks or an evening carriage drive, or more often by chamber music, more talk and games. Supper was served at eleven o'clock in the evening, and conversation went on well into the night, at least for Germaine and her intimate circle.

"Frau von Staël is a woman of great fantasy, and of tremendous excitability," Clausewitz told Marie in a letter of 5th October. "She has avidly saturated herself with German spirit and is completely filled by it. Apart from that she is completely French. This means that everything which she says after thinking, and which she takes from deep inside her, breathes this German spirit. On the other hand she lacks completely in her external behaviour, the quiet, tender dignity of German feminity, which is for me essential if women are to be interesting as women. With Madame de Staël this is less disagreeably obvious because she speaks almost incessantly about literature, and therefore she is always in touch with her most advantageous side." Clausewitz added: "She is busy discussing something almost all the time, but nobody can make a lively remark without her stopping and expressing her delight. This receptiveness of her mind makes her conversation and her company very pleasurable."[25]

Then there was acting, one of Germaine's chief excitements. The guests took part, with Madame de Staël, Madame Récamier, Wilhelm Schlegel and Benjamin Constant taking the leading parts. The audience came from as far away as Geneva, Lausanne and Berne; the theatre at Coppet flourished especially between 1807 and 1808. When Clausewitz was there, a great dramatic event was held, first at Ouchy on 22nd August, then at Coppet on 18th September: this was a celebrated performance of *Andromaque*, with Juliette playing the title role and Germaine playing Hermione.

So the summer days and nights passed for Clausewitz and Prince August: dinners, rehearsals, performances, excursions on the lake, rides, music, romances and endless talk. Clausewitz had never known anything in the least like it before, nor would he ever again. It was a novel way to finish a period as a prisoner-of-war. The sober Clausewitz struggled hard not to feel happy. He was torn between sadness, or feeling he ought to be sad, and enjoyment of the place and its remarkable residents. Misery gained the upper hand in the opening paragraph in his letter to Marie of 5th October: "Nowhere can I find comfort," he began. But the perpetual spring sunshine of Coppet shone down on him and warmed him, whether he liked it or not. "The landscape around Lake Geneva is among the most beautiful in the world and is unique even in Switzerland ... a picture of the promised land," the letter continued. White peaks were reflected in the blue water, and the autumn days were golden and glorious. "Flocks of birds act as companions to those who wander alone. Larks call as if they wanted to make us happy in the beautiful deceit of this sunny day, as if they were giving us a second spring. Everything here is still green and even in the fullness of life, so the little animals should be forgiven this little pretence, because even the human beings give themselves up to this sweet imagination, even the saddest." Coppet was at last penetrating through to him. He even attempted an occasional joke, which was unusual for him. "The people here are half French, as you say in your letter. But it doesn't bother me. I have very little traffic with them, and anyway, as I come from France, it is very happy for me to have only to deal with half, instead of complete, Frenchmen."[26] So Clausewitz relaxed, accepted what he was offered, and gradually filled himself full of heady radical opinions.

The wine of Coppet had completely intoxicated the handsome head of the Prince of Prussia. Romance between Juliette and August ripened. They made a fine-looking pair, but she failed to win Clausewitz's approval. He considered her, not without justification, "a very vulgar *coquette*."[27] One reason for his coldness toward Prince August's liaison was the fear that departure for home might be delayed after the passports had come through. Prince August was not to be deterred. One day he performed a considerable feat of oarsmanship to row Juliette across to Clarens to inspect the rock of

Meillerie, the setting of Rousseau's *Nouvelle Héloise*. There the couple swore eternal love; and after a performance of *Phèdre* at the chateau, in which she played Aricie, Juliette admitted the Prince into her private chamber and promised to be his wife.

The next step was to write to Monsieur Récamier in Paris and request a divorce. Impatiently they awaited a reply before the Prince left for Berlin. "We were convinced," she said thirty-five years later, "that we were going to be married, and our relationship was very intimate. Even so, there was one thing he failed to obtain."[28]

The day scheduled for the Prince and Clausewitz to leave had come: 28th October. Still no reply had come from Paris, and so August and his lady exchanged written promises instead: "I swear by my honour and my love to preserve in all its purity the sentiment that attaches me to Juliette Récamier, to take all steps that duty allows to unite with her in the bonds of marriage, and to possess no woman as long as there is hope that I may join my destiny with her's, August, Prince of Prussia." Juliette swore in similar terms, promising to have "no love or flirtation with any other man." So August and Clausewitz rode away for home, the Prince with Juliette's letter pressed to his heart and her ring in his pocket. Clausewitz, however, had brought something more substantial with him. He had made good use of his time at Coppet to deepen his knowledge of the French people and the French Revolution. The notes which he made during and immediately after the Coppet visit echo a good deal of Germaine's thoughts. Clausewitz had benefited from the walks, during which Madame de Staël had talked rapidly and emphatically, twisting a piece of paper or twig between her thumb and forefinger, an irritating lifelong habit; and he had learned from the discussions which took place when Germaine received favoured guests at her bedside in the mornings.

Clausewitz wrote down his various observations in his *Journal of a Journey from Soissons to Dijon via Geneva*, and in an essay on *The Germans and the French*, and after he had persuaded the Prince to visit the famous educational centre, the Pestalosis Institute at Iferten, he recorded more of his ideas in his *Pestalosis: a Fragment*. According to contemporary opinion, the Revolution had made France invincible. Clausewitz in his *Journal* disagreed, as did Madame de Staël. The Revolution had collapsed into despotism, he wrote, and as Machiavelli had written in *The Prince*, a corrupt people was incapable of liberty. Success during the Revolutionary Wars had resulted mainly from every Frenchman's fear of the guillotine, Clausewitz continued. But this tide had ceased to flow. Now that the Jacobin terror had given way to military dictatorship under Napoleon, the French nation was succumbing to lethargy. The French had never actually given proof of their allegedly superior moral qualities, he said, and to believe that the Revolution had endowed them with these in one moment was to be blind to the truth. History proved that the nation's character was not changed in a few days.[29]

The treatise *The Germans and the French*[30] raised the same subject on a more bitter level, and was probably written soon after his return to Berlin, with his French experiences fresh in mind. "I have passed ten months in France. I cannot refrain from informing others of the observations I have made," he wrote. Clausewitz described the French character in disparaging terms. The French had vivacity and skill, but were not far-seeing. They were conventional. Their language reflected their character, flimsy, commonplace, artificial, empty and full of wind. The German language on the other hand was more musical, varied, spontaneous, flexible in expression.

This emphasis upon the study of character through language may also have been influenced by Madame de Stäel; she had a similar interest in the subject, but took a very different view from that of Clausewitz. One passage in her book on the Germans gives substance to Clausewitz's criticisms of French conversation. She wrote that in France "words are not merely, as they are in all other countries, a means to communicate ideas, feelings and needs, but are an instrument one likes to play."[31]

In his essay, Clausewitz referred to the vanity of the French, especially of their generals, and their lack of frankness and their incapacity for serious work. He considered the French to be likeable, but to have a weak sense of humour. They knew no strong passion, except for money. But if they lacked vigour, they were also capable of great personal courage, described by Clausewitz as one of the finest of qualities. But then he undermined the compliment by saying that French courage was based upon conceit and excitement, and that as a rule their bravery lacked tenacity, and waned with their enthusiasm. Yet, for all this, the French were a powerful people. The Germans, as one might expect, had all the opposite qualities: originality, serious convictions, deep sentiment, application. But one serious failing sprang from the German taste for personal philosophical inquiry. This created an over-abundance of doctrines, a confusion of opinions, which made unanimity extremely difficult to achieve, both within the individual, and within the race. So believed the twenty-eight-year-old Captain von Clausewitz.

In early November, Clausewitz arrived back in Berlin and was reunited with Marie. But he was anxious to be off again. He wished to be reunited as soon as possible with Scharnhorst, who was then at Memel and still chairman of the Military Reorganisation Commission. Clausewitz at once contacted him to say he was back. He had already anticipated the joy of working with Scharnhorst again, and had written to Marie in September: "It is infinitely pleasant to share one's thoughts with someone you respect and with someone you trust. Such a love and devotion have I for two people only in the world, for you and my friend Scharnhorst. I would scarcely find a third to equal them, even if I looked all my life."[32] In October he wrote that the Fatherland and honour were the two "earthly divinities" to which he wanted to devote himself.[33]

On 27th November Clausewitz received a welcome letter from Scharnhorst at Memel: "My Dear Clausewitz. I have received your invaluable letter. I see that you did not receive the reply I sent to your previous one. So accept now my utmost sincere and heartfelt gratitude for the kindness, friendship and goodness which you have shown me in your letters. Your views are mine, or become so because of your letter. Your opinions give me strength to hold to mine. Nothing would make me happier now than to be at the same place as you."[34]

Scharnhorst mentioned how this reunion might be achieved. A "new formation" was being established, in which Clausewitz could be offered "more than one kind of appointment."[35] The formation in question was a reorganized General Staff, in which Clausewitz could help his former tutor in a secretarial role. Scharnhorst wrote of how well he expected they might work together in a letter of 1st December: "It gives me perfect pleasure to consider whenever I have a spare moment, that my mind is able to move towards that of a friend who knows me well, who does not misinterpret my feelings."[36] Clausewitz stayed in close touch with Scharnhorst, despite the latter's weakness as a letter-writer, a failing which Clausewitz and others had constant cause to complain about. On one occasion Scharnhorst sought out Carl's brother, Wilhelm, then stationed near Memel, writing to Clausewitz on 14th December: "Your brother in the Courbière regiment is an excellent person and has a high reputation."[37]

Clausewitz was anxious to set off for Memel. The Commission offered an ideal opportunity to help in work he would thoroughly enjoy—the improvement of the Prussian army. Napoleon also felt that the Prussians might benefit from Scharnhorst's work, and grew apprehensive. As early as 27th September Bonaparte wrote: "What is going on at Memel seems to me a bad joke . . . The King of Prussia has no need to keep up an army, he is not at war with anyone . . ."[38] Napoleon's power of action against the Prussians was circumscribed by the Treaty of Tilsit, which had officially ended hostilities between the two countries. But many people in Prussia, including Clausewitz, believed that Napoleon still regarded himself as Prussia's overlord, and that despite the Treaty he would seek the first opportunity to act as conqueror. This made it all the more imperative that the army should be reformed as rapidly as possible.

For the moment, however, Clausewitz had to wait impatiently in Berlin. He was still *aide* to Prince August. He would have to endure the dying days of Prince August's affair with Juliette for a little while longer. As long as August thought that he had a chance to capture Madame Récamier, he wished to stay in Berlin from where he could reach her more quickly. Clausewitz was tied to his side, involved in the frivolities of love-making, instead of the serious business of preparing for war.

SIX

The Prussian Army Reforms

"Let him who desires peace prepare
for war."
(Vegetius, *De Re Militaris*.)

JULIETTE RÉCAMIER RECEIVED a reply to her divorce request the very next day after Prince August and his *aide* had left Coppet. Her banker husband, struggling to extricate himself from acute financial troubles, said that he would consent if she so wished, but clearly he would be heart-broken. Madame de Staël told Juliette that she must press on regardless, but Juliette had doubts now that Prince August had gone, and now that an attractive American, Mr. Middleton, had arrived. She stayed at Coppet for a while longer, and did not return to Paris until December.

By now, Monsieur Récamier was more firmly against the idea of divorce. He even dared to suggest that after fifteen years Juliette must consummate their marriage. Juliette's letters to August in Berlin began to cool. The suffering Prince, who made Clausewitz suffer with him, insisted that she execute her written promise. Juliette made a feeble attempt at suicide, believing that she had thereby discharged her obligations. Cries of protest came from Berlin, but Juliette would not be moved. August went to Aachen, where the two lovers had agreed to rendezvous, but she failed to turn up; she sent her portrait instead. The Prince continued to live in hope, and would do so for the remaining thirty-six years of his life. He was buried still wearing her ring. But the episode was really over by the spring of 1808, not only for August, but for Clausewitz too. On 1st April they travelled to Königsberg in the far north east of Prussia, where the court and government had moved on 16th January, and where Scharnhorst was working with the Military Reorganisation Commission.

Master and former pupil were reunited. "I have seen Scharnhorst," wrote Clausewitz to Marie. "He was very friendly, and I spent between three and four hours with him. He had so much to talk about, about the events, our particular situation, the future, what had happened to him, that there is still much to tell, and much that would interest him. I could listen to him for many an hour. You can well imagine that there has not been time for me to speak to him about my situation." Clausewitz added: "The King has been very gracious towards me, that means he has spoken one or two words to me."[1]

On 8th April, following a recommendation from Scharnhorst to the King, Prince August was promoted to Brigadier-General, Chief of the East Prussian Artillery Regiment and of the overall Artillery Corps. From then on, although he was still officially August's *aide*, and although August did not take up his position for some months, Clausewitz was employed more in helping "the General." His impatience for Prussia to prepare for battle against the hated French was increased by the suffering of the country. Both on his journey home to Berlin, and then from Berlin to Königsberg, Clausewitz had seen how frightful conditions were. High indemnities had been squeezed from each province by the French, French officials were everywhere, and Napoleon's Continental System had thrown Prussia's economy into complete chaos. Throughout Prussia, sauntering in the streets, manning the garrisons, monopolizing the conversation at dinner parties, were French soldiers and officers, no less than 150,000 of them. They would never leave unless forcibly ejected. Clausewitz was determined to play his part in bringing this about.

While he was never a full member of the Military Reorganisation Commission, Clausewitz worked in close co-operation with its chairman. Later, in September, he wrote to Marie saying that he was Scharnhorst's "literary agent."[2] He also became fully acquainted with other leading reformers. It was now, in the spring of 1808, that the close friendship grew between Clausewitz and Gneisenau. Although the two men had met before, they had not really known one another well. At Königsberg, reintroduced to one another by Scharnhorst, the friendship became intimate. It was to mean a good deal to Clausewitz. Gneisenau was to be the second father-figure of his life after Scharnhorst. After the latter's unfortunate death in 1813, Clausewitz grew to rely upon Gneisenau more and more, with a dependence that that would last until Clausewitz's own death.

August Wilhelm Antonius Neithardt von Gneisenau was, like Scharnhorst, not a Prussian. He was born in October, 1760, at Schilda in Saxony. His father was a Saxon artillery lieutenant who served in the army of the Austrian Empire against Frederick the Great in the Seven Years' War (1756–63). A week after his birth, the mother and baby were involved in the flight following Frederick's last victory at Torgau. The mother died a few weeks later, from the exhaustion of the retreat and from the fright caused by dropping her baby at night out of the cart in which she was travelling. As his father was unable to look after him, the infant Gneisenau was handed over into the care of strangers. He was badly neglected. His unhappy treatment was reported to his grandfather Captain Müller—his mother's father—who lived at Worzburg; Captain Müller took charge of his upbringing. Gneisenau was sent to the University of Erfurt at the age of seventeen, with the aim of entering him into the army when his studies were finished. He joined the Emperor's service, and fought in Bohemia against Frederick the Great in the War of the Bavarian Succession in 1778.

Gneisenau then joined the army of the Margrave of Ansbach and Bayreuth. When the British were hiring mercenaries from the Margrave and other German princes in 1781 for the conflict with the Thirteen Colonies of America, Gneisenau enlisted to fight for the British Crown, and was posted as a Second-Lieutenant in a *chasseur* regiment. He gained little practical experience of fighting in America, since the war had virtually ended by the time he arrived. Nevertheless, he was able to study at first hand the tactics of irregular warfare.

After Gneisenau's return to Europe in late 1783, the petty wars in the small kingdoms of the Holy Roman Empire no longer appealed to him. He turned his coat and applied for employment with Frederick the Great on 4th November, 1785. He was accepted, and commissioned First Lieutenant in the Guard Regiment at Potsdam. During the Revolutionary War with France he served in Poland, was involved in Prussia's partitioning of the country, and rose to the rank of Captain. With peace Gneisenau, like many another officer, found little to do—except to get married in 1796 to Caroline von Kottwitz.

Gneisenau's anticipation of the outcome of the war against Napoleon in 1806 was as gloomy as that of Scharnhorst. "Oh my country, my *self-chosen* country!" he sighed.[3] Gneisenau fought at Saalfeld where Prince Louis Ferdinand was slain, and was himself wounded in the leg. During the retreat he was sent by Hohenlohe with Knesebeck to try to arrange provisions for the troops along the road to Stettin, and from Stettin he rode to the King's Headquarters at Graudenz, and then on to Königsberg.

It was at Königsberg that he first began to attract attention. He became acquainted with Princess Louise Radzivill, who had befriended Clausewitz, too, when he had first arrived at the Prussian court as adjutant to her brother August. Gneisenau had the sad task of giving her an eye-witness account of her other brother's death at Saalfeld. Throughout his life Gneisenau had far-reaching plans for action. He developed one such plan at Königsberg: a scheme for carrying on the war by a combined operation involving Prussian, Swedish, English and Russian forces, striking in from the sea with the help of the British navy. Nothing came of it, however.

From 4th April to 24th April, 1807, Gneisenau stayed at Danzig, helping Kalkreuth with the defence of the town. Then he received orders to proceed to Kolberg. Arriving there on 29th April he found that the garrison of some 4,000 men, soon reinforced to 6,000, was surrounded by about 9,000 French under Marshal Mortier. Ammunition was running short, but Gneisenau and his men managed to hold on, despite an increase of French strength to 16,000. The Prussians were still in possession when hostilities ended at the beginning of July. This successful defence brought personal fame to Gneisenau. His conduct was held up as an example of Prussian bravery when so many garrisons had tamely surrendered. It also brought close friendship with Blücher. The two men were later to work together as Commander and

Chief-of-Staff during the late 1813 campaign and in the 1815 campaign. The warrior Blücher was anxious for the fight to be resumed in 1807, and whole-heartedly agreed with the sentiments of his old tutor's prayer: "Thou seest, dear Heavenly Father, the sad plight of thy servant Colonel Belling. Grant him soon a nice little war, that he may better his condition and continue to praise Thy name. Amen."[4]

In a memorandum of 27th February, 1807, Gneisenau had made clear to the King that he believed the Prussian army should adopt the French emphasis upon light troops.[5] He had many other ideas, too. On 25th July, 1807, he was appointed a member of the Military Reorganisation Commission. Upon hearing of his new post, Blücher wrote to Gneisenau: "Go, and my best wishes accompany you! Remember me to my friend Scharnhorst, and tell him that I lay it on his conscience to provide for a national army."[6] Gneisenau always believed Scharnhorst to be a greater man than himself. As far as intellectual analysis was concerned, this was probably true. Scharnhorst was also an abler staff officer; Gneisenau's performance as Chief-of-Staff to Blücher was to be marred by impetuosity and bias. But he had a more sensitive mind than Scharnhorst, and felt the most tender and the strongest passions. He had a greater sense of the dramatic. His ideas were sometimes too lofty, and even Clausewitz was to criticize his judgement on occasion. But Gneisenau was warm, sympathetic, kind, and was to care for the vulnerable Clausewitz in a way which was different from, yet complimentary to, that of Scharnhorst.

Now all three men, at varying levels of seniority, were to work together in those critical months of 1808. Clausewitz was to witness, and to assist, the vital effort which would so transform Prussia's military competence by 1813, 1814 and 1815, compared with 1806. Their reforms would also provide the seeds of Prussian and German militarism which, helped by interpretations of Clausewitz's writing, would shake Europe and the world in 1870, 1914 and 1939.

Before Clausewitz returned to Prussia, the initial progress of the reform group had been spurred on by the realization that reforms were urgently needed, not only in the army but in the Prussian state as a whole. The reformers were also helped by the King's initial reaction to the defeat; Friedrich Wilhelm wished his army to contain only those units that had fought until the very end of the war; the rest must be struck off the rolls. This drastic upheaval entailed the loss of some of Prussia's oldest regiments, and Blücher himself appeared before the King proudly wearing the now illegal red uniform of his disbanded hussars. But it also meant that a good deal of dead wood was cleared away, and that old barriers between the regiments were broken down.

Despite the help given by the shock of defeat, Scharnhorst still had acute problems to overcome. Many of the old Prussian school still held influential positions. Nor was formation of a body like the Reorganisation Commission a new idea: some kind of inquiry into the disaster was only to be expected, and an investigation was not necessarily meant to produce fundamental changes. Moreover, the King's "Guidelines" may have seemed to offer an exciting chance for innovation, but Frederick Wilhelm himself was undecided on most major issues; he was frequently to change his mind, or hesitate over proposed reforms.

That the Commission did more than simply list those guilty of cowardice or incompetence during the fighting, and that deep and far-reaching Prussian reforms followed in the civil and military fields, was due primarily to two men: Stein and Scharnhorst. These two men were vastly different in character. The civilian minister, Stein, was emotional and temperamental and had an explosive way of expressing his opinion; the military reformer was noted for his coolness and for his withdrawn attitude. But they held similar views of what Prussia so urgently needed.

Stein, who had been dismissed by the King only a few months before, was now asked to return, following Napoleon's insistence in July, 1807, that the Chancellor, Baron Karl Hardenberg should stand down. It took some weeks for the proud Stein to be persuaded, during which time he received a pleading letter from Hardenberg written by the King's command, and a passionate appeal from Clausewitz's friend, Princess Louise. But on 4th October, 1807, the fifty-year-old Heinrich Friedrich Karl Baron von Stein became the leading Prussian minister; and although he was to serve less than fourteen months, his ministry left an indelible mark upon Prussian history. "The chief idea was to arouse a moral, religious and patriotic spirit in the nation," he said. "To instil into it again courage, confidence, readiness for every sacrifice on behalf of independence from foreigners and for the national honour, and to seize the first favourable opportunity to begin the bloody and hazardous struggle."[7] In December, 1807, he wrote to Hardenberg: "We must train the nation to conduct its own affairs, and to grow out of the present condition of childhood in which an overbearing government wishes to control the people."[8]

Only eleven days before this letter, Scharnhorst expressed a remarkably similar view to Clausewitz. Their purpose, he wrote, must be "to kindle a sense of independence in the nation; we must enable the nation to understand itself and to take control of its own affairs. Only then will the nation acquire self-respect and compel the respect of others. To work towards this is all that we can do. To break the chains of prejudice, hasten and nurture our revival without inhibiting its free growth—our work cannot go further than that."

In this letter, extremely revealing for someone as withdrawn as he was, and which began "nothing would make me happier than to find myself in your company," Scharnhorst unburdened his misgivings about the task he had been given to do. "I consider myself very little," he wrote. "I have the best will to do what I can, but I am not made for winning attachments and confidence by personal action. Without telling me, the King promoted me and entrusted the task of reorganization to me in conjunction with a very mixed Commission. I have not tried to make friends, and considering the difference of views and the absence of personal regard, I may expect attempts to alienate the King from me, although he is very gracious and has hitherto treated me with unmerited confidence. At this very moment a quiet and honourable appointment is open to me elsewhere." Scharnhorst, who was referring to the offer of employment in Britain, was slightly reassured by the King's attitude. He continued: "Doubtful as our prospects are, yet we have laboured for the internal regeneration of the military system, alike in respect of formation, promotion, practice, and especially spirit. The King has put all prejudice aside, and not only showed himself willing but himself supplied very many ideas appropriate to the new spirit and arrangements."[9]

Co-operation between Stein and Scharnhorst was of prime importance; the reforms which Scharnhorst, Gneisenau and the others wanted to introduce would inevitably have to spread beyond the army itself. The repercussions upon civil life entailed by military reforms had been a prime obstacle to reform before 1806. But now, with Stein working on parallel lines to Scharnhorst, the difficulty might be overcome. Friedrich Wilhelm himself seemed to appreciate the link between the two. The Cabinet Order appointing Stein read: "As the future arrangement of the military system as well as the transitional arrangement of the army is so intimately concerned with the financial state, with policy, and with the future constitution of the State, it is my will that you take part also in the deliberations of the Military Commission."[10]

But first of all, while Clausewitz was still a prisoner-of-war in France, Scharnhorst had had to struggle with some members of the Commission itself. Initially, three conservative-minded members formed the majority: Count von Lottum, Bornikowski and Massenbach. Massenbach was described by Clausewitz after his behaviour as Chief-of-Staff to Hohenlohe in 1806 as of unstable and superficial enthusiasms, with a feeble basis for his ideas.[11] All three disagreed with Scharnhorst's belief that the country was in need of revolutionary reforms. Scharnhorst and Gneisenau therefore remained outsiders for the first weeks. But gradually, with the help of Stein, who was still not in office, Bornikowski and Massenbach were eased out of most of the Commission's work.

On 9th October, five days after taking office, Stein's famous *Emancipating Edict* was signed. This, aimed at ending personal serfdom in Prussia, was based upon earlier work by Hardenberg, and the idea had been a favourite of Friedrich Wilhelm since his accession. "Every inhabitant of our States is competent, without any limitation on the part of the State, to possess either as property or pledge, landed estates of every kind," declared the Edict. "Every noble is henceforth permitted, without any derogation from his position, to exercise citizen occupations; and every citizen or peasant is allowed to pass from the peasant into the citizen class, or from the citizen into the peasant class." And according to Paragraph 12: "From Martinmas, 1810, ceases all villainage in Our entire States. From Martinmas, 1810, there shall be only free persons."[12]

The Edict did not have as great an impact as might be supposed. The Prussian peasant, although nominally a serf, had long had substantial rights. He had been far more of a proprietor than the English farm worker because he did, for practical purposes, own the land, even if on a degrading form of tenure.[13] Nevertheless, the Edict was an eminently suitable counterpart to the reforms which Scharnhorst had in mind for the Prussian army. With an improved status for the peasant civilian, it would be easier to improve the status of the peasant soldier.

In October another conservative, Karl Ludwig von Borstell, joined the Commission, but his appointment had been terminated within a few weeks by Scharnhorst's threat to resign. The reformers now pressed on with their schemes for better service conditions for the ordinary soldier, including changes in the harsh military discipline. At the same time proposals were drafted to abolish the nobility's special claims to officer positions, and to introduce universal military service in Prussia. After the ousting of the conservatives, the Commission's membership comprised Scharnhorst, Gneisenau, Goetzen, Boyen and Grolman. This was to be an excellent team. Hermann von Boyen wrote of the events in 1806: "There have been few campaigns in which such numerous, and often such incomprehensible, blunders piled on top of each other."[14] This man was to be extremely close to Scharnhorst. He was to be War Minister from 1814 until 1819, and again in 1841 until 1847. C. W. G. von Grolman was to become Chief of the General Staff during Boyen's first War Ministry. Apart from this central group of reformers, to which Clausewitz was to act as an unofficial secretary, a number of sub-committees were set up to deal with specialized problems. The commission itself had direct access to the King.

But first the Commission had to deal with the complicated and painful matter of punishing those guilty of neglect, incompetence or cowardice during Prussia's 1806 defeat. The group managed to bypass this by persuading the King to refer the investigation to a separate body. Eventually only 208 officers were found guilty of violating the Prussian code of honour by capitulating to the enemy, either without cause or with too little show of resistance.[15] Seven senior officers were condemned to death. One escaped, and the sentence was commuted to life imprisonment for the rest.[16]

In autumn, 1807, the Commission began its more important work. It proposed a reform which was to create one of the most heated arguments with the conservatives: the ending of the nobility's virtual monopoly of the officer corps. The King's *Ortelsburger Publicandum* of 1806 had stated that for the duration of the war every soldier had the right to an officer's commission. In September, 1807, the reform group recommended that this emergency measure should now be made permanent. A draft proposal of 25th September said: "A claim to officer rank shall in peacetime be warranted only by knowledge and education, in time of war by exceptional bravery, activity and quickness of perception."[17] This attempted reform was closely linked with Stein's Edict of the following month. According to Scharnhorst, noble status should no longer be the prime qualification for entry into the officer corps; educational and competitive examinations should be held. He pointed out that the Prussian nobility had not been noted in the past for their educational proficiency. Grolman was even more emphatic. "In order to fight, it is not necessary to belong to a special class," he said. "The sad belief that one must belong to a special class in order to defend the Fatherland has done much to plunge it into the present abyss, and only the opposite principle can pull it out again."[18] Scharnhorst firmly believed that the admittance of the *bourgeoisie* into the officer corps was an essential part of his overall attempt to bridge the gap between the army and the people. This problem, he maintained, and the army's unpopularity, had to be destroyed if full national support was to be given to Prussia's forces.

But this military equivalent of the civilian Edict met with stronger opposition than the change in the peasant's civilian status. Yorck, who was less opposed to reform than many people imagined, could not bring himself to agree with the encroachment of the *bourgeoisie* upon the officer class. He is reported to have told Prince Wilhelm, the King's youngest brother: "If Your Royal Highness deprives me and my children of our right, what is the basis of yours?"[19] Others protested still more vehemently against the idea.

The argument was still raging when Clausewitz arrived at Königsberg. So too was the debate over universal military service, which the Commission had unanimously recommended to the King in a memorandum of 15th March, only a few days before August and Clausewitz arrived at court. As early as 31st August, 1807, the Commission had announced that "all inhabitants of the state are its born defenders," and had proposed that the army should be reorganized into a standing regular force and a part-time militia, both to be recruited from the entire population without exemption, although Scharnhorst personally believed that some exemptions were unavoidable. Again, this was part of the attempt to link the army with the people. Clausewitz threw himself into the debate and reform attempts with unreserved enthusiasm. Apart from Gneisenau, he also made the acquaintance of Count Friedrick Dohna, soon to become a close friend, and of Major Grolman and Boyen. Above all, he had come to work at Scharnhorst's side.

With one eye on the French, and anxious for the time when the Prussian army would redeem itself against Napoleon, Clausewitz was convinced that the reforms were not only vital, but long overdue. Napoleon, he believed, was determined one day to annihilate the Prussian state. In an unpublished note earlier that year, Clausewitz had written that time was running out: "Fools that you are! It is now tomorrow is made. It is in the present that we prepare for the future. While you wait for the future it emerges, ill-figured by your hands. Life concerns you. What it will be, it will be because of you."[20] After reading Friedrich von Gentz's *Fragmente aus der Neusten Geschichte des Politischen Gleichgewichts in Europa*, in which the Prussian-born pamphleteer called upon Germans everywhere to awaken from their sleep, Clausewitz noted: "The preface of the fragments should be read to the Germans as a sermon every fourth week, and the Germans themselves should drum the content into the heads of our ministers."[21]

Clausewitz was constantly preoccupied with his fear that time was short. The weeks were too precious to waste, while the French threat loomed so large. It was not enough merely to engage in philosophical debate. Talk should be replaced by vigorous action. "Great, yes, indescribably great is time," he wrote to Marie on 17th August. "Few human beings grasp its meaning. To few of even the wisest scholars among us is it more than a tool, used to depict some kind of system, to demonstrate their brain power. All this is the vain playing of children and of fools."[22] Clausewitz therefore busied himself with Scharnhorst's work and with lobbying support for the Commission's proposals at the Königsberg court. He was totally committed to the reformers' cause. Prince August, too, was firmly in agreement with the idea of military innovations—which was probably just as well, as he was still technically Clausewitz's superior officer.

During the early summer it became clear that the King himself would go far towards meeting the Commission's recommendations. On 3rd August, his birthday, Friedrich Wilhelm issued three decrees. One was concerned with the regulations for officer selection, and represented a considerable victory for the reformers. Although the King reserved the power to appoint "from time to time" officers of his own choice, the opening passage of the new law was virtually word for word the Commission's proposal of 25th September, 1807. "From now on," said the King, "a claim to officer rank shall in peacetime be warranted only by knowledge and education, in time of war by exceptional bravery and quickness of perception. From the whole nation, therefore, all individuals who possess these qualities can lay title to the highest positions of honour in the army. All social preference which has hitherto existed ceases completely in the army, and everyone, without regard for his background, has equal rights and equal duties."[23] This was a complete reversal of Frederick the Great's system. The door which led to the exclusive, arrogant officer corps had been thrown wide open. But with the second proposed reform, universal service, Friedrich Wilhelm hesitated. The first of the new Articles of War for non-commissioned officers and privates merely stated: "In future every subject of the state, without regard to birth, will be obliged to perform military service, under conditions of time and circumstance yet to be determined."[24]

The third decree dealt with the question of discipline. To Scharnhorst, all three decrees were indissolubly linked. Corporal punishment could not be continued if privates had the chance of rising to the highest ranks, and if there was to be universal service. With their appeal for relaxation of the harsh military code, the reformers won their most resounding victory. The King declared that corporal punishment was to be forbidden in future, except in the case of soldiers who had been found guilty three times of serious offences; these were transferred to a special category. No longer would a soldier receive vicious floggings for minor breaches of discipline, or for more serious offences be made to run the gauntlet of two hundred men armed with salted whips, his hands bound, his feet hobbled, a ball of lead in his mouth to prevent him biting off his tongue in agony. Gneisenau was especially pleased with this reform. He had long advocated a relaxation of discipline, for example in an article printed in a Königsberg newspaper, entitled *Freedom of the Back*. Other humanitarian, or plainly practical, officers had urged a similar reform, as had Prince August and Clausewitz in the memorandum sent from France. A new system of military justice was also brought in, which was designed to protect the private soldier from arbitrary decisions of local commanders.

Overall, the reformers had reason to be satisfied with the 3rd August decrees. But the struggle continued and much remained to be done. Letters from Clausewitz to Marie show his feverish impatience and his gnawing fear that France might not allow Prussia proper scope to carry out enough reforms. "These times are grave for us, inexpressibly grave," he wrote two weeks after the King's decrees. "Few men realize it. Remember my prophecy, Marie. We shall see rising over our heads a black storm, and we will be enveloped in night and mists of sulphur before we expect it."[25]

Austria was preparing for war against Napoleon. In Prussia, a decision had to be taken as to what should be done if war broke out between her neighbour and France. In Clausewitz's view, the question was superfluous: Prussia should at once lend Austria her full support. During August, he worked on a mobilization plan which was drawn up by Scharnhorst, and taken to the King by Stein who added some suggestions of his own. According to the plan, Prussian troops should advance and join those from Pomerania on the middle Oder; while forces from Silesia should unite with the Austrians and occupy the fortresses of Glatz, Silberberg and Cosel. The plan continued: "At the moment of this advance of the troops, a universal insurrection is to break out in Pomerania, the New Mark, the Mark and the district of Magdeburg, Lower Saxony, Westphalia, Hessen, Thüringia and Franconia. On a single day an attempt will be made to gain possession of all the fortresses by treason or assault."[26]

The King first read the plan on 21st August. He then called a conference attended by Stein, Scharnhorst and Gneisenau. Clausewitz was in despair when he learned what Friedrich Wilhelm had said: nothing would be done without Russia's help, and in any case the King did not feel that he could depend either on his own people, after the experience of 1806, or upon

7—C

Austria, Prussia's rival. The reformers could only continue their attempts to extend and consolidate Prussia's own military innovations. Moreover, the August decrees were more declarations of principle by the King than tight regulations; they still had to be put in practice. One way of seeing that Friedrich Wilhelm and his officials did not renegue was to ensure that the army and the people fully understood the new Articles of War. Clausewitz himself played a part in spreading the news. He told Marie that Scharnhorst "has given me the job of writing out Prussia's new Articles of War and other regulations, making three copies for publication in the Halle Literary Journal, the Jena Literary Journal and the Gottingen Journal."[27] A similar article written by Clausewitz appeared in the *Königsberger Zeitung* on 9th September.

But in the same month, September, came the Paris Convention, in which Napoleon secured an even firmer grip on Prussian affairs. The Emperor made harsh demands: the Prussian army was to be limited to 42,000 men for a period of ten years. The restriction meant a complete upheaval of Prussian plans for army organization. Even before the Convention, the reformers had had to limit their ideas for the size of a new army to what shattered Prussian finances could withstand—finances which were made even weaker by the heavy burden of 150,000 French occupying troops, and by the indemnities which Napoleon had demanded. Throughout 1807 and 1808 the Commission had had to think in terms of reducing the overall size of the army, rather than expanding it. Recruiting was difficult, even if the soldiers could be paid. In view of Napoleon's almost complete domination of the European continent, foreign recruitment was impossible, and Prussia's own territory had been slashed by the defeat, reducing the population from which native forces could be raised. One idea had been put forward by Scharnhorst in July, 1807. This was the *Krümper* system, in which units would send a number of trained men on leave each year, and replace them with raw recruits. In this way replacements could be found more cheaply. But the plan was not put into operation for the whole army until 1809, and was to be interrupted in 1811.[28]

The Commission had therefore based its plans upon the assumption that Prussia could afford an army of only six divisions. Now, with the Paris Convention, the projected six divisions had to be scrapped. Instead, only one division was planned. This would comprise six combined brigades consisting of seven to eight infantry battalions and twelve squadrons of cavalry. In addition, there would be three artillery brigades.[29] The Paris Convention also banned Prussian measures to raise a militia. Finally, larger indemnities were demanded.

Scharnhorst, Gneisenau and Grolman tried in vain to persuade Friedrich Wilhelm to reject this emasculating humiliation. The atmosphere at Königsberg became strained, as Clausewitz remembered it had been at the court in Berlin before the 1806 campaign. The reformers feared that the

Convention would provide the King with an excuse for not putting through the proposals already accepted. Gneisenau, in particular, thought that Napoleon's latest demands would encourage the King's tendency to hesitate, and that Friedrich Wilhelm would merely agree to a partial reorganization of the old-style standing army, rather than to militia proposals which Gneisenau strongly favoured. Gneisenau felt that the old army "had contributed more than anything else to the enervation and degeneration of peoples, which destroyed the warlike spirit of the nation and its sense of community, by relieving the other sections of society from the duty of directly defending the State."[30]

Gneisenau was already forming plans for a popular insurrection in Prussia on the lines of a rising which had taken place in Spain. Stein supported him in this, and they planned to arm the population, not only in Prussia but in northern Germany as a whole. Friedrich Wilhelm dared not approve such a dangerous scheme without help from Russia. Nor was Scharnhorst as enthusiastic for the idea as his more volatile colleague, preferring to rely instead upon his *Krümper* system. At this stage Clausewitz too had reservations, but was soon to show his belief in the strength of irregular forces such as those planned by Gneisenau. Day by day, Clausewitz's apprehensions grew. Marie scolded him for only writing to her about his fears, and told him to relax more. "You reprimand me," he replied on 5th November, "but it is not my fault. It is not that I do not want to take life easy. One of my principles, my dearest love, is to enjoy life as much as possible. But one pain I cannot prevent; my mind is dominated by a terrible fear, always in my thoughts and which all the principles in the world cannot take away."[31]

The reformers then received another blow. Napoleon's suspicions had already led him to make his rigorous demands in the Convention of Paris. Now, French police intercepted an incautious letter written by Stein. The Minister's position became untenable. Napoleon pressed heavily for his dismissal, and Stein had to give up his office on 24th November. The military reformers had lost their most powerful civilian supporter. Soon afterward, Napoleon issued a warrant for Stein's arrest and had his estates at Nassau seized. Warned by the French Minister in Berlin, Stein fled, first to Austria and later to Russia where he became an invaluable adviser to Czar Alexander. It seemed as if progress made so far was to be halted, and even reversed. In December the Commission again urged the King to introduce universal military service, trying to persuade him to act upon his vague pronouncement of 3rd August. Friedrich Wilhelm refused.

Clausewitz became increasingly depressed. Far from going out and enjoying himself as Marie had told him to do, he criticized the pleasure-loving members of the court, including Queen Louise. He complained to Marie that, despite the shadow of war, the court was returning to its old frivolities; once he had seen the Queen still dancing at 2 a.m. He also told Marie that he had been ridiculed for not taking part in court life. But how could he, he asked, when the sky above Prussia was black and full of hissing serpents?[32] In a letter of 22nd December he wrote: "To live among a generation which has no pride and is incapable of sacrificing its present happiness and life to the supreme good—this clouds and embitters all joys of existence. With regard to the future, I am as pessimistic as possible. And in truth we do not deserve a better fate. Poor German Fatherland!"[33] The nation was being humiliated and dominated more and more by the arrogant French. "A nation in which I cannot say of a generous man that he is a generous man, nor to a friend that he is my friend—this nation is thrown into the worst slavery," he wrote on 27th December.[34]

Clausewitz added: "The path which we walk grows more and more narrow, our feet less and less steady. Is this a time when one should drown one's senses with artificial joys? Our Fate was already decided at the time of the Treaty of Tilsit ... I trace the course of Bonaparte's decision to annihilate us, and I am fully convinced that if the French had not found this opportunity, they would always have found another. The Spanish have never done anything against the French. The most vicious intrigues have since been introduced to serve as a reason for a catastrophe which had already been decided upon. That we have been ill-treated by the French without interruption since the Treaty of Tilsit, you cannot really appreciate unless you live here."[35]

Clausewitz would soon end his employment as *aide* to Prince August. Meanwhile, even if the attempt to bring about fundamental reforms to Prussia's army had been halted, important work was being done in the field of technical efficiency, all of which Clausewitz thoroughly approved. Basic equipment, from uniforms to ammunition, was being improved. With the introduction of the combined brigade system, with infantry, artillery and cavalry units grouped more closely together, there were exciting possibilities for a new, more flexible, tactical control. Ironically, this closer grouping resulted from the limitations imposed on the Paris Convention.

More important still in December, 1808, the King issued definite orders for the creation of a full Ministry of War, a measure which Stein among others had urged for many months. The royal orders stated that the new ministry would have authority "over everything which pertained to the military and to its constitution, its establishment and its maintenance, and ... everything which hitherto lay within the jurisdiction of the *Oberkriegskollegium*, the *Militardepartement* of the General Directory, the Provincial Magazine Department of Silesia and Prussia as well as the *Generalintendantur*."[36] Clausewitz wrote to Marie on 28th December that the removal of these many departments, which had overlapped, conflicted and competed with one another, would set adrift a whole "cargo of noble invalids."[37]

Six weeks later, to his great relief Clausewitz gave up his employment as August's *aide-de-camp*. He described this post to Marie as "entirely unmilitary," remembering perhaps how he had had to put up with

August's involvement with Juliette. He explained that he had not "had a single military duty for almost six years" before he began to help Scharnhorst.[38] Clausewitz wanted to return to real soldiering, including the chance to die honourably for his country. "If I should perish in great circumstances," he wrote to Marie on 2nd January, 1809, "I would not lose more than a handful of mortal happiness. But if I do nothing with my life except have unfulfilled desires, be nothing but the spectator of miseries and cares, my existence would hardly pay for the place which I have taken for myself upon this earth. May God preserve me from this." Reading such sentences as these, it was no wonder that Marie pleaded with Carl to go out and enjoy himself more. Perhaps she was growing used to the passion which her beloved Clausewitz had for the idea of dying in battle. This, to him, would be true happiness. Clausewitz's letter continued: "If only the fight had begun between virtue and evil. It is that which is the need of our times. It would strengthen us and pull us out of the abyss into which we have sunk, little by little. I would gladly perish in the struggle, but it has to be fought. And fighting to me means using all one's strength."[39]

A week later he wrote: "I said in my previous letter that the time spent in Königsberg was especially important for me, particularly with regard to my inner life. Among other reasons, I have never seen the traits of my mind and inner character so clearly. There was union in a single purpose with other people of many kinds, but at the same time having originality of character and ideas. In the presence of such startling contrasts, of such clear colours, one sees oneself best."[40] Since he was no longer Prince August's *aide*, he had even livelier hopes of being able to concentrate upon this work with Scharnhorst and the others.

The parting with August was warm. In a letter to the King on 16th February, 1809, the Prince asked for the rank of Captain, First-Class, for Clausewitz, saying: "He is an extremely active, scientifically educated officer, who conducted himself excellently during the war, and who distinguished himself at Auerstädt after Captain von Schonberg was wounded, and who led my grenadier battalion with skill."[41] The King approved his son's request for Clausewitz's promotion in a Cabinet Order dated 21st February, 1809. To his great delight, Clausewitz was also told that he would now join the General Staff, and become *aide* to Scharnhorst. According to Boyen, he became Scharnhorst's "foremost and most intimate worker."[42] His post was to be confirmed on 1st March, the day that Prince August took up his appointment as chief of the Prussian Artillery Corps. "It is as if, leaving a cold grave, I return to life on a beautiful spring journey," Clausewitz wrote to Marie.[43] Included in this letter, symbolically, was a cutting from a document upon which was Scharnhorst's signature.

During the next hectic weeks, Clausewitz was fully engaged with the Commission's work, spending long hours with documents and plans. He still kept himself apart from the court society. Nor, at the other extreme, was he interested in the "Bond of Virtue," the *Trudentbund*, formed in April, 1808, whose fanatical members were dedicated to preserving the nation's honour by any means necessary. Clausewitz disliked secret societies, just as much as he disliked opulent social occasions. He refused to take this extremist group seriously, despite its popularity among certain sections at the court.[44] Clausewitz preferred Scharnhorst's quiet company, or Gneisenau's more inflamed conversations, or walking alone when his eyes became too tired to read in the flickering candlelight of his room.

One long letter was a typical example of his wish to be alone, observing rather than joining in. "Yesterday I was on the bridge which crosses the magnificent Pregel. Absorbed in my thoughts I watched the flowing water. Suddenly I was conscious of a host of impressions on all sides . . . I found myself in the richest and liveliest part of Königsberg. It was a Sunday, when the first perfumed breeze of spring came on the evening air. Everything was in motion. Carriages rolled over the bridge with ladies dressed for the *fête*; merchants passed by, chattering of the certain future in vague uncertainties; a thoughtful statesman made his way through the crowd, unaware of the comings and goings around him, unaware of the decorations which glittered upon his breast and fascinated all eyes. A poor woman was helped across the bridge, her monotonous lamentations falling on the inattentive ears of the passers-by. From a high balcony a solitary flute player sends his satisfying tune down to the crowd. With greater strength a fanfare of trumpets comes down from the castle tower, and can be heard over all Königsberg."[45] This, to Clausewitz, was his beloved Fatherland: the rich and the poor, the bustle and the quiet, and standing above all to guide and to protect, the monarch and his proud army.

SEVEN

Hope and Despair

"A Nation can only hope to have a
strong position in the political world
if its character and practice in actual
War mutually support each other."
(*On War*, bk. iii, ch. vii.)

IN THE EARLY spring of 1809 it seemed increasingly likely that Austria would soon go to war against Napoleon. If so, Prussia might still follow her lead, and Clausewitz's dream of once more taking up the sword against the French would come true. Austria's Minister of War and generalissimo of the army, Archduke Carl, had introduced substantial reforms, including the creation of a national guard in the various Hapsburg lands. National sentiment against the French was running strongly in the German provinces, fired by the example of the Spanish. Count Philip Stadion, Austria's premier Minister, was also eager to throw off French domination. He urged that the opportunity created by Napoleon's Spanish preoccupations should not be let slip.

Meanwhile in March, 1809, the Prussian Ministry of War was officially formed; Scharnhorst, with Clausewitz as his *aide*, was to be the *de facto* Minister. The military structure was now divided into two branches, a General Department of War (*Allgemeine Kriegsdepartement*), and a Military Economy Department (*Militär Okonomiedepartement*). But having come this far, Friedrich Wilhelm typically hesitated: he refused to invest any one person with overall ministerial power. He was evidently frightened of giving any individual too much authority in military affairs; and in any case Scharnhorst, the obvious candidate, was junior to some less suitable but highly influential officers.[1] Instead, Scharnhorst was made Chief of the General Staff and Head of the General Department at the Ministry. The conservative, Count Lottum, was appointed Head of the Military Economy Department. But in effect Scharnhorst's quietly dominating personality made him Minister despite the King's reluctance to frame such a post. The two main departments worked closely together, and as a rule Lottum acquiesced in Scharnhorst's policies.

Clausewitz therefore found himself at the very heart of this new and crucial Ministry, as Scharnhorst's assistant. Scharnhorst's deputy was

Colonel C. W. G. von Grolman, but Grolman only stayed until May. He was then succeeded by Colonel von Hake, an officer who in later years was to cause Clausewitz anger and distress. Next in the hierarchy was Herman von Boyen, who assumed the functions of the General Quartermaster's staff. Clausewitz became deeply involved with the Ministry's many functions, especially those of the General Department. These included matters relating to promotion, pay, decorations, justice, training, education, artillery, engineering, fortifications, ordnance, and the development of new ideas. Above all, he was engaged in the practical details of unit dispositions, war plans and mobilization procedures. A flood of instructions, memoranda, minutes, plans, maps, flowed from his office, written or corrected by his hand; Scharnhorst and his assistant were working as "one mind, always in agreement." Clausewitz was extremely gratified with his new tasks.

Greatly to his liking and excitement, Austrian troops had re-opened hostilities with the French in April. Archduke Carl had called upon all Germans to raise the standard of freedom and drive Napoleon back over the Rhine: "We take up arms to maintain the independence of the Austrian monarchy, but also to regain for Prussia her freedom and national honour. The insolence that threatens us has already humiliated Germany. Our resistance is the last hope; our cause is the cause of Germany." For Clausewitz, the moment had come to avenge the defeats of Jena and Auerstädt, to punish the French for the humiliations which Prussia had had to endure, forcibly to eject the French from the soil of the Fatherland. Prussia, he had no doubt at all, would join the fight. "Yesterday we had semi-official information that the Austrians had occupied Hof on the tenth," he wrote to Marie on 23rd April. "Hostilities will follow as a matter of course, so now we anticipate the news of the first significant act of war. What a great moment this is! Infinitely more so than in 1805 and 1806, partly because it comes so close to reversing everything, and secondly because it is the eve of this great upheaval."

The time was ripe, Clausewitz firmly believed, but the struggle would be arduous, and the longer it lasted, the more certain would be France's downfall. "The fight of the entire Spanish nation for its freedom, Austria's tremendous endeavour, the situation in Germany, the comparative weakness of French military power—all these are great basic factors in the belief that all this cannot be taken care of with a few great strokes; in the length of the struggle lies the inevitable fall of the French and the salvation of the Fatherland. We have still been able to hope sometimes, since 1805, that through the character of the times, that through Bonaparte's mistakes, such a beautiful moment could come, a moment in which one might truly believe in the liberation. This moment has really come, although it was more by the working of Fate than by human effort. In any case, I have little faith in the intelligence of Governments." Clausewitz finished with an echo of the prayer of Blücher's tutor, Colonel Belling: "I hope and pray to God that he will give a war, and one that will last some years."[2]

Others hoped and prayed the same. Indeed, the immediate passionate response given by many Prussians to Archduke Carl's appeal has been cited as "the first tangible result of the reform programme of 1807-1809."[3] The atmosphere was completely unlike the "spiritless passivity" which followed Jena. Men like General Friedrich von Kalkreuth and General Karl Zudwig von Borstell, who had opposed the reforms, now openly insisted that Prussia should join Austria's struggle. Friedrich von der Marwitz and Karl Friedrich von Knesebeck went further, and were among the first to offer their services to Austria.[4] Clausewitz told Marie: "If I were to miss this chance, I would destroy all my life so far, which was no more than a preparation for this moment. Destiny offers her powerful hand, and I am resolved to grasp it."[5]

Friedrich Wilhelm thought otherwise. Some military talks were begun with Austria, but the Prussian King was still obsessed with Napoleon's power, frightened of a repetition of 1806, and anxious for a firm Russian committal to fight before he would take Austria's side on the battlefield. Clausewitz and many like him were appalled. To stand apart from Austria would be as foul a Prussian degradation as her bloody defeats at Jena and Auerstädt. It would be far worse than her cowardly neutrality before 1806. Honour, liberty, respect, the Fatherland—all of them now stood on trial before history. But many agreed with the King. Clausewitz sadly told Marie that he, and others like him, were becoming more and more isolated at court. A period of pain, heartsearching and dark uncertainty was beginning for Clausewitz, which would face him with a terrible dilemma: should he continue to serve his King, or should he go elsewhere, and risk being branded as a traitor? He had to decide the basic question of which came first, the King who personified the Fatherland, or the Fatherland itself. "If the King allows his troops to march with the French it will be quite impossible for me to remain in the service," Clausewitz told Marie. "Secondly, it will also be impossible for me to stand by as an onlooker."[6]

Others had already made up their minds, and were being bitterly condemned for it, often by their closest friends. "Grolman and the elder Dohna have asked for their dismissal, and a number of people have criticized them, among them a woman whom we both respect (Princess Radzivill), who has called their behaviour ungrateful and bad. I was very surprised at this verdict, and extremely upset, because it is very one-sided to put it mildly, and shows that even a woman with a noble spirit and intelligence is not free from the influence of her entourage and environment." Clausewitz continued: "Truly, many others will wish to resign. Those who are so loyal to the King that they cannot part with their salaries or secure posts; those who from an excess of patriotism prefer parades to the battlefield; those who speak endlessly of 'Prussia' so that the name 'Germany' will not remind them of wider and nobler duties—they are hardly the best."[7]

Prussian society was rapidly dividing into factions and hostility was growing between them. Gneisenau had already left Königsberg for his country house, where he elaborated plans for a "Free Prussian" Legion; the Legion was to be set up in Prague to fight against Napoleon with the Austrians if Friedrich Wilhelm refused to do so. These plans were known only to a few officers, of whom Clausewitz was one. But as Stein wrote from Austria on 20th April: "The King is confirmed in his obstinate hesitation by his friend [Czar] Alexander, and by the danger of the enterprise; and I fear that it will cost his councillors a great deal to change his mind."[8]

Clausewitz sent Gneisenau a stream of reports of the situation at Königsberg. "Here the same ideas and attitudes still reign," he wrote. "It is becoming more and more difficult. All hopes seem to grow more daring, and more hopeless. I am beginning to fear that we will even supply the French with troops although no-one will admit it. How I would like to be away from here! I cannot tell you how happy I would be to receive the call from you. But at the same time I become fearful lest you should fail. Certain others, among them Grolman, have decided upon something else. This however seems much less solid to me." Grolman, in fact, intended to join the British army in Spain, and eventually did so after a period as a staff officer in the Austrian army. In his letter to Gneisenau, Clausewitz wrote that he also was on the point of leaving Prussia and entering the Austrian service, although he would prefer to fight in Gneisenau's force. "I have decided to join to avoid being condemned to remain here, which would be the worst of all. But this will never stop me answering the first call in that connection (from Gneisenau), which is far more valuable and worthy of consideration. I assume that you will have spoken to Tiedemann. He would not be averse to joining you, for nothing will induce him to remain idle. He told me that you spoke to him within the last few days about your general intentions. I have kept them a secret from everyone."[9]

Scharnhorst, too, was anxious to do something. But if he withdrew from the King, Friedrich Wilhelm would be even less likely to take positive action. As Clausewitz reported to Gneisenau: "The relationship of the General to the King seems to me to have remained the same. Since Goltz left, he is the only soldier whom the King consults on details about political matters. But he still declines his advice. I believe that the General wishes to wait until the very last moment before he leaves, and I think this is right under the present circumstances . . . The King and Queen are well; Prince Wilhelm is still somewhat sickly . . . Princess Louise, Prince Radzivill and little Eliza ask me to send you a thousand greetings and a letter for the children . . ."[10]

Clausewitz and Scharnhorst anxiously studied the news which filtered back to the War Ministry from Austria. These reports told a story of early

Austrian hopes giving place to rising gloom. When the war was still only a few days old, Austria found herself in urgent need of an ally. She began with considerable advantages. By the spring of 1809, French forces in Germany had been reduced, partly by the demands of the war in Spain; as a result, Davout was only able to field a force of some 54,000 men at Würzburg. More French troops were diverted *en route* to Spain, and with other forces collected from Bavaria, Baden, Hesse and Wurtemburg, the French managed to gather about 120,000 men. The Austrians had about 240,000, with the militia and Hungarian insurrection forces adding about 100,000 more. Two corps of almost 50,000 men formed the army under Archduke John; 30,000 were deployed in Galicia, while the rest were placed under the command of Archduke Carl in the Danube area. The French army was split into two separate wings owing to confusion over plans. Davout commanded the left, and Masséna and Oudinot led the right wing seventy-six miles away from him. The original Austrian plan was to strike fast to exploit this French dispersion; the main Austrian army was to advance from Bohemia to the River Main to attack Davout's flank and force him back across the Rhine.

Then the Austrians changed their minds; they wished to avoid the risk that the main army might be cut off from Vienna by a rapid advance by Napoleon down the Danube. The Austrians now intended to move on Bavaria, and then turn to trap Davout between themselves and the two Austrian corps from the Upper Palatinate, commanded by the Count de Bellegarde. This switch resulted in a ten day delay and threw supply arrangements into disorder. Not until 10th April did the Austrian advance begin, and then bad weather, bad roads and supply deficiencies meant that the march from the Inn to the Isar rivers took eight days. Davout had time to concentrate 40,000 men at Ratisbon, and Napoleon himself was able to reach Dillingen. At considerable risk, the Emperor moved Davout across the Austrian front to Ingolstadt, and Masséna and Oudinot up to Pfaffenhof, to restore contact between the two French wings.

As the French were concentrating, Archduke Carl did the reverse. He moved his right and centre towards Ratisbon on 19th April, but as this exposed his communications he had to leave his left on the River Abens to give protection. Davout was allowed to move upstream to join Lefebvre, and the Austrian left centre under Hohenzollern clashed with Davout near Dinzling, and lost 5,000 men. By 20th April heavy fighting was under way, all along the banks of the Abens. Outnumbered and outflanked, the Austrian left wing was pushed back and forced away from the main body. Napoleon left the pursuit of the Austrian left flank to Bessiéres, and wheeled to engage the Archduke on 22nd April just south of Ratisbon. The Austrians were forced to retreat to the north bank of the Danube. Clausewitz grew increasingly frustrated. He believed that if only the Prussians could take the field, the situation in Austria could still be reversed. He was convinced, like

Scharnhorst, that France was no longer the power she used to be. Prussia's army, on the other hand, had been improved; there was a strong desire for combat; Napoleon was fully occupied. Why, then, wait for Russia? If Prussia entered the war, Russia would follow.

So Clausewitz believed, but not Friedrich Wilhelm. Letters to Marie in Berlin, or in Charlottenberg, continued to reflect Clausewitz's torment. While he paced his room in Königsberg, one Prussian officer in Berlin could stand the waiting no longer. Reports of the actions of Major von Schill came to the War Ministry. On his own initiative, Schill rode out with about a hundred hussars from Berlin in support of an insurrection believed to be on the point of breaking out in Westphalia. Other officers and men joined him as he advanced through Potsdam and Wittenberg to Dessau, claiming to act upon the King's authority. Clausewitz believed Schill's actions to be clumsy, but courageous.[11] Friedrich Wilhelm was both furious with this insubordination and in panic lest Napoleon should act against Prussia. He disclaimed all responsibility. On 4th May Major Schill learned of Austria's setbacks on the Danube, and heard that the Westphalian insurrection was now unlikely to take place. But still he pressed on, hoping to reach the North Sea coast, capture a port, and hold it until help arrived. Milhaud, the French commander at Magdeburg, sent out troops to intercept him, but Schill brushed them aside on 5th May and reached Stralsund twenty days later. He could have escaped by ship, but he decided to turn and face the enemy. By 31st May 6,000 Danes, Dutch and Holsteiners had gathered to oppose him in front of Stralsund, while he only had about a quarter of that number inside the town. So the unequal, hopeless, grave, and to Clausewitz patriotic, fight began. Bloody hand-to-hand fighting ended with the killing of Schill and most of his officers and men. "Schill's death affects me much," Clausewitz told Marie on 9th June, "just as if I had lost my dearest brother."[12]

The exploit was retold throughout Prussia. While Schill had been marching for the coast, Borstell had warned Friedrich Wilhelm that to discipline the insubordinate Major might easily provoke a popular uprising, especially in the streets of Berlin.[13] Blücher warned Friedrich Wilhelm that if he failed to support Austria, many more Schills would take action. "All this could be avoided if Your Majesty placed yourself at the head of your people, took advantage of their present mood, and strengthened your authority so that they will at once stand by you in any cause. The long-awaited moment has come."[14] Scharnhorst, in the closest daily contact with the King, urged him not only to sign an immediate alliance with Austria, but he offered a plan which he and Clausewitz had prepared to supplement the standing army with a trained reserve. This scheme was a revised version of the *Krümper* system; it would create a force from members of the propertied classes who could equip and mount themselves.[15]

The Chief of the General Staff repeated his belief, strongly shared by Clausewitz, that if Austria should fall, Napoleon would turn upon Prussia.

"If this war with Austria ends happily for France," said Scharnhorst, "no-one will any longer hinder the complete sovereignty of Napoleon in Europe. Destruction of the royal dynasty and perpetual war for the interest of France will therefore be the fate of Prussia's royal house and people. What awaits Prussia has already overtaken Sardinia, Etruria, Spain and the Pope . . . Prussia cannot expect a continued existence from Napoleon."[16]

But the King refused to be moved, despite an uprising against the French in Hesse, and despite the effort of Brunswick to light the flame of war in his territory. Clausewitz and everyone else was impotent. More officers left to serve abroad. Blücher offered his sword to Archduke Carl, writing to Gneisenau: "God knows with what grief I quit a state and an army in which I have lived for fifty years."[17] Clausewitz told Marie that so many soldiers were leaving the country to fight elsewhere that soon only cowards would remain. He now took further steps to join the Austrian army. He contacted Colonel Streigentesch, the Austrian *attaché* at Königsberg, and asked him to supply the relevant papers.[18] He also considered sailing to Britain and perhaps fighting with the British army in the Spanish Peninsula, as Grolman intended to do. Clausewitz's admiration for the British, the most relentless enemies of Napoleon, was high; but he criticized their planning of the European diversion through which they hoped to help the Austrians; according to Clausewitz, the British expedition should have been landed on the Escaut river, not on the Weser.[19]

Friedrich Wilhelm still refused to take any serious steps to join Austria, and laid down certain conditions which must first be met. Russia must not object, Britain must lend proper support, and he must personally be convinced that Austria and Prussia would win. Nobody could possibly give these assurances. Yet Austria was in desperate need of support. Napoleon had pressed right on to Vienna, reaching the Austrian capital on 10th May. Archduke Maximilian managed to hold out for two days, but then had to evacuate the city. The French capture of Vienna meant that the Army of Inner Austria, which had earned a good deal of success in Istria under Archduke John's command, had to withdraw because its lines of communication were menaced. In turn the Tyrol had to be abandoned, although the insurgents and Chasteler's regular Austrian troops, too, had won notable victories.

Napoleon's aim was to move on from Vienna and secure his passage to the north bank of the Danube. Initially he was checked, but still hoped to cross the river near Vienna *via* the island of Löbau, which the Austrians had neglected to fortify. Archduke Carl's army was still not fully deployed when, on 20th May, Masséna's corps began to use this island stepping-stone to force a bridgehead. The French then occupied the villages of Aspern and Essling on the north bank. The battle of Aspern-Essling quickly began. The two villages were taken and re-taken with vicious fighting continuing throughout the day. Next morning, as Davout's corps poured across the bridges from the island, Napoleon launched his main blow against the Austrian centre and gradually forced it back.

Then, much to Napoleon's consternation, the bridge over the main stream of the Danube collapsed under the pressure of Austrian boats floated downriver laden with stones. The turbulent waters of the Danube, swollen by melted snow, cut off the rest of Davout's corps and the urgently needed ammunition. At that moment the Archduke threw his reserve grenadiers into the fight, and the French were pushed onto the ridge between Aspern and Essling. On the afternoon of 21st May came a two hour lull, as both sides flagged from exhaustion. Then, Austrian pressure on the two French wings became so violent that Napoleon had to order his bugles to sound the retreat. With great difficulty and many casualties the corps of Lannes and Masséna withdrew across the remaining smaller bridge on to the island of Löbau. Lannes himself had been killed. Napoleon had been dangerously near to defeat. French losses totalled over 30,000, compared with 24,000 Austrians. The battle was of a very different character to any which Napoleon had so far fought; a thrill of hope reverberated throughout Europe. It also increased the anger and frustration of officers at Friedrich Wilhelm's court. If only Prussian help had been on hand, the outcome might have been total disaster for the French. The most that Friedrich Wilhelm would do was to write to the Austrian leaders: "One more victory and I am with you."[20]

Desperately Clausewitz clung to the belief that something might still be done; and that he could play a part, if not for his own country, then perhaps fighting and even dying in a foreign army. "Although the horizon is very black," he told Marie on 9th June, "I sense within me a courage and vitality which threaten to damage my assessments, but which are still welcome. Perhaps death is most beautiful when life is most intense."[21] A fortnight later he wrote: "The thought is very good to me that one day I will delight in firing the bloody bullet at the arrogant, odious Frenchman. While people face one another in war, one may be aware of the glory of existence. Those who have lived for years in slavery, scarcely allowed to have hostile thoughts about the French, let alone speak out with the thunder of cannons, must undertake a sad war with pride."[22] French efforts to suppress Prussian thoughts as hostile as those of Clausewitz were hardly surprising.

Clausewitz now waited anxiously to see whether Austria would be able to use her advantage. Much depended on whether the Army of Inner Austria could block the French Army of Italy, and Marmont from Dalmatia, from reinforcing the weakened Napoleon. It is hard to know which Clausewitz and the other Prussians found hardest to endure: to see Austria almost topple the mighty French army, believing that if only they had been there the defeat could have been total, or to see Austria let the chance which now presented itself slip uselessly away. The advantage was not driven home. Austria dismally failed to concentrate all her available troops. By the end of June, Napoleon had nearly 170,000 men in the vicinity of Löbau, and the Austrians under Archduke Carl were outnumbered three to two. Belatedly, Archduke John was ordered to bring up his Corps from Hungary, but he arrived too late. Aspern and Essling were too strongly held by the Austrians for Napoleon to try and renew the previous engagement. So Bonaparte made a feint, and then attacked to the east of the villages on 4th July. Troops led by Oudinot, Masséna and Davout pushed rapidly forward, and the Austrians gave up their advance position, falling back upon a stronger line. Unfortunately, the line was so long that the orders took almost four hours to pass from one flank to the other.

On the evening of 4th July Napoleon launched a direct attack. Bernadotte took the village of Wagram in the Austrian centre, only to be driven out again. Next morning Archduke Carl took the offensive, pushing back the French left, and left centre, by ten o'clock in the morning. Napoleon made a brilliant counter-attack to drive a wedge into the Austrian advance. French troops pierced the Austrian centre, Wagram was retaken and Davout gained valuable ground on the right. The stubborn Austrians managed to retain reasonable order, and the French were too exhausted by battle to press further forward. And, with the arrival of Archduke John, Napoleon was forced to consolidate his position. Losses had been about even on both sides. But Archduke Carl was anxious for a truce. It was clear to him that Napoleon's downfall could not be secured by Austria alone. At Znojmo, where spirited if indecisive fighting had taken place during the morning of 11th July, the Archduke, at about midday, asked for an armistice. Talks began, and the armistice was signed at two o'clock in the small hours of the next morning.[23]

Reports of these negotiations threw the Prussian Ministry of War into added consternation. Nor did the military situation seem to necessitate an armistice. The Austrian army was still strong; the French had been severely jolted. Once again, Prussian intervention could have been decisive. But within Austria, Stadion's opponents had gained more power; Metternich now wanted peace; Archduke Carl resigned after an internal squabble, and the Archdukes John and Joseph soon did likewise. Metternich replaced Stadion as Foreign Minister and Count Lichtenstein, who became Commander-in-Chief, also wanted peace. Russia, like Friedrich Wilhelm, was still determined to stay out of the war. England's Continental expedition had been useless, as Clausewitz had feared it would be. So the Austrians agreed to the harsh terms presented by Napoleon.

The resulting Treaty of Schönbrunn of 14th October marked the nadir of Hapsburg power. The whole of Germany lay at Napoleon's mercy. At Königsberg, Scharnhorst and Clausewitz were in complete despair.

II

Peace came before Clausewitz could reach either Austria or England; it came before Gneisenau's plan for an insurrection could bear fruit; it came before Blücher went to Austria. Even Scharnhorst had been completely powerless. Officers who had gone away on foreign service returned, or travelled to Britain and then on to Spain. Carl wrote to Marie on 31st July: "I have grown older these last few weeks. I can almost say that with this step all magic has vanished from my life. To me, to fight against the enemy here in Germany for the Fatherland, was the best the world could offer."[24] The atmosphere at Königsberg was shrouded in gloom. Only the King and his supporters were cheerful, the self-satisfied Friedrich Wilhelm believing that events had proved him right. Had he not saved the Prussian army from almost certain defeat? The reformers, shaken and discouraged, profoundly disagreed. They reacted in their own, individual, characteristic ways to the peace.

Blücher, for example, who had promised Friedrich Wilhelm that with 30,000 men he would throw the French from Germany, aged rapidly and took more heavily to drink. "The fate in store for us is horrible," he wrote to the King.[25] Then partly in obedience to the King's wish to get him out of the way of the French, he angrily retired with his bottles to Stargaard. Alarming tales of the old general's conduct reached Scharnhorst and Clausewitz at Königsberg. The sad drink-befuddled soldier believed that he had been made pregnant by an elephant; then he became convinced that French agents were persecuting him, and had made the floors of his rooms too hot to walk upon. Boyen said: "When he was sitting he kept his legs raised from the ground or else he jumped around on tiptoe."[26] For the moment the future partner of the Duke of Wellington was, to say the least, incapacitated. Gneisenau resigned from the Prussian army, partly as a result of pressure from Napoleon. But he continued to serve the state as a secret agent, carrying out diplomatic missions to London and to the Russian capital at Petersburg; all the time he kept up correspondence with his friend, Clausewitz.

As the reformers were gradually dispersed, reaction grew against them at the court. For a time in late 1809 even the King's confidence in Scharnhorst was shaken. Scharnhorst defended himself with his *"Comparison between the former and the present conduct of business in the upper part of the Military Department."* In this document he attacked the military conservatives by pointing out the improvements which reforms had brought. "I must go on to speak of the new arrangements in the army itself," he wrote, "since every possible objection that can be urged against this has been laid before Your Majesty, as I think I have observed on many occasions. I might feel easier about this knowing that most of the ideas of the new system are simply Your Majesty's, put into effect by the Commission. But how few know this! And even for Your Majesty many points require fuller explanation."

Scharnhorst continued: "What would the adversaries of the new system have . . .? Are noblemen's children to have the privilege of being appointed officers in their crass ignorance and feeble childhood, while educated and energetic men are set below them without hope of promotion? So much the better, no doubt, for the noble families, but ill for the army . . . Or is promotion not to go according to accomplishments? Is old age to monopolize the higher posts? If so, active, lively and ambitious men, whose minds soon wear out their bodies, must be kept back, and lazy, dull blockheads, with few exceptions, must come to the fore." Scharnhorst repeated the basic desire which had driven the reformers: "To raise and enliven the army's spirit, to unite it more closely with the nation, and direct it to its great and important vocation, this is the principle which lies at the root of the new arrangements, and it should be studied first by those who would judge of them."[27] Clausewitz and Scharnhorst continued to work at the War Ministry, hoping and praying that another chance of war would soon come, that next time it would be seized, and that in the months between they could improve the army still more.

In December, 1809, the King and court returned to Berlin after an absence of three years. It should have been a happy occasion, but it was the reverse for those who felt that the King should have been returning in triumph, with the French driven from the Fatherland. Scharnhorst retired straight to bed with a feverish cold. But at least Clausewitz was re-united with Marie, able to see her every day instead of only during snatched visits. Still no marriage date had been fixed: continued opposition came from Marie's strict mother, and Clausewitz, still only a Captain, continued to feel the lack of money. Moreover, he was preoccupied with his work at the War Ministry, which he undertook in a state of near frenzy.[28] Clausewitz remained Scharnhorst's closest collaborator, helped by Captain Count Friedrich von Dohna, who had married Scharnhorst's daughter Julia in Königsberg the November before. Dohna looked after Scharnhorst's personal affairs, while Clausewitz continued to act as his *aide* on the business side.[29] In addition, Clausewitz was in charge of protocol in the plenary sessions of the Ministry. In all, it was difficult and complex work.

Then in January, 1810, another blow fell. Under pressure from his many other commitments, Napoleon tried to squeeze additional money from Prussia. He demanded payment of the indemnity written into the treaty of 8th September, 1808, fixing the sum at 154,000,000 francs. Friedrich Wilhelm pleaded for more time. Napoleon replied that if the money was not forthcoming, Prussia had two choices: either to cede him the province of Silesia, or to raise the money by reducing the Prussian army to a royal guard of 6,000 men. Aware of the reforms which Scharnhorst and his team had been carrying out, and of the dangers if Friedrich Wilhelm had joined Austria in 1809, Napoleon evidently wished the second choice to be made. His peremptory demands plunged Berlin into crisis.

"Prussia will be involved in a new catastrophe," Clausewitz wrote on 29th January, to Gneisenau, then at Stockholm, "from which she will scarcely be able to extricate herself from complete extinction if no saving conditions appear. But even if she goes down with honour I hope to go down honourably with her, or at least to sacrifice my own existence." He continued: "I do not know what I shall do. Austria? Russia? England? Hardly. The bankruptcies here have no end. All that has been nurtured in this sandy desert throughout the centuries, in the form of well-being, prosperity, culture and trade, may now wilt in a decade."[30]

Scharnhorst mounted a vigorous attack upon the French demands. He persuaded the Dohna-Altenstein ministry to suggest that secession of at least part of Silesia was preferable to the complete destruction of the army. He met with stubborn resistance, but continued to struggle. Reporting the state of affairs in Berlin to Gneisenau, Clausewitz described the political skirmishing, and the fight to keep up with the army reorganization despite the French demands. He wrote on 8th February that as far as Gneisenau's return was concerned, "the General thinks that there need be no obstacle. This is my own opinion too, and my wish, so that we have you near us again . . . sooner or later you must return here. Lottum has asked to be released from his post. His weak state of health, and an ill-considered opposition to the General, are the causes. Hake has taken his post and in turn Boyen has taken Hake's post. In military affairs we still advance, but following the law of the crooked line, with all its deviations. Questions of service, conscription, police and militia give rise to a great number of meetings with no result, because so few people have the proper wisdom and strength of character. Princess Louise, Prince Radzivill, Ribbentrop and above all the General send their kindest regards. The first has read your letters from Bothenburg. She is a first-class woman and is always concerned about you."[31]

The political intrigues in Berlin continued. But most of the Prussian middle-class was uninterested in politics, and still doubted the need for war against Napoleon. Clausewitz would probably have agreed with Madame de Staël's opinion; in her *De l'Allemagne* completed in those same weeks of 1810 she wrote "The spirit of the Germans seems to have no communication with their character: the one cannot tolerate any limits, the other will submit to any yoke."[32] Clausewitz's former hostess diagnosed that the Germans were peaceful to a fault unless goaded by some great spur. They held an undue regard for rank, were indifferent to politics, and submitted themselves to foreign occupation.

Opposition to Scharnhorst grew, as it did to the governing ministry which shared his view that to cede Silesia was preferable to emasculating the army.

Then, to Scharnhorst's consternation, this Dohna-Altenstein ministry collapsed. It now seemed that the Prussian army would be pruned beyond all hope of recovery. But Hardenberg, who became State Chancellor in June, managed to avert a further crisis. By a brilliant piece of statesmanship he managed to convince Napoleon's envoys that Prussia could pay the indemnity without having to take either of the other two drastic steps. Yet the money still had to be found; there would have to be vicious economies and taxation. Army funds were drastically reduced, and Hardenberg's money-raising methods caused widespread hatred, especially among the highly-taxed landholders in Brandenberg and East Prussia. More people were turned against the army—the apparent cause of financial hardship—and national unity which had been so carefully created now disintegrated.

Moreover, Napoleon now wanted a second price to be paid if he were to allow time for his financial demands to be met: Scharnhorst mu;t leave the War Ministry. Friedrich Wilhelm had to agree. In a sense, Scharnhorst was the sacrifice offered to avoid the virtual destruction of the Prussian army. Clausewitz was shocked by rumours of the dismissal which were soon confirmed by Scharnhorst himself; in June "the General" began his enforced retirement. But something was salvaged; Scharnhorst continued his supervision of the staff and engineering functions, and his influence upon the work at the War Ministry remained. According to the King: "Major-General von Scharnhorst should continue, so far as it could be done secretly, in the same relation to the officials of the War Department as hitherto in respect of the Ordinances and initiative of the more important matters of business."[33] But unity and energy at the Ministry were weakened; and military improvements, which Clausewitz and the others believed should be begun as rapidly as possible, were held back. This disruption was precisely Napoleon's aim; the French Emperor also insisted that some recent military measures, especially those designed to improve Prussian fortifications, should be scrapped, or at least postponed.

At this time of dark gloom for Prussia Queen Louise died, on 19th July. Her death cast a terrible shadow over Friedrich Wilhelm. "The lonely, joyless life of the King reacted on those around him," wrote the Queen's friend Countess Schwerin. "Things grew ever more still and less brilliant in the Berlin world. The age seemed to have grown sadder, and more evil."[34] The lonely King seemed to personify his lonely, outcast nation.

Once Scharnhorst had been removed, Clausewitz's own position became uncertain. Again, something was rescued. Officially Clausewitz was transferred back to full General Staff work on 19th July, relinquishing his post as Scharnhorst's adjutant in favour of Tiedemann. But unofficially he continued to work at the General's side for another year. "I have left the War Department with the General, and I shall carry on with his office business," he wrote to Gneisenau on 26th July.[35] Despite the recent setbacks

Clausewitz was determined to be cheerful. His letter to Gneisenau continued: "Apart from that, half against my will, I am to become a 'Professor.' Together with Tiedemann I am to teach tactics at the War School. In addition, I am to give lessons to the Crown Prince. You see, my duties are now as peaceful as planting cabbages and, lacking property, I am quite happy."[36] The last remark was a reference to Gneisenau's new landed status, found for him by the efforts of Scharnhorst and Clausewitz. Through the help given by these two friends, the King authorized Gneisenau to have a fee-farm or copyhold, so that he could support his family. When he had heard the good news Gneisenau had written to his wife from Petersburg on 6th June: "The idea of this plan was a ray of light. It was successful and my hopes were realised because of my loyal, sympathetic friends. When you write (to Clausewitz) tell him of my sincere regard, which you are well aware of, and share in it with me. The friendship which he gives me comes from a rare and noble heart."[37]

So Clausewitz, nominated a Major on 29th August, began to teach at the War School. His involvement with tactical lectures was another way in which reforms could be introduced into the Prussian Army. Efforts to revise the rigid tactical doctrines which had contributed to the Prussian defeat in 1806 were among the most radical measures undertaken at this time. Three main steps were taken to introduce the reforms: Instructions issued in 1810 and 1811, especially those drafted by General Yorck; lectures given at the War Academy by Tiedemann and Clausewitz; and the Army Regulations of 1812. All three were closely linked.

Yorck was appointed Inspector-General of the Light Infantry brigades in February, 1810. On 17th March he submitted the first of two training Instructions for the King's approval. The introduction to Yorck's draft highlights the difference between his approach and that of others in the past: "The relevant application of real circumstances sets apart the thinking officer from the officer who acts mechanically." There should be more flexible tactics, Yorck continued, "in which man does not cling to man." According to Scharnhorst: "The Instruction is so outstanding, so intelligently integrated, so closely bound up with the principles of war, and these are stated so accurately and justly, that I have read this excellent essay with as much profit as pleasure."[38]

Despite his removal from the War Ministry, Scharnhorst was still Chief of the General Staff. Thinking on very similar lines to General Yorck, he was formulating tactical directives for the army as a whole. One passage of his work read: "Good marksmanship is always the most important thing for the infantry: it always decides the action. Before the war we taught the men to load quickly, but not well, to fire quickly, but without aiming. This was very ill-considered; we must therefore work with all our might to root out this error."[39] But for the rigidly-trained, rigid-minded Prussian officers and soldiers these radical ideas needed time to be accepted and learned.

Years of parades, of repeated drills, of the same shouted commands and mechanical movements, could not be ended rapidly.

On 22nd April, 1810, Yorck was commanded by a Cabinet Order in Clausewitz's handwriting, to ensure that light infantry officers "entered into the spirit of the Instructions you drafted."[40] This was still wishful thinking. The summer manoeuvres that year attempted large-scale realistic exercises for the first time, but they revealed serious deficiencies. Another Cabinet Order severely criticized the performances of the troops, and for the manoeuvres of 1811 Yorck issued a further series of Instructions "to clear up lack of confidence and execution." One important section in these Instructions, which were published on 16th May, 1811, stated: "It has often been assumed that light infantry tactics amounted to nothing more than either firing standing still or moving in a scientifically formed open line. On the contrary, light infantry tactics consist in the ability of combining, according to the situation and terrain, movement in close formation with well-aimed fire which can only be obtained through open order."[41]

For the massive task of changing the practice and attitude of an entire army in so little time, an obvious instrument was the basic education of young officers. Here, Scharnhorst relied heavily upon the help of his two former pupils, Clausewitz and Tiedemann. He himself found time to deliver some of the lectures, which showed how important he considered military education to be. The Berlin Academy had been extensively reorganized by the ever-active Scharnhorst. When the *Allgemeine Kriegschule* (General War School) opened on 2nd May, 1810, it not only replaced the institution in which Clausewitz had been a student, but also the Artillery School.

The first term started on 15th October. Clausewitz and Tiedemann soon found that they had very different methods of approach, but together they fitted extremely well. Tiedemann was mainly concerned with indicating the drawbacks of the old rigid linear formations and their consequent lack of flexibility. As Clausewitz said, Tiedemann's lectures "worked out and illuminated very well the disadvantages of the old tactical methods."[42] But Tiedemann stayed with the old and did not venture far into discussions of the new. Clausewitz, on the other hand, concentrated upon explaining the revolutionary tactics which were then being introduced. His method was vigorous, exciting and compulsive. In his lectures, as in his writing, Clausewitz came far more to life than in his everyday conversation. Here he was dealing with something which passionately interested him. He had adequate time to prepare himself; he had a captive and attentive audience, and he had no need to worry about having to give an opinion without being able to think carefully beforehand—something he always dreaded. In these months, Clausewitz became far more like the author of *On War*. He was utterly sure of himself; his personal shyness and reticence fell away.

"I shall try to remove preconceived opinions and root out prejudice," he declared at his first lecture. He then proceeded to put forward ideas, in some cases far in advance of their time, which may have sometimes shocked his students, but always captured their interest. Clausewitz paid a great deal of attention to the basic distinction between open and close order fighting, and betweeen "little wars" and larger, more conventional ones. "By little wars we understand the use of small units in the field; actions involving 20, 50, 100 or 300 or 400 men make up the little war, unless they are forming part of a wider action."[43] In other words, these small actions were more like a guerrilla operation. (The word "guerrilla" itself came from the Spanish, "small" after the fighting in the Peninsula.) It involved units being detached, or specifically trained soldiers being used, for light operations, and acting independently and flexibly. It was the ultimate contrast to the linear formations in which Prussian tactics had become petrified.

Here, Clausewitz was pushing on far ahead. The Prussian army was being instructed to accept the use of light infantry in open order tactics, operating like the French *tirailleurs* at their best. This was just becoming permissible to the conservatives, but instruction so far had been based upon using these units only in a regular war setting. But with his emphasis upon the "little war," Clausewitz went much further ahead, and discussed the role that detached, irregular units could play in civil wars and insurrections. This was completely unorthodox and was abhorrent to many regular officers, as the idea of guerrilla warfare would be for almost another 150 years. It was felt to be unmilitary, below the accepted standards of war, and unacceptable. Moreover, Clausewitz's lectures on guerrilla warfare were interwoven with political connotations, try as he might to avoid them. He insisted that armed uprisings were merely a "method of fighting"—in other words, "in its relation to the enemy."[44] But the natural consequence of this was alarming. If the people were armed, was there not a danger of the *bourgeoisie* turning against their own rulers, and against the upper class? In any case, the regular conventional officers declared, it was they who could and should do the fighting, not some ill-disciplined rabble. Clausewitz and other officers like him, including Gneisenau, disagreed. They maintained that circumstances might often dictate drastic new steps. Yet the traditional view was to endure for many decades. Not until after his death was Clausewitz proved correct: that men could be trained as irregular troops, and could fight actions which either could not have been fought by regular soldiers, or not as effectively.

Clausewitz returned to the subject in *On War* (Book VI, Chapter XXVI), when he again crossed the accepted boundaries of formal tactics. His lectures formed the basis of this Chapter, in which he wrote: "A people's War in civilized Europe is a phenomenon of the nineteenth century. It has its advocates and its opponents: the latter either considering it in a political sense as a revolutionary means, a state of anarchy declared lawful, which is as dangerous as a foreign enemy to social order at home; or on military grounds, conceiving that the result is not commensurate with the expenditure of the nation's strength. The first point does not concern us here, for we look upon a people's War merely as a means of fighting, therefore, in its connection with the enemy; but with regard to the latter point, we must observe that a people's War in general is to be regarded as a consequence of the outburst which the military element in our day has made through its old formal limits; as an expansion and strengthening of the whole fermentation-process which we call War." He added, in a passage significantly echoed by modern writers like Mao Tse-Tung and Che Guevara: "According to our idea of a people's War, it should, like a kind of nebulous vapoury essence, never condense into a solid body . . . Still, however, it is necessary that this mist should collect at some points into denser masses, and form threatening clouds from which now and again a formidable flash of lightning may burst forth."[45]

Having perhaps astonished his students with the unorthodox content of his lectures, Clausewitz talked of the new forms of regular warfare. He attempted to define the difference between the soldier who moved and fought mechanically, and the skirmisher, who used more initiative. The latter, he said, "possesses an enterprising spirit, a confidence in himself and his luck, which someone who has always served in the line can hardly imagine." On the other hand, the skirmisher "is more respectful of danger in ordinary battle than troops fighting in close order. This is an absolutely necessary quality of light troops . . . in whom the most extreme daring must alternate with intelligent caution, depending on the circumstances. The free play of intelligence, the clever merging of boldness with caution—this is the quality that renders the little war so extraordinarily interesting."[46]

Clausewitz also continually underlined the fact that the light infantryman and the line soldier could be the same person, and that the tactics of both could be amalgamated. All forms of war were interconnected, he said. War was not the realm of exclusive groups of specialists. "We employ a classification according to which war is divided into large and small types. But the frontiers between the little war and the large-scale merge into one another." To Tiedemann, skirmishers were important auxiliaries, whereas to Clausewitz they were an integral part of all infantry groups. Prevailing circumstances alone should determine the exact formula, and even then both kinds would generally be used. "In skirmishing, the infantry never completely deploys into open order, but a suitable number of men always remain in close formation . . . wherever you wish to thrust forward in attack, you must have soldiers in close formation in readiness. Yet although close formations appear generally more suitable for the attack, clear advantages are attached to the skirmish line, even in regular combat."[47] So, carefully and methodically, Clausewitz revealed to his pupils the full changes that were being brought about in Prussian infantry tactics, which also affected strategy, and which would be heavily relied upon in the coming struggle with the French. Emphasizing the use of light troops, the interplay between open and close order and, at the far extreme, the use of guerrillas, Clausewitz showed just how far tactics were being altered from those which had formed the basis for the military doctrine of less than six years before: he showed the shift from the old to the new forms of war.

The third and final step which was to bring about the revolution of Prussia's Frederickian methods of fighting, the Regulations of 1812, would soon be completed. But meanwhile Clausewitz had personal business to attend to. At long last he was to be married to the faithful Marie. Clausewitz had had no reason to doubt for a long time now that Marie wished to be his wife; her letters had been loving and intimate. Apart from her mother's objections, the main delay had been caused by Clausewitz himself. He had been so preoccupied with his work that after the first flush of romance the references to his love had been appended to his letters almost as an after-thought. Not that his feelings towards her had weakened. It was his nature to become immersed in something to the exclusion of everything else; and usually thoughts of war precluded thoughts of Marie. It would always be so. But now Clausewitz was in Berlin. He was a Major, a member of the General Staff, military tutor to the Crown Prince and to Prince Frederick of the Netherlands, and a lecturer at the *élite* War Academy. There were, pre-sumably, fewer grounds upon which Marie's mother could oppose the match. Finally, on 17th December, 1810, Carl and Marie were married in a simple ceremony at St. Mary's Church in Berlin.

Domestic financial problems still troubled him as they would for some years to come. Clausewitz was earning about 1,500 thalers, not a large sum, and he and Marie had only a small amount of money to buy and furnish their first home. "Clausewitz and Marie were married with much love and few means," wrote Marie's friend Caroline von Rochow. "They were delighted with each other and lived happily in a tiny building, where the entire household effects consisted of a sofa and six chairs covered with calico, and a few other pieces of furniture. She counted herself lucky when she could treat relatives or good friends to a leg of mutton when they came for dinner."[48] Marie herself believed that their marriage would benefit from the long wait which had gone before. "A love which led more quickly to its goal, which had to fight fewer internal and external obstacles, would have saved us much pain. But it could not possibly have been so rich in happiness and pleasure." She continued: "I would like to have seen, met and come to know him a few years earlier so that I could have had the happiness of our marriage before the final disappearance of youth. But I cannot regret the long probation period which we had to bear."[49]

Clausewitz soon returned to business, especially to his involvement with the important and far-reaching Army Regulations. Work was begun on the manual in January, 1811. On the 14th of that month the King appointed two commissions to draft new tactical regulations for the infantry and the cavalry; Scharnhorst was to be chairman of both. Clausewitz, Krauseneck

and the Royal Adjutant, von Natzmer, were responsible for the infantry
sections, advised by Yorck and Blücher. During 1811 each chapter of the
new manual was submitted in turn to Friedrich Wilhelm for approval. Since
he wanted certain changes, the manual could not be issued to the troops before
the beginning of 1812. The Regulation was shorter than the manuals used
by other armies at the time, but it was compact; and like Clausewitz's lectures
and Yorck's instructions, it was a complete contrast to previous documents.

The Regulation opened with questions of drill, which it said should be
based upon the "natural, free and unforced posture of the individual."[50]
Then came instructions for firing. Again, there was a marked difference to
the old rule of massive unaimed volleys. At the proper signal, "every man in
the first rank raises his weapon, aims as well as possible, fires, reloads
without the least hurry, and makes ready again. Now the man behind him
aims, fires and loads in his turn." Orders were given for company and
battalion formations, for the deployment of the battalion third ranks and
the fusiliers, and for the use of forces. In a passage reminiscent of Clausewitz's own lectures, the manual stated that a gradual build-up of pressure
should be achieved through constant interaction of the four successive lines
of troops which made up the brigade: the fusiliers, the two lines of ordinary
infantry, and the cavalry. There should be fluid reinforcement of units,
substitution, withdrawal, the shifting of force from one point to another, and
the replacement of entire lines of battle. In other words, flexibility was
essential. The enemy must always be kept guessing; the army should be
manipulated to snatch every opportunity, to seize and exploit the unexpected, and above all to grasp and retain the battle initiative.

The 1812 Regulation was the culmination of all the reformers' efforts. Its
contents would not have stood a chance of being put into practice if the
previous reforms had not been attempted, and largely adopted. The relaxation of discipline for example allowed greater individual initiative, the
adoption of light infantry tactics, the issue of instructions, and perhaps as
important as any of these, the creation of a real atmosphere of reform.

Meanwhile, as the committees had worked on the manual throughout
1811, the European situation had again become unsettled. The first clear
signs of a break between France and Russia were becoming apparent. As in
1809, it seemed as if Prussia was to have a first class chance of striking
against Napoleon. Once again Friedrich Wilhelm refused to act. The group
described by Clausewitz as "the good party" tried all it could to make the
King move. In the summer of 1811, for example, Gneisenau drew up a
detailed memorandum urging Friedrich Wilhelm to mobilize his army on the
first signs of war between France and Russia, and to allow an insurrection to
be organised against the French, pleading that the Prussian people should
be summoned to the colours to fight for the Fatherland. When he received
this document, Friedrich Wilhelm scribbled in the margins: "Nobody
would come!" "Good, like poetry!" and: "If a single preacher were to be

shot, the whole thing would be over." Gneisenau angrily retorted: "Religion, prayer, love of one's ruler, love of the Fatherland—these things are nothing else than poetry! The heart is never uplifted unless attuned to poetry. The man who acts only by cold calculation becomes an inveterate egoist. Upon poetry is founded the security of the throne."[51] But nothing could be done to induce the King to begin active preparations for war.

Clausewitz, his work on the Regulation finished for the moment, went on leave with Marie in August, 1811. They passed more than two months at the spa at Kudowa in Glatz province. One reason for his visit was to take the waters, but he also spent much of his time studying local geography for military purposes, especially in case an insurrection could be organized. He drafted a *Defence Plan for Silesia* which he sent to Gneisenau; he knew that his friend had been recommended as the future Commander-in-Chief of the province. This appointment would form part of the plan to strengthen Prussian defences by achieving greater co-ordination between the districts. The French build-up of forces in 1810 and early 1811 in central and northern Germany—contrary to the terms of the Tilsit treaty which stipulated their withdrawal from Prussia once indemnities had been paid—had frightened many people. If France attacked Prussia the small Prussian garrisons scattered throughout the country might fall before the Prussian army could concentrate. It was therefore decided to send senior officers into the provinces with emergency powers to act upon their own initiative. One such appointment was that of Yorck, as Governor of West Prussia in May, 1811, upon Scharnhorst's recommendation.

In his *Defence Plan for Silesia*, Clausewitz envisaged that volunteers would fight with fowling pieces and pikes if necessary,[52] and that the Prussians would make use of the fortresses of Neisze, Kosel, Glatz and Sulberberg. He believed that Gneisenau could make "a Spain out of Silesia," and placed considerable hope in the abilities of the hero of Kolberg. But Gneisenau himself, seeing how his plan for a national uprising had been received by the King, was unsure whether he really wished to be Commander of Silesia. He wrote to Clausewitz to tell him so.

Clausewitz hastily replied on 13th September to try and persuade him. "What you have said about yourself made me almost impatient, before I realized that great modesty often characterizes a great man, and that one must accept this. If you eventually emerge as a victorious Commander-in-Chief of Silesia, would not the world call you a great man then? I would call you this now, in anticipation, but I stop myself in case I am thought a flatterer. Why would you not be happy in accepting the Silesian commander's baton? Are you not able to be strong in spirit, with a sustaining courage in moments of anxiety and horror? Is not this the essence of all great Field-Marshals? I do not exaggerate your abilities, and if you have a different trust and knowledge of human nature, then lean upon mine. I have been so little mistaken up to now that I believe this very strongly. If you wish to decline this post, who else would be equal to it? Grawert, Tauentzien, Kliest or Borstell, if you force the King to choose? Surely you would always blame yourself if you not merely failed to grasp such a position of power firmly, but actually refused it outright, allowing it to fall into such hands?" Clausewitz ended: "In the army no one enjoys such complete confidence as you ... for you are the unsilenced voice, especially in Silesia. I know of no one else who would be so trusted here."[53]

Clausewitz's appeal failed. Gneisenau wrote back to say that he had refused the post. Clausewitz's angry reply illustrates not only the close relationship which existed between himself and Gneisenau, a superior officer, but also how his feelings could run away with him. "It is essential that the right man stands in the right place," he wrote. "I feel impelled to speak my mind, and to warn of the danger involved in making this appointment. I know that what is needed in war, more than skill, ability, judgement and everything else, is authority. Tell me, for God's sake, who has this? Who has the courage to give a clear yes or no? The one who is appointed must be a man like you or the General for whom one has respect and trust, and who can uphold the required authority of the high command."[54]

Relations between France and Russia were steadily deteriorating. It was an uneasy period, with a lowering international sky. "The storm of 1812 had not yet broken," wrote the poet Pushkin, "Napoleon had yet to put the great people to the test. He was still threatening, still hesitating." If Napoleon moved against Russia he would first occupy Prussia. For weeks Friedrich Wilhelm's carriage stood waiting in the castle courtyard in Berlin, ready for the King's flight to Königsberg should the French launch an invasion, and his army be unable to stop them. Act now, urged the reformers, before it was too late. But Friedrich Wilhelm refused to move without Russian support and, although he repeatedly wrote to Alexander, this help was not guaranteed. Nor did many senior Prussian officers have much time for Gneisenau's and Clausewitz's schemes for an insurrection. Guerrilla warfare was still an abhorrent idea. Boyen, who supported Gneisenau's scheme, later commented that "in the army, with the exception of Blücher, Yorck and Gneisenau, the great majority was against guerrilla warfare in so far as now and then they took note of it. The great majority of officers could not equate their tactical training with such a method of warfare."[55]

If Clausewitz's War Academy lectures had begun earlier, or had reached a wider audience, the idea might have been more widely accepted. But now even Gneisenau felt despondent; Clausewitz, still desperately hoping, continued to scribble down his ideas. While at Kudowa, apart from devising his operational plan for Silesia, he drafted a scheme for the creation of a legion of German volunteers.[56] In this he relied heavily upon English money and upon the landing of an English force at the mouth of the Weser; but he believed that the German middle class could raise a 6,000-strong guerrilla force within a few months, in imitation of the Spanish uprising. These 6,000 insurgents, together with the English, could turn a corner of Oldenburg into a second Torres-Vedras. But the English would not be drawn into promising substantial help; they believed they were doing quite enough in the Peninsula. In any case, Prussia under Friedrich Wilhelm must first recover the prestige lost in 1806. The "good party" was still a minority, and plans such as those drafted by Gneisenau and Clausewitz were still ignored at home and abroad.

Scharnhorst was meanwhile hurrying from one capital to another, sometimes in disguise to escape French notice; dressed as a wounded Russian colonel returning from Turkey, as Boyen's servant, or as a common labourer. In a letter to Yorck he described those days as a "stormy, shaky condition . . . a dark and darkening future, a labryinthian confusion."[57] But in October he secretly visited Petersburg and managed to obtain a concession from the Czar: Alexander promised that if Napoleon were to occupy part of Prussia, or strengthen his forces on the Vistula, the main Russian army would advance upon the Vistula through the Duchy of Warsaw, and an army corps of twelve battalions would be sent simultaneously to East Prussia to defend Königsberg. To show that the Russians would act at once, the Czar also authorized his General von Wittgenstein, who remained with three Russian divisions two days march from Tilsit, to move without waiting for fresh instructions from Petersburg, if Yorck in West Prussia requested help.

Friedrich Wilhelm was faced with an even more complicated dilemma. He could now count upon some Russian support, but this would not save his entire kingdom. On the other hand, he was becoming heavily pressed by the French party at court to seek an alliance with Napoleon to remove the threat of a French invasion completely. Austria's attitude was the key to the problem; if support came from that quarter Prussia might yet hope to defeat the French. Scharnhorst therefore rushed to Vienna immediately after his Petersburg mission. Metternich received him cordially. But the Austrian Minister, like many in Friedrich Wilhelm's own court, was suspicious of the Russians and scathing about the Czar's promises. Austria therefore refused to turn against the French, and Metternich would not promise help even if Prussia faced possible annihilation. Many Austrians still blamed Prussia for their own defeat in 1809.

Back in Berlin, Chancellor Hardenberg had begun to study the advantages of a military alliance with Napoleon, and threw his considerable influence against any mobilization plan. Late in the autumn of 1811, Napoleon stepped up the pressure. Either Prussia must enter his treaty network, the Rhine Confederation, or sign an unconditional offensive/defensive alliance with France. At this last, desperate stage, the reformers saw one ray of hope. Faced with the new French demands, even Hardenberg advised an alliance with Russia against Napoleon. But Friedrich Wilhelm was still not convinced, and the French party at the Berlin court gained the upper hand. The chief spokesman of this group was Ancillon, backed by General Grawert. Described by Gneisenau as the "court parson", Ancillon maintained that Napoleon cherished friendly intentions towards the Prussians, otherwise, he added, the Emperor would have destroyed them long ago.

Friedrich Wilhelm made one last appeal to Alexander to send an envoy to negotiate with the French on Prussia's behalf. The Czar replied on 22nd February, 1812, that he would only give help "against an attack at once unjust and groundless, and induced only by the insatiable ambition of Napoleon."[58]

The French Emperor had almost lost patience with the dithering Prussians. He had a force of nearly 300,000 men on the borders of the country, and French troops were already crossing the frontier from Magdeburg and Swedish Pomerania into Prussian territory. The commander of the artillery of the Grand Army received secret instructions to prepare siege trains for Spandau, Kolberg, and Graudenz. To be realistic, Friedrich Wilhelm could do nothing but accept the French demands; but Clausewitz and those who felt like him refused to be realistic. They wanted to fight, even if it meant defeat. His notes and comments both then and later, including the unpublished *Über die Kurftigen Kriegsoperationen Preussens gegen Frankreich* written soon after the Peace of Vienna (1815) showed his strong belief that Prussia should have gone to war in 1812, despite the high risk of her being destroyed. At the worst, Clausewitz believed, a war could only hasten the fate which Napoleon had already envisaged for Prussia; nothing would be lost by taking up arms now, and honour at least would be saved. "One is obliged to undertake an operation against chance of success," wrote Clausewitz, "when it is impossible to do anything else."[59]

But Friedrich Wilhelm believed there was something else. On 24th February, 1812, he put Prussia's signature to a French alliance. Prussia was to supply a corps of 20,000 men for Napoleon's use, which resulted in nearly half the line army being swallowed up by the Twenty-Seventh Division of the Grand Army. Upon oath, the King had to promise not to augment the forces that remained in Prussia. The country lay wide open to the forces of Napoleon; and it had to provide for the upkeep of his army on its way to Russia, undertaking to supply oats, hay, liquor, in huge quantities. French troops occupied Berlin. The King and his court scuttled away to Potsdam, where Friedrich Wilhelm wrote a pathetic letter to Czar Alexander, saying that he had had to think of the salvation of his own monarchy, but that at heart he still remained the friend and ally of the Russian ruler, and hoped that in this sense they would carry on the war together. As Prussian troops were now fighting the Russians, it was hardly likely that Friedrich Wilhelm's letter would be well-received.

To Clausewitz, the worst thing possible had happened; not only was

Prussia joined with France, but he himself might have to fight under Napoleon. He poured out his anger in a long document consisting of three highly emotional declarations; this he submitted to Gneisenau and Boyen who added marginal notes of their own. The three *Bekenntnisse* were not published until 1869 because they were too inflammatory. Certain passages in this document were the most powerful which Clausewitz ever wrote; and according to the historian Heinrich von Treitschke, Clausewitz's protest was "a classic memorial which even today (1879) must profoundly move every German heart."[60]

In the first of his three declarations, Clausewitz denounced those who believed that men who wanted war to the death must be mad and dangerous revolutionaries, or at least irresponsible prattlers and scribblers. Clausewitz angrily condemned the flatterers and subservient officials at the court who lacked all character, and were "lost to vice, and forgetful of their obligations." In a paragraph reminiscent of Emile Zola's famous *J'accuse* letter Clausewitz continued: "I believe: *that* people have nothing to honour more than the dignity and liberty of their existence; *that* they must defend these to the last drop of blood; *that* they cannot fulfil a more noble duty, nor obey a more noble law; *that* the shameful blot of a cowardly capitulation is never wiped away; *that* this drop of poison in the blood of a people is transmitted to posterity and will cripple and undermine the energy of later generations; *that* the honour that once was, cannot be disgraced; *that* the honour of the King and the Government is the unique safeguard of the nation and must be at one with the people; *that* in general a people is invincible when it fights nobly for its liberty; *that* defeat after a bloody and honourable battle assures the revival of liberty and is the seed of a new life. No! The patriots were not misguided enthusiasts. On the contrary it was they in the general panic who had the clearest view of the situation. With a clear conscience they struggled against the storms of corruption and cherished a sense of duty in their hearts. Posterity will be their judge."[61]

Clausewitz's second declaration consisted of an *exposé* of the current situation. The Continental System had ruined European commerce, he wrote, and had led to general bankruptcy; the uncertainty of the future had unsettled national credit; the spirit of enterprise had been discouraged and complete stagnation had followed. But the French alliance would not help, Clausewitz added. He repeated his conviction that, since the Peace of Tilsit, Napoleon had never ceased to humiliate Prussia and to threaten her total destruction, and that he planned to pit Prussia against Russia, and then to destroy her. With every concession, Prussia's strength to resist had diminished, he said. War must be declared against the French. The chance of failure was indeed greater than the chance of success—on this point Gneisenau, in an attached note, disagreed—but even so, Prussia would have all the desperate courage of despair.

In the third section, Clausewitz discussed Russia's military strength and how Prussia could help her against Napoleon. Once again he returned to the theme of a national uprising. This would use all men between eighteen and sixty years old who were not already in the regular army, and arm them with rifles, scythes or picks, giving each a bag of supplies, a straw-padded cap to soften blows, and an insignia marking the province to which he belonged. He went on to give details of the irregular force, or *Landsturm*, which was later to emerge in a modified form in the War of Liberation. Men of two or three villages would form a company, he wrote, and several companies or troops would constitute a column. They would avoid large-scale battles, but would obstruct the enemy in the provinces, by hindering French officials, capturing detachments and attacking convoys, conducting ambushes, and lending support to the regular army. These irregulars would be proudly taught to scorn French sabres and bullets, and "we shall reply to cruelty with cruelty."

Clausewitz refuted the idea that the Prussian terrain was unsuited to partisan warfare. Some parts were inaccessible for regular forces, especially the swampy forests, and these were excellent areas for the guerrillas to use. Nor were the Germans themselves unsuited as partisan fighters: Clausewitz maintained that in some respects they were better than the French, who were "indiscreet and conceited." In a short appendix, he listed the advantages of a defensive war, and described the main features of the new form of warfare. Once more, the passage was a forerunner to *On War*: the time of intrigues and petty interests was over, he wrote; no longer would professional armies fight without conviction or ferocity, or wars be conducted according to polite rules. The war against Napoleon, Clausewitz concluded, was a war for all men. The document remained unseen except by the few people whose advice Clausewitz had sought. The contents did nothing to help him in that tragic month of February, 1812, but served as a valuable foundation for his later thoughts upon the same subjects.

Meanwhile, Clausewitz had to consider what to do. Yet, with his inflamed sense of honour, dignity of the Fatherland, and hatred of the French, he really had no choice. He told Marie of his decision to take the most drastic step of all. He would join forces with Prussia's enemy, Russia. In his February document Clausewitz had pictured how a man might take such a decision. "He walks away from the scene, abandoning the happiness of his life and the subject of his devotion, knowing that he cannot serve the enemy of his Fatherland, whom he detests from the bottom of his heart. Such a man, in this moment, would like to show the calm deliberation of a cool judgment."[62] Certain other Prussian officers took the same step, although the number who actually did so when the French treaty was signed was far smaller than historians in the last century estimated. At the most, there were about two dozen.[63] Among them were Boyen, who resigned as Director of the personnel section at the War Ministry; Tiedemann, who had refused to replace Boyen; and von Dohna, Scharnhorst's son-in-law. Scharnhorst himself was not permitted to resign, but the King gave him unlimited leave to visit Silesia. Gneisenau received permission to go, and went to Vienna. The resignations constituted a political demonstration unparalleled in Prussian history: service to the Fatherland took first place above service to the leader of the Fatherland; if the leader was judged to be acting wrongly, to desert him was not to betray Prussia, but to serve her.

Stein, who also left for Russia, wrote: "To my eyes, the dynasties are entirely immaterial at this critical moment. They are nothing but instruments."[64] And Gneisenau commented: "The world is divided into two sides: those who, whether they like it or not, serve the ambition of Napoleon, and those who fight them. Thus, not territories and frontiers divide us, but principles." This division now meant that Clausewitz would be fighting on the opposite side not only to the Prussian force under Napoleon, but also, on a personal level, to his two brothers who would be in that force.

On 31st March, 1812, Carl bade farewell to Marie and left for Lignwitz in Silesia, where he intended to join Scharnhorst while the King considered his request to resign. Even if the request were refused, he still intended to cross the border into Russia, to take up arms against the same army which he had worked so hard to reform.

EIGHT

Clausewitz in Russia

"War is nothing but a duel on an
extensive scale."
(*On War*, bk. i, ch. i.)

CLAUSEWITZ WAS IN a miserable state when he left Berlin, worried and frightened by the step he had taken, and suffering from a terrible headache which was increased by the jolting of his carriage. Eventually he hired a post-horse to ride on to Frankfurt, where he spent a few sad hours with his brother Wilhelm and sister Johanna. Soon he and Wilhelm would be fighting on opposite sides. Then he continued to Lignwitz, still tormented that he may have made a mistake in leaving Prussia. Here, he wrote his first letter to Marie.

"I have travelled the road which I passed along with you last year, my dear wife, when I was so happy. This time I was in the sweat of fear and cursing every stone. The farewells at Frankfurt were very painful for me, and increased my headache. You see, my dear wife, I am not made of unfeeling *papier-maché* as people tend to believe after seeing me in Berlin." He added: "I do not wish to say much of my feelings about travelling on the road which we used so happily last year; I need my strength and must not be swept away by the sorrow which overshadows my whole being. Despite the blurring caused by the pain, I still recognize many of the places we visited together last year, and about which we have talked, and all this moves me very much. I hardly dare compare this time with that, because I would be completely mastered by my sorrow."[1]

In Breslau he received two letters. One was an assurance from Petersburg that he would be commissioned in the Russian army as a First Lieutenant with an income of 1900 thalers—an increase of about 400 thalers on his Berlin salary. The second letter, of 23rd April, was a curt dismissal from the King: "Following your application on the 12th of this month I give you herewith your dismissal. Friedrich Wilhelm."[2] "So the final step is taken," said Clausewitz. "I can no longer carry the flag which I have devotedly followed with my life for twenty years."[3] He wrote again to Marie on 26th April: "The misfortune of the Fatherland has reached its summit, for her noblemen are slaves who take up swords against themselves at their master's command. To any intelligent man, the few forms of freedom are a worthless mockery, because what Prussia has become within a few months, so will Austria become, and even sooner. We really have nothing left to fear. Instead, we have everything to hope for, because in this condition everything that happens, every new move or upset in the political world, is a reason for hope. So I face the future with optimism."[4]

Reaching Lignwitz, Clausewitz was re-united with Scharnhorst. He also had a military duty to perform before he left Silesia and entered the Russian army. Hurriedly he completed a memorandum which he was writing for the instruction of his royal pupil the Crown Prince, Friedrich Wilhelm. If it had been available to a wider military readership, this 11,500 word treatise would have been as important as Yorck's manuals and Clausewitz's own lecture notes in the literature of Prussian reform. Entitled *The Most Important Principles for the Conduct of War to Complete My Course of Instruction of His Royal Highness the Crown Prince*, the memorandum began: "These principles, though the result of long thought and continuous study of the history of war, have nonetheless been drawn up in haste, and so will not withstand severe criticism in regard to its form. In addition, only the most important subjects have been chosen from a great number, since a certain brevity was necessary." Then followed a miniature and more personal version of *On War*, one which reflected the peculiar circumstances in which Prussia now found herself. Indeed, the *Principles* were an important step towards *On War*. As Marie wrote twenty years later: "A paper with which he finished the instruction of H.R.H. the Crown Prince contains the germs of his subsequent works."[5] The *Principles* show how far Clausewitz had developed his lines of thought by 1812; and they show how even before his experiences in 1812, 1813, 1814, and 1815, he accurately assessed the fundamental features of the shift from the old to the new forms of war.

The Crown Prince was urged to think strictly in terms of the new and more flexible Prussian tactics, and to disregard those who tried to fob him off with the old. These tactics, as outlined in the *Principles*, would be of far more value in battle than the previous ideas of rigid formalistic, operations. "Any person who may present this matter differently to Your Royal Highness is a pedant, whose views will only do you harm. In the decisive moments of your life, in the turmoil of battle, you will some day feel that this view alone can help where help is needed most, and where a dry pedantry of figures will forsake you."

Clausewitz inserted his own opinion of how Prussia should have faced the French threat. "Whether counting upon physical or moral advantages, we should always try, in time of war, to have the probability of victory on our side. But this is not always possible." He continued: "Often we must act *against* this probability, *should there be nothing better to do* . . . Therefore, even when the likelihood of success is against us, we must not think of our undertaking as unreasonable or impossible; for it is always reasonable if we do not know of anything better to do, and if we make the best use of the few means at our disposal . . . We must therefore familiarize ourselves with the prospect of an honourable defeat. We must always nourish this thought within ourselves." After stressing that "no military leader has ever become great without audacity," Clausewitz went on to discuss tactics. Many of the points which he made here later reappeared in *On War*; one example was his theme that "the most important thing in war will always be the art of defeating our opponent in combat."

Warfare had three main objects, he wrote: to conquer and destroy the armed power of the enemy, to take possession of his material and other sources of strength, and to gain public opinion. There were a number of important rules. "The first and most important . . . is to use our entire force with the utmost energy . . . The second rule is to concentrate our power as much as possible against that section where the chief blows are to be delivered." In *On War* these two rules, marking the shift away from the previous wars of manoeuvre, were blended into statements like this: "The greatest possible number of troops should be brought into action at the decisive point."[6]

In his *Principles* Clausewitz continued: "The third rule is never to waste time . . . the fourth rule is to follow up our successes with the utmost energy." He summarized the principles in the section headed: "Application in Time of War." Again we find a strong resemblance to his later writing, for example this passage: "The conduct of war resembles the workings of an intricate machine, with tremendous frictions, so that combinations which are easily planned on paper can be executed only with great effort . . ."

Clausewitz finished with an exhortation to his pupil, who, like Clausewitz's brothers and many friends, would soon be on the opposite side in the war. "A powerful emotion must stimulate the great ability of a military leader, whether it be ambition as in Caesar, hatred of the enemy as in Hannibal, or the pride in a glorious defeat, as in Frederick the Great. Open your heart to such emotions. Be audacious and cunning in your plans, firm and persevering in their execution, be determined to find a glorious end, and fate will crown your youthful brow with a shining glory, which is the ornament of princes, and engrave your image in the hearts of your last descendants."

After sending off the memorandum to the Prince, Clausewitz spent a few more days with Scharnhorst before resuming his journey from Silesia. He had long talks with the General and discussed with him the state of the Prussian, French and Russian armies. Scharnhorst believed strongly that the Russians should use the vast space of their country as a weapon in the coming campaign by luring the enemy into hostile territory. The need for this policy was a direct result of the Franco-Prussian treaty, he said. Scharnhorst had put this view to Metternich in Vienna the previous December, when he said that the alliance with Prussia gave Napoleon 100,000 men, "with 300 field pieces, and eight fortresses well armed and provisioned for six months; it deprives Germany of the hope of recovering her independence, enables Napoleon to call Poland to arms, and makes it impossible for Russia to wage any but a defensive war."[7] But this view of the best, if not the only, possible Russian policy, which Scharnhorst repeated to Clausewitz, was not shared by the Czar. Alexander still hoped for a glorious victory if the French threw themselves against the entrenched positions at Drissa, just inside the Russian border. One of the strangest aspects of the situation in which Clausewitz found himself, when he decided to join the enemy of Prussia, was that as Scharnhorst's *aide* at the War Ministry he knew more than most Russians the details of Prussia's mobilization and troop deployment plans. This knowledge could have been of real value to Russia, but this apparently occurred to no-one, least of all Clausewitz himself.

He and "the General" rode together in the countryside around Glatz and Silberberg, where only a few months before Carl had stayed with Marie while writing the treatise for Gneisenau. Despite the sadness of departure and the memories the district had for him, his letters to his wife were no longer as despondent as before. "Sadness has gently taken hold of me, yet has not made me depressed," he wrote;[8] although later he added: "Being with you is my only happiness. If war does not snatch me into its whirlpool soon, I will become very homesick for you, my beloved sweetheart. Every stroke of your dear handwriting is precious to me. Not hearing from you is the most terrible experience, and one which I have to expect in the future."[9]

In May, Clausewitz rode on to find this whirlpool of war. He carried with him letters of recommendation, including one from Gneisenau: "Herr von Clausewitz . . . is one of the most talented of people and full of profound knowledge of military science."[10] On 6th June Clausewitz arrived at Vilna, in the Russian territory of Polish-Lithuania, and the bustling headquarters of the Czar and General Barclay de Tolly, commanding the First Army of the West. There, Clausewitz dressed in his Russian Lieutenant's uniform. A number of Prussian officers had already reached the town, including, to Clausewitz's great delight, his friend Gneisenau. Gneisenau had ridden from Vienna with Count Chasot, a hot-headed Prussian who had left Prussia during the 1809 campaign in Austria. But Gneisenau had already made up his mind to leave for England, despite an excellent reception from the Czar.

"He had come to the conclusion," wrote Clausewitz in his memoirs of the 1812 campaign, "from the whole appearance of things, that he could find in Russia no fitting theatre for the active exercise of his profession. He spoke no Russian, and so could fill no independent command. He was too old and too senior in rank to consider taking some subordinate post on the staff of a general or corps, as I and other officers did. He could therefore only have fought the campaign in the Czar's suite. He knew well what this involved, or rather, did not involve. The Czar's headquarters were already overrun with distinguished idlers. To attain either distinction or usefulness in such a crowd would have needed the dexterity of a real intriguer, and a close familiarity with the language. He was lacking in both.''[11]

It was clear to Gneisenau and Clausewitz that the Russian preparations for the expected French offensive were seriously deficient, and in some respects dangerously wrong. The Russian army itself had a number of defects: the Commissariat was corrupt, the discipline over-harsh, and many officers were incompetent. Not the least difficulty was the Czar's intention to take overall personal command of his armies. He had never commanded before or even served in the field. His military knowledge rested primarily upon tuition given to him by the Prussian-born Lieutenant-General von Phull. Clausewitz had first met Phull when Phull was a Colonel lecturing on strategy at the Berlin War School in 1803. His military talents were dubious. He had failed to realize the developments which had taken place in warfare, and was described by Clausewitz as a "complete pedant."

Phull, Massenbach and Scharnhorst had been the three Chiefs of Staff during the 1806 catastrophe. Phull had done little to distinguish himself at that time. Indeed, his conduct had been very peculiar. After the defeat at Auerstädt he had burst into insane laughter, according to Clausewitz, and had jeered at the Prussian army for not having followed a plan of his. "He said on his flight, taking off his hat: 'Adieu the Prussian monarchy.' " Clausewitz wrote: "He was a man of much understanding and cultivation, but without a knowledge of actual things. From the earliest period, he had led such a secluded and contemplative life, that he knew nothing of the happenings of the daily world . . . The more recent phenomena of war had made no impression on him. I never saw a man who lost his head so easily, or who, intent as he always was upon great things, was so often overwhelmed by the least intrusion of reality."[12]

Clausewitz was appointed Phull's *aide-de-camp*. After only a few days in this post he believed that his previous judgement of the General was if anything too lenient. Yet the Czar relied heavily upon Phull, despite the fact that the Prussian had lived in Russia for six years without making any effort to learn the language. "The Czar felt that Phull was to be considered as an abstract genius," wrote Clausewitz.[13] Clausewitz believed that Phull was advising the Czar to follow a mistaken strategy against the French. Phull declared that the Russians should depend upon forward defensive positions at Drissa, before withdrawing, rather than retreating deep into the country early on as Scharnhorst and a few others advocated.

Time was running out, and much remained to be done. Napoleon had massed an army of 420,000 men near the Russian frontier. Any day now he would throw it over the Niemen. Yet because of his reliance upon Phull, the Czar had made little attempt to prepare himself for command. General Barclay de Tolly, who was also his War Minister, in fact undertook the duties of Commander-in-Chief; he issued the daily orders, received reports, made announcements. Phull, on the other hand, was isolated and was

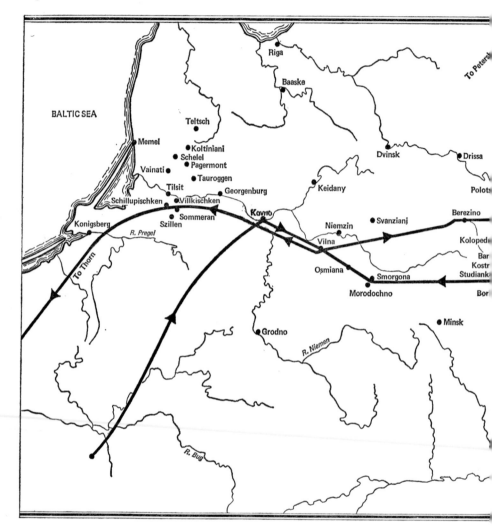

regarded by the Russians with "envy, disfavour and distrust"; he had no
knowledge of the people around him, no firm appointment, and even lacked
an *aide* until Clausewitz arrived. This situation seemed incredible to Clausewitz. As he said, "the Russian army was 180,000 strong, if taken at a high
estimate; the enemy, at the lowest, 350,000—and Bonaparte was their
leader."[14]

  Clausewitz learned that Phull's plan was to have the Russian First Army
in the West withdraw into entrenched positions around the middle Dvina,
leading the French against them. The Second Army of the West, under
General Pyotr Bagration, would then press forward on the right flank and the

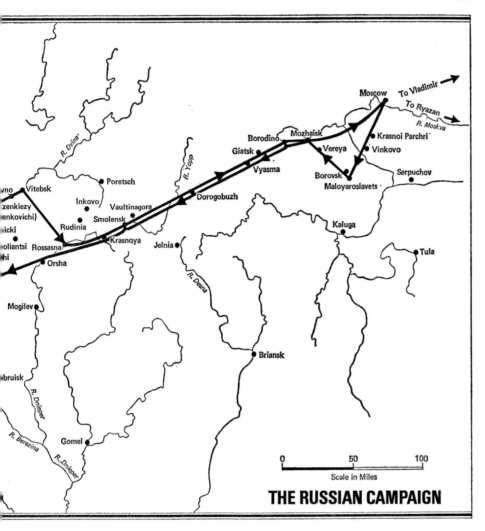

THE RUSSIAN CAMPAIGN

rear of the enemy. Phull's scheme was based upon the sound belief that the real resistance should be offered inside the Russian frontier, in order to extend the enemy's lines of communications. But Clausewitz had serious doubts about the details. The position at Drissa was, he believed, wrongly sited. The First Army was too weak. Above all, Drissa lay much too near the frontier. He also learned that no firm plans had been made as to what would be done after Drissa, except for a vague idea that the Russians should fall further back. "I asked General Phull which line of retreat he contemplated, that upon Moscow or upon Petersburg? He replied: 'It must depend on circumstances.' It is plain that clarity and determination were absent, for an alternative of such importance could not be left to future chance."[15]

Senior headquarters officers, notably General Barclay de Tolly, and Bennigsen, tried to make the Czar change his mind and plan for a battle near Vilna itself. "A kind of intrigue was started," wrote Clausewitz. At that time, Barclay's forces were spread along a wide line from Samogita to Velhynia; Barclay hoped that the French would cross the frontier on an equally wide front. If they did, the strength of Napoleon's force advancing on Vilna would be diluted, and the Russians would be able to handle it. Clausewitz disagreed with this idea too, calling it an "absurd calculation." But opposition from the senior officers at least had the merit of shaking the Czar's confidence in Phull.

The Russian headquarters continued in confusion, while Napoleon made his final preparations. Two weeks after his arrival, Clausewitz was able to state his own opinions. The Czar ordered him to travel to Drissa to inspect the progress of the fortifications, which the Russian army would rely heavily upon; and he was also told to survey stopping places for the army during its withdrawal to the Drissa positions. Clausewitz left Vilna on 23rd June, escorted by a junior Russian officer. During the night of 24th–25th June, the French Grand Army began to cross the Niemen. For the next three days, the French flowed onto Russian soil, regiment after regiment, troop after troop, in four uninterrupted streams at Yurburg, Kovno, Olit and Merech. Ominously, the weather was already very hot. Inside the Russian territory the French found a deserted, brooding, silent landscape, sullen with dark forests and wide empty fields. Fifty miles away in Vilna a hubbub broke out late in the evening of 24th June, when Czar Alexander learned of the invasion while attending a ball given in his honour.

When he reached Drissa, unaware at first of the French advance, Clausewitz was almost arrested as a spy by the officer in command of the fortifications. "I had nothing more to show than an order written by General Phull, and General Phull was not considered as an authority." Clausewitz's position was greatly embarrassed by his own inability to speak Russian, a constant disadvantage to him, and by the fact that Phull's order was written in French, the most unfortunate language to choose. But eventually he managed to convince the Russian officer of his identity. He inspected the works, and was very disturbed by what he found. He saw a great many entrenchments but the ground was sandy, and the entrenchments weak; Clausewitz ordered the works to be strengthened with palisades and felled trees. He then discovered that the bridges over the River Dvina, needed for the army's withdrawal, were not yet being erected. The Russian officer in charge confessed that he had no idea how to build them. Clausewitz promised to have an engineer sent out. A number of important fortifications were missing, including defensive positions on the right bank of the river. In all, the Russians would be in acute danger of total defeat if they used Phull's encampment.

Meanwhile Napoleon was advancing at speed. Clausewitz, hurriedly finishing his inspection, was told that the Russian Imperial headquarters had moved back to Svanziani, with Barclay's First Army headquarters between the town and Napoleon. Clausewitz arrived at the Czar's position on the same day that French troops entered Vilna. Clausewitz was given an audience with Czar Alexander. He intended to criticize the state of progress at Drissa, and to extend his personal brief by developing his opinions of the whole campaign. He realized that it would be a difficult audience because Phull would be there. "I was his *aide*. I had been received by him at Vilna in the friendliest manner; and I had been recommended by him to the Czar."[16] But Clausewitz could never hide what he believed, especially with regard to something as serious as the whole operational scheme for the Russian army, with the French not many miles away. He tried to be as discreet as possible, both in what he said and in his written memoir. Soon afterwards he was told by the Prince of Oldenburg that the Czar knew that Clausewitz had not fully spoken his mind. According to the Prince, Alexander intended to see Clausewitz on his own so that he could speak more freely. Clausewitz was in a difficult position. Since he was Phull's *aide*, other officers at the Imperial headquarters tended to identify him with his superior, and to someone as sensitive as Clausewitz this was very painful. When Lieutenant-General Count Lieven arrived, the ex-Russian Ambassador in Berlin who had helped Clausewitz find a post in Russia, Clausewitz called on him to talk about his troubles. The Count also brought news of Scharnhorst, who was pressing his view that the Russians should retreat deep inside their frontiers. Lieven, who thoroughly agreed with this idea, told the Emperor what Scharnhorst had said, and Clausewitz did the same with Phull. But both the Czar and his chief adviser needed time to become convinced. The implications of a long withdrawal were immense: it would mean abandoning many miles of Russian soil to the enemy, with a heavy strain upon army and civilian morale.

Clausewitz was given another unpleasant task. Phull felt that General Barclay was falling back too slowly upon Drissa, and feared that the French would reach the Dvina before him. Indeed, the first French had arrived at Vilna only an hour after the last Russians had left. Phull therefore sent his *aide* to Barclay's headquarters with orders for the General to hurry. Clausewitz noted that he was "ill-received." Barclay's rearguard units had achieved one or two successes against the French vanguard troops and were full of confidence. Their commander had no desire to pull them back and continued to delay doing so.

Barclay was experiencing a dilemma which would become more and more acute: told to withdraw on the one hand, he was criticized for not engaging the French on the other. Shishkov, the Czar's secretary, summed up the latter point of view. "How terrible!" he wailed. "To lose Vilna only five days after the opening of hostilities! To run away, to abandon so many towns and so much territory to the enemy, and with all that, to boast of such a beginning! What more could the enemy wish for? Nothing, except perhaps to advance unhindered to the very gates of our two capitals! Oh, merciful Lord, my words are washed in bitter tears."[17] Clausewitz sympathized with Barclay to some extent. Viewing Drissa as he did, he thought it would be a disastrous mistake to go there. But he was disturbed by Barclay's "lack of obedience."

Napoleon had to wait at Vilna to put urgent administrative matters in hand and to allow his supplies to catch up with the advance. Already, serious French logistic deficiencies were being revealed. The Russians gained valuable extra time. Yet, for the moment, confusion and indecision still reigned in the Czar's headquarters. One morning a report came that the Russians were being outflanked during the slow withdrawal to Drissa. The Czar hurriedly summoned Phull and his *aide* to ask what should be done. According to Clausewitz, the senior officers merely argued, while Phull paced up and down the room, and it was left to the junior officers to reach a decision. Clausewitz and two others, including Colonel von Toll who was becoming a close friend of Clausewitz, and was soon to distinguish himself as a staff officer, "put our heads together to investigate the matter on the map, which was spread out on a table between us." Clausewitz doubted the accuracy of the report. "I believed that things should be allowed to carry on unchanged. In a council of war, he who advises inaction usually carries his point, and this was no exception." Next day the news was indeed proved wrong. Russian troops began to file down the roads leading to the entrenchments at Drissa.

It was becoming clear that Phull no longer enjoyed the Czar's confidence, partly as a result of reports such as that delivered by Clausewitz at the end of June. Clausewitz tried to persuade Phull to change his mind. In addition, he believed that the Russian army was suffering from a command divided between Phull and Barclay, and he even frankly told his superior officer that Barclay should be left in sole command. He was confident that Phull would agree because "he had no trace of egotism in his character."[18] On 8th July the Czar inspected the works at Drissa; his doubts over Phull's scheme were quite evident when he saw the layout of the entrenchments.

Then fortunately for Russia, Phull's plan was shattered. According to Clausewitz, the reason was the failure of General Count Bagration, with the Second Army, to advance as intended against the French flank and rear. Clausewitz attributed this failure to a breakdown of Russian courage; he was thankful for this, believing that an offensive by the Second Army would have brought about its destruction. Clausewitz was too harsh on Bagration; in fact, rather than displaying any lack of courage, he and his men had fought bravely and skilfully to manoeuvre their way out of a French trap. In any event, Bagration was now moving on a line which would let him unite with the First Army; General Barclay protested strongly against having to do battle at Drissa and asked that the two Russian armies be joined. Czar Alexander had had enough. He was persuaded to hand over control to Barclay. His part in the direction of the army grew less, and before long he was to leave the forces for the twin capitals of Moscow and Petersburg to organize reserves and reinforcements.

Disaster had been avoided by the narrowest of margins. If Napoleon had been able to advance from Vilna immediately or if the Second Army had taken the offensive as planned, the 1812 campaign would have finished soon after it had begun. Of this, Clausewitz was convinced. He believed that a main reason for Alexander's abandonment of the Drissa plan was the ending of his confidence in Phull. "It was only the excess of his [Phull's] weakness and incapacity which, by causing his extinction before the catastrophe could happen, had saved the Russian army from destruction."[19]

The Russian situation had been recovered a little, but uncertainty as to Phull's personal position increased. Members of the Imperial headquarters even refused to talk to him. Finally, upon Clausewitz's advice, Phull went to the Czar to say that he accepted the need for Barclay to have sole command. Alexander asked him whether he wished to stay with the Imperial staff, or go to Petersburg. Phull chose the former. As it happened, General Barclay objected to the Imperial staff's attachment to his own headquarters, and after the Czar himself had gone, arranged for this Imperial group to be a day's march in advance of the army during the withdrawal. This would push the elderly gentlemen out of harm's way. Clausewitz added that Barclay's method of removing the Czar's staff placed it "under the category of the heavy baggage, which was very galling to the officers."[20] One by one these senior soldiers were called away by the Czar, or found excuses to leave, and General Phull himself eventually left for Petersburg. "My job with General Phull has finished," Clausewitz wrote on 19th July in one of his few letters to Marie during those months. "I do not know what my new position will be, but I am convinced that it will be more acceptable."[21]

Clausewitz asked Count Lieven for help again, and through his intervention was given an appointment on the general staff, attached to General Count Peter Pahlen. General Pahlen was considered to be one of the finest cavalry officers in the Russian army, and was to command the rear guard covering the retreat along the right bank of the Dvina. Not yet forty years old, Pahlen was "simple in his habits, open in his character; not indeed endowed with great intellectual powers or scientific knowledge, but with a lively understanding."[22] He also spoke German fluently.

To his consternation Clausewitz found that he had been promoted too far. Instead of being either the General's second officer or *aide-de-camp*, he was to be first officer of the general's staff and first Quartermaster. In view of his inability to speak Russian, Clausewitz felt unequal to the job and, after Pahlen had received him "with a kind of stately indifference," he told him so. Pahlen refused to change the appointment. "I immediately found myself in a false position, and all I could do was to work hard to earn the respect of the Russians by avoiding neither tiredness nor danger."[23] Under Pahlen he was soon to have abundant experience of both. The exhausting, demoralizing, and finally triumphant, Russian retreat now began. It was to be one of the most terrible military campaigns in history for victor and vanquished alike. In *On War*, Clausewitz was to draw more examples from his 1812 experiences than from any of the other campaigns in the struggle against Napoleon.

General Barclay had begun to break camp at Drissa on 14th July after only six days in the area. He then made a flanking movement to turn down the Moscow road towards Vitebsk. The Russian commander, Clausewitz commented, "found reason to thank God for his extrication from the mouse-trap."[24] Another of Clausewitz's future commanders, the German-born Prince Ludwig Adolf Wittgenstein, was left on the middle Dvina with about 25,000 men to cover the road to Petersburg. Barclay was facing growing opposition from his own senior officers, especially from his rival, General Pyotr Ivanovich Bagration. His chief of staff, Ermolov, was Bagration's friend and secret correspondent.

Barclay had no firm plan of operation. As Liprandi, senior Quarter-master of the Sixth Corps, wrote later: "I venture to conclude that neither before Smolensk nor until Moscow itself did we have any defined plan of action."[25] Count von Toll, Quartermaster-General of the First Army, with whom Clausewitz was in close contact, wrote in his memoirs that no one on the Russian staff at that time had the least idea of the part which the vast geographical expanse of Russia could play. The French still had a chance of catching up before Barclay and Bagration could unite at Vitebsk, where the Russians hoped to take up strong defensive positions. But Napoleon's forces did not begin moving from Vilna until 16th July, forty-eight hours after the start of the Russian withdrawal from Drissa. The French were already suffering from hunger. About 3,000 diseased and wounded soldiers had to be left behind in the town; horses were becoming thin and mangy and many were dying on their feet.

On the Russian side, relations between Barclay and the prickly Bagration, who was worshipped by his troops, were by now deplorable. Bagration, to the south of Barclay, wrote on 8th July: "First they stretched me like a gut, while the enemy broke into our lines without a shot. We began to retire, no one knows why. No one in the army, or in Russia, doubts that we have been betrayed."[26] Threatened by Davout's approach from Minsk, and with his 45,000 Russians spread thinly over the marshes by the Berezina, Bagration had been in a critical position. He had seemed trapped, but had skilfully swerved further south, reaching Bobruisk where he quickly crossed the Berezina. In the fighting retreat he destroyed an entire French light cavalry regiment, and then ordered Rayevsky to hold Davout at Dashkova while he crossed the Dnieper at Novy Bykhav on 25th July. After this brilliant operation, Bagration's temper was understandably worsened when, instead of being commended, he was censured for not going to Minsk. Even Clausewitz failed to appreciate the success of the move. He merely noted that Bagration's force had made "a futile attempt to break through at Mogilev," whereas Bagration had in fact saved his army and fooled Davout. The General felt completedly justified in his outburst on 15th July: "One feels ashamed to wear the uniform. Honest to God, I feel sick."

But Napoleon was also angry. He had found that his two Marshals in the north, Oudinot and Macdonald, would be unable to lend much support for his advances. Napoleon had expected Marshal Oudinot to unite with Marshal Alexandre Macdonald to threaten Petersburg, which was defended by Wittgenstein. But Macdonald had failed to push forward as planned, owing mainly to lack of confidence in his troops. Of the 32,500 men under Macdonald's command, two-thirds were Prussians—among them Clausewitz's brothers—and the rest were nearly all Westphalians, Bavarians, plus a small number of Poles. Only the Prussians showed a real fighting spirit. But full use was not made of them. Macdonald scattered his army by besieging the port of Riga and getting stuck at Dünaburg despite a number of successful engagements, including one at Baaske. In the siege of Riga, Wilhelm von Clausewitz, now a company commander, received the *Pour le mérite* for his conduct, and Major Friedrich von Clausewitz fought bravely in command of an East Prussian *Jäger* battalion.[27] Meanwhile Oudinot, without support, clashed with Wittgenstein on 30th July at Kliastitsi, and moved back to Polotzk, where he remained inactive for some time.

After a ten-day march in stifling heat the main Russian army reached Vitebsk. "I still have not heard a shot," Clausewitz wrote to Marie during the march, "and great events have still to take place. The rear guard actions so far have been on the whole to our advantage." The language problem was becoming acute. "It is true, as I have told myself a thousand times— though others disagree—that without knowing Russian one is quite useless. My whole desire is at least to see the war itself, and to win something for my own country." Clausewitz added: "I must be satisfied with the reception I have had here. The Czar especially is very gracious towards me, and the Grand Duke has treated me with honour and respect beyond what I deserve." On the other hand, he told Marie, "the young dandies in the Emperor's suite have a somewhat repelling coldness."[28]

The march to Vitebsk gave a taste of the hardships to come. "I have not changed my clothes for three weeks," Clausewitz told his wife. His hands were raw from the rubbing reins; the heat was intense. He believed that the withdrawal from Drissa had taken too long, and had expected to see the French, coming down the other road from Beshenkovichi and Vilna, catching them up before they reached Vitebsk. But, Clausewitz added: "General Barclay de Tolly commands the army with greater power than he did before, which was very necessary. I do not think he is a bad general."[29] This view of Barclay differed from that held by most Russian officers.

The commander now moved through Vitebsk and placed his army on the left bank of the Dvina; a stream lay to the front and the town itself lay on the right flank. The French were close behind. In an attempt to delay them, Barclay ordered Count Ostermann-Tolstoy's Fourth Infantry Corps back to block the Beshenkovichi road; and at the small town of Ostrovno, less than ten miles from Vitebsk, his hussars clashed with an advance detachment of French cavalry on 25th July. After putting these troopers to flight, the Count's forward troops rode on, only to run straight into a French cavalry brigade. Most of the Russians were hacked down. Ostermann-Tolstoy's main force came up soon after, and in front of him the Count saw a dense mass of cavalry: it was Murat's division, leading the Grand Army itself.

Fierce fighting continued throughout the day; then the Count made a withdrawal and barely managed to avoid defeat on the 26th before Barclay rushed reinforcements forward under Konovnitsin. From eight in the morning until three in the afternoon Konovnitsin's force was attacked on two flanks by Beauharnaise and Murat, and suffered heavy artillery fire and continuous cavalry charges. Inevitably, he was pushed back. Joachim Murat, the King of Naples and Eugéne de Beauharnais ordered a rest for their exhausted men, but at that moment Napoleon rode up in person and demanded an immediate pursuit. The remains of the decimated Russian force continued to fight, and reached the village of Komarovo by nightfall.

About the same time, Pahlen's rearguard force, containing Clausewitz, arrived at Vitebsk along the Drissa road. Despite its weariness the unit was immediately hurried forward to help the battered Russians hold up the Grand Army massed along the Beshenkovichi road. When Clausewitz and the rest arrived the track was strewn with Russian corpses, bloated and stinking in the terrible heat. But the French had been delayed. Two miles behind the advance position, where Clausewitz awaited the next French attack, Barclay was gaining valuable time. It was generally believed that Barclay would accept battle at Vitebsk. Clausewitz was convinced that this would be a fatal error. He considered that the Russian positions were unsuitable, and knew that Barclay would be outnumbered; he only had about 75,000 men to Napoleon's 150,000. "I was in despair at the idea," he wrote. Barclay was also beginning to have serious doubts. Meanwhile he relied upon his small force on the outskirts of the town to hold the French at bay while the rest of his troops were organized.

At first light on 27th July, the expected French assault was launched against Pahlen's defensive lines. The ground was wooded and hilly, unsuited to cavalry operations. Not realizing this, Pahlen grouped his cavalry in the small open space available, as if he were operating on a wide plain with plenty of room for manoeuvre. As a result, the Russian cavalry-men, Clausewitz among them, were cooped into a restricted area on the right wing between a river and a wood, and suffered badly from French artillery fire. With each salvo horses and men were thrown into bleeding heaps. They waited for the order to move; none came. The troopers had to wait for the next salvo, and the next. Burned by the sun, covered in dust, the men stared ahead into the shimmering haze, watching for a French advance.

But unfortunately, the enemy infantry and cavalry assaults were, as Clausewitz put it, "languid" compared with the previous actions and artillery fire. The Russian infantrymen were spread thinly about on high ground; with good cover but with the view in front obstructed by trees and brushwood, they repulsed sporadic charges from five o'clock in the morning until mid-afternoon. Casualties remained moderate. Then, as the sun slowly fell, Clausewitz heard that Barclay had finally decided not to risk a major battle at Vitebsk. The withdrawal would be continued. "It can be said the Russian army was saved from destruction for the second time," wrote Clausewitz. "I felt so delighted and relieved that I was ready to thank God on my knees for thus diverting our steps from the mouth of an abyss."[30]

At last Pahlen's cavalry moved behind cover; then they were ordered back behind the Lutchesa river to take up positions just evacuated by Barclay's main army. Clausewitz thought that Pahlen had been extremely lucky. The French attacking his positions had been the advance guard, directed by Napoleon in person; but believing the Russian army still to be in its Vitebsk positions, Napoleon had been conserving his main effort. Moreover, the French infantrymen had been demoralized by the stubborn resistance of the Russians during the previous few days. Clausewitz was unimpressed by his commanding officer's handling of the engagement. "The action fought by General Pahlen left a very unsatisfactory impression on my mind," he wrote. "The deployment of his force was not in accordance with the principles and views which I had formed for myself about the handling of troops in action." The cavalry should have been split into smaller groups and placed behind the infantry, to give greater depth and better protection, and the various units should have been arranged to give increased mutual support. But "as I had not been attached to Count Pahlen for more than a week, I had naturally only acquired a small influence with him."[31]

Moreover, there was the language barrier. "Reports come in, discussions take place, orders are given, all in Russian . . . How can I, in such a moment, ask for a translation either from the commanding officer or from someone else who can speak the language? Before I can grasp anything, they have moved on to something else . . . This was the first battle in which, by my position, I might have influenced the deployment of the force. Yet it was fought in a manner directly opposed to what I thought. And I felt so completely useless that I would have preferred to fight as a subaltern in the line."[32]

Clausewitz's troubles soon ended, in part at least. Among the reinforcements sent to Pahlen's force to restore his losses came a higher ranking staff officer, to whom Clausewitz became subordinate. Clausewitz ceased to be responsible for troop dispositioning. Despite his self-disparagement about his conduct in the fighting near Vitebsk, Clausewitz, now a Captain in the Russian army, later received the decoration of Knight of the Order of the Holy Vladimir from the Czar, for the manner in which he had "stood under fire and fulfilled his duties with success."[33]

Pahlen's force was still to form the rearguard, positioned on the far side of Vitebsk to delay the French while the main army continued to withdraw. The 3,000 infantry, 4,000 cavalry and forty guns were expected to block the road for as long as possible. As they waited, Napoleon realized that his enemy had once again escaped; the Grand Army rode into the deserted and silent city of Vitebsk. If Napoleon had ordered an immediate advance, Pahlen and his men would have been in a desperate position; the whole weight of the Grand Army would have leaned against them. But once again Bonaparte delayed. He had urgent diplomatic business to attend to, especially in connection with the war in Spain; his supply system was still grossly deficient; his army was showing increasing lack of cohesion. The Grand Army, a massive international force whose regiments had greatly varying standards of discipline, efficiency and morale, was almost unmanageable, even for Bonaparte.

Napoleon delayed, trying to solve pressing administrative problems, and merely sent out light reconnaissance units into the scorching countryside around the town. Not until 10th August did the French Army begin to move. Barclay had again avoided battle. But criticism of him mounted. The nobility in Moscow and Petersburg, and the great majority of middle-class citizens and landowners, were growing panicky at the news of the advancing French. Why was Napoleon not being stopped? In the army itself, Barclay de Tolly was known as *Boltai da i tolko*—"all bark and no bite," or literally, "nothing more than talk."

The Russian line of withdrawal was towards Smolensk, the nearest point at which Barclay and Bagration could meet. Barclay, marching his men in three columns, was given fourteen days' start by Napoleon, who, even after his eventual order to move, failed to throw out his right wing to cut the road—an "inconceivable" mistake, in Clausewitz's view. Each day as the withdrawal on Smolensk continued, Clausewitz could make out the moving black figures of the French advance units not far behind. Pahlen's rearguard kept a short way in front of them. Dust hung in the air, showing the Russians how near their pursuers were. There was occasional skirmishing, but no significant action. The Russians suffered, nevertheless. Corruption was ruining the Czar's Commissary Department. Essential stores which were to have been stockpiled at points along the route were found insufficient, or in some cases missing completely. In their effort to leave nothing for the French, the forward Russian regiments left nothing for the centre and rearguard of their own army. Villages were plundered and the terrified

Facing page Gneisenau, from a portrait in Apsley House

peasants fled. Soldiers and horses began to starve. Medical services for the wounded, after actions such as that outside Vitebsk, were crude. Some of the most serious Vitebsk casualties received no treatment at all; Kozodavlev, Minister of the Interior, reported to the Czar on 6th August: "Many of them arrived from Vitebsk unbandaged, because there were only two doctors. There is a complete shortage of medicines and bandages, and worms are eating many of the wounded alive."[34] The Russians were encouraged by one thought: if they were suffering, then the French were, too.

Clausewitz heard the intelligence reports which had reached the Russians, describing the state of Napoleon's army. "In the first weeks of their advance, the French had undergone an enormous loss in sick and stragglers, and were in a state of privation which gave early warning of their rapid consumption."[35] News came to the Russian camp of roads littered with the stiff and swollen carcasses of French horses and with the disabled sick and stragglers. Because of the shortage of fodder horses were already having to be fed on green forage.

On 1st August the two Russian armies under Barclay and Bagration were united near Smolensk, having evacuated a territory sixty miles deep and losing, Clausewitz estimated, about 10,000 men and twenty guns, a loss he described as "trifling." The union of the two armies was a severe setback for Napoleon. But Barclay, nominally the overall Russian commander, was again undecided as to whether to withdraw further, or accept battle. Many more officers opposed the retreat, and wanted to turn and fight; a view supported by the success of the flank forces. Colonel Toll was one of those who insisted the retreat had gone far enough and that there should be a sudden switch to the offensive. Clausewitz still disagreed.

But on 8th August, General Barclay reluctantly decided to fight. First, however, he had to find the main French force. He set off towards Rudinia, only to receive reports during the first day's march that the French were on the road to Poretsch. He halted the advance; General Platoff attacked Murat's forward units at Inkovo before receiving the order to stop, and took 500 prisoners. To Clausewitz, it was a mistake to develop the Russian advance against the enemy. The French were too scattered and could not have been brought to a decisive engagement. The Russians might have been able to drive some French units before them, but little would have been gained. It was a point of view he was to outline again in *On War*: an offensive is only worthwhile if likely to achieve notable results. Clausewitz disagreed with Colonel Toll's belief that much could be obtained through a quick surprise action. "Such surprises in strategy seldom produce a positive victory, but merely an acquisition of ground, and a favourable introduction to a battle. To obtain a decisive victory it is essential that a respectable portion of the enemy's force should be reached, brought to blows, and hemmed in."[36] But once more Barclay was persuaded to take the offensive. After staying four days on the Poretsch road he set off again for Rudinia. By then it was too

Facing page "*The father of my soul,*" *Gerhard von Scharnhorst*
(1755-1813)

late. The French, forewarned, had already begun to advance on Smolensk. Barclay and then Bagration hurried back to the town. As the Russian ammunition base, Smolensk had to be retained, or at least the French must be stopped from seizing the Russian supplies.

"Barclay was unsure at this moment whether his own head stood on his shoulders," commented Clausewitz. "Owing to the continued plan to move on to the offensive, preparatory steps to find a good defensive position had been delayed." He continued: "The Russians were now thrown back upon the defensive. They had no clear idea where, or how, they should place themselves. They would probably have resumed their retreat at once, if Barclay had not turned pale at the thought of what the Russians would say."

Meanwhile the French advance on Smolensk was being hindered by a Russian detachment under Neverovsky on the road from Lad. After giving desperate resistance, his men were slowly pushed back by forces flung forward by Ney and Murat, but the Russians retained order and were not routed. According to Louis Philippe Ségur, Napoleon's principal secretary: "The Russian cavalrymen seemed rooted to the ground. A number of our first attacks ended in failure about twenty paces from the Russian front. The retreating Russians would again and again suddenly turn to face us and throw us back with musket fire." Messengers flogged their horses to warn Barclay of the growing threat to Smolensk: the main Russian army was rushed to the city to face the French onslaught. But Barclay decided to keep only 15,000 men in Smolensk itself; this force would hold the French at bay while the magazines were cleared; after this Barclay, having partly satisfied those who wanted action, would continue the retreat covered by Bagration. The remnants of Neverovsky's division, at only a sixth of its strength after the struggle on the Lad road, were merged with Rayevsky's men in the suburbs of Smolensk.

At six o'clock in the morning, 16th August, the French bombardment began. Soon after came the first infantry assaults. The battle raged throughout the day. Casualties were massive, especially among the French; the Russians had the benefit of protection from the houses and high walls. That night Barclay fed in Dokhturov's corps, and battle was resumed next day. For almost thirteen hours there was a continuous artillery bombardment. Gradually the Russians were pounded from the outskirts, where almost all the houses were ablaze, back into Smolensk itself. Bloody street fighting continued into the night, illuminated by the glow of burning houses.

From outside the city, where Clausewitz stood, the whole city of Smolensk seemed to be on fire. Then, in the middle of the night, the Russian guns suddenly fell deathly silent. Soon after came a massive reverberating explosion. The last of the ammunition in the stores had been deliberately blown up. Barclay issued the order to withdraw. The weary, filthy defenders retreated to join the main army, and the Russians moved on, with a brave rearguard made up of men under Konovnitsin and Colonel Toll. At daybreak on 18th August the French took possession of Smolensk. They found many acres of black smoking ruins, and piles of charred and broken bodies. An eye-witness, Ivan Maslov, wrote: "The burning suburbs, the dense multi-coloured smoke, the red glow, the crash of exploding shells, the thunder of cannon, the rattling rifle fire, the beating of drums, the moans and groans of old men, women and children, the whole people falling on their knees with arms outstretched to the skies—such was the picture that greeted our eyes and tore at our hearts." The scene in the Old City was especially horrible. Here, the Russians had been unable to evacuate the wounded before the fire spread. One French officer wrote: "These unfortunates, abandoned to a cruel death, lay here in piles, charred, almost without human form, among the smoking ruins and flaming beams. The positions of many corpses showed the ghastly torments that must have preceded death."[37] Once again the Russians had fought with outstanding courage. In some cases, the troops had been so eager to open fire upon the advancing French that they had stood out in the open, and would not take cover until driven by their officers' swords. Some historians have laid great stress on Russian drunkenness in the battles of the 1812 campaign but this has been exaggerated. In his memoirs, Clausewitz made no mention of Dutch courage.

Clausewitz estimated the Russian losses at Smolensk at about 20,000. Now both armies, already tired before battle began, were approaching complete exhaustion. Some French commanders were urging Napoleon to call a halt. Berthier told Bonaparte: "It would be better to make two campaigns of it." Narbonne, Madame de Staël's lover and *protégé*, had already pleaded with the Emperor: "I take leave to beg of you, Sire, not to take this wonderful flower of France into the depths of Russia."[38] But the retreat and pursuit would continue, with Moscow the ultimate objective. As Napoleon warned: "A capital which is occupied by an enemy is like a girl who loses her virginity."

For the moment there was a diversion. After retiring a short distance, Barclay delayed moving further until the night of 18th August. Then, after dark, the Russians marched in two columns by a roundabout route along the Poretsch road, towards Petersburg, before turning back across to the Moscow road. Clausewitz could not understand why the main Moscow route could not have been used at once. The maneouvre was too complicated, he said, and gave Napoleon a better chance of cutting the Russian line of retreat. Once again Clausewitz found that Bonaparte's failure to do this was "incomprehensible." Clausewitz had a theory as to the origin of the complex operation: "I believe that Colonel Toll involved himself here a little in the subtleties of staff-officer science. At least, I afterwards heard much praise for the scientific detour of the army."[39]

Soon after came a sharp and sudden engagement at Vaultinagora between Ney and the Russian rearguard. The French lost 7,000, the

Russians 6,000. Clausewitz said Barclay distinguished himself "by his best quality, and the only one which justified his selection for high command: a perfect composure, firmness and personal bravery." An attempt by Junot to outflank the Russians was delayed for too long, and his force was further hindered by an engagement with Bagration's outlying troops. By the time Junot at last came to the Moscow road, seeking to trap Barclay between himself and Napoleon, it was too late. The Russians were further on, withdrawing towards Dorogobuzh. This spelled the end of Junot's career; disgraced, he lost his sanity a few months later.

Russian conduct so far had been generally in line with the best strategy for the campaign: a long retreat, with the Russians turning at intervals to strike back at the advancing French. In terms of either side's strength, the strategy was working well. Clausewitz estimated that "the Russians lost in these actions some 30,000 men. But we can reckon that, between this point and Borodino, they were reinforced by 20,000. The diminution was therefore only about 10,000. The French were 182,000 strong at Smolensk, and 130,000 at Borodino. Their diminution, therefore, reached 52,000, of which 16,000 were detached. The loss of the French then, in these actions and in sick and stragglers, was 36,000. So the two armies were approaching equal numbers."[40] Clausewitz emphasized that although Russian operations were conforming to the best strategy, this was largely a matter of luck, with no conscious decisions on the part of the commanders. Barclay was "ill at ease, and felt conscience-stricken to be nearing Moscow without having had a general and arranged battle to try to convert the French advance either into a halt or a retreat. His staff felt the urgency of such a battle still more strongly."[41] At the time, Clausewitz was far from optimistic about the outcome of the campaign. Nor did he think that the new British Continental expedition would help. He wrote to Marie while *en route* from Smolensk between 12th and 24th August: "The war situation is still rather bad. But if we were to lose the great battle that lies before us, it would be far worse, because the landing in Zeeland will not hurt Napoleon's little finger." He added: "I doubt if we will win, but all would not be lost if we could only carry on for two campaigns." If this were to happen, he said, "I hope to be more useful in the next, because I will learn Russian during the winter."[42] On the night of 24th August, Napoleon set out from Smolensk with his main force. On either side of the road the fields and crops were devastated. Ruined houses were still smoking.

Barclay and his staff, meantime, continued to survey the ground as they withdrew, seeking a position from which they could give battle. Colonel Toll, who usually went in front of the army to reconnoitre the countryside for the next day's march, was accompanied for a time by Clausewitz. As they rode along together, Colonel Toll decided that he had located a good defensive position at Usviate, behind the Uja river just west of Dorogho- buzh. After looking at the site with Toll, Clausewitz disagreed. "The position was indeed very advantageous, but I could hardly say very strong." Eventually, said Clausewitz, "I thought that if we are to fight today or tomorrow, then better here than elsewhere."

But opposition came from Bagration, who preferred a site further on. "Colonel Toll, who was very obstinate and not very courteous," said Clausewitz, "was unwilling to give up his idea and started to argue, which threw Bagration into a violent temper. 'Colonel,' he said, 'your conduct will earn you a musket across your shoulders.' This phrase in Russia is not merely a mode of speech, for such a degradation could happen even to the most distinguished under the rules of service, and the threat was not to be despised." Unwilling to aggravate Bagration any further, Barclay agreed to scrap Toll's idea. Instead, the army would occupy an area near Doroghobuzh chosen by Bagration. To Clausewitz, this was even worse. "The position seemed detestable to me. In front there was no difficulty of access and no clear view. I was in despair at this change. Colonel Toll was in a sullen fury."[43] Once more, in Clausewitz's view, the Russian army narrowly escaped disaster. Barclay decided to move back further still. On 24th August the army renewed the retreat.

On the 27th, positions were again about to be taken up, this time at Vyasma; but they were abandoned when reserves which arrived under General Miloradovitsch were fewer than expected. Instead, Vyasma was set ablaze to stop the French using it as shelter. Two days later, Barclay called a general halt a mile from Giatsk to fight his battle; he had some fortifications made. But once again, the engagement did not materialize. This time the reason was the arrival of Kutuzov, appointed Commander-in-Chief of the whole Russian army. In future, Barclay was merely to command the first Army.

A change of leadership had been forecast for some time. Many in the army believed, said Clausewitz, that Barclay was dismissed for his indecision, which had stopped him fighting a battle, and for his "foreign behaviour." Barclay was the son of a Livonian clergyman, and had served in the Russian army since his youth; he was Russian in all but name. But he spoke the language badly, and this, in Clausewitz's view, was enough to set him apart. Barclay was probably right when he addressed himself to the Czar on 29th August: "Had I been guided by blind, senseless ambition, Your Imperial Majesty would have received reports of battles, and, even so, the enemy would be at the gates of Moscow, because we did not have sufficient forces to resist him."[44] Barclay was opposed by powerful men, including Constantine, the Imperial heir-apparent, and above all, the embittered Bagration. Bagration would no longer speak to his commander and resorted to written notes, some of which were extremely spiteful. Moreover, Barclay's chief adviser, Lieutenant-Colonel Vollzogen, was hated by many Russian officers, including Colonel Toll. Clausewitz reported: "I heard an officer who

returned from the headquarters pour out his bitterness, saying that Vollzogen sat there in a corner like a fat and poisonous spider."[45] Vollzogen was
rumoured to be one of Napoleon's spies. According to Bagration: "The
entire army is suspicious of *aide-de-camp* Vollzogen. He is Napoleon's man
more than ours."[46]

Mikhail Illariorovich Golerischev Kutuzov, sixty-seven years old, was a
veteran soldier. A Turkish bullet had put out one of his eyes at Alushta
when he was only twenty-nine. He was a disciple of the Russian hero, Count
Alexander Suvaroff, conqueror of the Turks, Tartars and Poles, who had
fought Napoleon in Italy and who had died in 1800 leaving glowing
reports of Kutuzov's ability. Suvaroff said of him: "He's crafty, crafty! And
shrewd, shrewd! No one will fool him!" Kutuzov was lazy, and cunning. He
disliked the Czar, and the feeling was mutual, but Alexander knew of no
better choice.

The new commander was determined to outwit Napoleon. He wanted a
serious battle even less than Barclay. Although he knew he would have to
engage Napoleon before Moscow, he intended this to happen only once.
With cunning, he hoped to avoid Barclay's fate. Kutuzov was given a
tumultuous welcome. The army thought there would now be great and
glorious battle. But as Clausewitz commented: "Barclay had been trundled
back from Vitebsk to Vyasma, like someone staggering along trying to regain
his balance, and to start with Kutusov couldn't recover a firm footing for
the army."[47] This was the General's excuse for avoiding an engagement. So,
much to the dismay of everyone who wished to fight the French, Kutuzov
ordered the continuation of the retreat two days after his arrival.

Thick smoke rising from burning wooden houses hung in the air behind
them as the troops moved wearily on. The condition of both armies was now
deteriorating rapidly. At the end of August the heat was still overpowering,
and French soldiers came to blows among one another for a taste of brackish
swamp water. The Russians took steps to prevent the enemy obtaining
provisions from the land; Cossacks circled vulture-like around the French to
pick off the stragglers. More and more soldiers died on the dusty road. Nor
were the Russians much better off. Hunger and thirst caused more casualties than French grapeshot or musket fire. Clausewitz wrote: "Lack of water
was the worst aspect. I remember vividly the suffering from thirst. I drank
greedily from the filthiest of pools. How this must have affected the cavalry
may easily be imagined."[48] Writing to Marie from near Doroghobuzh, he
said: "The difficulties of this campaign are extraordinary. For nine weeks
now we have been on the march. For five weeks we have had no change of
clothes. Heat, dust, filthy water and often near-starvation. Until now I have
spent each night in the open, with few exceptions, because few people live in
this locality and their pitiful huts have been destroyed. Despite these
hardships I feel better than I did in Berlin. Gout tortures me now and then.
I have toothache practically all the time, because since Vilna I have had

three hollow teeth. I am also losing my hair; and my hands, which have not seen gloves for a fortnight, look like yellow leather."[49]

There was no hope of rest. Napoleon's main force was always in sight o the Russian rearguard, now commanded by Konovnitsin. Konovnitsin's men were forced to fight at frequent intervals. The days were filled with the sound of musket fire crackling in the background, and occasionally cannon, and always the pall of black smoke behind. Clausewitz had now been transferred to the main body of troops, and attached to Count Uvarov's First Cavalry Corps as Quartermaster-General. Then the Russians turned once more on the scrub slopes to face their pursuers. The position was again chosen by Colonel Toll, now Kutuzov's Quartermaster-General. Clausewitz viewed it critically: "It was certainly not the best among the many which Toll had thought fit for battle."[50] Nearby lay a small village, so far untouched by war.

Its name was Borodino.

NINE

From Borodino to Moscow

"There rises the sun of Austerlitz."
(Napoleon before the battle of
Borodino.)

I

ALMOST DESPITE THE Russians, events still worked to their advantage. As Clausewitz realized: "Bonaparte had involved himself in such a difficult operation that things naturally began to work for the Russians, and a good outcome was assured without much effort on their part. Kutuzov would certainly not have agreed to the battle of Borodino, from which he probably expected nothing, if he had not been pressured by the court, the army, and the nation as a whole. He probably looked upon it as a necessary evil. He knew the Russians, and understood how to deal with them."[1]

Russia's defensive position at Borodino looked better at first sight than it really was, according to Clausewitz. The right wing was protected by the river Moskva, which did not seem to be fordable, while the front was covered by the River Kolotscha, which flowed through a reasonably deep valley. These points had attracted Colonel Toll. The main defect was the angle to the proposed battlefield of the Smolensk-Moscow road; the road ran parallel to the River Kolotscha for some way, then crossed the river and cut away at Gorki hamlet. If the Russian army stood parallel to the stream in front, to use its cover, it would also stand obliquely to the line of retreat on the road: its left flank would be exposed. Moreover, half a mile from the main road was a second track to Moscow from the village of Jelnia; the track led straight behind the rear of the Russian position parallel to the stream. The enemy could then make a simple advance to threaten any Russian withdrawal. To avoid this risk, the left flank would have to be set further back. As a result the line would bend: the right wing in a strong position, the centre lying further back from the stream, and the left further still. As this Russian arc was concentrated into a rather small area, it made a better target for the French artillery. The left flank was to some extent wasted; having to be placed where it could protect the line of retreat, it occupied an inferior area; to support it more men had to be moved back on to the old Moscow road.

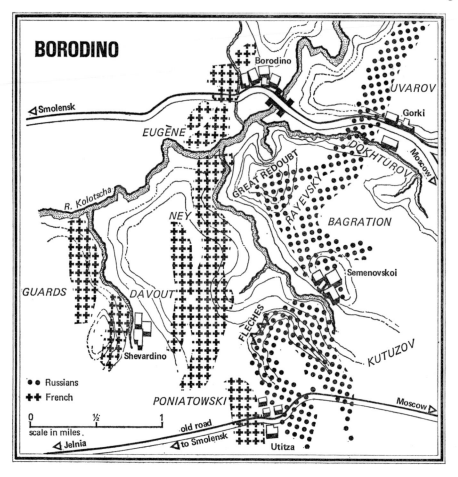

Late in the afternoon of 5th September, French forward troops appeared before the advance Russian redoubt near the village of Shevardino; the redoubt was held by some of Bagration's men. Clausewitz, with the main army, made light of this preliminary to the Battle of Borodino in his memoirs, the *hors d'oeuvre* as he called it. But the struggle at the redoubt was marked by extreme bravery and stubborn resistance on the part of the Russian detachment. Several French cavalry attacks were beaten off. Then, two French infantry divisions and three regiments of another division were thrown against the small position. French eye-witnesses described how the Russians, cheering, met the enemy and counter-attacked with bayonets; but all the defenders were slain, including artillerymen who had preferred to stay by their guns rather than retreat as they could have done.

The noise of guns, muskets, screams and shouts eventually faded by the evening, to be replaced by the ominous sound of murmuring men, and the creaking of French gun-carriages as the main infantry columns arrived to face the Russians. Napoleon deployed them as soon as they came up: Eugène's men on the right; Poniatovski's corps on the left; Murat, Ney, Junot in the centre; and the Imperial Guard at the head. Both sides slept little that night. Napoleon felt that the Russian camp fires were going out one by one as the small hours went by; his constant fear was that Kutuzov would try to slip away. But at dawn the Russian bugles sounded, drums began to beat, the men came to arms, and the two massed armies awaited battle.

But no battle came that day. Napoleon continued his preparations, spending hour after hour inspecting the positions, talking to the men, issuing orders. He had already decided to fight with massive artillery bombardments, and he placed his guns accordingly. Riding through the Russian lines, Clausewitz could see the French hard at work. Towards lunchtime a brief commotion broke out among the men around him. Kutuzov was inspecting his troops and the holy ikon of the Smolensk Mother of God was being carried round the positions. That evening Napoleon issued a stirring proclamation to his regiments: "Let them say of you: he was in the great battle under the walls of Moscow."

On 7th September, dawn began to streak the sky at five o'clock. Thirty minutes later the sun crept up behind the Russian lines. Its light filtered across the scrub and slopes in front and reached the French positions, glinting on the bayonets, breast-plates and gun-carriages. Clausewitz watched the mounting enemy activity. He knew that the fight was about to begin. At six o'clock, according to his memoirs, the French guns opened their bombardment and began one of the bloodiest battles recorded in history. Clausewitz was positioned with Uvarov's cavalry, on the right wing of the Russian line. The right and the centre were both led by Barclay. Dokhturov commanded the centre, and Kutuzov, a relation of the commanding general, led the reserves. The left wing was under Bagration. The Russian left consisted of about 25,000 men with 8,300 reserves; and the rest totalled about 75,700, plus 7,000 Cossacks and 10,000 militiamen, which gave the Russian force an overall strength of nearly 128,000, with 640 guns. Clausewitz estimated the French total at 130,000, with 587 guns.

As the earth-shaking French artillery opened up its bombardment at the Russian right and centre, French troops under Delzen advanced upon the village of Borodino itself; the village, which lay on the French side of the River Kolotscha, was defended by a *Jäger* detachment. But soon after, as Clausewitz had rightly guessed, the main French offensive was directed at the more vulnerable Russian left. Troops led by Davout, Murat and Ney attacked Bagration's positions, as Napoleon hoped to turn the Russian flank.

Russian artillery and musket fire tore holes in the advancing enemy lines and the first French assaults were repulsed; Davout's horse was shot under him and he was carried away, badly concussed. Several other senior French officers were also either killed or wounded. The struggle in this left sector raged around Russia's fortifications near the small Semenovskoi brook, where the positions had been hurriedly built and were technically unsound. Clausewitz wrote: "They stood in sandy soil, open at the rear, destitute of all external devices ... none of them could hold out against a serious assault, and in fact most of them were lost and regained two or three times."[2] These *flèches*, soon littered with dead men and horses, were repeatedly attacked. Vorontsov's division was slaughtered almost to a man. Neverovsky took over, his men running forward in their frenzy to bayonet the onrushing masses of French, lunging to tear open the bellies of the horses, dragging men down from their saddles, screaming as they stabbed at the enemy.

But Davout's men managed to secure a foothold in the *flèches*. The struggle swirled around the nearby Great Redoubt. More and more French guns were trained on the Russian positions in an effort to batter them down: first 150, then 300, and then 400, over two-thirds of Napoleon's artillery. Clausewitz, over on the Russian right, watched the terrible effects of this massive bombardment. The front line was shifting so wildly that the French gunners often had no time to alter their range, and blasted at their own men. Under a storm of grapeshot French troops from the 7th Light, the 17th and 30th of the line, and the second Badenese Regiment crossed the Kolotscha and scrambled up the slopes and on to the plateau near the Great Redoubt. Despite the terrible artillery fire, they continued to advance. The Russian positions were seized, the front broken.

Bagration ordered a counter-attack. The Russians advanced with fixed bayonets, only to be thrown back again and Bagration was wounded with grapeshot which smashed one of his legs. He struggled for a moment to stay astride his horse, knowing that if he left the field the effect on his men might be disastrous. But his knees could no longer grip, and painfully he slipped from his saddle. He lay propped against the side of an earthwork, his clothes blood-soaked, uniform unbuttoned, a gaping wound above one knee, his pale bloodied face covered with black powder. Soon after, he died.

The Russian positions on the left flank remained in French hands; and Napoleon turned his guns and cavalry on to the Russian centre. Again and again the French cavalry thundered forward, the charges so close to one another and so powerful that there seemed to be just one solid mass of surging horses. Horses whose riders had been shot down ran wildly about, adding to the confusion. The roar of the artillery drowned the screams and shouts, even the noise of the rifle fire. General Miloradovich's *aide* tried to attract Eugène of Würtemberg's attention, and unable to make himself heard in the din he raised his arm, only to have it torn off by a cannonball. Thrown down from his horse, he raised his other arm, still trying to gain Eugène's attention. Disgraced, Barclay wanted nothing but to die. He rode forward to where the artillery fire was at its most intense: and survived.

Miloradovich, not to be outdone, rode even further on, dismounted, sat down, and announced that he intended to have his breakfast. The battle raged all around him. Still the Russian centre refused to budge, while on the left the Russian lines managed to re-form.

Enduring the artillery fire on the right flank, deafened by the noise, seeing the chaos and hell to his left through the drifting black smoke and the vivid flashes of the guns, Clausewitz was about to move into action with Uvarov's cavalry. For a while he had been sitting astride his horse, near Kutuzov. According to Clausewitz, Kutuzov "had been listening to all the reports and discussions like one who had no idea whether he stood on his head or his heels, but from time to time said, '*C'est bon, faites le!*' "[3] Then Colonel Toll rode up with a new plan to end the stalemate which had developed. Not long before, General Platoff had been ordered to take 2,000 Cossacks to find a ford on the Kolotscha on the Russian right. This he had done; then, having crossed the river, he had found that the area was undefended by the French. Seeing that the enemy left flank near Borodino was unprotected, General Platoff believed that here was a perfect opportunity for a Russian cavalry attack. Toll informed Kutuzov of the idea. Clausewitz had doubts about it; the cavalry assault would be too small to cause more than a slight diversion. But "enthusiasm blazed up like lighted straw; several voices proposed to make this known to all the troops" to give them encouragement.[4] And Kutuzov replied: "*C'est bon, prenez le!*"

Clausewitz's version of this event differs from many accounts of Borodino. According to other historians, this idea was part of Kutuzov's plan for the day's battle; according to Clausewitz the scheme was proposed on the spur of the moment by someone else. Uvarov was ordered to make the attack with 2,500 cavalry. As his Quartermaster-General, Clausewitz helped organize the men. But as he worked, he still had serious qualms. If the French only threw cavalry against them, Uvarov might succeed. But Uvarov might also be opposed by infantry, and "we know well what happens when a single arm is opposed by two others." With this gloomy thought, Clausewitz rode off with his commanding officer. Guided by the Prince of Hesse, who had been sent back by General Platoff, they trotted across the river above Stararoie into French held territory. The din of battle continued, as both sides were locked together in a death struggle around the Russian positions.

Uvarov's force turned towards Borodino itself, but owing to the swampy ground the cavalrymen had to incline to the right. Sure enough, as General Platoff had reported, the French had failed to defend this flank adequately. Moving as fast as possible, the Russian detachment confronted a surprised French cavalry brigade, and a group of enemy infantry amounting to "a regiment, or a strong battalion." The French cavalry immediately drew back. "The infantry, however, was bold enough to remain, and formed a square," wrote Clausewitz. With their backs to the brook running to

Borodino, this infantry unit from the Italian Division—which had previously taken Borodino village—was in a strong position. "General Uvarov
wanted to attack at once. I urged that the artillery should first be opened up
on them. But the Russian officers were worried in case the enemy should pull
back and escape." Clausewitz remembered his own experiences in the
retreat after Auerstädt; but now the role was reversed, and he was convinced that the Russian cavalry would suffer the worst against an infantry
square.

The troopers were advanced and formed into line. The order to charge
was called out. Clausewitz watched the cavalrymen move off at a fast trot,
then a canter. As he had warned, they were repulsed by the Italian volley.
The horsemen straggled wearily back to the Russian position, were
re-formed and the order to charge was repeated. Again, horses and riders
were brought to the ground by the steady Italian musket fire. Still Uvarov
insisted upon the attack. A third charge was made and repulsed. Then
Uvarov took Clausewitz's advice. Small mobile guns were dragged into
position and fired almost point blank at the brave but vulnerable Italian
square. The infantrymen suffered one devastating salvo, then hastily withdrew into hilly ground, leaving their dead and wounded behind. The
Russians trotted past the dead and dying who had fallen in the churned
mud of the small valley.

But the French had been alerted, and the Russian attack had been
delayed by the Italian resistance. As many as 5,000 enemy infantrymen
ran out from Borodino and scattered themselves in the thick brushwood on
the slopes by the village, firing down upon the approaching Russians as they
deployed. Behind the infantry the French cavalry was drawn up. In front of
the enemy position flowed a stream which horses could only cross at a small
dam. The French were therefore in a position which was almost impossible
for cavalry alone to assault. Some of Uvarov's men near Clausewitz
advanced too close and were immediately cut down by musket fire. Clausewitz and the rest hurriedly reined back just out of range, and waited. A
quarter of a mile to the right, General Platoff with his 2,000 Cossacks tried
to find a way across the marshy brook.

At any moment the French might bring up their artillery on to the slopes,
and batter the Russian cavalry back over the marsh. And yet, according to
Clausewitz, the Russian command was placing more and more hope in the
small force led by General Uvarov and General Platoff. The main battle
was still gripped in a bloody deadlock. Casualties were rising; the smoke lay
thicker on the ground, and neither army was gaining the upper hand. But
the French had one advantage. The Russians had used up most of their
reserves in propping up the damaged left flank and centre; they had even
moved troops from the right wing to the most critical areas. On the other
hand Napoleon still had reserves in hand: Clausewitz could see "the French
Guards, some 20,000 strong, standing motionless in heavy columns like a

thunder cloud.''[5] He continued: "The Russians could not carry out any offensive movement other than that led by General Uvarov. All eyes were now turned upon him."

But Uvarov could not move. Frustrated, the General and his staff officers tried desperately to find a way of attacking the French in front without being badly mauled. An *aide-de-camp* rode up, then a general staff officer, then an Imperial *aide-de-camp*; all of them demanded to know whether a charge could be made. But Uvarov only had 2,500 cavalrymen to attack 5,000 infantrymen, who were well protected and supported by cavalry; and to get to them the Russians would first have to cross the stream. To attack would have been suicidal, said Clausewitz, and should only have been attempted by "some young fire-eater who had a reputation to make." Firing to the left increased, and through the brushwood came yelling and charging Cossacks. Some of General Platoff's force had managed to ford the stream further up. A group from Uvarov's squadrons galloped away to join them, dashing off "like a burning rocket," managing to splash across the stream and enter the brush during the confusion. But it was a hopeless gesture. Uvarov ordered the rest of his men not to follow. Moments later, Clausewitz watched the Cossack survivors return, horses and riders covered with blood. With French cavalrymen now threatening to trap them, the Russians had to draw back to the main positions.

This, to Clausewitz, was the lowest point of the battle of Borodino. "I can still see the weariness and exhaustion which the struggle assumed. The infantry masses were so reduced that perhaps no more than a third of the original strength remained. The rest were either killed, wounded, engaged in removing the wounded, or rallying in the rear. Large gaps were everywhere apparent. The massive artillery engagement, undertaken by nearly 2,000 guns, was now only heard in single shots; and even these seemed to have lost the force and thunder of their original voice, and now coughed in a hoarse and hollow fashion. The cavalry made its attacks at a weary trot.''[6]

In his memoirs Clausewitz belittled the result of General Uvarov's cavalry action. While its effect was not decisive, it certainly achieved more than he gave it credit for. The Italian regiment which opposed the operation certainly did not underestimate the threat; according to one of their reports: "The movement not only afforded the hope of a useful and powerful diversion, designed to free the centre . . . but it promised the Russians the prospect of new and immense results. Every unforeseen incident in war is a time for terror.''[7] The final destruction of Rayevsky's battery had been delayed; and Napoleon refused a second request for reinforcements by Ney, Murat and Davout to attack the Russian left. If General Uvarov had not threatened the French flank, the "thunder cloud" formed by the *élite* French Guard may not have been motionless, as Clausewitz observed it, but would probably have been pitched against the battered Russian army.

Now the redoubt, held so long and desperately by Rayevsky's dwindling corps, was finally re-taken. French cavalry charged from the rear as Eugène's infantry was flung in a dense mass against the front. The Russians met the onrushing infantrymen with their bayonets, making their deadly lunges, and throwing the pierced bodies into the ditch beside them, only to be hacked down by the French cavalrymen from behind. The French took possession, and slaughtered all the survivors.

II

Evening came, and a light rain began to fall. Borodino, described by Napoleon later as "the most terrible of all my battles," came to an exhausted end. The shattered remains of the two armies drew apart, Napoleon giving his order to retire before Kutuzov. But the Russians had suffered the worst. Out of 112,000 men, 58,000 were lost, more than one man in every two. French casualties were 50,000 from the total of 130,000. The expenditure of ammunition had been colossal: the cannons had fired 120,000 times, and three million cartridges had been used.[8] Corpses of every European nationality lay so close together on the battlefield that it was impossible to walk without treading on them. Ditches were overflowing with the torn bodies of horses and men. During the night the Chief Surgeon of the Grand Army, J. D. Larrey, performed 200 amputations, 74 per cent of which were successful. Only 700 Russian prisoners were taken. And as Napoleon surveyed the field of battle, Ségur marvelled at the behaviour of the Russian wounded lying near them. "They did not let out a single groan," in marked contrast to the screaming and moaning French. When darkness came the maimed and dying were left where they had fallen. It was a gloomy night, and the weather was closing in. Camp fires were lit on the hills as regrouping signals for the various units; and throughout the night wounded men staggered towards the flickering lights.

Meanwhile Mikhail Kutuzov was trying to decide what his next step should be. One commander after another reported to him, telling him of losses, of ammunition shortages, of equipment and weapon deficiencies. He was told that the sixth, seventh, and eighth Corps had been almost annihilated. Only 300 of Voronstov's 4,000-strong Grenadier division had survived; only three officers and ninety-six soldiers still lived out of 1,300 men in the Shirvansk regiment. But, remarkably, the Russian army did not feel defeated. Many expected that the battle would be resumed the following day. Before the grey light of dawn illuminated the smoking, hideous battlefield of Borodino, Kutuzov had made up his mind: he had fought the engagement which everyone had wanted: now he could continue the retreat deeper into Russia. He ordered the army to move out in four columns on to the Moscow road, pretending that he was merely seeking another battle position.

But he had taken a second decision, which was the most closely-guarded secret of all; to surrender Moscow itself. Clausewitz thoroughly agreed with the Russian commander's decision to withdraw. "No improvement could be expected from a renewal of the action. The position was broken in upon, the line of retreat menaced, the next step in the progress of calamity would have been total defeat. The army was still in order, and could withdraw without disorder. In deciding to start a retreat Kutuzov unquestionably acted wisely."[9]

On the morning of 8th September, the march to Moscow began. As the Russian army moved out, the wounded had to be left behind, and, as after Smolensk, their fate was terrible. Those who could, hobbled or crawled down the road after their comrades, but hundreds perished by the roadside and in the nearby villages. Many were burned to death when the French set fire to the houses. Moscow lay fifteen miles away. Clausewitz learned that the army was to move by short stages and that he himself, still attached to General Uvarov, was to return to the rearguard. The rearguard consisted of 10,000 infantry, just under 10,000 cavalry, and was under the overall command of General Miloradovich. At noon on 8th September, Napoleon ordered Murat to pursue Miloradovich with his entire cavalry force. Contrary to some accounts of the campaign, Clausewitz maintained that the rearguard was not hard pressed by Murat's troopers: "The two groups usually came in sight of one another in the afternoon, marched towards each other, and skirmished and cannonaded for a few hours; then we retired a short distance, and both sides formed their camp." He added: "This march displayed weariness and strategic disability on both sides."[10]

A more serious clash occurred on 10th September, when the French appeared at Miloradovich's bivouac positions an hour before sunset. The Russian rearguard commander "could not give way unless his force was to give up its intended quarters for the night and, as the ground was favourable, he decided to fight." In the engagement, Clausewitz's horse was wounded.[11] The Russian infantrymen who were occupying a scrub-covered ridge were attacked by the French cavalry and infantry, and were gradually pushed back into an inferior position. But they continued to fight for another hour, until by eleven o'clock it had grown too dark for either side to make out the other. Clausewitz observed that on this occasion, too, the French attacks were less energetic than before. The rigours of the march, and the punishment at Borodino, were taking a rising toll.

On 13th September, the Russian army came within sight of Moscow. Once again Kutuzov planned to suggest that he would fight a battle for the city, and then seem to be dissuaded from doing so. "The cleverness of this old fox," wrote Clausewitz, "was more useful at the moment than Barclay's honesty."[12] In the afternoon of the 13th, Kutuzov called a conference in a peasant's house at the village of Fili, attended by all the senior generals of his army except Miloradovich, who could not leave his troops. Most of those

Facing page *Czar Alexander I of Russia, from Monnier's portrait of 1806*

Above *The reception of Alexander I of Russia at Memel by their Majesties Friedrich Wilhelm and Louise of Prussia*

Left *Field-Marshal Barclay de Tolly (1761–1818), the Russian infantry commander*

present spoke in favour of a battle. Kutuzov was stubborn, and was reported to have said: "You fear a retreat through Moscow, but I regard it as far-sighted. It will save the army. Napoleon is like a stormy torrent which we are as yet unable to stop. Moscow will be the sponge that sucks him in."[13] But the only general to offer him full support was the unfortunate Barclay. Abruptly, the Russian commander ordered that the withdrawal should be continued, and his dejected army was told of his decision.

Already, a stream of carts and carriages, horsemen and pedestrians were leaving the city and, when the Russian army began to enter the streets on 14th September, thousands more flocked to join its retreat. Moscow was thrown into utter confusion and panic. If Napoleon were to launch an attack, a terrible disaster would follow for soldiers and civilians alike. Clausewitz was still outside the city with the rearguard when General Miloradovich was ordered to contact Murat to arrange a truce while Moscow was cleared; Miloradovich was to say that if this was refused, the people of Moscow would put up a desperate and costly defence.

Miloradovich sent forward the white flag to the French advance positions. In reply the King of Naples sent his subordinate, General Sebastiani. "A long conference followed," said Clausewitz, "to which we of the staff were not admitted." Then the two Generals mounted their horses and rode some way together. "I saw that General Miloradovich's proposals had met with no difficulty. It was clear that the French wanted Moscow in a complete state, and if the Russian request was agreed to, any Russian plan to set the city ablaze would be avoided." With agreement reached, the rearguard could leave their watch over the French and enter the chaos of the city.

Clausewitz saw hundreds of the peasants, who could not easily escape, come flocking around General Miloradovich, "crying out for protection. Groups were standing in the streets watching our march. People were weeping. The streets, too, were so blocked with the carriages of the refugees that the General had to send forward two cavalry regiments to force room for us. The most painful sight was the wounded, who lay in long rows at the edges of the road. They had hoped to be given transports so they could escape with the army. But they had to be left, lying there helpless. These wretched beings probably all perished."[14] Clausewitz rode past Moscow's magnificent wooden palaces, nearly all of which would soon be destroyed, and which Madame de Staël had also seen only a few days before describing them as "green, yellow, pink, and sculptured like dessert decorations."[15] Then, as he passed the Kremlin and the 300-foot bell tower of Ivan the Great, two battalions of the Moscow garrison merged with the army; as they left the city, these garrison troops began to play military music.

Miloradovich rode up to the commander, shouting: "What idiot told your band to play?" The commander replied that a garrison must play music when leaving a fortress, under a regulation laid down by Peter the Great. "Where do the regulations of Peter the Great provide for the

11—C

surrender of Moscow?" bellowed back Miloradovich. "Order that damned music to be stopped!" In silence the army trudged on. Clausewitz was now on Miloradovich's staff, since Uvarov had fallen ill. As he left Moscow, he was wondering which road the army was taking: it could either proceed on a straight line to Vladimir, or turn south on the Ryazan road. Clausewitz was anxious that it take the Ryazan route. Soon after Borodino he had discussed the possible route with Colonel Toll, who had agreed that the army should change direction; but his reasons were different. To Toll, the south offered more fertile country and hence more food for troops and horses: to Clausewitz it offered space in which to play hide and seek.

The choice was crucially important; and Clausewitz, in his memoirs, says that contrary to the opinion of many other historians, Kutuzov was neither the sole author of the decision to go south, nor was the decision itself suddenly made. "Even the younger staff officers often discussed the idea. Its conception and discovery did not spring from the head of a commander or adviser, like a Minerva from the head of Jupiter." In a passage almost identical to a famous extract in *On War*, Clausewitz added: "In war all is simple; but the most simple is still very difficult. The instrument of war resembles a machine with great friction, which cannot, as in ordinary mechanics be adjusted easily, but has always to take into account a great many different factors. War is, moreover, a movement through a dense medium." Kutuzov acted under conflicting emotions, opinions, ideas, and threats; and from it all the Russians did what they did. And because they went south, first on the road to Ryazan, then cutting back, the French advanced no further than Moscow and became, as Kutuzov said they would be, sucked in. Also, when the French retreat began, the Russians having moved south and then turned back again, were in a position to outflank them.

Meanwhile the Russian rearguard took up positions just outside the abandoned city of Moscow. It had been agreed with General Sebastiani that the head of the French advance guard should not enter Moscow until two hours after the Russians had left. But the Russians had hardly had time to take up their positions when two French light cavalry regiments moved out of the suburbs, and lined up in front of them. Miloradovich immediately sent forward another flag of truce, demanding a meeting with Murat. The French commander again refused to talk and sent Sebastiani instead. He told the angry Miloradovich that the Russians had taken longer than had been expected, and the French agreed to wait. So the French advance guard and the Russian rearguard stood facing one another as the refugees poured out of the doomed city. Clausewitz saw the carriages, *dorzhkis,* handcarts, *cabriolets;* people were crying, their faces dust-covered and tear-stained; babies were being trundled away in wheelbarrows, household goods were piled upon backs and crowds milled upon the road; the old were helped or carried in litters or left to stagger on alone. The frantic flight from the city continued for many hours. But already, as Clausewitz sat astride his horse, watching, "I saw wreaths of smoke rising from several places in the furthest suburbs." He thought that the fires, which were small at that time, were just part of the general confusion.

The Russian army drew away from the city and the main French forces marched in. Murat moved into the streets at about midday. The centre of the capital was now deathly quiet, most of the inhabitants having reached the outlying suburbs on their flight into the countryside. The French cavalry went through the narrow alleys expecting an ambush at any moment, but apart from a few shots fired near the Kremlin, the only noise was the clatter of their own horses' hooves upon the cobbled streets.

Napoleon decided to stage a triumphal entry the following day. In the evening the first reports came to him of the fires in the city. During the night the wind rose, moaning through the deserted streets, fanning the flames, and more fires began to break out. At three o'clock in the morning Napoleon was awakened to be told that the heart of Moscow was in flames. On 15th September, when the Emperor rode out to the Kremlin, almost half the city was ablaze. Sparks flew from one frail wooden building to another, helped by the wind; and that night Napoleon was woken by a garish light streaming in through the window of his room in the Kremlin, as the glare from the fires turned night into day. Only with difficulty was Bonaparte able to flee in time. The streets were choked with smoke and dust, houses were collapsing on all sides, and many of the Old Guard perished as they rushed Napoleon to the Petrovsky Palace on the outskirts of Moscow. The fire was still smouldering weeks later; over three-quarters of the city had been destroyed. Moving away from Moscow, Clausewitz could see the glow behind him each night. "On this march I saw Moscow burning without interruption, and although we were seven miles distant, the wind sometimes covered us with ashes. Even though the Russians were already broken in to sacrifices of this kind, after the burning of Smolensk and other towns, yet this one filled them with terrible sorrow, and incensed them against an enemy who they blamed for this act of barbarity, a result of the enemy's hate, insolence and cruelty." The French were meanwhile blaming the Russians for the fire, and were hanging those suspected of arson. Bonaparte's officers believed it to be a massive and carefully planned operation.

Clausewitz doubted this. "In the army the fire was looked upon as a great misfortune, a real calamity," he wrote. Nor, at first, did he believe that Rostopchin, the blustering Governor-General of Moscow, was chiefly to blame, despite the widely-held view to the contrary. Clausewitz met Rostopchin eight days after the start of the fire, and accepted the man's frenzied denials of responsibility. Clausewitz thought it more likely that the fire was an accident: "The confusion which I saw in the streets as the rearguard moved out; the fact that the smoke was first seen to rise from the outer edge of the suburbs where the Cossacks were active, both convinced me that the Moscow fire was a result of the disorder, and of the habit the Cossacks had of first thoroughly pillaging and then setting fire to all the houses before the enemy could make use of them." He continued: "That the French were not the agents I was firmly convinced, because I had seen what value they placed upon possessing it undamaged; that the Russian authorities had done the act appeared to me, at least, not proved and the eager and solemn assurances of the man held as the principal agent seemed to leave no room for doubt. Had Rostopchin so acted, as if making a great and necessary sacrifice, he would not have solemnly denied it. I could not, therefore, believe that the fire of Moscow had been started deliberately."[16] Later he changed his mind and admitted that he may have been deceived by Rostopchin. But Clausewitz was never as firmly convinced as others were of Rostopchin's guilt. "It is one of the strangest happenings in history that an event which so influenced the fate of Russia should be like a bastard born from an illicit love affair, without a father to acknowledge it."[17]

Clausewitz realized that Napoleon was in a desperate situation at Moscow. This was not primarily due to the destruction of the city, although "many necessities were no doubt destroyed, of which they [the French] might have made use." There were wider reasons for the threat to Napoleon. "An army of 90,000 men, with exhausted troops and ruined horses, the end of a wedge driven 120 miles into Russia, an army of 110,000 men on their right, an armed people around them, forced to show a front to all points of the compass, without magazines, with insufficient ammunition, with but one, entirely devastated line of communications—this was not a situation to pass a winter in."[18]

At the time, many Russians did not appreciate this. The army, said Clausewitz, was in "a condition of grief and despondency." Clausewitz himself was about to leave it. General Miloradovich had given up his command of the rearguard on the march from Moscow. This in turn meant that Clausewitz had to be transferred. He reported to the main headquarters for orders. There he found instructions which had arrived some weeks before from the Czar, and which had been lying around forgotten: these appointed him Chief of Staff at the Riga garrison, far away to the west, which was still under attack by his countrymen. He presented himself to Barclay who, as War Minister, had to issue him with the official passport. General Barclay told him: "Thank your God you are called away from here. No good can come of all this." Many in the army, said Clausewitz, both wanted and expected peace; he strongly disagreed. The French, he thought, would be destroyed if only the Russians would keep up the fight.

"I trembled at the thought of peace, and I saw, in the calamity of the moment, the means of salvation," he wrote.[19] As he told Marie in a letter at the end of September: "On the whole our position is not bad, but already the people are inclined to despair. We have lost a battle, but with measure:

we have nearly equal numbers now. Because of our retreat towards Kaluga, the enemy will not be able to keep Moscow. He will have to release part of his conquered provinces. I think that the subjugation of Russia is out of the question."[20]

Clausewitz was nevertheless worried. He told Marie: "I think a bad peace will overtake us." Indeed, he had a personal reason for sadness. The post he was to take at Riga was previously held by his close friend Karl von Tiedemann, his colleague at the War School both as a student and more recently as lecturer. The two of them had consistently followed parallel careers, succeeding one another to various appointments. It had happened again, but this time in tragic circumstances. At Riga, Tiedemann had been active in trying to persuade the Prussians to leave the French. He had written numerous notes and had sent them to the Prussian commanders, first Grawert, then Yorck. He had even gone forward to the enemy outposts to speak to the Prussians in an attempt to convince them that they were on the wrong side. On 22nd August, during an attack on the Prussian lines near Dahlenkirchen, Tiedemann had been fatally wounded by a pistol shot from a Prussian hussar. When news reached Berlin that this young officer, one of the renegades who had deserted Prussia, had been killed by one of his own countrymen, there was delight in some circles of society, "to whom," wrote Countess Sophie Schwerin, "the word of command constituted their political conscience."[21] According to Yorck: "This man has fallen as a victim to his passions and his political opinions. It is a good thing that he is dead."[22]

So Clausewitz lost one of the closest friends of his own age. He now had to make the difficult journey to the Baltic coast to replace him. At Riga his superior would be General Essen, himself engaged in trying to bring the Prussians over from the French. Clausewitz was not particularly sorry to leave the Russian army. If he had received the order from the Czar on its arrival, he would have missed Borodino and Moscow, which he would have regretted, but "to be attached to General Essen certainly promised me a more agreeable activity than a post with a division or cavalry corps of the main army, where, because of my ignorance of the Russian language, I could only perform even the most simple duties with great effort. Because of this the campaign so far had been doubly severe for me."[23] Clausewitz described this language problem in a letter to Gneisenau. "I have carried out the duty of an ordinary officer with the greatest difficulty. I cannot tell you how disagreeable this time has been, and how few the happy moments. Despite everything I have not regretted the step I took ... But I have longed for service in a German unit. One is like a deaf mute here: the other people seem to act idiotically and yet cannot be told to stop."[24] He made the same complaint in a letter to Marie, even before he received the Czar's order: "I have the greatest desire to serve again in a German corps, where I can use my skills effectively."[25] When he heard the news of his appointment to Riga, he told her: "The difficulties and negative side of my situation came to be so great that I was almost inconsolable. Then the long awaited orders from the Czar came for me to go to Riga, to replace my unforgettable friend Tiedemann, who has died there with glory. This employment frees me from a thousand great and small inconveniences."[26]

So, on 25th September, after a number of irritating postponements, Clausewitz was handed his *podorschna* (passport) at Krasnoi Parchri. He intended to travel by post-horse to Serpuchov, Tula, Ryazan, Jaroslav and Novgorod to Petersburg, where he would obtain a new uniform to replace the tattered, stained, flea-infested clothes he wore; then he would travel on to Riga. But the language problem surfaced again. Travelling only with an *aide*, he was suddenly surrounded by a group of rough-looking militiamen near Serpuchov, and arrested as a spy. He kept repeating the few Russian words he knew; he showed them his *podorschna* and his document case full of official Russian papers, and the Russian order for his new appointment signed in the Czar's own hand; he pointed to his Russian uniform. But all this was not enough to allay the suspicions of the militiamen. His *aide* was Polish, and most of the militiamen thought Clausewitz was French. Nor was he any better off when he insisted he was Prussian, since Prussia was also their enemy. Luckily, the militiamen decided not to shoot him there and then. Instead, they forced him to ride back with them to the army headquarters which he had left not long before. Clausewitz knew that if he tried to make the journey alone again, the same thing—or worse—would probably happen; so he remained, stranded. Impatiently he had to wait, cursing his inability to speak the language.

Then he tried again, this time with his fellow-Prussian Count Chasot, who had originally come to Russia with Gneisenau from Vienna. With Chasot and Clausewitz was Baron Bode, of the Saxon service. Both Bode and Chasot had belonged to the Prince of Oldenburg's staff during the campaign, and were now to go to Petersburg to help the Prince form the proposed force of Germans serving in the Russian army: the Russo-German Legion.

As the group rode on, escorted by a Russian officer, Chasot explained to Clausewitz the details of the Russo-German Legion, a force with which Clausewitz was soon to become closely involved. As far back as 1810, Peter, Duke of Oldenburg, whose small state had been annexed by Napoleon, had suggested to the Czar that use should be made of the bitter discontent in the German armies, particularly that in the Prussian force. A former commander of the Oldenburg army, Colonel Arentschild, was sent into Prussia by the Czar to engage officers "who might be out of employment and might have no further engagements with other sovereigns." But at that time, 1811, Colonel Arentschild had little success; Prussian officers still hoped that Friedrich Wilhelm would go to war with Napoleon. After the treaty between Prussia and France, and the opening of the 1812 campaign, the idea was hopefully revived. Colonel Arentschild tried to form a corps from German deserters; and when Stein came to Russia, and a German expatriates committee was formed at Petersburg, fresh impetus was given to the proposal.

The formation of the German Legion was however delayed, for several reasons. The plan made a distinction between German prisoners and those of other nations fighting for Napoleon; German prisoners should be sent to special centres at Revel and Kief. But the representatives of the German Committee at the army headquarters, Prince August of Oldenburg, Count Chasot and von Bode, found this was often not done; the Germans were usually treated with as much contempt or cruelty as the French. Another drawback was the physical condition of the prisoners themselves. The poet Arndt, who was also involved in this work while in Russia, wrote: "We dreamed of a speedy increase of the Legion to some ten or twenty thousand, but God looked upon it, or rather had already looked upon it. The prisoners had grown dry, dead and nerveless in marrow and bone—what with marches, cold, want, and harsh treatment from their Russian drivers as they were dragged along roads of snow and ice; and so they died off like flies. I saw samples enough of these unhappy starved and frozen youths."[27]

Chasot and Bode were on the way to report progress when Clausewitz went with them to Petersburg. Chasot fell ill *en route*, and the group usually had to make an early stop each night instead of pressing on. At these halts they found the whole country was buzzing with news of the campaign, with one rumour flying after another. Accurate information was hard for the Russians to obtain. When they reached Jaroslav, the Czar's sister the Ekaterina Pavolvna, heard that the three young officers had just come from the main army, and summoned them to give her the latest news. "She asked me for my opinion of what Bonaparte would do," wrote Clausewitz in his memoirs, "whether it would be a direct retreat, and by what road. I said I was sure that the French would make an early retreat, and that I thought it would be made on the road they had advanced along. She seemed to have formed the same opinion. She conveyed to me the impression of a woman formed to govern."[28]

Clausewitz did not reach Petersburg, with its dazzling white buildings and bustling court, until mid-October. Military events had quietened down by then, but the diplomatic world was in turmoil. In Moscow, Napoleon was attempting to obtain peace—a peace which, he insisted, must be signed in the ruins of the city he now occupied. The French leader had staked everything upon the seizure of Moscow. This, he had believed at the outset of the campaign, would be the method to bring victory, as his seizure of other capitals had been in the past. His entry into Moscow had, on the face of it, repeated what had happened in Austria in 1805 and 1809, and in Prussia in 1806. These precedents suggested that the Russians would speedily submit; Austria and Prussia had yielded after their capitals had been taken. But there was another, more ominous, example: national resistance in Spain had not collapsed after the taking of Madrid in 1808; on the contrary, it had become steadily more determined and successful. Clausewitz wrote in *On War*: "When Bonaparte marched to Moscow in 1812, all depended upon whether the taking of the capital, and the events which preceded the capture, would force the Czar to make peace, as he had been compelled to do after the battle of Friedland in 1807 . . . if Bonaparte did not obtain peace at Moscow, there was nothing for him but a strategic defeat."[29]

Day by day, Napoleon hoped for an emissary from Alexander; but none came. He could only wait, while the cold weather approached, while his marshals grew daily more anxious, while bread and fodder became scarcer. The discipline of the Grand Army was disappearing rapidly; the French veterans as well as the Germans, Poles and Italians were beginning to degenerate into a rabble. Still Napoleon waited, while Alexander refused even to acknowledge his urgent letters. On 3rd October, the French leader told his generals that he intended to burn the remains of Moscow—fewer than 5,000 houses of the original 30,000—and then advance on Petersburg, where Marshal Macdonald would join him. The generals were appalled. To march on Alexander's second capital would mean marching into the Russian winter. Napoleon then decided that General Caulaincourt should journey to the Czar with a peace proposal, but Caulaincourt protested that this would reveal the difficulties of the French position. Napoleon finally agreed to send his *aide* Count de Lauriston instead, and he set out to arrange a meeting with Kutuzov in order to obtain a pass.

In Petersburg, Alexander and his court were also in confusion. Many feared that Napoleon would indeed advance from Moscow. But Clausewitz believed that the longer the Russians held on, the greater would be the French defeat; at all costs, an early peace must be prevented. In Jaroslav, the Ekaterina Pavolvna, before and after her discussions with Clausewitz, pleaded with her brother to continue the campaign. "Moscow has been taken . . . but do not forget your resolve: no peace of any kind. There is still hope of restoring your honour." Alexander replied that there was no question of peace. Fortunately for Russia, and eventually Europe, the Czar was more firmly resolved than ever before. On 20th September, soon after the Russians had evacuated Moscow, Alexander had issued this Proclamation: "Let no one despair. Indeed, how can we lose courage when all classes of the realm are proving their courage and constancy?—when the enemy finds himself with his remaining troops so far from his own country in the midst of a great nation, surrounded by our armies, one of which faces him and three others threaten to cut off his communications, and prevent him bringing reinforcements?"[30]

His sister still had to be convinced. "People are blaming you, and blaming you loudly," she wrote. "What you should do is not for me to say. But do save your honour."[31] In reply, Alexander blamed the fall of Moscow on Kutuzov. When Lauriston met Kutuzov in early October, with Napoleon's overtures of peace, the Russian commander made a report to his Czar. Alexander told him: "When you set out to command the army which was entrusted to you, you knew of my express wish to avoid all negotiations with the enemy and all peaceful relations with him. After what has happened, I must today emphatically repeat that my resolution must be firmly maintained by you in its full extent."[32] No negotiations would take place. But Clausewitz believed that something else still threatened a possible Russian victory. If Kutuzov engaged in battle with the French, the Russians could still be disastrously defeated.

For the moment, Kutuzov was showing greater military wisdom than ever before. Taking the Ryazan road, he had wheeled south to the old Kaluga road, and then moved to Krasnoi Parchri. In this way Kaluga and the south were protected from a possible French offensive. At the same time, Cossacks had been ordered on towards Ryazan to confuse Murat who was following behind. Kutuzov had carried out a successful flanking movement; now he wanted to play for time, believing that the longer Napoleon stayed in Moscow the better it would be for the Russians. But some of his generals, including the influential Auguste de Bennigsen, wanted a battle. Kutuzov refused to consider this. Kutuzov was also opposed by General Sir Robert Wilson, the British Commissioner with the Russian army. General Wilson was sending back confidential reports on Kutuzov's conduct both to his own Government and to the Czar, and was playing an arrogant and energetic part in the intrigues at the Russian headquarters.

Napoleon meanwhile had realized that chances of peace talks were hopeless: the Grand Army must withdraw. On 14th October, he ordered that French artillery coming to reinforce the Grand Army should not proceed beyond Smolensk. But he waited just a few more days before moving from Moscow. For Joachim Murat's self-esteem, this was a few days too long. On 18th October Russian forces advanced against his units, which were camped near the small river of Chernishna: Kutuzov had finally yielded to the pleadings of his generals for a battle. Colonel Toll had scouted the French positions and had found them badly organized, with French patrols inadequate because the horses were weak from hunger. Chances of a Russian success were therefore good, but Kutuzov himself did not appear for the engagement and left everything to General Bennigsen. After the initial clash the French rallied, then retreated in good order. Bennigsen called for reinforcements, but Kutuzov refused and the battle of Tarutino was allowed to finish. Bennigsen was enraged at being denied Kutuzov's full support, which he believed would have made the battle decisive. His outburst was so violent and defamatory that Kutuzov finally threw Bennigsen out. Kutuzov had formed his plan, and he intended to follow it as closely as possible.

On the night of 19th October, the main French army began to leave

Moscow. The movement began on the 120th day of the campaign, the thirty-ninth day after arriving in Moscow. The journey home was five hundred miles in length, but initially the men were cheerful: laden with loot—liquor, silver bowls, icons, ornaments, dresses, jewellery—they sang as they marched through the streets. As when the Grand Army arrived, there were no crowds to see it leave; but now the buildings around were mostly a mass of rubble, with charred timbers still smouldering and spitting sparks at Napoleon's men. For the next four days massive explosions tore through the remains of the city. On 21st October, the Kremlin itself was blown to pieces. The noise was heard by nearby Cossack patrols, and on 22nd October, one detachment ventured cautiously to the city. No Frenchmen were to be seen in the streets. The retreat had begun. "Perhaps my work in the Fatherland is closer than we believe," Clausewitz wrote to Marie at the end of October. "Matters at this moment are very good. We might easily have a good result. And a decisively unhappy one is almost impossible. However, we must not triumph too soon."[33]

Burdened with loot, Napoleon's 100,000 men marched straight towards Krasnoi Parchri. Napoleon intended to collect the remnants of Murat's force at the town before marching towards Kaluga, and then turning back towards Smolensk. The Emperor was determined to return by the way he had come, rather than retreat through the southern provinces. Some of his critics said that he should have taken the latter route, in order to utilize the undamaged villages. Clausewitz was the first military writer to say Napoleon was correct. If he had gone south, he explained, "the French army would have been starved in a week." He continued: "I could never understand why it has been so obstinately contended that Bonaparte should have taken another line for his retreat, than the one by which he advanced. Where could he have drawn his supplies from, except from his prepared stores? What could an exhausted country do for an army which had no time to lose ... what commissary could go in front to collect supplies ... what Russian authority would have obeyed his orders?"[34]

Clausewitz maintained that Napoleon must first move towards Kaluga to remove the threat from the Russian main army. If he had marched direct from Moscow to Smolensk, Kutuzov could have reached Smolensk before him. But if Bonaparte managed to manoeuvre the Russians back, and suddenly switched the direction of the French retreat, valuable time could be gained. He might even have led Kutuzov into a disastrous mistake and exposed his army to a decisive defeat. Besides, Kaluga contained Russian stores which the French might be able to capture.

While he was still in Petersburg, Clausewitz heard two unpleasant pieces of news. Firstly, new arrivals from the Prussian court said that King Frederick Wilhelm was about to discipline him for his entry into Russian service. "Already there is to be a court case against me," he wrote to Marie at the end of October. "That the King must do something against us, I understand, but why should he honour me with his anger? It would make me very bitter, because I have done nothing to deserve it." Clausewitz continued: "In any event, we must now console ourselves with the thought that even in the most evil-minded eyes, our only interest was that which Europe recognizes as its own. And this I believe will justify our conduct before God and the world."[35] Secondly, Clausewitz heard news of General Essen. Essen was to have been his superior officer at Riga, but had been replaced by the Marquis Paulucci, whom Clausewitz disliked and had no wish to serve. "This officer," said Clausewitz after meeting Paulucci when he first arrived at Vilna four months before, "was a restless genius, with a strange faculty of persuasion. Heaven knows how they had decided that, with such qualities and abilities as his, he was so fitted for the great movements and emergencies of war. Moreover, he combined with much wrong-headedness a good deal of ill-nature."[36]

Once the French retreat had started, it was obvious to Clausewitz that if he went to Riga, he would miss the action. He therefore visited the Duke of Oldenburg in Petersburg, and begged for the post of Chief of Staff in the Russo-German Legion which the Duke was raising. Meanwhile, as German recruitment was still difficult, and as the Legion was not yet fully formed, Clausewitz did not want to be left with nothing to do. He asked the Duke to see whether the Czar would allow him to join Wittgenstein's army. This force was operating in Lithuania and promised to play a leading part in blocking the French retreat. Much to Clausewitz's delight, Czar Alexander granted the two requests. Clausewitz prepared to join the fighting once more. Just before he left Petersburg, early in November, Clausewitz wrote excitedly to Marie: "Who would have thought that the end of 1812 would have been so good. Shall I guess what will happen? Napoleon will have to retreat 150 miles through destroyed provinces with an army which is already destroyed. It will be through human failings, not fate, if Europe is not saved now." He added: "Should all hope disappear, should Europe be smashed completely, I hope to go with the German Legion to England."[37]

But one matter was still making him uneasy: the actions of the King and his officials at home in Prussia. Carl himself was out of harm's way at the moment; but Marie could be involved. "I hear that they will make you a court case," he wrote to her. "I only fear that you and my brothers may have difficulty over this, one way or the other. Otherwise I would not mind. This worries me very much, and I grow ever sadder at the thought that our reunion may be so far away. I comfort myself with the thought that, one day, Germany will think of us with gratitude, and will praise at our graves the good intentions for which we have sacrificed our lives."[38]

In the meantime, there was nothing that Clausewitz could do, except help to beat Napoleon. Re-kitted, refreshed and ready for action, Clausewitz set out from Petersburg again in the second week of November, travelling by way of Poskov and Polotsk to Czasnicki, Wittgenstein's head-quarters—where he arrived just too late for a battle. Wittgenstein had been occupied in blocking any move upon Petersburg by French forces under Oudinot, St. Cyr or Victor. The three French corps totalled 98,000 men; Wittgenstein's strength, according to Clausewitz, was never above 75,000. "He had thus neutralized for the offensive a superior mass of the enemy, lost no ground, but instead gained such a superiority that he was now ready to take part in the operation, devised at Petersburg, for cutting off the French army."[39] The army headquarters was feeling very self-satisfied. When Clausewitz arrived the officers told him they had fought seventeen pitched battles; and on 15th November, at Smoliantsi they had clashed with Victor and forced him back. Clausewitz was much impressed by the record and by his fellow-officers at Czasnicki. "Such a result gained against French troops and Bonaparte's lieutenants deserves the name of a glorious campaign," he wrote.[40]

Count Ludwig Adolf von Wittgenstein was born in Westphalia in 1769. He had begun his military career in 1793, serving Prussia before he had moved to Russia. He was described by Clausewitz as "full of good will, activity, and enterprise. His understanding was a little deficient in clearness, and his activity in solid energy." Wittgenstein's Chief of Staff was the Saxon-born Major-General d'Auvray, a good-humoured man, noble, full of zeal, but "a little deficient in practical soldiership." Clausewitz added: "He was not to be trifled with, as he could lay about him on occasion, which was often necessary." The "prime mover" in the army was another Prussian, Major-General Diebitsch. Diebitsch was Count Wittgenstein's Quarter-master-General—"Fiery, brave, enterprising, quick in resolve, of great firm-ness, with good natural understanding, somewhat confident and imperious, carrying others along with him, and ambitious."[41]

Clausewitz himself was slightly intoxicated by the self-satisfaction of his new colleagues. Wittgenstein had only begun to act effectively on 19th October, when joined by the Petersburg militia. He had compelled St. Cyr to retreat from Polotsk and had occupied the town, following this up by occupying Vitebsk on 6th November. But he was frightened of Napoleon. In addition, he was soon about to show his lack of "activity in solid energy." His hesitation was to have unfortunate results.

While Clausewitz had been riding south to join Wittgenstein, Napoleon and his army had been retreating towards the area in which Wittgenstein was operating, and Kutuzov had again been labouring under criticisms from his generals and the Czar. During his own retreat, Kutuzov had been urged to give battle to stop the French advance on Moscow; now, during the French retreat, he was being urged to fight a battle to stop Napoleon's flight to the frontier. Kutuzov was just as reluctant as before to engage the enemy. He had no intention of trying to bring Napoleon to battle, even if Wittgenstein and the other general in the area, Chichagov, were thereby threatened. Kutuzov intended to stand back and watch the Grand Army die. Even if the Grand Army managed to survive the horrors of the retreat Kutuzov would still not be greatly concerned, as long as the French quit Russia. He saw his duty as the liberation of his country, not of Europe. Nor, as he firmly told Sir Robert Wilson, was he interested in relieving Britain's suffering from the Continental System.[42]

In pursuit of this policy, the Russian commander refused to rush forces into the town of Maloyaroslavets, when the French clashed there with Dokhturov's corps. Instead, Kutuzov went round the town and took up positions on the road to Kaluga; he stood back watching as the houses burned and the streets changed hands again and again, and eventually the French prised out the Russians and snatched possession. Another battle was fully expected to follow the next day, 24th October, this time with the main Russian army. But Kutuzov ordered a withdrawal further down the road to Kaluga. Then he turned again, and waited. For the very first time in his career, Napoleon withdrew from a general battle, as Kutuzov had expected and hoped. Napoleon himself turned; and retreated first to Maloyaroslavets then to Borovsk, Vereya, and Mozhaisk.

It was then, perhaps, that the real French retreat began. Behind came the Russians, with Kutuzov now pushing forward as fast as the French, not to seek a battle, but to keep the French on the move. By day clouds of smoke were billowing up ahead; by night a deep red glow lit up the October sky. Although the weather had grown much colder, the frost had not yet arrived. But even now, before the French had reached Smolensk, the hunger, misery, and exhaustion of Napoleon's forces were reaching terrible proportions. Hunger, not the cold, destroyed the French army. First the horses were eaten. Then the troops began to eat their dead comrades—a common occurrence even before Smolensk was painfully reached. The roads were scattered with emaciated bodies; and increasingly the bodies had half-gnawed bones. This disaster befell the French for a number of reasons. The stay in Moscow had been prolonged—and Napoleon had expected a Russian capitulation; existing supply deficiencies were therefore aggravated. This supply system, overstretched and vulnerable, had repeatedly suffered attacks from Cossacks and partisans; stocks stored along the route were therefore less than planned, and they had been reduced still further by corrupt officials and above all by the removal of food and stores to feed and equip reinforcements or replacements on their way to Moscow. Stocks were therefore inadequate; nor had officials been warned that the Grand Army would be in desperate need of them. Moreover the main body of the army arrived at the replenishment points after the horde of men from the administrative units, who had left Moscow earlier. Famine therefore rapidly accelerated.

With the growing horror of the retreat came an escalation of bitterness and barbarity by both French and Russians. Several thousand prisoners dragged along by the French were given no food; and if any of these wretches staggered or lagged behind, they were shot, bayoneted or clubbed to death. Neither did the Cossacks show mercy. Sir Robert Wilson noted on 5th November: "Today I saw a scene of horror rarely encountered in modern war. Two thousand men, naked, dead or dying . . . hundreds of unfortunate wounded crawling out of the woods . . ." The Cossacks, falling on a French detachment, had done their swift and terrible work. Russian peasants also joined the struggle as the partisan war reached its climax. Men, women and youngsters were recruited to ambush, harry, track down and exterminate the faltering French. They were motivated by the burning of Moscow, the cruelty of the French themselves, and simply by the intoxicating animal lust to slaughter. These peasants showed, as the Spaniards already had, how a nation's living strength could be employed. It was a further vindication of the message contained in Clausewitz's lectures on irregular warfare, a message which would be developed in *On War* after Clausewitz had lived through 1812. Yet at the time the partisan activity was looked upon with suspicions by the Russian Government: the officials feared, as they had in Prussia, that a class war might erupt between the serfs and their landlords.

Constant pressure upon the French army forced it to abandon baggage, loot, guns, sick and wounded. All were seized by the hovering Russians. And near Mozhaisk the fleeing Grand Army came upon a special and prophetic horror. The French found a plain covered with rotting remains of horses and stiffened men half-eaten by wolves, littered with broken weapons, rusty sabres. At first the French did not recognize the place: the scarred battlefield of Borodino.

Clausewitz had begun to feel the cold of the rapidly approaching Russian winter in the first week of November. On 8th November, as Napoleon reached Smolensk at the head of his disintegrating army, the first fingers of frost touched the ground. As the last of his soldiers arrived at the town a week later, snow was settling. At Smolensk the French army expected to find adequate stores. The stocks had been relied upon for the survival of the Grand Army: throughout the retreat so far the men had been told: "Your hunger will finish at Smolensk." But now the stocks were discovered to be totally insufficient. Inadequate amounts had reached the city from France and Prussia, after the Cossacks had finished their attacks on the convoys, and officials at Smolensk had sold some of that which did arrive to local Jews—who re-sold it again to the Russians. All that was left in Smolensk was seized and devoured by the rabble of the Grand Army within three days. The men were now almost impossible to control; only the Imperial Guard preserved firm discipline. On 14th November, Napoleon led his troops on again.

Marching parallel to the French, Kutuzov experienced the recurring difficulty of avoiding battle. He still intended to let the Grand Army destroy itself, with the help of the Russian winter. But even men like Toll and Kovnonitsin, who worshipped Kutuzov, pleaded with him for a general engagement. In Petersburg, the Czar agreed to a scheme behind Kutuzov's back which was aimed to stop the French at the waters of the Berezina. By then, Alexander believed, the French would be so weak as to be defenceless. Despite Kutuzov's reluctance, the French were engaged at Krasnoya, and suffered heavy casualties. Moreover Ney, in command of the French rear-guard, was in a desperate position. Leaving Smolensk on 17th November, together with about 8,000 wounded and women fleeing from Moscow, Marshal Ney's force of 7,000 infantrymen and 450 cavalry was attacked and virtually surrounded just before the Dnieper river. He was asked to surrender and refused. Instead he marched doggedly forward with 3,000 men through the thick snow of the trackless forest, and emerged on the bank of the Dnieper. The river was covered with the first thin ice of winter; Ney stepped on to the ice first, and it creaked but held. Others followed. But under the weight of the advance, the ice splintered and cracked, and many fell through to perish in the freezing water. Only Ney and 800 of his troops reached the other side. On the bank they had left lay the wagons full of the sick and wounded, screaming and cursing at being left so helplessly to die at the hands of the waiting Cossacks.

At Orsha, where Ney rejoined Napoleon, the French had only about 30,000 soldiers fit to fight. Czar Alexander was even more firmly convinced that they could be massacred at the River Berezina. Again without inform-ing Kutuzov, the Czar sent out instructions to Wittgenstein and to Chi-chagov who was operating to the south-east of him. Kutuzov, on the other hand, was apprehensive about the state of his own troops. Their condition deteriorated rapidly after Krasnoya. As Clausewitz himself experienced, the cold was growing more acute, and the Russians were inadequately provided with winter clothing. Deaths and desertions mounted; in six weeks the main Russian army had lost over 50,000 troops and now numbered no more than 35,000. Kutuzov knew that Wittgenstein had over 35,000, and Chichagov some 25,000. But Kutuzov did not feel that he could rely upon these two generals. Wittgenstein was believed to have an obsessive fear of Napoleon, and Pavel Vasileivich Chichagov was not a soldier, but a sailor with the rank of Admiral. Therefore Kutuzov still thought it best to let Napoleon's army crawl, bloody and broken, back over the Russian frontier. On the other hand, a number of factors tended to support the Czar's plan to kill or capture Napoleon "for the sake of Europe." Admiral Chichagov's vanguard occupied Minsk on 16th November, capturing massive quantities of stores which had been awaiting Napoleon; and on 15th November, Wittgenstein had won his success over Victor; the three Russian armies were now poised for the final pounce upon the Grand Army. The Czar intended that this should happen whether Kutuzov agreed or not.

Clausewitz had apparently arrived at Count Wittgenstein's headquarters

TEN

Tauroggen

"Does not the sight of the sufferings
of their hungry, thirsty comrades
pierce the hearts of the Commanders
and his Generals a thousand times?"
(*On War*, bk. iii, ch. i.)

10

BUT THE THREADS were not drawn tightly enough. Napoleon snatched at a loose end, pulled, and, Clausewitz said, "entirely saved his old honour and acquired new."[1] When he heard that Admiral Chichagov's troops had taken Borisov and blocked the French passage to the bridges, Napoleon sent urgent orders to his commanders Dombrowski, Oudinot and Davout, to concentrate all available force upon the town to secure the crossing. Oudinot advanced rapidly. Seeing the threat, Chichagov sent out General Pahlen—Clausewitz's former commander—to hold the road with his cavalry. Clausewitz was lucky not to have still been on the General's staff—Pahlen's men were completely routed. Oudinot continued to press forward, pushing the Russian infantry into the woods near the town of Borisov and sending Chichagov scurrying back over the Berezina. Oudinot then occupied Borisov and waited for his Emperor. Napoleon fixed Russian attention upon Borisov by a number of feints, while he had two bridges thrown over the river farther north near Studianka. His engineers worked night and day, using thousands of nails they had brought on their backs from Smolensk especially for this purpose.

Wittgenstein could still have reached the area in time to attack the French before they began to cross the river. But he did not, and has been blamed for it ever since. According to his critics, he spent five days inactive after clashing with Victor at Smoliansti; then instead of marching south to chase Victor towards Radulichi, he seemed for no good reason to move in the direction of Barany. As a result he reached the Berezina after Napoleon's troops had begun to cross.

Close to Wittgenstein, Clausewitz had a unique chance to study the reasons for the General's conduct during those critical few days; and he saw Wittgenstein's actions in a different light from later critics. He fully agreed that Wittgenstein was sometimes slow to attack, and that he made mistakes during this period. But Clausewitz made a considerable effort in his memoirs to explain his commanding general's position. The Czar, too, was much to blame, Clausewitz wrote. Meddling as he did in the Russian operations, Alexander had ordered Wittgenstein to deal not only with Victor but also with Oudinot, by throwing him back on Vilna.[2] It was virtually impossible to do both at the same time. "Beyond this, the instructions were that Wittgenstein was to occupy the Ula from Lepel downwards and then wait for further events. Count Wittgenstein had to keep his headquarters near Czasnicki. He remained quiet, therefore, for a week after the action of Smoliansti."[3]

Each day, Wittgenstein awaited orders. He knew very little of what was going on elsewhere. Clausewitz made it clear in his memoirs that no intelligence reports were sent to him, either by Kutuzov or by the Czar. Not until 20th November did he find out for himself that Victor and Oudinot were moving towards the Berezina, "which indicated the approach of the French main army. Before, nothing more had been known about the whereabouts of the army than that it had arrived in a very weakened state at Smolensk."[4] But that had been ten days before. Not until 22nd November did Wittgenstein hear of Chichagov's move to Borisov, Clausewitz continued. Wittgenstein then started the move to join him. He then learned that the main French forces were nearer to the Berezina than he had thought, that Napoleon had left Orsha, and that Kutuzov had only sent an advance guard of 20,000 men against him. News of General Pahlen's defeat reached Wittgenstein, but the Russian general believed that Chichagov still held the town of Borisov.

Wittgenstein had three alternatives: to join Chichagov, to strike south against the Smolensk road and Napoleon's flank, or to follow Alexander's instructions and guard Lepel by moving towards the Ula. With hindsight, Clausewitz said, it was easy to say that Wittgenstein should have marched sooner for the Berezina. Yet as Clausewitz wrote in On War: "In war all is simple, but the most simple is still very difficult ... War is moreover a movement through a dense medium."[5] This medium was made dense by the appalling conditions, by the difficulty of knowing what was happening, and by the often incorrect reports which reached Wittgenstein. Clausewitz also wrote in On War: "A great part of the information obtained in war is contradictory, a still greater part is false, and by far the greatest part is of a doubtful character."[6] The main French army advancing under Bonaparte's personal command, was, according to Wittgenstein's information, still 80,000 strong. At the lowest estimate it was 60,000, said Clausewitz. In fact, the real fighting strength of the Grand Army was now below 30,000. Clausewitz continued: "Observation by reconnaissance was very difficult, because it was impossible to distinguish in the moving mass those still bearing arms from the others. In short, it is both conceivable and excusable, that in Wittgenstein's headquarters it should have been supposed that a mass of from 90,000 to 100,000 men was in their front."⁷ To rush against the flank of this force with only 40,000 Russian troops, without chance of reinforcement, would have been sheer suicide. Moreover, believing that the Berezina at Borisov was held by Chichagov, and that the French had no means of bridging the river, Wittgenstein thought that Napoleon would either have to turn north or south when he reached the obstacle, and aim for a crossing either at Lepel or Bobruisk. Lepel was Wittgenstein's responsibility. So he reached his decision. He would stay and cover Lepel. Clausewitz gave his verdict: "Wittgenstein acted as most men in his place would have acted, and not in a way which can be absolutely condemned."⁸ In defending his commander, Clausewitz was to some extent defending himself: as a member of Wittgenstein's staff, he shared in the blame for the final decision. Nevertheless, his verdict was an accurate one, except that he makes no mention of another factor, Wittgenstein's fear of Napoleon.

Early on 25th November, Wittgenstein's army moved up the snow-covered road towards Lepel from Kolopedniczi. Advance patrols were sent out to probe the countryside to see whether Wittgenstein's supposition had been correct, and Napoleon had indeed turned north. But by evening on 25th November, no contact had been made. Wittgenstein became increasingly worried that he had made a mistake; and he decided during the night that the French were not after all making for Lepel. Very early on the 26th he called a conference of his staff. Clausewitz and the others were told that the army would turn and advance south for Kostritza and the Berezina. After a forced march in difficult conditions, Wittgenstein's troops reached Kostritza on 27th November, where the General learned that the French were making their crossing only three miles away at Studianka.

The French Guard had entered Studianka during the night of 25th November, at the same time as Wittgenstein was heading north, and forty-eight hours before he returned to Kostritza. Napoleon arrived at daybreak on 26th November and immediately ordered that the crossing of the river should begin. A Russian detachment under General Chaplits was the first to report the move, Chaplits' troops opened fire upon the French, but this was insufficient to stop Napoleon's men from moving over the hastily-constructed bridges.

The crossing continued throughout daylight on the 26th, during the night, and then the following day. At 2.0 p.m. on the 27th, Napoleon and the Old Guard went over. The French army was forming up on the western bank, and Victor's Corps was the only other effective fighting group left to come. Napoleon had given orders that the fighting men should go first; then if there was still time, the hordes of unarmed French, the wounded, sick, women and children could follow. If there was no time, the bridges were to be detonated.

Not until 28th November, as Victor's troops were beginning to cross, did

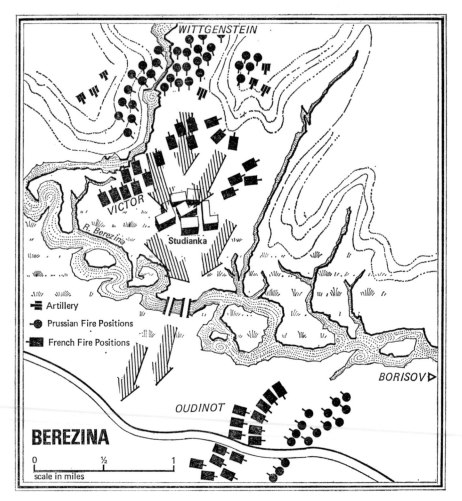

the Russians make a determined attack. Chichagov had heard of the activity around Studianka on 27th November, but had put it down as another diversion, and had remained at the village of Shabashovichi some twenty miles to the south on the west bank. He moved up far too late. Wittgenstein, reaching Kostritza on 27th November was much nearer to the crossing point. But he then made his biggest mistake of all. Instead of thrusting directly at Napoleon, Wittgenstein decided to move east round the French and attack from the rear, believing that Admiral Chichagov would stop the crossing from the other bank. Clausewitz was not with the army at the time, having been left further north with many of Wittgenstein's troops to cover the left flank. This absence of part of his force may have influenced Wittgenstein's decision. Another reason was his fear of Napoleon. Clausewitz half acknowledged this, writing that Wittgenstein's roundabout route "showed a certain timidity, a too great anxiety to preserve his corps from all injury." Clausewitz commented: "On this occasion, General Wittgenstein cannot be acquitted of a certain share in the escape of Bonaparte." He added: "On the 27th, Wittgenstein could not indeed have stopped the passage completely, but he might have made the French loss much greater."[9]

Clausewitz arrived during the early afternoon of 28th November, when the Russian attacks on the remainder of the French force on the east bank were still taking place. It was a hopeless, one-sided affair. The French were only intent upon escaping across the swirling Berezina. Even Victor's troops were stricken with panic. Clausewitz now saw one of the blackest sights in all history, there upon the banks of the Berezina. The first French troops to cross had done so in good order, with the Guards still maintaining their discipline. But confusion soon increased, and when the attacks by Count Wittgenstein's troops and the Cossacks began late on the 27th, confusion became chaos. The bridges were inadequate and the over-worked French engineers had to carry out one desperate repair after another. The thousands of people milling around the frail structures, pushing, struggling, screaming for a foothold, quickly went beserk. Those clinging to the edges were mercilessly hacked down by the Cossacks; those packed into a solid mass in the centre were blown to pieces by cannon fire from the Russian guns, dozens of Frenchmen torn apart by a single shell. Men and women who were already weak and insensible from hunger, clawed at one another, climbed over one another, in their frantic attempts to reach the sanctuary of the shaking bridges. Hundreds were trampled under foot and suffocated in the blood-stained slush.

Apart from the fighting troops who remained from Victor's division, at least 25,000 people tried to cross on the 28th when Clausewitz reached the area. They included women and their children, some of whom had fled from Moscow with the French, others the wives of soldiers who had accompanied their husbands on the campaign and who had been trailing behind the army. The men were mostly half-dead, many with limbs lost in battle or through frost-bite. All were half starved; none were armed. These non-combatants were hemmed in between the river and the Russian army, all attempting to funnel on to the two makeshift bridges. Into this mass were crammed carts, waggons, sledges, carriages.

Early on the 28th one of the bridges collapsed. Frantic efforts were made to repair it, but by midday it was impassable.[10] The other was so narrow it could only take two or three people abreast. It was growing colder, perceptibly, and the river was icing over, but not sufficiently to walk on. Many tried to swim, but perished in the freezing currents. Others waded out and tried to clamber on the bridge further from the bank, but as they grasped the wood their hands were kicked and cut by those struggling to cross. Early on the 29th Clausewitz saw thousands of people still left on the east bank. At nine-o'clock French engineers destroyed the remaining bridge, despite the indescribable shrieks of those left stranded. The Russians closed in. Trampled by horses, slaughtered by bullet or cannon fire, frozen to the ground by the deteriorating weather, men and women were stripped by the Cossacks and thrown in the snow—they died in many different and terrible ways. Clausewitz, riding in the middle of it all, saw the hundreds of stiffening corpses, the dying, the phantom-like humans who screamed out for food and help. He wept as he rode among them. "What ghastly scenes have I witnessed here," he wrote to Marie. "If my feelings had not been hardened it would have sent me mad. Even so, it will take many years before I can remember what I have seen without feeling a shuddering horror."[11] He wrote in his memoirs: "I felt as if I could never be released from the terrible impressions of the spectacle. I only saw a small fraction of the famous retreat, but in this fraction of some three days' march, all the horrors of the movement were accumulated."[12] Amid the panorama of death were thousands of fearful incidents; one man crawled to the broken bridges, the raw stumps of his legs leaving two red trails in the snow; a woman, who had fallen half through the ice had frozen there, one of her arms half severed, the other clutching a breathing, suckling baby.[13]

"Wittgenstein took about 10,000 prisoners on those two days, among them an entire division," said Clausewitz.[14] But most of the captives could not possibly have been fit to fight: Napoleon had already taken his best men across. As for the rest, it was estimated that over 10,000 people died upon the banks of the Berezina.[15] When news of the disaster filtered out, sympathy for the French grew in some sections of European society; the Russians were criticized for their barbarity at the Berezina and for their alleged burning of Moscow. Clausewitz reacted with indignation. "I hear we are being condemned," he wrote to Marie. "In God's name, anyone present at the scenes of these tragedies, anyone who has seen the misery, does not feel that any condemnation is justified when the German Government has contributed to the distress and pain."[16]

Bonaparte had managed to bring 60,000 people over the river, including some sick and wounded, and was joined on the other side by a further 20,000 who had remained on the flanks. But of this 80,000 total, half were to perish on the next stretch of the retreat between the Berezina and Vilna. Even more than before, it was bad weather and hunger, rather than Russian sabres, which slaughtered the French. Of those who clung to life, thousands had lost hands, feet, noses and ears from the appalling frost. Their skin turned purple, then blue-brown and finally black as it rotted from their bodies. Fingers and toes snapped off like dead twigs. According to a German soldier serving with the French: "Ravages of cold were equalled by those of hunger. No food was so rotten or disgusting as not to find someone to relish it. No fallen horse or cattle remained uneaten, no dog, no cat, no carrion, nor indeed the corpses of those that died of cold or hunger. It was not unknown even for men to gnaw at their own famished bodies."[17] Some went insane. Most lapsed into lethargy, known as "the Moscow depression." Others, those most likely to survive, degenerated into mere animals.

The cold often brought enemies together as men from both armies huddled around the same roadside fires. The Russians suffered almost as much as the French. They too were starving, Clausewitz said, "since we could not send on far in advance, and our continual progress made it impossible to fetch supplies from any distance on the flanks." He added: "I saw the road, which had only been passed by the advance guard, already marked out by bodies of Russians who had collapsed under the cold and fatigue." Clausewitz's face was scarred by the biting cold, and remained marked for the rest of his life. "Wittgenstein lost a good quarter of his force in the last four weeks," Clausewitz wrote. "He had left Czasnicki with 40,000 and reached Vilna with scarcely 30,000."[18]

After the Berezina and before Morodochno, the temperature never rose above twenty-six degrees below zero. After Morodochno, it dropped even lower; when the French reached Vilna, the temperature fell to nearly forty degrees below zero. Many of the French units had simply ceased to exist by that time. General Loison, whose troops were among the first to reach the town on 9th December, tried to defend it against the Russians who arrived next day, but 12,000 of his 15,000 men had perished from cold and hunger in the space of just three days. Even the Guard was reduced to fewer than 500 men. Most of those still alive were quite unable to offer any kind of resistance: gunners and cavalrymen with their hands frozen off, infantry-men with their feet half rotted away. Nor, despite a number of incredible efforts, were the Russians themselves capable of fighting. Many units suffered worse than Wittgenstein's force, and the main Russian army found it impossible to go beyond Vilna. Fewer than one third of the men who had left Maloyaroslavets with Kutuzov ever reached Vilna; continued opposition was mainly undertaken by the Cossacks. Two massive national armies had been destroyed, not by battle, but by hostile weather. The Russian winter was no colder than in normal years, but the men were ill-equipped to fight it. They had marched on and on, French and Russians, Poles and Prussians, Italians, Westphalians, Bavarians, until they could go no further.

On 14th December, Napoleon's army crossed the Niemen, watched with horror by the French units who had been left to guard the river. Count Louis Philippe Ségur gave this terrible description: "Instead of the 400,000 companions who had fought so many successful battles with them, who had swept so masterfully into Russia, they saw emerging from the white, ice-bound wilderness only 1,000 infantrymen and troopers under arms, nine cannon, and 20,000 stragglers dressed in rags, with bowed heads, dull eyes, ashen, cadaverous faces and long, ice-stiffened beards. This was the Grand

Army."[19] Napoleon was not present to watch the death throes of his army. He learned of the last tragic events when he was in Paris. On 6th December he had left his force in the small town of Smorgona, leaving Murat in command and travelling on in a sled with Caulaincourt. In Warsaw, referring to the tragedy, Napoleon coined a *cliché*. "There is only one step from the sublime to the ridiculous," he said. Napoleon had urgent business to attend to. Europe might rise up against him on all sides to take advantage of his defeat in Russia: a new French army must quickly be created. There was the threat, too, from Prussia. If Friedrich Wilhelm tore up his alliance with France, if the Prussian army which was still fighting for France were to change sides, then Napoleon's entire European empire would be in danger of ruin.

Clausewitz was soon to help try and bring about this Prussian switch. The effort had been made before by others, including Tiedemann. At the first news of Napoleon's difficulties in Russia, General Yorck, who had replaced Grawert on 13th August as commander of the Prussian troops, had been approached by Essen, the commandant at Riga. Essen had urged General Yorck to turn upon Marshal Alexandre Macdonald, arrest him and throw him into the fortress at Riga. Yorck did not even bother to reply. He had already made known his attitude to this kind of plan in his comments upon Tiedemann's unfortunate death: "It is a good thing that he is dead; now we shall have more peace. In the last days of his life he also made himself contemptible, not only by often inciting our troops to desertion—in vain, fortunately—but by shamefully proposing to Major Crammon on the 6th [of August] at Schlock that he and his battalion should capitulate."[20] When Paulucci succeeded Essen as Governor of Riga, he too had failed to persuade General Yorck to shift his allegiance.

But now two new factors had to be considered: the French defeat and the shaky relationship between Yorck and his superior commander, Macdonald. As the remnants of the main French army struggled on towards the River Niemen, the Russians feared that Macdonald might move down from near Riga to give them cover. Wittgenstein therefore received orders to move north-east to cut Macdonald off. In fact, Clausewitz said, Macdonald had received no order from Napoleon to come south. His instructions were not sent until Murat had issued them at Vilna, and even then the orders did not reach Mittau until 18th December. The messenger, a Prussian, was frightened of falling into Russian hands and made a detour via Tilsit. Meanwhile Macdonald was greatly agitated, his worries increased by the crisis between himself and General Yorck and the consequent lack of trust that he had in the Prussian army. On 19th December, having received Murat's order from Vilna, and confirmation of the terrible rumours whispered about the fate of the Grand Army, Macdonald moved south. He split his army into four columns, three of which were formed from Prussian troops under Generals Massenbach, Kleist and Yorck. The roads were bad, and the snow lying

Facing page: top *A smoky view of the Battle of Borodino*; bottom *another view of the same*
Overleaf: *The appalling horrors of the retreat from Moscow*

Above *Casualties of the French retreat from Moscow*

Left *The Russian commander, General Mikhail Kutuzov (1745–1813)*

Below *Napoleon watches the burning of Moscow from the ramparts of the Kremlin*

thick on the ground. Yorck was separated from Macdonald by about six miles.

The Russians were already moving up to meet Macdonald's army. Having given his exhausted troops some rest at Niemzin, Count Wittgenstein had begun his march on 17th December, heading towards Georgenburg by way of Kiedany. In view of the expected clash with the oncoming French, Wittgenstein had pushed out two smaller corps in addition to the usual advance guard. One of these corps, consisting mainly of Cossacks, was commanded by General Diebitsch, whom Clausewitz served as chief staff officer. By 20th December, this corps had reached Koltiniani. The Russians had no idea of Macdonald's exact location. They guessed that he would be moving towards Memel in order to use the Curische Haff, the narrow strip of land between the lake at the Niemen estuary, and the sea. General Diebitsch therefore advanced in that direction only to discover that Macdonald was already behind him. He turned about and marched to Verni and decided to try to intercept Macdonald next day at Koltiniani. After an early start, Diebitsch's corps reached the town at ten o'clock in the morning, where the General learned that the main Franco-Prussian force had already passed through. But the rearguard had still to come; Diebitsch planned to cut it off. For Clausewitz, this decision brought a personal dilemma. His brothers Friedrich and Wilhelm were serving with the Prussians; and he believed that Friedrich, a Major, might be commanding this rearguard which he and the Russians were about to attack. The prospect was horrible. The Prussians would be outnumbered, and his brother might be killed or captured. Clausewitz believed that Friedrich's capture would be almost as intolerable as his wounding or death. "The thought of seeing him taken prisoner was more painful than that of being opposed to him under fire."[21]

Clausewitz was therefore "indescribably satisfied" to discover from captured Prussian stragglers that the enemy they were about to engage was commanded by General Kleist. But the Russians also learned that this rearguard consisted of far more men that they had thought: four battalions of infantry, two cavalry squadrons and an artillery battery. They themselves, with only 1,400 men, would be the outnumbered force. General Diebitsch decided upon a deception, and asked Clausewitz to ride forward and try to arrange a truce with Kleist; the Prussian General might then believe that he, and not Diebitsch, was in the inferior position. "I replied that as a Russian officer, I was ready to undertake any duty assigned to me. But it would be better if a Livonian or a Courlander should go, who could speak German, and who would be more acceptable to General Kleist than one of the Prussian officers who had left the Prussian service to the great annoyance of most of the Prussian commanders."[22]

General Diebitsch agreed, and another officer, Major von Reune, was sent instead. Reune was instructed to tell Kleist that his road ahead was blocked by a considerable Russian force, and that talks should be held to avoid useless bloodshed. Reune did so. Kleist replied that he had no authority to negotiate, since his superior officer, General Yorck, was not far behind. This indiscreet admission revealed to Diebitsch and Clausewitz that their small force stood in the very centre of Macdonald's whole deployment, somewhere between Macdonald and his Prussian corps. This made Diebitsch's position extremely dangerous from a military point of view, but it offered the chance of opening armistice talks between the Russians and Prussians. Clausewitz believed that "the possibility of coming to an understanding with the Prussians was of highest value."[23]

Generals Yorck and Kleist had 10,000 men between them. In their front, at Koltiniani less than a mile from their forward troops, was Diebitsch with his 1,400 Cossacks. Macdonald, with 4,000 men, was six miles on the far side of Koltiniani. Macdonald's other corps, under Grandjean and totalling 6,000 men, was at Tauroggen, four miles to the south of Koltiniani, and on the far side of the town from Yorck. The Prussian General was therefore without support. If he could be persuaded that he was severely threatened—indeed, as he lacked a strong cavalry force of his own, Diebitsch's Cossacks could cause much damage—he might agree to talk. Clausewitz wrote: "These considerations, however, under different circumstances, would not have caused General Yorck to pause for an instant." But this time the Russians hoped that he would use the situation as an excuse for an agreement.

Growing anxious about Yorck and the whereabouts of the Russians, Marshal Macdonald was hesitating in his advance south. He sent scouts to try and reach the Prussian Corps which was following him, in order to acquire information. Each was intercepted by the Russians. Both Yorck and Macdonald were kept in ignorance of what the other was doing. Yorck met Kleist during the early evening of Christmas Day, was informed of the contact with the Russians, and agreed to talk with General Diebitsch himself. That same evening Clausewitz rode forward with Diebitsch; they arrived at the Prussian camp at sunset. The two Prussian generals, representing enemy sides, were closeted privately together while Clausewitz waited outside.

Diebitsch told Clausewitz on the ride back to their camp that Yorck had not given a firm answer to the armistice proposal. Diebitsch had told him frankly of the size of the Russian force under his command, and had said that while he could not hope to stop Yorck completely, he could sever the Prussian baggage train and artillery. He also outlined to Yorck the terrible condition of the main French army; and told him that the Czar had ordered that the Prussians were not to be treated in the same fashion as the French. Finally, Diebitsch had offered to give up any advantages he might have through the present military position, if Prussian neutrality could be secured. Yorck had refused to commit himself. But he had hinted, Diebitsch told Clausewitz, that he might eventually come to an agreement if he could preserve the honour of his force. At the moment he could not justify such an action. In the meantime the two generals had agreed there should be no military action during the night. In the morning, to give Yorck more time to think, the Prussian general would make a reconnaissance and march towards Lavkove, as if attempting to turn the Russian flank; Diebitsch would counteract this by moving to Schelel, so that the Russians would again be in front of the Prussian force. At the end of the meeting Yorck had said: "You have a number of Prussian officers with you: send me one of them the next time."[24] Asked whether he would be willing to undertake this role, Clausewitz agreed.

Back at Koltiniani, which they reached at about ten o'clock at night, Diebitsch asked Clausewitz for his opinion of Yorck. Clausewitz had encountered the fifty-three-year-old General a number of times, for example when he had been Scharnhorst's *aide* and Yorck had commanded the light infantry; and also when Yorck had been advising on the infantry sections of the 1812 Regulations which Clausewitz had helped draft. Hans David Ludwig Yorck von Wartenburg had been born at Königsberg and originally his family had come from England. He had not belonged to the inner group of Prussian reformers. Some of Scharnhorst's ideas were, he thought, ill-advised, for example the admission of the *bourgeoisie* into the officer corps. But after the 1806 campaign, in which he had fought bravely, he fully realized the need for tactical improvements. Initially Julius von Grawert had commanded the Prussian army serving under Napoleon in 1812, following a suggestion by Bonaparte himself. But Grawert had suffered poor health, and increasing doubts were felt about his ability to withstand French pressure. Apparently upon Scharnhorst's advice Yorck had been appointed to the unusual position of Second Commanding General. General Grawert fell ill and Yorck assumed full command. Not long after, Macdonald's Tenth Corps, into which the Prussians had been incorporated on 6th June, had crossed the Russian frontier.

Yorck could now make the momentous decision which could radically alter affairs, not only in Prussia, but in Europe too. If he acted with sufficient boldness the indecision which had paralyzed Prussia in 1805, 1809 and 1812, which had led to the catastrophe of 1806 and to Prussia's alliance with the French, could now finally be ended. Clausewitz had mixed feelings about Yorck. He said Yorck had "a fiery and passionate will, hidden by apparent coldness; a powerful ambition, suppressed by constant resignation. He was distinguished by strength and boldness of character. He was honest." Then Clausewitz added: "But he was gloomy, choleric and reserved, and a bad subordinate. He did not make friends easily. He was motivated by the desire for fame, and his natural abilities supplied the means for it. His worst feature was, that under the guise of being downright and straightforward he was in fact close and reserved. He talked loudly when he felt unsure, and was despondent when confident." Clausewitz concluded: "He was unquestionably one of the most distinguished men of our [the Prussian] army."[25]

Clausewitz felt that he must warn Diebitsch of Yorck's "close disposition." He said: "I was much afraid that the General might make use of the night to put us to rout and force his way through to Macdonald. I therefore advised Diebitsch to take great care." This was done. Two Cossack regiments were posted in front of Yorck, with a third to the Russian rear. Cavalry horses were kept harnessed, the men ready to fight.

During Christmas night it seemed as if Clausewitz's misgivings had been correct. "We had dismounted at a house, lain down upon straw without undressing, and had just closed our eyes, when pistol shots were fired in the village and in our rear. They were not single shots, but a general discharge lasting some minutes. We jumped up, and I said to myself: 'That is Yorck on our rear, as I guessed he would be.' We mounted."[26] Rushing through the dark to where the skirmish had taken place, Clausewitz found that it had been another Prussian patrol sent by Massenbach to try and reach Yorck with a message from Macdonald. The patrol had clashed with Cossacks outside Koltiniani, then the Prussians had reined their horses around and had disappeared into the darkness of the night.

Dawn on 26th December saw the start of the charade of moving both the Prussian and Russian forces while Yorck wondered what to do. But the operation went wrong, almost with serious results. Instead of marching in the direction agreed with Diebitsch, Yorck went towards Schelel because the roads were bad and because he did not wish to put his horses and men to unnecessary hardship. Partly in view of Clausewitz's warning the night before, General Diebitsch was suspicious. "A lively interchange of flags of truce was the result," said Clausewitz, "in which I was constantly employed."[27] Clausewitz's first attempt to open negotiations with Yorck about a switch to Prussian neutrality was a failure. Yorck refused to see him for fear of compromising himself, and reprimanded the officer at the outpost for having allowed Clausewitz to enter the Prussian positions without special permission. But it was all part of the charade. As Clausewitz said: "This was a comedy."[28] Yet he was fully aware of the implications. If General Yorck agreed to talks, his personal situation would be critical. If negotiations were successful and if the Prussian army left the French, Yorck would have committed the most outrageous act of treason imaginable—if Friedrich Wilhelm chose to regard it so. Clausewitz waited. At last, General Yorck sent an officer to start the discussions with him. To Clausewitz's great delight, the officer was "one of my most intimate friends," Friedrich von Dohna, husband of Scharnhorst's daughter Julia; he had been joint *aide-de-camp* to "The General" with Clausewitz in Berlin.

Dohna was not serving with Yorck. He, like Clausewitz, had left the Prussian service in 1812. He was now a Lieutenant-Colonel in the newly formed Russo-German Legion to which Clausewitz had been invited as staff officer. Legionary troops under General Lewis had followed Yorck from Riga, and Dohna's superior officer had sent him forward to Yorck as a negotiator. From what Dohna told Clausewitz, it appeared that Yorck was seriously considering an agreement, but wished to postpone it, briefly, while he moved nearer to the Prussian frontier. Apart from the fact that he was awaiting the return of an *aide* whom he had sent to Berlin for instructions, it would make a better military show if he tried once or twice again to unite with Macdonald before coming to terms with the Russians. Unwittingly, Macdonald was encouraging an agreement between the Russians and Prussians. Had he remained in Tauroggen and Vainati, Clausewitz said, where he was on Christmas day, or had he returned there on 26th December, negotiations would have been impossible: Yorck would have had no reason for not joining with the French. But because Macdonald continued his march, the Russians remained between the two forces, and Yorck could still suggest that he had been "deserted by Macdonald." While appreciating this point, Diebitsch was still alarmed about the delay in coming to terms. He was still suspicious of General Yorck; and should he be manoeuvred so that the Prussian General could suddenly seize Tilsit, Diebitsch would find it difficult to explain himself. General Yorck continued to delay reaching a decision; and he was steadily but slowly advancing on Diebitsch: the Russians were forced to move back to Schelel on the 26th, Pagermont on the 27th, and through Tauroggen to Villkischken on the 28th, only two miles from Tilsit, and Yorck was at Tauroggen. Only a light screen of Cossacks was deployed between them; little could have prevented a union of the two forces. Yorck was certainly inclined to reach an agreement with the Russians, if he could get away with it, but he faced another difficulty in joining up with Macdonald: he had already compromised himself to some extent by not having done so before.

On the night of 28th December, Clausewitz rode to see Yorck, but still without any result. On the 29th, he tried again, taking with him two documents which were to take the shape of an ultimatum. The first document was a communication from General d'Auvray, Wittgenstein's chief of staff, addressed to General Diebitsch. It reprimanded Diebitsch for not having finished the talks with Yorck; more important, it added that on New Year's Eve, Wittgenstein's advance guard would be at Schillupischken, and Wittgenstein himself nearby at Sommeran. The main Russian force would then be deployed on the road west from Tilsit, cutting off the retreat of Macdonald and Yorck to Königsberg. The letter finished with a personal message to Yorck: should he continue to hesitate, the Russians would treat him as any other hostile commander "and all question of friendly agreement on any conditions would henceforth cease."[29] The second document was a letter from Macdonald to the Duke of Bassane, which had been intercepted by Wittgenstein's scouts. Dated 10th December at Stalgen, it told Yorck exactly what Macdonald and the French thought of him and his Prussians. "The shell has at last burst with General Yorck," Macdonald had written. "I consider that unless the gentlemen of the Prussian staff can explain themselves, it is my duty to show more firmness. The body is sound, but they are ruining it. The spirit is prodigiously changed." The French General continued: "Just a few favours, a few rewards, and I shall easily set it up again, provided of course that the officers as specified are promptly thrown out. They will not be missed, because two-thirds of the army detest them."[30] Diebitsch and Clausewitz calculated that this letter, with its arrogance, its attitude of French master to Prussian dogs would anger the proud Yorck sufficiently for him to push the French aside.

And so Clausewitz arrived once again at Yorck's headquarters for the critical meeting, perhaps their last chance of reaching an agreement. Yorck was in a foul temper. Just before Clausewitz had arrived he had been given a message from a French trooper who had managed to slip past the Russians. The note, from Macdonald, was terse and supercilious: "General Yorck is expected with impatience at Tilsit."[31] Yorck's excuse for talking with the Russians, that he had received no orders from Macdonald, was now gone. Nor had he received instructions from Berlin, despite his urgent request. He did not know what to do, and he was angry as a result. As Clausewitz had said: "He talked loudly when he felt unsure." So, as Clausewitz went into his room, Yorck spoke in an extremely loud voice.

"Get out," he bellowed. "I have quite finished with you. Your damned Cossacks have let a letter from Macdonald get through, ordering me to unite with him. So all doubt is finished. Your troops do not arrive. You are too weak. I have to march. Now please, I want no more talk, or I shall lose my head." Quietly, Clausewitz replied: "I cannot answer that. But please allow me a candle, since I have some letters to show you." Yorck hesitated. Clausewitz added: "Your Excellency surely will not put me in the embarrassing position of having to leave without executing my mission." Yorck called for more candles, and ordered Colonel Reeder, his Chief of Staff, to come in from the antechamber. The letters were read out; a moment of silence followed. Abruptly, Yorck said: "Clausewitz, you are a Prussian. Do you really believe that d'Auvray's letter is honest? Can Wittgenstein's troops really be in those positions on 31st? Can you honourably swear to it?"

"I give Your Excellency my word for the honesty of the letter, based on what I know of General d'Auvray and the other officers in Wittgenstein's headquarters. I cannot swear that the deployment will be carried out exactly as he says, because as Your Excellency knows, in war one is apt to fall behind schedule."

Yorck fell silent again for a moment. Then he put out his hand to Clausewitz. "Yes. You have me. Tell General Diebitsch we shall talk early tomorrow at Poscherun Mill, and that I have now firmly decided to separate from the French and their cause."

A time was fixed for eight o'clock the following morning. Clausewitz turned to leave. Yorck called after him: "I will not do things by halves. I shall get Massenbach as well for you." He called in an officer from General

Massenbach's cavalry, and pacing up and down he asked: "What say your regiments?" The officer was enthusiastic about the idea of being rid of the French alliance, and he added: "Every man in the unit feels the same." "You young ones can talk," General Yorck replied. "My old head is shaking on my shoulders."[32]

Clausewitz returned to headquarters, and excitedly told Diebitsch the news. Then he had a hurried meal, and returned to tell Yorck that Diebitsch agreed to the meeting at eight o'clock the next day, 30th December. In the morning Clausewitz went with Diebitsch and Count von Dohna to the Mill at Poscherun. After waiting anxiously for an hour, they saw Yorck riding up with Colonel von Reeder and his *aide-de-camp*, Major von Seydlitz. Fittingly, all those present at the signing of the historic Convention of Tauroggen were Prussians. From now on, Prussia's army would be neutral in the struggle between Russia and France. It was to be assigned to a district in Prussian Lithuania on the Russian frontier. If Friedrich Wilhelm were to reject the Convention, it was agreed that the army would refuse to serve against the Russians for a period of two months.[33] "It was," said Clausewitz, "a wonderfully pleasant feeling."[34] Diebitsch flung his arms about Clausewitz's neck and wept with relief when the talks were successfully completed.

Elated with the Convention and with his reunion with his fellow-Prussians, including his brothers Fritz and Wilhelm, Clausewitz wrote to Marie from Tauroggen: "I write to you with marvellous feelings from this place, dearest Marie, from which I stepped onto Russian soil nine months ago—the Prussian headquarters. You will easily understand what came to bring me here from the news you will have got by the time this arrives. I have found my brothers, and they are well, in body and soul; and I am honoured, decorated with medals, although not French! I have had a beautiful day of re-union. Tomorrow Fate will separate us again, but at least now we will not oppose one another."[35]

The Convention of Tauroggen had immense implications in the military, diplomatic, and internal Prussian political fields. It was the first step in the War of Liberation. The course of military operations was immediately altered. With Yorck's 14,000 troops, Macdonald could have stopped the Russians from holding up Napoleon's assembly of new armies in East Prussia and Silesia. Before, Napoleon had had the whole of Germany for his operational base; now the centre of this base, Prussia, was no longer reliable. Instead, the French were compelled to withdraw further back out of Prussia, which in turn allowed the Russians to cross their frontier unmolested and to penetrate what was formerly Napoleon's territory. On the diplomatic side, Napoleon could now expect a Prussian declaration of war against him. Boyen wrote: "Without Tauroggen and the rising of the East Prussian estates, Scharnhorst would very likely have failed to overcome the French party and the King's indecision."[36]

The Convention was one of the few, and the most important, of the actions taken in the years of Prussian reform which was in flagrant disregard of the King's wishes. Clausewitz described General Yorck's decision as one of the most daring in history because of its violation of rules and tradition. Yorck had broken an alliance signed by his King, had placed the King's army in a neutral position—both without Frederick Wilhelm's consent. Indeed, down through the years since 1812, Yorck's action has been praised in Germany by those who have held that the head of state did not have final authority over matters of state conscience; and Yorck's decision has been condemned by those who believed that the head of state did have such ultimate power. Others have argued that Yorck acted, believing that it was what Friedrich Wilhelm wanted.[37] Others have believed that Yorck followed secret instructions sent by the King. Neither of these theories has been proved. Yorck received no guidance from Berlin, and indeed he deplored the lack of it. When orders concerning the changed military and political situation reached him on 29th December, they were vague, apart from stating that if a retreat to East Prussia was necessary, Yorck was once again to govern the province.[38] Clausewitz certainly did not believe Yorck was signing under secret orders from his King.

Immediately after the Convention was agreed, Yorck wrote a long letter to Friedrich Wilhelm explaining his action. "I willingly lay my head at your Majesty's feet if I have done wrong. I would die with joy and resignation at least to avoid having failed in my duty as a true Prussian and faithful subject. Now or never is the moment when Your Majesty may tear yourself from the extravagant demands of an ally whose intentions towards Prussia, in the event of his success, were involved in a mystery which justified anxiety. This is the view by which I have been guided. Heaven grant that it may lead to the welfare of our country!"[39]

While awaiting a reply, Yorck wrote two other important letters, one to his fellow-Prussian, General Massenbach, the other to his French superior, General Macdonald, in which he told them both of what he had done. Massenbach, at Tilsit, after some hesitation, marched to join forces with Yorck. Macdonald, said Clausewitz, "behaved himself very nobly" when he heard the news of the loss of the Prussian troops. Those remaining with his French corps were allowed to leave to join their countrymen. The Prussians as a whole, Clausewitz continued, gave the decision to become neutral a joyful reception. For Clausewitz himself, the Convention meant no change in his employment. Before he could rejoin Prussian service, he would need the King's consent. And for the moment, Friedrich Wilhelm refused even to acknowledge the existence of the Convention, and he began to take action against Yorck.

Meanwhile, upon hearing of the Prussian secession, Macdonald had hurried from Tilsit to Mehlaucken, aiming to retreat to Königsberg. General Diebitsch and the other forward unit of Wittgenstein's pursuing army were close behind. But the Russian advance guard, under General Scheppelov, made a drastic blunder, marching on 31st December to Szillen instead of Schillupischken because he confused the names. He was immediately deprived of his command. The Russian pursuit slowed. The troops were exhausted, the roads were bad, communication lines were over-extended. Above all, it seemed all over.

On New Year's Day, 1813, General Yorck had entered Tilsit to rest and refit his men. Word of Friedrich Wilhelm's disapproval reached him there a week later. Clausewitz believed that one reason for the King's opposition to the Convention was the lack of full information in Berlin about the extent of the French disaster.[40] Undoubtedly, Friedrich Wilhelm was still frightened of Napoleon and of what the Emperor would do as a reprisal for Prussia's action. Added to this there was the King's natural hesitation; and the dislike of agreeing to something which had been forced upon him by one of his generals. Whatever the reason, in mid-January Lieutenant-Colonel von Natzmer, the King's *aide-de-camp*, arrived at Wittgenstein's headquarters with a message for Yorck, whose positions were behind those of the Russians. Wittgenstein demanded to know the nature of the message. He was told in reply that Yorck was to be removed from command, and replaced by General Kleist, and that there was to be a full inquiry into Yorck's conduct.

General Yorck's reaction was straightforward and determined: he refused to give up his command. Believing that Macdonald was massing troops at Danzig and might turn upon his Russian pursuers, Yorck was prepared to disregard his new neutrality and help Wittgenstein. On 8th January he entered Königsberg. Five days later he wrote to Bülow: "What kind of opinions are held in Berlin? Have men stooped so low that they dare not break the chains of slavery that we have meekly worn for the past five years? Now or never, we must regain our liberty and honour. With bleeding heart I tear the bonds of obedience and wage war on my own."[41] It was a repeat of Schill's action in 1809, only on a massive scale. Ordering part of his forces west to cover Danzig, Yorck proceeded to enlist help in the neighbouring districts. The strongest support of all came from Stein, who was now back from advising the Czar. There was no time to lose, said Stein; the country had to be prepared, the army made ready, the people organized, for the War of Liberation.

While the King continued to hesitate, Stein and Yorck began their work, in which Clausewitz was to be involved almost at once. Yorck was a rebel. So too were those who helped him, including Clausewitz. They had turned upon their King, or so Friedrich Wilhelm believed; but that mattered little, because to them Prussia, the Fatherland, came first. Now was the chance to obliterate the shame of Jena and Auerstädt, and avenge the humiliation of the long years that had followed. As Yorck said, it was now or never.

ELEVEN

Eighteen Thirteen

"We may be sure that it was not
overlooked by the bold
Bonaparte—that he was keenly
aware of the terror which the
appearance of his sword inspired."
(*On War*, bk. ii, ch. v.)

CLAUSEWITZ STRONGLY SUPPORTED Stein's belief that to defeat Napoleon and liberate Prussia, all reforms put forward after 1806 should be fully put into practice, and that the whole Prussian nation should be rallied to make war upon the French. This national organization, this enlistment of all Prussian people, was started at Königsberg, although the King still seemed determined to act against Yorck and to help the French. As late as 24th January, 1813, Napoleon told Eugène Beauharnais that he expected Friedrich Wilhelm to supply him with much-needed cavalry.

The means of organizing the people would be the militia and the *levée en masse*. At Stein's invitation, Clausewitz hurriedly prepared a scheme for this comprehensive use of the nation's entire manpower. Based upon the ideas of Scharnhorst and Gneisenau, and upon his own opinions already put forward in the third *Bekenntnis* of 1812, Clausewitz drafted detailed proposals for the *Landwehr* and the *Landsturm*. The *Landwehr* was to supplement the strength of the main armies, and the *Landsturm* was to act as an irregular insurrectionary force. Men aged between eighteen and forty would be recruited into the *Landwehr*, in a proportion of one to every fifty citizens. The recruits would be armed with rifles, and provided with a cartridge pouch and hatchet, and would wear the insignia of their corps. They would be divided into companies and battalions; one battalion, of about 1,000 men, could be used in conjunction with each regular regiment. Clausewitz therefore believed that the *Landwehr* would enable the regular armies to achieve numerical superiority. Older men aged between forty and sixty, would be enlisted into the *Landsturm*. The role of this force would be to support the main armies by all possible means: enemy communication lines would be attacked, enemy tax commissioners killed, sabotage and guerrilla operations carried out.[1]

Clausewitz worked on this project in Konigsberg throughout January. The scheme would apply specifically to East Prussia, but he envisaged that it might provide a model for the rest of the country. The need for such an organization was becoming daily more apparent. Napoleon was busily engaged on one of his most remarkable feats: the creation of a new army within the space of four months. As Caulaincourt wrote, "France was one vast workshop." Napoleon's aim was to raise no less than 656,000 troops. Already, in the previous November, he had ordered a new conscription for 1813, which he estimated would produce 137,000 recruits; and even on the terrible road from Moscow he had ordered that extra National Guard units should be raised which would total a further 80,000 men.

By the end of January, Clausewitz was hard at work finishing his *Essential Points in the Organization of a Defence Force and a Militia*. In this, he envisaged that most of the male population of Lithuania, East and West Prussia should be enrolled in the *Landwehr* and *Landsturm*. Clausewitz had been given every encouragement by General Yorck, who was still in command at Königsberg in direct defiance of the King's wishes.

Yorck had written again to Friedrich Wilhelm, early in January: "Your Royal Majesty's kingdom, though smaller than in the year 1805, is destined to become the liberator and protector of your people and of all Germans."[2] Friedrich Wilhelm disagreed, but Yorck carried on his work regardless. One young officer in Yorck's army even went so far as to write to his father in distinctly treasonable terms: "Our King sits inactive in Berlin. He pays not the slightest attention to us here. But I hope General Yorck will act ... Everyone watches with high expectations. He is now our King. He concludes peace and makes war. There is already little love lost for our King; if he does not declare against France now, anything might happen."[3] Indeed, Friedrich Wilhelm dared not proceed against the Königsberg rebels: his fear of the possible reaction was only equalled by his fear of Napoleon if he did not act.

General Yorck called a special session of the East Prussian states. Appearing in person before it, he demanded the formation of a *Landwehr* of 20,000 men with 10,000 reserves, chosen and organized in the manner which Clausewitz had suggested. At the same time a special military commission, chaired by Yorck, examined the details of Clausewitz's scheme. The project was fully approved, but the commission made some additional suggestions, including one for an exemption system, which Clausewitz disagreed with. Nevertheless, Clausewitz's draft was still substantially the basis of the system finally adopted by the East Prussian states on 9th February. The whole area at once began to organize itself.

With the adoption of this plan to put civilians into uniform, East Prussia was virtually committed to the War of Liberation. Friedrich Wilhelm realized that he could hesitate no longer. Other provinces, apart from East Prussia, were becoming restless. The King was in danger of being disregarded by his own people: if he failed to act soon, the Prussian people would act for him. Everywhere the people were turning against the French. Napoleon's soldiers, still filtering painfully back through the countryside from Russia, were abused. Berlin was no longer safe for French troops. Street urchins jeered at those who had survived the Russian winter. Cavalrymen who had lost their mounts were insulted by offers of help to lead their non-existent horses, and the urchins offered shoe-shines to the infantrymen who hobbled through the city with bare, frost-bitten feet. The King had already taken one definite step, by authorizing the formation of volunteer *Jäger* detachments on 3rd February. The reformers had long sought his permission for this. Friedrich Wilhelm had also left Berlin for Breslau, to place himself further from the clutches of the French. But he still stopped short of a firm decision to go to war.

Scharnhorst was now back at the King's side, and he stepped in with decisive influence. The Austrian envoy at the Prussian court reported on 25th February: "The day before yesterday, General von Scharnhorst assured me that the King, after a long private struggle, had finally acquiesced in his view."[4] Faced with the prospect of a massive popular uprising, which was already being organized in East Prussia, Friedrich Wilhelm at last signed an offensive and defensive alliance with Czar Alexander, at Kalisch on 26th February. By the terms of the alliance, Russia undertook to provide 150,000 men, and Prussia would send a minimum of 80,000 regular troops to the field. The Convention of Tauroggen had been vindicated. The news was received at Königsberg with jubiliation and massive relief. A Board of Inquiry soon exonerated Yorck, on the pretext that military necessity had forced him to act independently. The military charade played out with Diebitsch had, after all, saved Yorck from disciplinary action. But the King continued to view Yorck with disfavour. Clausewitz was also to be regarded with some dislike by the King, but at least the legal proceedings against him, about which he had heard when he was in Petersburg, were dropped.

On 4th March the French evacuated Berlin. The Russians entered on the same day. When the Russian general, Czerbitcheff, appeared at the royal theatre that night he was thunderously applauded for over twenty minutes. On 13th March the treaty with Russia was published, and Prussia, to Clausewitz's fierce joy and satisfaction, at last declared war upon France, an event for which he had been praying and waiting for six long years.

Clausewitz had another reason for rejoicing: in March he returned to Berlin and to Marie. He had been away from his wife for over ten hazardous months. Inevitably, she found him much changed by the ordeals of the tiring campaign and the Russian winter. At Königsberg he had been as thin as a skeleton, and when he reached Berlin he was still very gaunt. His red hair was sparser and was frosted with grey, and his face was darkly blotched by ice sores. Above all, his personality had altered. Always withdrawn by nature, events had made him more so; he easily alternated between short bursts of wild enthusiasm and deep depression. He was even more sensitive than he had been before; if he had been hardened by his fearful experiences at Borodino and Berezina he was also more vulnerable in himself.

Especially, Clausewitz suffered now from his treatment at the hands of the King. This was to have a far-reaching effect. As Prussia was now allied with Russia against France, Clausewitz naturally wished to return home. But he would have to pay the price for daring to disagree with the King's treaty with France in 1812, for having left Prussia to fight for the Czar, and for his involvement in Yorck's decision at Tauroggen. Clausewitz soon found that he was looked upon with disfavour, despite the help he had given in the Prussian army reforms, despite the part he had played in the *Landwehr* proposals. "In Russia I wrote to you that I could not distinguish myself," he had written to Marie soon after his arrival at Königsberg. "In Germany I must. I will not travel by way of Breslau, because I could not go through there unnoticed, and it is hard to decide whether the King is less gracious to me if I take notice of him, or no notice of him. Apart from that none of my friends are with the King."[5] On 11th March Clausewitz applied to the King for readmission into Prussian army service. He enlisted the help of Scharnhorst, still the Chief of the General Staff, and of Gneisenau, who was now the Quartermaster General. Both wielded powerful influence which they used on his behalf; Clausewitz could have found no better sponsors. Scharnhorst noted on 19th March: "I have made another attempt to move Clausewitz into service." Two days later he wrote to his friend: "My dear Clausewitz. I can only write a few words. I flatter myself with the hope soon to be reunited with you. I have never failed to recognize your great value, and I realize it even more at this time, when I have a great deal to do. I shall only be able to manage if you are with me, only if I can join my thoughts with yours so that we can proceed in partnership on a straight course."[6]

"General Scharnhorst is expected tonight," Clausewitz wrote to Marie when he was still at Königsberg. "I am very happy to see him again. He has asked the King to take me back into the army. The King has said: 'Clausewitz. Hmm. Yes, I'll find out whether he served well with the Russians.' "[7] Clausewitz had to wait. Meanwhile he wrote to Marie again in a manner which showed his excitement at the thought of fighting the French: "That I am now well and happy is the main subject of what I have to tell you. With a fine little army, led by my friends, to go with such an army to a beautiful country, for such a purpose, at a beautiful time of the year, such is more or less the ideal of earthly existence."[8] But in mid-April Clausewitz received the King's reply, issued on 19th March: "In consequence of your letter of the 11th, I have commanded that your process should be cancelled. You can only be readmitted to the service of the Fatherland when you have won the right for special consideration by great distinction in the coming campaign."[9] An angry Clausewitz wrote to Marie from Oldenburg: "The words 'great distinction' had been added in the King's own hand because it was not bitter enough for him."[10]

Ironically, two days before Friedrich Wilhelm issued his refusal, a royal order had announced the creation of a Prussian *Landwehr* on the East Prussian model. Clausewitz's proposal was heavily drawn upon, including his scheme for recruiting all men aged between eighteen and fifty who were not already serving in the regular army or the *Jäger*. A month later, Clausewitz was also to see his *Landsturm* ideas incorporated into another edict. This made all men so far unaffected responsible for home defence and partisan operations. These two measures were Prussia's closest approach to univeral conscription. Both of them drew upon Clausewitz's ideas. As he wrote: "I have the views of a Prussian officer. I have the full confidence of Scharnhorst and Gneisenau. And I have never had so much to do and had so much influence."[11] Yet Clausewitz himself failed to gain a commission in this new "nation in arms." His rejection in 1813 affected him for the rest of his life.

Scharnhorst saw no hope of changing the King's mind at the moment, and suggested that Clausewitz should be the Russian general staff officer at the Prussian headquarters. The army itself would be commanded by Blücher, with Scharnhorst as his Chief of Staff. Clausewitz agreed. He arrived at Blücher's headquarters at Dresden, from where he wrote to Marie: "I would rather it had been a friendly surrender of my person to Scharnhorst." He added on 22nd April: "I am too proud to ask the General again. I returned to Prussia, only just as it happens, so that I might better serve my Fatherland in war, and no setback shall prevent me."[12] But at least Clausewitz would be fighting close to Scharnhorst. Blücher was eager to begin. As Scharnhorst had recently said, in a reference to the old warrior's mental breakdown in 1809: "Blücher must lead us though he has a hundred elephants in his belly." Once more, Clausewitz was spinning towards the "whirlpool of war." By mid-April, Napoleon was ready to take the field with 226,000 men and 457 guns. His forces were organized into two armies: the Army of the Elbe under Eugène, and the Army of the Main which he commanded himself. His manpower total was less than he had hoped for, but the acquisition of such a strength was still a unique effort. On the other hand, the French cavalry force was insufficient and badly trained. In April this arm only consisted of about 15,000 horses, of which only half was really fit for service. This weakness was a result of the disaster in Russia, where virtually all Napoleon's cavalry had perished; the help which the Emperor had expected from Prussia would not now come, and too few cavalry horses were left in France. The younger cavalrymen lacked training and experience, and their equipment was deficient.

As a result of the extension of military conscription, Prussia managed to mobilize an army of 280,000 in 1813, amounting to 6 per cent of the entire population. But too little time had been available for instruction, in some

cases only nine weeks, and for producing equipment. Weapons were therefore scarce; and the proportion of trained to untrained soldiers was relatively small. In March, 1813, the first line units only comprised 68,000 men,
and these were to be severely depleted in the opening phase of the war.[13]
Nevertheless, optimism and determination could be sensed in Prussia,
qualities which had been completely lacking in 1806. Frederick Wilhelm
was astonished by the response to his address to the people, *An Mein Volk*, on
17th March, and by the swarms of volunteers who thronged into the local
recruiting stations. Optimism and enthusiasm also softened Clausewitz's
bitterness. He had very little confidence in Friedrich Wilhelm and disliked
the King's advisers, Knesebeck and Ancillon. But Clausewitz had firm faith
in Blücher, in the Prussian army, and in Scharnhorst. "If we lose courage in
these conditions we deserve to be flogged," he wrote to Marie on 1st April.[14]

Very soon the Prussians marched to fight. Blücher advanced from Dresden towards Altenburg. Clausewitz was extremely excited by the prospects
ahead. Only the continuing attitude of the Royal family cast a shadow over
his pleasure; the Crown Prince, the former pupil to whom Clausewitz had
sent his *Principles of War* before going to Russia, refused even to talk to him.
This, said Clausewitz, did not annoy him as much as people like Leute, the
Crown Prince's Governor, "who show me a kind of affected hostility and
turn their backs upon me."[15]

On 15th April, Napoleon left St. Cloud for Mayence, where he arrived
two days later. On 25th April, he moved on to Erfurt, the assembly area for
most of the French forces, then went on to Eckartsberg. Already the lack of
cavalry was restricting French forward reconnaissance. Napoleon intended
to advance towards Leipzig and then Dresden, to force the Russians and
Prussians to accept battle or fall back behind the River Elbe. Eugène's army
was to cover him: if the allies advanced against Napoleon, Eugène would
threaten their right flank. Bonaparte had two major aims: first to win a
decisive victory to restore his prestige; and second to seize Berlin. He
wanted to thrash the Prussians back into subservience, and avenge his
Russian defeat. So, by the evening of 30th April, the Army of the Elbe was
drawn up around Merseburg, while the greater part of the Army of the
Main was in the vicinity of Naumburg. Clausewitz had written to Marie
from Altenburg on 25th April: "In a few days the curtain will rise and we
will not be far from a great battle. The preceding events make the difference
between 1813 and 1806 very noticeable. I am very busy because I do most
of my work for the General [Scharnhorst] . . . I am very happy and
content."[16] The Russians and Prussians were to act together as a single
force, the Russian part totalling about 110,000 men of whom 30,000 were
cavalry and Cossacks. The overall allied commander was the senior Russian
officer, and since Kutuzov had died on 28th April, the person appointed
was Wittgenstein, Clausewitz's last commanding officer in Russia, and now
a Field-Marshal. By the end of April, Wittgenstein had deployed the main

allied army in the area between Zwenkau and Altenburg, south of the Naumburg-Leipzig road and east of the Mulde River. His force consisted of 64,000 infantry, 24,000 cavalry and 552 guns.

Both sides manoeuvred for battle positions. On 1st May, Bonaparte ordered Eugène to advance from Merseburg to Schladebach, and deployed his own army at Lützen, Weissenfels and Naumburg. Bonaparte entered Lützen in the evening of the 1st, and next day Ney was commanded to stand fast at the town. Ney was also ordered to occupy in strength the nearby villages of Klein Görschen, Gross Görschen, Rahna and Kaja, all of which lay south of Lützen, to cover Eugène's advance on Leipzig, as well as the movements of the rear elements of the main army upon Lützen. On the allied side, Russian cavalry patrols reported that the French were spread across from Weissenfels to Leipzig, and that the flank at Kaja only had a weak guard. Ney had neglected to reconnoitre the area adequately in the direction of Peggau and Zwenkau, and the French outposts had failed to realize that the enemy was only about two miles away from them. Wittgenstein immediately decided to take advantage of the French mistake. He aimed to shatter the French flank guard, thrust in his forces, and cut the main French army in half. Late on 1st May, Blücher was told that Wittgenstein intended to make his attack next day; the Prussian commander was ordered to undertake a night march to Peggau, on the right bank of the Elster. Blücher set out at once.

Clausewitz had an unusual and difficult appointment. While his post was largely a fiction to enable him to fight with the Prussians, he was still technically the Russian liaison officer with Blücher's force. Yet since he could only speak a few words of Russian, his ability to act as a go-between was limited. Moreover, his duty as liaison officer was difficult for other reasons. From early in the campaign there was disagreement between the senior officers of the two armies. Blücher held a very poor opinion of the Russians and of their commander, and an incident during the night march early on 2nd May reinforced this. Towards morning Blücher discovered that Yorck's corps was moving on the same route which he had been ordered to take, including the same bridge over the Elster river. This mistake, which Blücher blamed upon faulty Russian staff work, could easily have resulted in dangerous confusion. As it was, the consequent delay prevented Blücher's troops from having a much-needed rest before the battle. Blücher, not the most amiable of men when aroused, naturally selected the "Russian" liaison officer as the target for his anger.

On 2nd May, 1813, Prussian swords were drawn for the attempt to drive the French out of the Fatherland. Concentrating upon the villages of Rahna, Gross and Klein Görschen, the allied assault was launched at about eleven o'clock in the morning. Napoleon himself was absent for the first few hours. Not expecting an engagement that day, he had left Lützen early in the morning and had ridden forward to join Lauriston, who had been

ordered to drive Kleist from Lindenau and to occupy Leipzig. While he was
on the road approaching Leipzig, Napoleon heard the violent bombardment which opened the battle of Lützen, also called the battle of Gross
Görschen. Ney, who was with him, galloped back to his corps; Napoleon
ordered all the troops on the Leipzig road to march upon Kaja before he
returned to the area of fighting. Marmont and Bertrand, west of Lützen,
were also commanded to send troops to the battlefield.

Field-Marshal Wittgenstein's aim was to take the villages and so push
through to the level ground around Lützen, where his superior cavalry force
could operate to the best advantage. Clausewitz, on his horse almost
continuously since 2 a.m., was positioned with the rest of Blücher's staff,
who were sheltering under the meagre cover of a low hill facing Gross
Görschen. They waited for the infantry to take Gross Görschen. But after
repeated assaults, the French still clung on to the village, and Blücher could

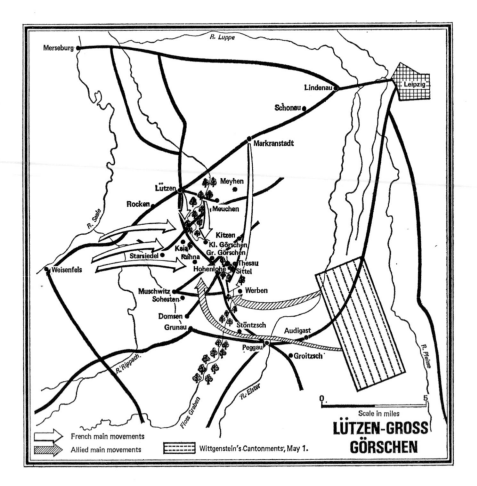

LÜTZEN-GROSS
GÖRSCHEN

stand the inactivity no longer. At about midday he abruptly reined round his horse and galloped off to find Wittgenstein and obtain an order to attack, much to the consternation of his staff; Blücher was a difficult man to keep up with. Locating a startled Wittgenstein, Blücher was persuaded to be patient. Once again Clausewitz had the unnerving experience of sitting astride his restless horse while shell and shot burst all around. Most of the time he was near Blücher, who, said another member of his staff, "with the most absolute imperturbability, remained for the most part at the dangerous places, untiringly smoking his pipe. When it was smoked to the end he would thrust it out behind him and call 'Schmidt!' whereupon his orderly would hand him one freshly filled and the old gentleman smoked away at his ease." Blücher's staff officer continued: "Once, for a time, we halted quite near a Russian battery, and a French bomb fell directly in front of us. Everyone shouted: 'Your Excellency, a bomb!' 'Well, leave the damned thing alone then,' said Blücher calmly. He stood by until it burst and then, and only then, changed his position."[17]

Napoleon galloped up to the fierce fighting at 2.30 p.m. His Third Corps was in a desperate condition as it tried to hold onto the smoke-covered villages. As usual, Bonaparte's arrival at once raised the spirits of his men as he hurried quickly from one unit to the next to rally the flagging French. According to Marshal Auguste Marmont: "This is probably the one day of his whole career on which Napoleon incurred most personal danger on the battlefield. He exposed himself constantly to danger, leading back to the charge the defeated troops of Third Corps." On that day, not only Napoleon and his staff, but on the other side Blücher and the group of Prussian staff around him, were constantly in danger. Everyone was in the thick of the battle. The struggle became a grinding trial of brute strength, as both forces tried to lock on to the villages, especially Gross Görschen. The result was a wild *mêlée*, in the thick smoke, of fighting, cursing and dying men. Backward and forward pushed the line between the two armies; French and Prussians drew apart, and then surged forward to clash again; wave after wave of yelling infantrymen ran forward at the villages, but still the French refused to loosen their hold upon the battered houses in the centre. Prussian cavalry were thrown in. Clausewitz himself led one squadron charge, then another, despite the fact that he was a staff officer and normally had no right to lead a thundering line of horsemen. His men hacked their way into the solid mass of French troops, and with the combined shock of Prussian and Russian infantry and cavalry attacks, Gross Görschen was taken. Then it was lost again. The quadrangle formed by the villages became a raging inferno. Of all the battles in which Clausewitz fought, he had never been so near the centre of the maelstrom. "The battle was extremely fierce and I was right in the middle of the enemy," he told Marie the next day. "Since we could not influence the command of the skirmish, we [the members of the staff] could only fight with sword in hand."[18] At one time his small cavalry unit was completely surrounded by French infantrymen. Desperately Clausewitz and his men tried to cut their way through the enemy battalion. Many of the Prussians were dragged down from their horses and bayoneted by the enemy. Clausewitz himself was wounded: his head was gashed behind his right ear by "a little Frenchman."[19] But gradually Clausewitz fought through to freedom, his horse's flanks bleeding, its fetlocks sprayed with blood from the dead and wounded it had trodden over.

Then the surviving troopers reformed; again came the order to charge. Horses were now almost too weary to move at more than a trot; the tired arms of the cavalrymen could barely lift the sabres. Survivors, fewer still than before, returned to await another order, Clausewitz among them. "To play such a direct part in the fight would at any other time have been a distinction for an officer of the general staff," Clausewitz told Marie. "But at Gross Görschen everyone did this or something similar, and it was impossible to say that one had done better than the others."[20] Nevertheless, Clausewitz still privately hoped that his conduct in the midst of battle would meet Friedrich Wilhelm's conditions for his re-entry into Prussian service. His attempt to win "the right for special consideration by great distinction" spurred him on to risk his life again and again in the bloody struggle for those few battered houses.

Just before four o'clock in the afternoon, General Blücher and his cavalry joined Yorck's troops and made yet another charge, this time against Klein Görschen and Rahna. In the bloody pandemonium Blücher himself narrowly escaped death. His horse was shot and a bullet struck the General's side. Seizing another mount, Blücher sent a member of his staff to Yorck, instructing him to assume command, and then hurried back behind the fighting to have his wound attended to. So much blood was seeping through his uniform that he thought the injury must be serious; but the surgeon told Blücher he had only received a flesh wound. Blücher waited impatiently for the bandage to be fastened, and then mounted his horse and rushed back into the thick of the battle.[21]

More French troops were hurrying on to the battlefield and Napoleon was gaining numerical superiority. Gradually, the French began to recover under the Emperor's brilliant tactical direction. At about half past five, as Macdonald closed in on the right of the allied army, and Bertrand and Marmont on the left, Napoleon ordered a battery of eighty guns to be formed south-west of Kaja. While the allies were being battered by this cannon fire, the Young Guard was lined up in four columns and, supported by the Old Guard and the Guard cavalry, advanced to the famous battle cry of "*La Garde au Feu!*" The time was half past six; Rahna, Gross and Klein Görschen were stormed. Mortier, leading the Young Guards, fell under his wounded horse, and 1,069 of his *élite* troops were slaughtered.[22] But steadily Wittgenstein's flanks were pushed in, and the allied centre collapsed. Learning that Kleist had been ousted from Leipzig, and that their lines of retreat were now threatened, the allies began to fall back further; darkness spread over the deserted battlefield. The withdrawal to the Elster bridges and the road to Dresden was made in perfect order, covered by the cavalry. Yorck launched a further attack upon Kaja, where Napoleon was based, only to be repulsed.

According to an official account of the battle of Lützen, written immediately afterwards: "The whole quadrangle was so thickly sown with dead and wounded that it seemed as if several battalions had bivouacked there."[23] Field-Marshal Wittgenstein believed that night alone had saved the allies from costly defeat. If two more hours of daylight had followed, the momentum of the French attack could have sent the Prussians and Russians reeling with their backs to the River Elster. Blücher angrily disagreed. He demanded one last charge with his cavalry; permission was given. Once again his exhausted troopers climbed stiffly into their saddles, wheeled their drooping horses into line, and waited in the darkness. The order came, and Blücher's men thundered through the night at the French position near Kaja, where Napoleon stood in a square formed by his Guard. A French officer described the attack: "The burning villages lit the skyline. Suddenly, on the right flank of the French army, a line of cavalry dashed up with a noise like muffled thunder, coming right up to the square behind which was the Emperor. I believe that had they advanced quickly 200 paces further, Napoleon and his whole staff would have been captured."[24]

The French were too weak in cavalry to pursue the allies; and Napoleon's victory had only been achieved with the heavy loss of 18,000 men killed, wounded and captured. Two thirds of these casualties came from Marshal Ney's Third Corps. Clausewitz estimated the allied dead and wounded at between 10,000 and 12,000 although later estimates put the figure as high as 15,000. Since the Prussian staff had been so involved, the casualties included many of Clausewitz's friends and acquaintances, as he told Marie in his letter the next day. And among the wounded was Scharnhorst; but Clausewitz did not believe "The General" to be seriously hurt. "General Blücher is severely bruised," he told Marie. "General Scharnhorst was shot in his leg, but it is nothing serious, and he is back. Hedemann has a contusion. Only two officers from the Guard Fusilier battalion are neither dead nor wounded. Karl Röder is wounded . . . Fabian Dohna is wounded. Prince Leopold is dead, and many others of our acquaintance all of whom I cannot name."[25]

Clausewitz gave Marie more details of the battle when he wrote to her again five days later from Proschwitz, near Meisen. "Wilhelm [his brother], whom I spoke to in the midst of most ferocious rifle fire, is perfectly well . . . Scharnhorst led the skirmish on the right wing against the three villages. He went straight at the enemy several times with sword drawn, at the head of cavalry and infantry, right into the enemy, encouraging his troops, waving his sword and shouting, 'Long Live the King!' His wound, which he received at about six o'clock is not dangerous. He can already undertake a journey to Vienna. Gneisenau was on the left wing, also leading cavalry and wielding his sword. Old Blücher was very brave too, as you can well imagine." Clausewitz continued: "We hope that a strong diversion will come from the Austrians, which has already been mentioned by the King in a letter to the army." And he finished: "I am well, and with Gneisenau. We all miss Scharnhorst very much."[26]

Gneisenau had taken Scharnhorst's position as Chief of Staff to Blücher while "The General" rode to Vienna to try to persuade the Austrians to join the allies. In making the journey, Scharnhorst neglected his wound. The jolting of the carriage reopened the gash, and infection began to spread. Scharnhorst's condition began to deteriorate rapidly. He wrote to Gneisenau on 10th May from Zittau: "My friend, I beseech you to take my papers into your safekeeping, or give them to Clausewitz, in order that they may be looked after for me, and pass them on to nobody else, whoever he may be. Give my regards to Clausewitz. Take my sons into your care."[27] The following day he posted some military instructions to General von Knesebeck, the King's adviser, and wrote: "I am on the move once more, after being delayed twenty-four hours in Zittau by a terrible inflammation and a fever in which I raved continuously. Now I am once more on the road. I still hope to be of some service at my place of destination."[28]

Meanwhile, as Scharnhorst tried to win Austrian support, the Prussian and Russian armies struggled to recover their foothold against the French pressure. Although Napoleon's victory had been costly and indecisive, the allies were forced to abandon the line of the Elbe. A new strategy now had to be agreed. "The General" was indeed missed; he might have been able to help soothe the quarrels which broke out between the Prussians and Russians. After the fighting on 2nd May, Bülow had been left to defend Berlin with about 30,000 Prussians; the rest of the allied army moved back by way of Dresden to Bautzen. At Bautzen the allied strength was reinforced by 13,000 Russians commanded by another of the generals whom Clausewitz had met in 1812, Barclay de Tolly. But both Blücher and Gneisenau were increasingly critical of the Russian high command. Gneisenau said that he could not imagine why Wittgenstein had abandoned the Elbe; the French had not pressed so hard. "The chief evil from which we suffer," Gneisenau wrote to Hardenberg, "is the leadership of the army. Count Wittgenstein is unequal to it."[29]

Napoleon decided to establish his main advance depot at Dresden, and entered the town on 8th May. As reinforcements arrived, he deployed his army to threaten both Berlin and Bautzen; an extremely difficult manoeuvre but one which could split the allied force and increase the dissension in the senior command. The Prussians, he hoped, would become obsessed with the safety of their capital. Bonaparte also shuffled his commanders.

Eugène was dispatched to Italy, to raise an army in case war broke out with Austria; the Elbe and Main armies were first merged, then split into two wings. Napoleon appointed Marshal Ney to command one, while he led the other himself. At the same time, he tried to cajole and bully the allies into peace talks. The Austrians were delaying joining the alliance against him, despite diplomatic pressure from Prussia, and he tried to turn this hesitation to advantage. On 17th May, Caulaincourt was instructed to travel to the allied position and seek an interview with Czar Alexander. The Czar would be offered an armistice as a first step towards a peace conference at Prague. Napoleon's move failed at first when the Czar refused to grant Caulaincourt an interview on 19th May. The overall position was therefore unsettled. At Blücher's headquarters unease was growing about future relations with Russia. Clausewitz was fearful for Scharnhorst's health. He, Gneisenau and other friends of the General waited anxiously for news. Little came, except the information that Scharnhorst's condition was failing to improve.

Napoleon then tried to step up the campaign by putting pressure upon the town of Bautzen. He ordered three of his Corps, supported by a fourth, to move in the direction of the town. Marshal Ney was also commanded to approach. At the same time, two of Ney's Corps were ordered to advance on Berlin. Soon afterwards Napoleon modified his plan, and ordered all of Ney's force to concentrate on Bautzen, but by the time the cancellation of the first command reached Ney, some of his force had already set out for Berlin. The arrival of this part of Ney's army at Bautzen was therefore delayed. Under the nominal command of Wittgenstein, the allied army of 64,000 Russians and 32,000 Prussians was positioned on the eastern bank of the River Spree, near Bautzen itself. Napoleon reconnoitred the enemy deployment on 19th May, and decided to attack frontally on 20th May; Ney was ordered to strike from the north on the 21st and to fall upon the allied rear. Napoleon hoped that Ney's assault would sever the allied line of communication and force Wittgenstein back against the Bohemian mountains. Napoleon believed that Austria would then refuse to join the alliance against him; and the defeated Prussians and Russians would have to accept a dictated peace.

Clausewitz was still with Blücher's staff, positioned on the slopes to the north of the village of Kreckwitz. Blücher's troops formed the right flank of the allied army. To Gneisenau's annoyance, Wittgenstein had decided to fight a defensive battle; he also believed that Wittgenstein had sacrificed the chances of a decisive victory by his cautious disposition of forces.[30] Sure enough, after the first day's fighting on 20th May the allies had been pushed back from Bautzen and from the river. For Clausewitz and the other officers on Blücher's staff, this opening to the battle of Bautzen was a frustrating disappointment. The cavalry was barely used, because the plan was still to fight upon defensive lines; when cavalry charges were made, they were both costly and ineffective. This time Clausewitz and the other staff officers remained in the headquarter's group and took no part in the charges themselves. The night spent on the hills was uncomfortable; the men dug redoubts or tried to sleep, or perhaps watched the French camp fires below them around Neider-Gurig. Napoleon's troops could be heard preparing for the next day's struggle. Consulting his maps and laying his plans at the bishop's palace at Bautzen, Napoleon was still determined to win a decisive victory.

At four o'clock, early on the morning of 21st May, Clausewitz heard the French duty squadron sound the bugle call for the cavalry to mount and the artillerymen to prime their weapons. Just before six o'clock the guns flashed in the valley below. The allies replied, and the cannonade continued along a front of nearly eight miles. Napoleon's plan was to pin the enemy down while Marshal Ney forced the decision by outflanking the main allied position. As the guns roared, Marshal Ney's army steadily moved towards the villages of Wurschen and Baruth, behind Blücher's position on the allied flank. Meanwhile, Napoleon's main infantry forces advanced against the Russian and Prussian positions. Clausewitz could see the lines of enemy infantrymen as they left their cover at the valley bottom and began to climb the difficult slopes; to the left of Clausewitz's position a particularly heavy bombardment took place, as the French guns tried to blast a passage for

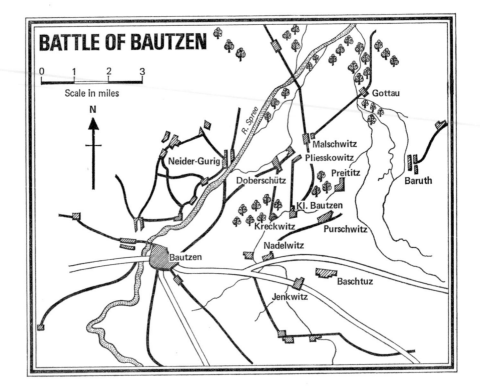

BATTLE OF BAUTZEN

Marshal Mortier's troops to seize Nadelwitz and Kreckwitz. Then Blücher's men were engaged by Betrand's units which swarmed up the slopes in a frontal attack. Bloodily, they were shot and bayoneted back down the slopes, and dozens of dead lay sprawled just in front of the Prussians. And so the day went on amid the thunder of artillery, the whining and explosion of shells, as the French advanced, retired, advanced again; and all the while Marshal Ney was edging round the allied flank.

Owing to a disagreement between the Czar and Field-Marshal Wittgenstein, too few forces were sent to meet Ney's threat. By four o'clock, only Kleist's troops held the line which stood between Ney and his attack upon Blücher's rear over the Bloesser-Wasser river. Once again, Wittgenstein decided to withdraw. Orders were sent to General Blücher, who moved his men out in good order. Once again the French losses were higher than those of the allies, 22,500 against 10,850. Napoleon is reported to have exclaimed: "What, no result? No trophies, no prisoners—and such butchery?" To preserve contact with Austria, the allies fell back on Silesia. Napoleon's pursuit was not begun until 22nd May; Oudinot was left to gather up his Corps and then march upon Berlin. On 27th May the main French army crossed the Katzbach; two days later Davout and Vandamme reoccupied Hamburg, and on 1st June, the allies having by now withdrawn to Schweidnitz, Napoleon entered Breslau. On the same day, to the intense disgust of Gneisenau and Clausewitz, an armistice was agreed. Five days later the truce was extended until 20th July, and later to 16th August. To Gneisenau, this cessation of hostilities was unnecessary and deterimental. from every point of view, including the psychological. Clausewitz agreed, although his opinion was not voiced in the same harsh terms.

Meanwhile Clausewitz suffered a greater, and more personal anguish. Scharnhorst was clearly on his death-bed. His wounds had failed to heal; infection and inflammation increased, and he became daily weaker. At Prague, although still desperate to continue his diplomatic missions, Scharnhorst could travel no further. There he died on 28th June.

Clausewitz was overcome with grief. "The last news of Scharnhorst was that he was dead, as you will have already heard," he wrote to Marie on 30th June. "You will know how sad I am. Although he is irreplaceable for the army, for the country, and for Europe, I find it difficult to think of all that, and at this moment I can think of nothing but the personal loss of this dearest friend of all my life. No-one else can take his place and he will always be missed by me. I cannot tell you how deep is my grief." Clausewitz continued: "How hard it must have been for him to leave this world: he had so much left he wanted to do. I would not have cared to attend his dying moments, since it would have affected me badly, but I still regret my absence among those who paid their respects and showed their devotion at the end, because of the thousands who owed him gratitude and love, no-one owes him more than I. Except for you, nobody has shown me so much kindness, and nobody has so influenced the whole happiness of my life."[31] Scharnhorst's memory would never fade. Clausewitz was always in need of him; nobody could take his place, not even Gneisenau. As late as 31st July, 1830, Clausewitz was to write to Gneisenau: "The more I learn, the more I am convinced that we owe everything to Scharnhorst."[32]

Gloom at Blücher's headquarters, caused by the armistice and by Scharnhorst's death, was increased for another reason. General Barclay de Tolly was now given *de facto* supreme field command of the allied armies, and Wittgenstein was relegated to the same level of seniority as Blücher—and Gneisenau soon found Barclay as unsatisfactory as his predecessor. "We are burdened with heavy chains," he wrote, "and have little hope that things will improve, because there is no-one to seize and combine the elements of victory."

Officially the armistice was designed to permit the discussion of peace terms at Prague. But apart from this, Napoleon wished to be certain of Austria's position, and to split the allies further apart. Perhaps most important of all, Napoleon was in a weak military position. The lack of French cavalry had prevented him from making both Gross Görschen and Bautzen more decisive; and no less than 90,000 of his men were on the sick lists. Napoleon had too few effective troops left with which to fight a battle; and a defeat would probably have brought Austria in against him. French logistic problems were still far from a solution. Ammunition was short, and the Cossacks and partisans were causing severe disruption to French lines of communication. On 10th June, therefore, Napoleon retired to Dresden to patch up his forces. Gneisenau feared that the armistice might be used by the changeable monarchs of Russia and Prussia as a means of obtaining full peace. Again, Clausewitz agreed with him. Having created enthusiasm for war among the people and in the army, it might be difficult to sustain it during the cessation of fighting.

So in the weeks after the temporary ending of hostilities Clausewitz wrote *The Campaign of 1813 up to the Armistice*. Drafted at Gneisenau's request, the document was apparently meant to justify the truce to the troops, and to the people. Clausewitz tried to show the benefits which could result and to boost the morale of the soldiers, by reviving their confidence. In a brief survey of events since Jena and Auerstädt in 1806, Clausewitz outlined the military reforms, the war preparations, and the attempts to prepare fortresses for the struggle against the French. The remains of the French army had been thrown out of Russia, he said. Now a Prussian army was in the field, and had won successes, for example at Möckern, and had held the enemy at Gross Görschen and Bautzen. The Prussian army was fulfilling many of the hopes of the Fatherland, as God asked of the defenders of a just and sacred cause. When the armistice ended, Clausewitz wrote, the army would enter the field once more. Victory, if not certain, was very likely. No-one should despond, he went on. The best use should be made of the truce; plans should be laid for the future; the armistice should not be scorned or disregarded by those who merely lived for the sound of battle. "He, who carelessly lets the truce flow past, who only listens to the uproar of unrolling events, cannot go forward with courage and confidence, with cool judgement and a clear view of the future." Clausewitz completed the paper, published that year in Glatz and in Leipzig the next, with a direct appeal to the troops: "Friends, I dedicate these lines to you. If I have done your hearts good and raised your spirits, my object is achieved . . ."[33]

Indeed, the army had performed well. While no decisive victory had been won over Napoleon, neither had Napoleon defeated the allies. Territorially the Prussians seemed to be the losers, but strategically Napoleon's forces were overstretched. The policy of arming the people was reaping rewards; partisans in the *Landsturm* still menaced Napoleon's tenuous supply lines. On 25th May, for example, Halle had been raised, and on 30th May a French artillery convoy, escorted by 1,600 troops, had been ambushed and captured near Hablerstadt. The standard of fighting by the French was deteriorating. French troops were organized far less efficiently than they had been during Napoleon's rise to fame. The latest conscripts were trained in haste, and were inexperienced. In Spain, French tactics had been shown to be deficient, and Clausewitz referred to "the somewhat ponderous thrusting methods of the French commanders."[34] The Prussians on the other hand, although very inexperienced too, were constantly improving. Benefits accrued from the close study of the tactical techniques proposed by the reformers; a correct blending of skirmishers and column was aimed at, although full co-ordination was still not always achieved. Napoleon is supposed to have said after the battle of Bautzen: "These beasts have learned something."[35]

With the signing of the armistice, more improvements could be introduced before the war entered the next round. The troops had been blooded, and use could be made of this experience; logistics could be reorganized; better equipment supplied; extra training undertaken. Above all, here was a chance to strengthen the *Landwehr* and the volunteer *Jäger* detachments. Already the *Jägers* had shown their value as officer reserves to replace battle losses.[36] And the *Landwehr* supplied the means for rapid expansion of front-line strength. In the summer of 1813 the *Landwehr* was built up to thirty-eight infantry regiments and thirty cavalry regiments, which gave a total of about 120,000 men trained to fight side by side with the regiments of the line. As Clausewitz and the other reformers had suggested, the men wore special insignia, and were already acquiring a sense of personal prestige; and because of the *Landwehr*, the Prussians could now send an army of 162,000 into the field.

Napoleon failed to win Austrian support, and a declaration of war against France was issued from Vienna on 12th August. Two days before, the armistice had been renounced by Russia and Prussia. Hostilities would soon

be resumed. The allies could now mass a colossal army. Moreover, Bernadotte, Crown Prince of Sweden—who had previously been one of Napoleon's commanders—was won over to the allied cause on 7th July. The
allied field force totalled over 520,000 men; in addition, there were 143,000
reserves and 112,000 garrison troops, to give a terrifying total of 776,000
soldiers. Napoleon, after a prodigious effort, managed to assemble 442,000
men, in addition to which he had 126,000 in the second line and in
fortresses on the Elbe, in Poland and in Prussia. Bonaparte quite wrongly
imagined that he outnumbered the enemy.

War could now be waged on a more devastating scale than ever before; a
gigantic, convulsive clash between nations-in-arms was threatening to engulf
the whole of Europe. With the massive energies now released, generals and
monarchs found themselves venturing into the unknown. Clausewitz fully
realized the changing nature of war, and would one day study the full
implications in *On War*. Meantime, he wrote: "The old ways of war ended
with the French Revolutionary struggle. This was forced upon us by the
French sword. By revolutionary methods, the French had burned away the
old concept of war, as if with acid. They unleashed the terrible power of war
from its former confines. Now it moved in its naked form, dragging massive
force with it . . . However, a new system of war was yet to be clearly
perceived. War was handed back to the people, from whom it had been
taken away in part, by the use of select standing armies." Clausewitz
continued: "Now war had thrown off its shackles. This was all that could be
understood of the new development. What would be built upon this broader
and firmer basis would only become apparent little by little."[37]

A way of controlling this unwieldy force in the field had to be evolved.
Before, the commanding general could manage by himself. Napoleon tried,
and eventually failed, in trying rigidly to concentrate all authority in his
own person. In Prussia, the instrument of command was the General Staff.
With common instruction, common doctrines, similar outlook, the staff
officers could be dispersed throughout the huge army to provide continuity
of policy. Cohesion could be obtained. Working closely with their respective
generals, the staff officers could blend their individual characteristics and
skills into the overall strategic framework of strategy and tactics. Staff
officers could thus wield a strong influence. Indeed, in *On War* Clausewitz
warned that this power could be excessive: "The authority acquired by
those who are at head of, and best acquainted with, this branch of military
service, gives them a sort of general dominion over people's minds, beginning with the General himself, and from this then springs a routine of ideas
which causes an undue bias of the mind."[38] But an intelligent staff system
could bring flexibility to size, suppleness to strength.

Clausewitz himself belonged to this Prussian staff officer network. Perhaps
the most marked feature of the general staff during the 1813 and 1815
campaigns was that the members of the reform group provided most of the

staff personnel. Among the most distinguished were Scharnhorst and Gneisenau, who acted as chiefs of staff to Blücher; Boyen who served with Bülow; Grolman with Kleist; Rauch with Yorck; and Clausewitz with Walmoden in 1813 and 1814 and with Thielman for the final 1815 campaign. Much depended upon the relationship between chief of staff and commander. One of the first to sense the value of the partnership was the most strikingly individual of all the Prussian generals, Lebrecht von Blücher. "Gneisenau," he wrote, "being my chief of staff and very reliable, reports to me on the manoeuvres that are to be executed and the marches that are to be performed. Once convinced that he is right, I drive my troops through hell towards the goal and never stop until the desired end has been accomplished—yes, even though the officers trained in the old school may pout and complain and all but mutiny."[39] When receiving an honorary degree at Oxford after the war, Blücher said: "Well! If I am to become a doctor, you must at least make Gneisenau an apothecary, for we two belong together always."[40]

The leashes were slipped in the summer of 1813 to let loose a creature of war whose strength and violence were as yet unknown. Clausewitz, as both an observer and participant, was to gain the knowledge and experience to write the crucial chapters of *On War*.

TWELVE

Napoleon at Bay

"The defensive form of war is, in
itself, stronger than the offensive."
(*On War*, bk. vi, ch. i.)

CLAUSEWITZ WAS STILL deeply affected by Scharnhorst's death, by the loss of the "father of my soul." In addition, he was still being denied readmission into Prussian service. Friedrich Wilhelm continued to look upon Clausewitz as an outcast, despite his brave performance in the fighting of spring 1813, especially at Gross Görschen. Since he was neither in one army nor the other, neither in a full Prussian nor a full Russian post, Clausewitz was even barred from receiving decorations for his conduct. "Scharnhorst has asked General Blücher to propose me for decoration," Clausewitz had written to Marie just after Gross Görschen.[1] Blücher put forward his name to Czar Alexander and to Friedrich Wilhelm. The Czar accepted the rest of the applications, but struck out Clausewitz's name "as he is a foreigner." Clausewitz was then passed over by the King of Prussia.[2]

Gneisenau wrote to Marie from Reichenbach in the first days of the armistice, mentioning that he had applied for her husband's re-engagement in Prussian service,[3] and Clausewitz himself referred to this attempt in a letter to Marie on 10th June: "Gneisenau has been appointed Governor-General of Silesia and to be commander of the Silesian *Landwehr*. He has asked the King if he can take me to help him. The answer has still to come back."[4] But Clausewitz did not expect the request to be successful. Nor was it. Only one day after he had written to Marie, telling her of Gneisenau's attempt, Clausewitz said in another letter: "The King has refused to allow Gneisenau to give me a job. I have no idea yet what I shall do."[5] Then, on 25th June, the Duke of Oldenburg asked the Czar whether Clausewitz could be appointed to the Russo-German Legion, as Chief of Staff to the commander, the Swedish-born General Count Walmoden. This position, which Clausewitz was originally to take up in Russia, would carry an annual salary of 2,500 thalers. Clausewitz was torn between wanting this appointment, with its chance of worthwhile employment and "very good salary," and the desire to be with Gneisenau, upon whom he relied even more now that Scharnhorst was dead. "How loath I am to leave Gneisenau," he told Marie in a letter from Peilau on 31st Iune, "and how great the difference will be between him and Walmoden. At the same time, I am quite happy about this transfer."[6]

On 3rd July Clausewitz learned that the Czar had formally accepted the Russo-German Legion appointment. Three days later Clausewitz received his transfer instructions. The Legion, a new version of the one formed during the last months of the 1812 campaign, now consisted of two infantry regiments, one battalion of *chasseurs*, two hussar regiments and a mounted battery. Its strength was 6,000 men, and was soon to be increased to about 9,000. Much to Clausewitz's disappointment, this force was to operate in the north, some distance away from the likely centres of action.

At the end of July, after visiting Marie for a few days in Berlin, Clausewitz rode out to Schwerin, the Legion's headquarters. He was granted an audience with the Czar on 8th August. Besides commanding the Legion, Count Walmoden also commanded the corps to which it belonged, and he chose Clausewitz as the Chief of Staff and Quartermaster-General of this entire military group. According to Clausewitz, he was received by his new superior "neither with friendliness nor disdain."[7] He received a further briefing on 12th August at Grabow and was told that the main threat to the allies in the north was posed by Davout's corps at Hamburg; Count Walmoden was to use his force as an army of observation, and it soon became clear to Clausewitz that his commanding officer intended to carry out his duties by means of constant, wearing manoeuvres, a type of operation that Clausewitz intensely disliked.[8]

Since he was not closely involved with the main action during this period of the war, Clausewitz had an excellent chance to stand back and view the war as an expert observer. The allied field forces, apart from observation groups such as Walmoden's, were divided into three armies: the Army of Bohemia, under the Austrian Prince Karl zu Schwarzenberg; the army of Silesia, commanded by General Blücher; and the Army of the North, under Prince Bernadotte. Napoleon decided to launch two operations: in the south a defensive strategy based upon Dresden, and in the north an offensive from Hamburg. The Hamburg offensive, in the area covered by Count Walmoden's corps, was to be directed against Berlin by Oudinot, with the support of Davout's and Girard's division. At that time, about 12th August, Napoleon believed that the main allied army was concentrated in Silesia. But after he had left Dresden for Bautzen, he learned on 17th August that part of General Blücher's army had been detached for Bohemia. Napoleon revised his strategy. He now intended to attack Blücher first, and having defeated him, turn upon the armies of Bohemia and the North.

On 19th July the allies had agreed at Reichenbach that, to avoid this very danger, if one were threatened an immediate withdrawal would be made, to give time for all the allied forces to unite. General Blücher had accepted command of the Prussian army with great reluctance when he learned that the aim was to retire, if threatened. Nevertheless, he withdrew according to plan when the French forces moved towards him in Silesia. Blücher then undertook a series of exhausting marches and counter-marches to manoeuvre the French into a position where he would have the advantage. By the flooded waters of the River Katzbach, Blücher ferociously turned back upon the French. Macdonald's force was routed by the Prussians on 26th August after grim, hand-to-hand combat with bayonets and musket butts. Gneisenau, once more Blücher's Chief of Staff, wrote: "It was exactly like a battle of ancient times. Towards the end of the day there was a time when firing ceased completely until more cannon could be dragged up over the sodden ground. Only the cries of the combatants filled the air, while the decision was left to bared weapons."[9] A few days later, with Blücher in relentless pursuit of the French, his Chief of Staff added: "The roads between the Katzbach and the Bober are evidence of the terror that fell upon the enemy. Corpses that have been run over are still sticking everywhere in the mud."[10] Meanwhile Prince Karl of Schwarzenberg had marched his Army of Bohemia towards Dresden. He arrived in front of Napoleon's main supply depot on 25th August, and was determined to attack the next day. But Napoleon arrived back in time the following morning. Prince Karl decided to withdraw before the Emperor could strike, but in the confusion the signal to attack was given by mistake. Chaos increased, and Napoleon's 70,000 men easily repulsed the 150,000 Austrians. On 28th August, while Napoleon was still at Dresden, Vandamme advanced to Kulm and was heavily defeated after clashing with the Russians; one Russian corps engaged him while another attacked the French rear. About 13,000 French prisoners were taken, including Vandamme himself.

At about the same moment that he was told of Vandamme's defeat, Napoleon received confirmation of another. On 23rd August, Oudinot had been defeated by Prince Bernadotte and Bülow at Gross Beeren, a few miles south of Berlin, and forced to retire upon Wittenberg. Friedrich von Clausewitz had been present, commanding the Fourth East Prussian Infantry Regiment. With great bravery, Carl's brother had defended Trebbin against Oudinot's advance guard on 21st August; he had held the town with only four companies, with the French bombarding the Prussian positions with concentrated artillery fire and then throwing three regiments into the assault. Despite these setbacks, Napoleon was still determined to strike at Berlin. All the manoeuvring, all the heavy fighting so far, had failed to produce a strategic decision for either side. Then on 6th September, Marshal Ney—who had replaced Oudinot in the north—suffered a massive defeat at Dennewitz. Once more, the Clausewitz family was bravely represented by Friedrich.[11]

And at last action came for Carl. He wrote to Marie from Dannenberg on 19th September: "After much backward and forward manoeuvring we have finally managed to spike the guns of Marshal Davout. Because of a large

Above *The disorderly crossing of the frozen Berezina River by two improvised bridges*
Bottom *Bagetti's watercolour painting of the weary French troops winding their way to the Berezina*

Overleaf *Napoleon army crossing the River Danube shortly before the Battle of Wagram (1810), from the painting by Jacques Swebach in Apsley House*

number of intercepted letters we knew what his intentions were. A French corps of up to 10,000 men was supposed to go to Magdeburg to reinforce the garrison there, and at the same time to sweep enemy patrols from the left of the river."[12] Count Walmoden had resolved to intercept this French corps, commanded by General Pecheur. He had ordered Clausewitz to work out details for the operation, and on the night of 13th September had moved about 15,000 men and twenty-eight guns from Dömitz over the River Elbe into French-held territory. "In three days a pontoon bridge, beautiful as the Pont Neuf in Paris, had been thrown over the Elbe," wrote Clausewitz. On the morning of the 16th, the Russo-German Legion was deployed in hidden positions near the fortification of Breshau. Scouts reported that the French were approaching.

But General Pecheur, growing fearful at the sight of Cossacks in the area, slowed and finally stopped his march when his force was near the Gärda river. Count Walmoden had an urgent discussion with Clausewitz. As a result, the Legion was ordered to advance to engage the enemy before General Pecheur could retire. The troops were hurried forward and ordered to attack the moment the French were seen. The clash between the two forces was short, but bloody. The Legion had lost the advantage of surprise, but still caught the French off-balance, and the infantry and cavalry rushed in before the enemy could recover. Clausewitz was responsible for disposition-ing the troops, and stayed at the heart of the fighting until the French began to withdraw. The Legion pressed forward with more cavalry charges, and the French withdrawal gave way to a retreat. Clausewitz believed that this retreat could have been turned into a rout, if only Count Walmoden had made full use of troop deployments that he had suggested, and if only the General had been more determined. "If the dispositions had been accepted in their entirety, nothing, absolutely nothing, of the enemy corps could have escaped. We would have taken General Pecheur himself, and we would have had 800 to 1,000 more prisoners, if we could have persuaded the Count to let the cavalry continue their pursuit for one more hour, as it was not yet completely dark." Clausewitz told Marie: "The Count, between you and me, is not particularly enterprising. He is not thrusting enough. Apart from that, he is first class."[13]

The engagement was still an impressive and decisive victory for the Legion. The French corps had been smaller than anticipated. Instead of twelve battalions, it consisted of eight battalions, ten guns and four cavalry squadrons; but this still amounted to a powerful force. Yet only some 2,500 Frenchmen escaped from the battlefield. They retreated first to Luneburg and then attempted to slip over the River Elbe, but according to Clausewitz only 500 or 600 reached the far side. The rest were cut down by Cossacks. Clausewitz added: "We have taken eight cannon, 1,500 prisoners among whom is the Brigade General Mittchinski, one Colonel, two adjutants of General Pecheur and several staff officers. The enemy had 2,000 dead and

Facing page *General Hans David Ludwig von Yorck* (*1759-1830*)

wounded." The Russo-German force had lost fifty officers and 500 men, dead and wounded. Clausewitz assured Marie that he himself was unhurt; but a friend had been seriously injured—"poor Lützov has not been mortally wounded, but he has been injured in a very disagreeable way which I cannot describe here."[14]

Unfortunately Count Walmoden was unable to take full advantage of his victory. Clausewitz told Marie: "We heard from prisoners that Marshal Davout was planning to attack us on the right bank of the Elbe. We only had two hundred men on that side and the half-fortified position at Dömitz. We therefore had to get everything done as quickly as possible in order to get back over the river to meet the French threat."[15] So Count Walmoden withdrew on the day after the engagement. Only a Cossack force and one battalion was left on the left bank. Back over the river Clausewitz heard that the threat from Marshal Davout was a false alarm: the Legion was to continue the boring task of "watching and waiting."

Clausewitz had conducted himself well at the action on the Gärda. He had shown considerable coolness, clear judgement and determination. There was no sign of Clausewitz's over-caution which was to appear later, and which sprang from his constant inclination to take the most pessimistic view. Count Walmoden praised his Chief of Staff in his report on the battle. But in a bitter note to Marie on 21st September, Clausewitz wrote: "I have no idea what the Count will do for me in this matter. But knowing the way he acts and thinks, I doubt whether it will be very much. They will probably consider it enough to give me the order of St. Annen, which will annoy me very much. My great ambition at the moment is to be a Colonel."[16] Clausewitz felt that when decorations were awarded he would suffer as he had done before, and that at the most he would be given a Russian award, such as the St. Annen, rather than a Prussian medal. But in one respect, Clausewitz was typically over-pessimistic. The day after writing bitterly to Marie from Dömitz, he was indeed promoted to Colonel in the Russo-German Legion.

The engagement between Count Walmoden and General Pecheur affected French strategy in the region. "The French have been so frightened by the *débâcle* at the Gärda, that they have cleared the whole left bank of the Elbe," Clausewitz told Marie. This news, and information that Cossacks were active in the area, reached Napoleon at about the same time as a premature report that Prince Bernadotte had crossed the Elbe with 80,000 men at Rosslau. The French Emperor decided to abandon all territory east of the Elbe, except bridgeheads; he ordered Macdonald to retire to the left bank. With high sickness and casualty rates among his troops, Napoleon could no longer face a threat on such a wide and vulnerable front.

Clausewitz told Marie on 20th September: "This war must be made to move like a Catherine wheel, violently spinning through an impulse from within."[17] Even as he wrote, the spin was growing more violent. Throughout Germany, opposition to the French invaders was rising. So far the war had been fought by the allies on defensive lines—and the campaign was to be used by Clausewitz as an example of defensive conflict in *On War*. But as Clausewitz wrote in *On War*, this strategy of defence, although the strongest form of all, was only so if a switch was made to the offensive at the critical moment. "A swift and vigorous assumption of the offensive—the flashing sword of vengeance—is the most brilliant point in the defensive."[18] And now in Germany, this sword was drawn against the French. Communications were attacked; Cossacks fell upon isolated French units; in the north Prince Bernadotte threw bridges over the River Elbe and appeared in full force before Wartenberg; and above all, General Blücher made the most decisive move of the campaign, worked out closely with his Chief of Staff Gneisenau. Marching rapidly northward, Blücher went to join Bernadotte. Napoleon was now threatened by a force of 140,000 men in the north, while Prince Karl of Schwarzenberg and his 180,000 men in the south began to advance upon Leipzig. Blücher's move had brought an end to the campaign of withdrawals and manoeuvres and a start of the offensive. Napoleon was being forced into a corner. Clausewitz pointed out in *On War* that Napoleon was compelled to adopt a defensive position in view of the disproportion of forces. "Bonaparte, who was once in the habit of falling on his enemy like a wild boar, have we not seen him, when the proportion of force turned against him, in August and September, 1813, turn himself hither and thither as if he had been pent up in a cage?"[19]

But Napoleon was far from trapped. He still had the advantage of interior lines, able to attempt to destroy one army and switch to meet the other. On 2nd October Napoleon decided that Blücher and Bernadotte should be dealt with first. By 8th October about 150,000 French troops were concentrated at Wurzen, east of Leipzig. Napoleon then lunged towards Duben in an attempt to pin down General Blücher, but the Prussian general had already slipped out of reach and was with Prince Bernadotte near Halle. Napoleon was now to be taunted, like a cornered animal. Napoleon knew that if he allowed himself to be lured too far north, Leipzig would be threatened by Prince Karl of Schwarzenberg. He therefore decided to try and induce Schwarzenberg to advance, then, when the Austrian general was involved with Murat, to fall unexpectedly upon him. Napoleon himself remained at Eilenburg, south of Duben, until 14th October, the bait. But on 13th October, Blücher sent word to Schwarzenberg, who was advancing slowly towards Leipzig: "The three armies are now so closely together that a simultaneous attack, on the point where the enemy has concentrated his forces, might be undertaken." The campaign was reaching its climax.

In the north, Clausewitz knew that a great battle would soon be fought. Anxiously, he studied reports from the area around Leipzig. The battle would mean life or death for all that he and the other reformers and patriots had fought for. Germany would either be liberated, or placed under even harsher French domination. Defeat would mean the dismantling of the

Prussian army; any forces Prussia would be allowed to retain would be forced to fight for Napoleon in his search for further conquests. But victory would bring triumph for Prussia's new military strength. Fighting broke out around Leipzig on 16th October. The initial allied plan was for General Blücher and 54,000 men to strike at the north-west of the city, while three separate forces were to push forward from the west and south. On 16th October, General Blücher drove the French from the villages of Radefeld, Stahmeln and Wahren, and by nightfall General Yorck had taken Möckern. Marmont and his French units were forced to fall back almost to the outskirts of Leipzig. Meanwhile the allies in the west and south had advanced in four columns on a wide front against villages held by the French. Napoleon intended to break through the allied centre at Güldengossa with a massive cavalry assault, followed by infantry attacks on the columns.

Murat advanced with between 10,000 and 12,000 cavalrymen, supported by the foot soldiers. His charge was successful. The French cavalry plunged deep into the allied formations and cut through well to the south of Güldengossa. Then came the sound of heavy gunfire from the north, as the Prussians advanced on Möckern. Napoleon, who had not expected General Blücher to attack that day, rode off to direct the French defence, and in his absence the chance created by Murat's assault was neglected. The French infantry went forward too slowly; Murat's horses were blown; and the allies were given precious time to bring up reserves. By evening, the French were being forced back again. Napoleon made some preparations for a withdrawal on the night of 16th October. Betrand was told to be ready to secure passages over the River Saale and River Unstrut at Merseburg, Freiburg, Weissenfels and Kösen. But the French army itself was not to retire until the 18th October. The delay had dire consequences.

Neither side fully engaged on the 17th. The allies were waiting for the arrival of Prince Bernadotte and Bennigsen. But at breakfast time on the 18th the allied guns opened their bombardment. Napoleon ordered Betrand to slip away to secure the river passages. Slowly the French advance outposts were driven back; and early in the afternoon Bennigsen and Bernadotte arrived with their troops, which were immediately thrown into the attack. Gradually the French lines were forced to contract. As the sun fell in the sky, Napoleon dictated his orders for a retreat to the west, where a gap still remained in the allied lines. With darkness, the battle of Leipzig died down. But in the city itself, and in the French army, terrible confusion reigned. The sky was filled with a red glow over the burning houses. According to an allied eye-witness: "Their baggage, their artillery, their broken regiments, the soldiers who had spent many days without food, were held up for want of bridges over the streams around Leipzig. The cries of innumerable wounded echoed in the narrow streets, as our shot and shell fell upon them. Over the battlefield, so recently filled with the thunder of 2,000 guns, there now reigned the stillness of the grave."[20] The remnants of Napoleon's army escaped and crossed the River Saale at Weissenfels on 20th October. Napoleon left behind him 70,000 killed, wounded and captured. The allies had lost 54,000.

To Clausewitz, the battle of Leipzig was a perfect example of the results of superior numbers. This message was to be hammered home in *On War*: a superiority of men at the decisive point brings victory. In October, 1813, the disproportion of the troop strengths had reached its climax, Clausewitz wrote. At Leipzig Napoleon was obliged to "seek shelter in the angle formed by the Parth, the Elster, and the Pleiss, as if waiting for the enemy in the corner of a room, with his back against the wall."[21] On 9th November, Napoleon reached Paris. For the first time in his life he had been decisively beaten in a European battle. Now, Clausewitz believed, Napoleon and France should be delivered the final death blow.

"We must cross the Rhine," Clausewitz wrote on 1st November in one of his frequent letters to Gneisenau. "The operations must continue without rest until the peace." If need be, the war should be pursued all the way to Paris. Demoralized, the French forces would be unable to stop the allied advance. "All previous arguments against operations inside France and even up to Paris are now baseless, and out of date. A rebellion in the [French] army, and in the provinces, would meet us half way. The corner stone of a durable peace would be laid, under conditions which would be easy to keep."[22] Both Gneisenau and Blücher agreed with Clausewitz. Blücher, who was now a Field-Marshal, believed that the allies should push on "to the last breath and last horse." Both he and his Chief of Staff, Gneisenau, were intent upon shedding as much French blood as possible. Gneisenau relished the thought of the chase and the revenge; he wrote: "The highest satisfaction in life is to avenge oneself upon an arrogant enemy."[23] He was motivated more by this than by political realities, as he would be again after Waterloo.

Czar Alexander, too, demanded the complete defeat of Napoleon; but for different reasons. He wanted the Emperor to be replaced by Prince Bernadotte. With France removed as a potential counter-balance to Russia, the Czar would be able to master all Poland, and, with this frontier strengthened, devote himself to the conquest of the Near East. But this Near Eastern policy would clash with Austrian interests; Chancellor Metternich therefore opposed the Czar. So the allies continued to quarrel among themselves at Frankfurt, where the joint headquarters were now established.

Leipzig had seen the peak of allied co-operation; thereafter this co-operation rapidly declined. Conflicting interests emerged more strongly. Austria and Prussia clashed over schemes for the future of Germany, and each struggled to dominate the coalition of various states which would comprise the new nation. This political struggle hindered military operations against the French and Blücher insisted that the military point of view should be taken first. "It is true that we accomplished much," he wrote later, "but not nearly as much as we might have done. By rights, Napoleon ought not to have come through, and God forgive those whose tardiness and laziness were to blame. But the devil is ever at work and envy is not idle!"[24] Napoleon had time to recover slightly; and when the allied armies did finally invade France, spearheaded by the Prussians across the central Rhine on New Year's Day, 1814, the Austrian army under Schwarzenberg still sought peace with Napoleon, rather than his destruction. This lack of common policy was clearly reflected in the disunited conduct of the campaign in France. Napoleon made full use of it.

Despairing letters flowed between Clausewitz and Gneisenau. Clausewitz was still serving with Count Walmoden, first in the Netherlands, then in Flanders, but always away from the main scene of fighting. If Clausewitz had been at Gneisenau's side, as both of them wanted, he would have felt still more frustrated and disappointed over the allied actions. To Blücher and Gneisenau, all opportunities were still open at the start of 1814. On 11th January, Joachim Murat, King of Naples, deserted to the allies in the hope that by doing so his throne—which Napoleon had given him—would be more secure. Three days later King Frederick VI of Denmark followed. Frederick's change of allegiance allowed Count Walmoden's force to move away from the area near the Danish frontier, where it had still operated as an army of observation. On 25th January, Prince Karl of Schwarzenberg was between Langres and Bar-sur-Aube, while General Blücher was near Brienne, then held by Victor and Macdonald. On the same day, Napoleon left Paris to lead his forces, and on 29th January he hurled his troops at Blücher to prevent him joining Schwarzenberg. But Blücher withdrew, and then advanced again to repulse Napoleon at La Rothière, forcing him to pull back to Troyes. Flushed with Field-Marshal Blücher's success, a diplomatic congress was opened at Châtillon on 3rd February which negotiated with the French until 19th March. At the talks, the allies offered France the frontiers she had had in 1792, before the Revolutionary wars had broken out.

Meanwhile an allied war council decided to send Blücher towards Paris from the north-west with 50,000 men; Schwarzenberg was to move towards the capital from the south-west via Sens, with 150,000 troops. This unstrategic division of forces stemmed from the political division among the allies; Austria still drew back from an attempt at a total French defeat. Clausewitz was among those who warned of the dangers, if Schwarzenberg failed to give Blücher full support, and of "the wretchedness of the state leaders."[25] Moreover, to Clausewitz the Austrian commander was an excellent example of the old-fashioned type of general, who believed in "algebraic actions" rather than in the new forms of flexible warfare on a mass scale. The contents of Book V, Chapter XVIII of On War were probably directed at Schwarzenberg, in which Clausewitz criticized those who worshipped the "sacred relics of military erudition" in empty phrases like "commanding positions, key positions, strategic manoeuvres." These expressions were "hollow shells without any sound kernel."

Blücher himself had to face Schwarzenberg's insistence that certain operations should be conducted in certain ways, for no better reason than the old theoretical manuals said so. For example, Schwarzenberg urged Blücher to occupy the "commanding position" of the Plateau of Langres, which is also the watershed of France. Blücher impatiently replied that the only advantage he could see in doing so was that if he stood upon the summit and urinated, some of his water would flow down into the Mediterranean and some down into the Atlantic.

Clausewitz was over harsh in his criticisms of Schwarzenberg. His information came second-hand from Gneisenau who, with Blücher, was guilty of several errors of judgement during the 1814 campaign. The same errors would recur the following year. The Prussian commander and his Chief of Staff saw events in too narrow a view. They wanted to press on regardless of diplomatic considerations, regardless even of the state of their troops. They wanted revenge, and were determined to have it. As Gneisenau wrote to Stein in January, 1814: "We must take revenge for the many sorrows inflicted upon the nations, and for so much arrogance. If we do not, then we are miserable wretches indeed, and deserve to be shocked out of our lazy peace every two years and threatened with the scourge of slavery." Gneisenau added: "We must return the visits of the French to our cities, by visiting them in theirs. Until we do, our revenge and triumph will be incomplete. If the Silesian Army reaches Paris first, I shall at once have the bridges of Austerlitz and Jena blown up, as well as the Arc de Triomphe."[26] With this attitude, shared by Blücher and Grolman, the Prussian military chiefs were in effect trying to supersede the civilian authorities. Clausewitz, in 1814, largely agreed with Gneisenau and Blücher. But when they formed the same attitude the following year, Clausewitz was to believe they were wrong—and in *On War* Clausewitz would severely criticize military leaders who overstepped the proper boundaries of their role.

In 1814, therefore, Gneisenau and Blücher were not quarrelling with Schwarzenberg simply over strategy, but over something far more fundamental. Unlike the Prussian commander and his Chief of Staff, Schwarzenberg did keep diplomatic as well as military considerations in mind. Indeed, he could hardly forget them. The unfortunate Schwarzenberg was constantly harried and hounded by the civilian chiefs, and by the allied monarchs. During the whole of the autumn campaign of 1813, Schwarzenberg suffered from the presence of three of the allied sovereigns at, or uncomfortably close to, his headquarters. These were Emperor Francis of Austria, Friedrich Wilhelm of Prussia, and Czar Alexander of Russia. With them went their advisers. The situation only slightly improved in 1814. The monarchs insisted upon involving themselves in the campaign, and plagued Schwarzenberg with their messengers, such as Clausewitz's colleague in Russia,

General von Toll, or, in the case of Friedrich Wilhelm, General von Hake. Schwarzenberg, normally mild-mannered, exclaimed: "It really is inhuman what I have to tolerate and bear, surrounded as I am by feeble-minded people, fools of every kind, crazy project-makers, intriguers, asses, loud-mouths . . . I often think I shall collapse under their weight."[27]

Moreover, of the military commanders, Schwarzenberg was most affected by the dissension among the allies. While Field-Marshal Blücher was determined to push on for Paris, and was supported by the Czar, the Austrians believed that Napoleon should be persuaded, rather than forced, to conclude a peace. Chancellor Metternich advocated a military strategy which was designed to avoid bloody encounters, and told Schwarzenberg in January to advance "cautiously" and to "utilize the desire of the common man in France for peace by avoiding warlike acts." Relations between the Austrian minister and Czar Alexander deteriorated, but Metternich continued to press Schwarzenberg to avoid further forward action. At one point, Schwarzenberg supplied Metternich with a report which stressed the deficiencies of the allied armies: this was valuable ammunition for Metternich in his struggle with Alexander. The showdown came on 26th January, when the Austrian Chancellor warned that if Russia intended to force Napoleon to abdicate, Austrian troops would no longer take part in the campaign. Alexander replied by threatening to march on Paris alone, or with his Prussian ally: as the Russians had lost fewer men at Leipzig and had greater reserves than Austria, the threat was a serious one. A compromise was reached at Langres on 29th January, when the allies agreed that military operations should be resumed under the direction of Schwarzenberg, who would pay "appropriate attention to military expediency."

Blücher and Gneisenau refused to modify their attitude. Impetuously, they wanted to rush headlong to Paris, and brought upon themselves criticism from some of their own Prussian colleagues. General Müffling, a future distinguished Chief of the Prussian General Staff, believed that they spent far too much time delivering emotional speeches, and that Gneisenau's planning was weak because he placed too much emphasis upon bravery as the determinant of victory; he had too much confidence in his own ability to inspire this courage whenever it was needed.[28]

Clausewitz was rather prejudiced, giving too much support to Gneisenau, and too little to Schwarzenberg. While he modified his opinion of the merits of Gneisenau's strategy the following year, Clausewitz failed to change his views of Schwarzenberg whom he criticized by implication in *On War* and more directly in his *Campaign of 1814*. Unjustly, Clausewitz completely disagreed with the Austrian commander when Schwarzenberg complained to his wife about the actions of the uncouth, hot-headed Prussian Field-Marshal and his Chief of Staff: "Blücher, and still more Gneisenau, are urging the march on Paris with such perfectly childish rage that they trample underfoot every single rule of warfare. Regardless of their rear, and

of their right flanks, they do nothing but plan parties in the Palais Royal."
Schwarzenberg added: "That is indeed frivolous at such an important
moment."[29]

Napoleon seized upon the splintered, disunited enemy advance. Operating on interior lines he conducted a brilliant campaign. In the middle of
February the Prussians were attacked, scattered, and suffered heavy casualties. Already weakened by lack of supplies from home, Blücher's men now
fell victim to a resurgence of local French patriotism. Peasants rose up
against the invaders to cut communication lines, ambush foragers, and
slaughter isolated patrols. Clausewitz, and several other Prussians, still felt
that peace would not come until Paris was taken. But the allies continued to
offer a settlement, while Napoleon redoubled his efforts to detach Austria
from the coalition. Eventually, on 1st March, the allies found a strong
enough basis of agreement to conclude the Quadruple Alliance of Chau-
mont. In this, they pledged themselves not only to the pursuing of the war
and avoiding separate negotiations, but also to enforcing peace against
French violation for twenty years.

Field-Marshal Blücher had already resumed his advance, but withdrew
again when Napoleon moved against him. He clashed with Bonaparte on 7th
March at Craonne, but two days later surprised Marmont at Laon and
routed him. Taking part in the engagement, with notable distinction, were
Friedrich and Wilhelm von Clausewitz, the latter as a Brigade Major.[30]
Despite every setback and criticism, the indomitable Blücher marched on.
He earned the nickname of "Forward," and he spared neither his troops,
nor himself. Napoleon retired to Soissons; but he moved against Schwarzen-
berg when he heard on 17th March that the Austrians were reaching for
Paris to the south of him. On 20th March the battle of Arcis-sur-Aube was
fought between 23,000 French and 60,000 Austrians, and ended with
Napoleon's withdrawal to Sézanne.

Napoleon had the hopeless task of trying to hold off two armies, and he
only had meagre forces with which to do it. He made one last desperate
gamble, marching east to attack Schwarzenberg from behind to induce the
Austrians to turn around and away from Paris. But Napoleon's plan was
revealed when one of his letters was intercepted by Cossacks: Alexander
persuaded Schwarzenberg to resume his advance on Paris and to link with
Blücher. With the road to his capital left open by his withdrawal into
Lorraine, Napoleon could do little to stop the allied advance. The French
Emperor had fought well, but the end was approaching. In *On War*,
Clausewitz argued that Napoleon could have fought even more effectively if
a different strategy had been adopted. "No-one has yet asked the question,
what would have been the result if, instead of turning from Blücher upon
Schwarzenberg, he had tried another blow at Blücher, and pursued him to
the Rhine? We are convinced that it would have completely changed the
course of the campaign, and that the Army of the Allies, instead of

marching to Paris, would have retired behind the Rhine."[31] In view of the
Austrian attitude, Clausewitz was probably right as far as Schwarzenberg
was concerned. But everything would have depended upon whether Czar
Alexander would have still wished to continue alone, and if so, whether he
would have been strong enough to do so.

As news of the Prussian setbacks and advances had reached Count
Walmoden's headquarters in the Netherlands, both he and Clausewitz had
redoubled their efforts to bring the Russo-German Legion closer to the main
area of fighting. Clausewitz wanted to be in at the kill. He wrote to his
friend Gneisenau to enlist his support despite the fact the Gneisenau was
fully engaged in the hectic advance on Paris, and was also occupied with the
squabbles with the allies, and would have little time to spare. At Count
Walmoden's suggestion, Clausewitz asked Gneisenau if he could help persuade the King to attach the Legion to Blücher's force, and, if possible,
integrate it within the Prussian army. "If you do this you will give orphaned
children a Fatherland," he wrote.[32] Among those orphans would be Clausewitz himself. The Legion had not, in fact, fulfilled the role for which it had
been originally designed. Stein, one of its most important founders, had
imagined that a British invasion force, helped by Sweden, would have
helped to liberate Germany. The Russo-German Legion would co-operate
with this Anglo-Swedish force, and form a link between the German
insurgents and the foreign army. But no foreign help came in 1812, and
early in 1813 Prussia took the place of Britain in Stein's view of how the
liberation might come about. The Legion was not needed to link the regular
army and the people: this army belonged to Prussia, and any link was made
by the *Landwehr* and the *Landsturm*. As a result, the Legion could do no more
than act as an auxiliary force to the allied forces, however well it might
conduct itself in this capacity.[33] Indeed, the Legion's performance was very
creditable, but it offered far too little scope for the impatient Clausewitz,
especially in the last days of the campaign.

Count Walmoden and his Chief of Staff waited for an answer to Clausewitz's request. On 25th March, Marmont's and Mortier's corps were
defeated by Blücher at La Fère-Champenoise, and General Pacthod's
National Guard put up an heroic but hopeless stand not far away. Rapidly,
the allies approached Paris. At the end of March, Napoleon's capital
surrendered, although Napoleon himself was still at large. The warhorse
Blücher was, for the moment, blown, his energy sapped by the struggle with
the enemy and allies alike. He wanted no more of it. He kept to himself in
his room high up in Montmartre while his ragged and dirty troops revelled
in the conquered French city below. Gneisenau urged him to take part in
the parades, but Blücher replied: "What have I to do with the Parisians?
What is Paris to me?"[34] Then the Field-Marshal fell seriously ill, and for six
days lay blind and prostrate.

Clausewitz was severely depressed as he awaited news of Gneisenau's attempt to merge the German Legion with the Prussian army. He tried to join the Dutch service, but nothing came of it. His future suddenly seemed bleak. Tension showed in letters to Marie. He wrote on 4th April, for example: "I do not know whether I am being conceited or whether I am thinking correctly, but I have an arrogant conviction that I did not deserve being thrown out and refused by every army."[35] At last, news came that the Legion had been accepted into Prussian service. Its troops would no longer feel outcasts. Yet this only made Clausewitz more miserable. The Legion as a whole had been passed fit for Prussian service, while he, one of the most patriotic of all Prussians, had previously been refused by the King.

Clausewitz set down to draft one of the bitterest letters of his life. Addressed to King Friedrich Wilhelm, and dated 12th April, it read: "The Russo-German Legion has had the good fortune to be accepted into the service of Your Majesty. I would feel justified in belonging to the Legion and sharing in this happiness if I did not remember Your Royal Majesty's previous judgement upon me, when I had held it my duty to place a special request before Your Royal Majesty. It is against my feelings to creep into Your Royal Majesty's army by the back door with a noble corps. And if I am not fortunate enough to be deemed by Your Royal Majesty worthy of serving in your excellent army, I will look upon my departure from the Legion as a necessary evil, which I would rather undergo than serve under the eyes of Your Royal Majesty without the same right to Your Royal Majesty's favour and goodwill which every other officer enjoys."[36] The letter, which Clausewitz had told Marie about on 1st April, was probably never sent. The day before it was written, Friedrich Wilhelm had issued a royal order appointing Carl von Clausewitz an infantry colonel in the Prussian Army.

At last, Clausewitz was back in the service of his Fatherland. Yet the return had come too late. On the same day as the royal order was issued, Napoleon Bonaparte abdicated. The long European war was over. Bonaparte had no other choice; his forces were exhausted, Paris had surrendered, the capitulation was signed at two in the morning on 31st March by Marmont at his mansion in the Rue Paradis. Napoleon's marshals wanted peace, Napoleon could only admit defeat, on Thursday, 7th April, 1814; the French tricolour was hauled down from buildings and from flag-poles throughout Europe. Hostilities had finished before Clausewitz had a chance to fight with the Prussians against the hated French. No other opportunity seemed likely; and now military service meant dull, routine, garrison life.

On the night of 28th April, Napoleon embarked in the British frigate *Undaunted*, berthed at Fréjus, and sailed for the Island of Elba. This generous treatment of Bonaparte was, Clausewitz warned, a dangerous mistake. Napoleon should have been "arrested for the atrocities he had committed."[37] As it was, some of the French marshals and part of the French army still supported their Emperor and, Clausewitz believed, the

French Government was composed of "malcontents." Although cooped up on Elba, Napoleon still remained a potential threat to Europe. On 30th May came the first Peace of Paris, negotiated with France by the four major allies. The terms actually gave France more territory and firmer boundaries than the "frontiers of 1792" proposal had seemed to offer. Czar Alexander had promised Louis XVIII's new *régime* that France under the restored Bourbon monarchy would receive better terms than those offered to Napoleon; Britain also wanted an understanding with the new monarchy; and Austria looked for a strong France to balance Russia. Talks about the new European balance of power continued in the capitals throughout the summer, prior to the general congress which was held in Vienna in late September.

In July the Russo-German Legion moved to Bonn, where it became simply the German Legion, incorporated into General von Kleist's Third Army Corps. Clausewitz went on extended leave. His health was suffering badly, not only physically—partly from gout—but also spiritually. He felt a reaction to the unrelieved strain of the previous two years; the exhaustion of the Russian campaign, from which he had had no time to recover before plunging into the work on the *Landwehr*; then the exertions and dangers of Gross Görschen and the other battles of early 1813; finally the wearying, frustrating operations after the ending of the armistice. His general debilitation was aggravated by the mental stress caused by his inability to re-enter Prussian service. For several months Clausewitz lived near Aix-la-Chapelle, where Marie stayed with him for some of the time. He began to put his notes in order and wrote about the local people and countryside. But chiefly, Clausewitz just brooded. He took the waters for his gout, and he took opium for his mind. Clausewitz had probably begun to take opium—a fairly common practice at the time—either in Russia, or soon after his return. But the drug did nothing to help him. He grew increasingly anxious that he would never be able to achieve all he wanted in Prussia's army; that his chances of promotion and of selection to posts he wanted had fallen. King Friedrich Wilhelm did not easily forget his grudges.

Clausewitz was not the only one to be penalized for his "desertion" to the Russians. Some members of the nobility had even had their estates seized. But such was Clausewitz's nature that his treatment at the hands of the King and the royal family seemed far worse. He took everything so very seriously. For the passionate patriot not to be allowed to serve his country was a serious matter indeed. Moreover, Clausewitz was always in an awkward position, never quite "in," never quite "out." He had been in the reform group and had done important work, yet he had never been quite as prominent, quite as influential, as the other members. While they could disagree with the King, and take opposite sides, they were strong enough to be allowed back into the fold. Even General Yorck returned, although the King never quite forgave him for the Convention of Tauroggen. Yorck was too powerful to be held back, but Clausewitz was in a far inferior position. Whereas a man of Blücher's temperament would reply to the King's treatment with a vigorous expletive, the sensitive Clausewitz suffered. So, that summer at Aix-la-Chapelle, Clausewitz became even more withdrawn; and the more he did so, the more he drew apart from the influential circle around the King. He never found it easy to make friends, and relied increasingly upon the staunch and loyal Gneisenau.

During the autumn and winter of 1814 the wartime allies quarrelled in Vienna over the structure of Europe. Both the Austrian Chancellor Metternich, and Britain's Lord Castlereagh worked on plans for a balance of power. Prussia, represented by Hardenburg, wished to end the weakness caused by the wide spread of her separate possessions; and both Austria and Prussia wanted to play the leading role in German affairs. Friedrich Wilhelm urged Hardenberg to press the Prussian case with extreme vigour; he also wished to cement his friendship with Czar Alexander, whom he looked upon as the protector of his monarchy. The Czar, on the other hand, was determined to consolidate his power in Poland. By 3rd January, 1815, relations had deteriorated so far that Britain, Austria and France concluded a secret alliance, promising to fight together if any of them were attacked by Russia or Prussia. In Berlin war with Austria was actively discussed.

Soon after, a European compromise was reached. The subsequent dealing out of territory altered the face of Europe for the next century. But many details had still to be settled. The Congress of Vienna was still in session when, on 4th March, the shattering news was received that Napoleon had escaped from Elba. He had landed in France three days before; by 20th March, he was back in Paris. The 1815 campaign, the "Waterloo Campaign," was about to begin.

THIRTEEN

Red Flows Ligny Stream

"To throw oneself, blinded by
excitement for a moment, against
cold death . . . can this be difficult?"
(*On War*, bk. i, ch. iv.)

FIRST OF ALL, Napoleon had to find an army. When he landed on the first
day of spring he had 500 grenadiers of his Guard, 200 dragoons and 100
Polish lancers. The horseless cavalrymen had to hump their saddles on their
own backs. Yet incredibly, by the end of May, 1815, Napoleon had 284,000
men, supported by an auxiliary force over 222,000 strong, and while a great
deal of this strength was rested upon paper figures, Napoleon's force included
the powerful army of the North under his personal command, consisting of over 120,000 men. The remainder were split between the Armies of
the Rhine, Loire, Alps and Pyrenees. In Vienna, the allies formed the
Seventh Coalition and busied themselves raising five armies. In Belgium an
Anglo-Dutch army of 93,000 men was deployed under the command of the
Duke of Wellington, and a Prussian army of 117,000 men under Field-
Marshal Blücher. An Austrian army of 210,000 troops, commanded by
Schwarzenberg was positioned on the Upper Rhine. Barclay's Russian
army of 150,000 men was deployed on the Middle Rhine, and an Austro-
Italian army of 75,000 men commanded by Frimont was situated in
northern Italy.

On 30th March, Clausewitz joined the Prussian General Staff. Anxiously,
he awaited news of his posting: where would he go, to whom, and in what
capacity? On 22nd April, Clausewitz was nominated Chief of Staff to the
Third Prussian Corps which was commanded by Lieutenant-General von
Thielmann. So Colonel von Clausewitz, as he now was, began his fourth
campaign against the French. He was one of the very few Prussian officers
who could claim to have done so.

The Third Corps was already moving forward. Late in April it crossed
the Belgium frontier and on 4th May, Gneisenau ordered General von
Thielmann to advance to positions between Huy and Ciney. Just over forty
miles away, lay a small village; it was called Waterloo. As always before
battle, Clausewitz was to be found in excellent spirits. "My health is quite
good now," he told Marie. "Only once have I taken opium, and a much

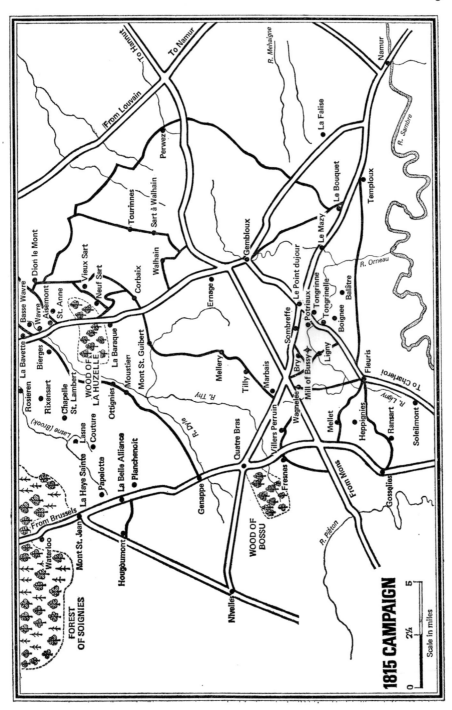

1815 CAMPAIGN

Scale in miles

0   2½   5

smaller quantity than usual, yet the result was much stronger—proof the body was no longer used to it. So although I am never without pain from my gout, especially in the morning, I have a feeling of resistance against the opium which is for me a sure sign that I feel better."[1] The Third Corps comprised four infantry brigades, the Ninth, Tenth, Eleventh, and Twelfth, commanded respectively by General von Borcke, Colonel von Kampfen, Colonel von Luck, and Colonel von Stülpnagel. Each brigade had from six to nine battalions of between 600 to 750 men, the total infantry strength amounted to 20,611 troops. The Third Corps' cavalry consisted of 2,405 horses organized in two brigades, commanded by Colonel von der Marwitz and Colonel Count Lottum, with a reserve under General von Hube. There were three foot batteries of artillery, three horse batteries and an artillery reserve, which gave a total of forty-eight guns.[2] General von Thielmann's Third Corps was the smallest of the four corps in the main Prussian army. The others were led by Ziethen (First Corps), Pirch (Second) and Bülow (Fourth), having 32,692 men, 32,704 and 31,102 men respectively.

In Belgium, the allied plan was simply to overwhelm Napoleon through sheer force of numbers. Wellington, Blücher and Schwarzenberg were to march directly upon Paris, and if one of them should be checked or forced to pull back, Barclay de Tolly was to reinforce them with the Russian army, while the others pushed on, and Frimont advanced up towards Lyons. The French frontier was to be crossed simultaneously by all armies between 27th June and 1st July; Wellington was in overall command of the forces in Belgium. Neither Wellington nor Blücher believed that Napoleon would take the offensive. The two commanders met for talks at Tirlemont on the 3rd May and decided to concentrate their armies on the line Quatre Bras-Sombreffe, ready for the move forward.

But Napoleon did decide to seize the initiative, enter Belgium, and defeat the Anglo-Dutch and Prussian armies in turn. First of all, he intended to drive through the gap which lay between the two armies before they could be fully joined. This meant advancing as rapidly as possible towards Brussels down the direct road through Charleroi which passed between Wellington's and Blücher's forces. Napoleon then intended to attack the nearest enemy, the Prussians, and then turn quickly upon the Anglo-Dutch force before Wellington could assemble his army strength. Ziethen, the Prussian commander near Charleroi, observed French camp fires burning at Solre and Beaumont on the night of 13th June, and dispatched warnings to Wellington and Blücher. The British commander acted less quickly than Blücher, who, at eleven o'clock on the evening of 14th June, ordered his Corps commanders to concentrate in the direction of Fleurus. General von Thielmann received his instructions during the night and at once ordered Clausewitz to prepare for the Third Corps' march forward to Namur. Bülow's Fourth Corps was to march from Liege to Hannut, while Pirch went forward with the Second Corps from Namur to Sombreffe. Ziethen and the First Corps were to prepare for the advance of the French on the Sambre river, and, if in danger of being overwhelmed by superior numbers, gradually to fall back to Fleurus and delay the French as long as possible. Clausewitz and the Third Corps force-marched during the day of 15th June and reached Namur late that night. As anticipated, the bulk of Ziethen's brave First Corps was driven back, but managed a skilful withdrawal upon Fleurus.

Meanwhile, Wellington had estimated that Napoleon would most likely try to advance by way of Mons and fall upon the Anglo-Dutch communications. During the early evening of 15th June, Wellington received a message informing him that the Prussians were massing between Sombreffe and Fleurus. But orders given by Wellington before he went to the Brussels ball organized by the Duchess of Richmond were still designed to cover his communications, and not to move towards Blücher. Not until later in the evening was Wellington convinced by dispatches that Napoleon was advancing on Charleroi. Then, almost too late, Wellington ordered his whole army to march upon Quatre Bras, to Blücher's right.

As Wellington's officers dashed to the front, some of them half-clad in ballroom clothes, Clausewitz was on the march again. At two o'clock in the early morning of 16th June, only a few hours after arriving at Namur, Thielmann's Fourth Corps was ordered forward to help Ziethen block the French thrust. During the early morning on the 17th June, Clausewitz and the rest of the troops were hurrying down the road to the sound of the guns near Fleurus, where Ziethen's First Corps desperately needed support. Ziethen's force occupied a salient along the Ligny brook behind Fleurus, with its right flank at Wagnelée, its centre at St. Amand, and its left flank at Ligny village. The Corps had taken heavy casualties, but had managed to hold off the French advance units. Thielmann's troops began to arrive at ten o'clock according to Clausewitz[3] and immediately deployed on Ziethen's left between Sombreffe and Le Mazy. Clausewitz quickly worked out dispositions to give a strong covering force along the Ligny brook. At the same time, Pirch's Second Corps also reached the area, and was immediately posted to Ziethen's rear. Among Pirch's brigades was one in which Wilhelm von Clausewitz served as a staff officer.

Frantically, the Prussians ran to take up defensive positions. But the strongest Corps of all, Bülow's, was still *en route* from Liege, sixty miles away. Through a series of misunderstandings and errors, partly the fault of Gneisenau's staff work, the Prussians would be deprived of more than 30,000 valuable men in the coming battle.

Blücher, therefore, could only concentrate 84,000 men on the field of Ligny. The area itself was of considerable strategic importance, since it covered the junction of roads from western and northern Belgium and from Germany and the River Rhine. The blocking of Napoleon was made even more crucial by the fact that six miles away Wellington was heavily engaged by the French at Quatre Bras. To control the important crossroads, the

French had to secure the high ground, notably near the villages of Bry and Sombreffe, and, to the east, the even higher ground at Tongrinne where Thielmann's Fourth Corps was deployed. But to gain the heights, the French would first have to take the villages clustered in the valley, through which the Ligny stream flowed. Here the main fighting was to take place: at St. Amand, La Haye, and Wagnelée on the gentle slopes to the west. The hamlets in the Third Corps area—Boignee and Balâtre—were also to be disputed, although not so fiercely. The houses in the villages, stone-built and with walled or thick hedge enclosures, offered the Prussians strong defensive positions.

Nevertheless, the Prussians were still in the tactically weaker position. The chief defect arose through the ground behind Fleurus being higher than the hills on the north of the valley where Blücher's units were positioned. This gave Napoleon's guns a greater range and made observation of the Prussian movements much easier. In addition, the folds of the land in the valley itself allowed the French to steal close, concealed until very near the point of contact.

That morning, Wellington had ridden over to talk with Field-Marshal Blücher and Gneisenau, at the mill of Bussy between Ligny and Bry. Wellington was very uneasy about the Prussian positions; Blücher, he believed, would be "damnably mauled." Gneisenau disliked and distrusted Wellington, considering him to be over-lucky and unwilling to lend the Prussians any support. When the British commander observed that the Prussians on the forward slopes would be vulnerable to French artillery, Gneisenau stiffly replied: "Our men like to see the enemy,"—a reference to Wellington's preference for keeping his forces on the hidden slope until the last moment, to keep them protected and maintain surprise. Others have agreed with Wellington's criticisms of Blücher's and Gneisenau's troop deployment. The Swiss military historian, Antoine Henri Jomini, called the position "detestable."

Both sides prepared for battle, and then came the worst part of all, the waiting. The men were nervous and tense, sweating in the strong sunshine. The officers, Clausewitz among them, checked their positions. Soon after midday, Clausewitz watched the French begin to move forward for the attack; the sun glinted upon weapons and buckles, gun carriages creaked, shouts of command were audible across the valley. On the Prussian side, the men were silent and still. Napoleon had ordered Grouchy to hold down the Third Corps with his infantry and cavalry force, supported by Exelmans and Pajol, while the French launched assaults under the command of Vandamme and Girard at St. Amand, and under Gérard at Ligny.

At two o'clock in the afternoon, said Clausewitz, the battle of Ligny began. For the first period the Third Corps was spared a major offensive, although many of its men were struck down by artillery fire. Clausewitz could see the clash in the valley below and to his right, only a few hundred yards away. He crouched behind a stone wall, and watched the lines of French troops advance across the yellow grain fields in the sunlight to storm St. Amand, held by three Prussian infantry battalions. At the same time, a thunderous artillery bombardment plunged the village of Ligny in dense and swirling black smoke. When the dust settled it seemed to Clausewitz that nobody could possibly be alive in the burning rubble. But then, as the columns of French troops approached, Prussians ran from the ruins to take positions behind the walls in the gardens.

Twice, French assaults were thrown back from Ligny. But at St. Amand the mass of French whom Clausewitz saw advancing towards the village swept all before them, and the surviving Prussians were sent reeling from the houses. Yet when the French tried to press on from St. Amand, they were met with devastating grape and cannister shot from Prussian batteries on the hills beyond, and Napoleon's men swayed back again. A Prussian counter-attack, with four battalions of men shouting and screaming as they charged forwards, succeeded in holding the lower part of the village. By this time, the thunderous artillery duel between the two armies had reached a terrible crescendo. Shells were exploding upon the grassy slopes around Clausewitz, and the Prussian guns answered from behind him, shells whistling over his head to smash into the flanks of the enemy assault below. Clausewitz could see the effect of the cannister shot, which scythed into the French ranks and sprawled the cut and bloodied bodies in the dusty field and sent many running in fear. But most continued to advance.

Now Thielmann's Third Corps was also engaged. Grouchy ordered French detachments forward to take Boignee and the outlying houses around Tongrinne. Clausewitz detailed reinforcements to run down the slopes to the cover of the walls and buildings. Some of the Prussian positions were taken, then retaken, in close-quarter fighting. More infantrymen were hurried over from Gérard's Corps to help Grouchy. One of these French troops described his terrible experience: "As we passed through the small hills, covered with corn, and caught sight of the nearest house, a veritable hail of musket fire rained down upon the head of the column with a frightful noise. From every hole in the old ruin, from all the windows and loopholes in the houses, from the hedges and orchards and from above the stone walls, the muskets showered their deadly fire upon us like lightning." The Frenchman continued: "The column set off again at a run and threw itself into the road that led down the hill across the hedges. From the palisades and the walls behind which the Prussians were in ambush, they continued to pour their musketry fire upon us. But woe to everyone we met! They defended themselves with the desperation of wolves, but a few blows from a musket or a bayonet-thrust soon stretched them out in some corner. A great number of old soldiers with grey moustaches had secured their retreat, and retired in good order, turning to fire a last shot, and then slipped through a breach or shut a door. We followed them without hesitation. We had neither prudence nor mercy . . . From the well-barricaded cottages they still poured their fire upon us. In ten minutes more we should have been exterminated to the last man. Seeing this, the column turned down the hill again. Drummers and sappers, officers and soldiers, pell-mell, all went without once turning their heads to look back. I jumped over the palisades where I should have thought it impossible to go at any other time, with my knapsack and cartridge-box at my back. All this did not take ten minutes."[4]

Napoleon's plan was still to take the Prussian right and centre, rather than to risk too many troops on the difficult hills defended by Thielmann and his Third Corps. So the main struggle continued around St. Amand, La Haye, Wagnelée, and Ligny itself. St. Amand, already taken by the French, was held. But Napoleon's troops were still stopped from advancing further by Ziethen's batteries. Girard's division took La Haye. When Pirch sent his Prussians down the slopes from Bry to counter-attack, entire ranks were bloodily slaughtered by French artillery fire. The survivors were pinned to the ground. Then, incredibly, they staggered to their feet again and moved forward. Scores more were cut down by the crackling musket fire from the village. Still they pressed on, and one after another, the houses of La Haye were wrenched from the French. Back swayed the enemy offensive. Girard himself was killed; but his troops fought on, and the Prussians had to withdraw and re-form, ready to launch a counter-attack organized by Field-Marshal Blücher himself. The old soldier stood up in his stirrups and shouted: "My sons! Carry yourselves bravely, do not let 'the nation' dominate you again! Forward! Forward in God's name!"

Blücher's famous rallying cry of "*Vorwärts!*" was at once answered by the familiar roar from the French: "*Vive l'Empereur!*" Men from Thielmann's corps were detailed by Clausewitz to hurry over to give support, and the Prussian charge began. Screaming "*Vorwärts! Vorwärts!*" the men plunged headlong against the blazing French guns, and hacked the enemy out of the buildings of La Haye. With the village back in Prussian hands, renewed efforts were made to push the French from Wagnelée. Again there was temporary success. The streets, with the French dead sprawled everywhere, were reclaimed by the Prussians. But when they advanced beyond the cover of the houses, Blücher's men came under terrible fire from French *tirailleurs* concealed in the thick waving corn. Disorganized, the Prussians retreated once more. So the vicious fighting went on, with Clausewitz watching and waiting for a renewed attack upon the Third Corps. His ears rang with the noise of battle. Through the drifting pall of black smoke he could see the successive assaults and counter-attacks: La Haye changed hands four times; St. Amand was fought over again and again. More men were ordered to leave the Third Corps to reinforce the battered Prussian left. Clausewitz and Thielmann had to reorganize their depleted forces as best they could.

Fighting at Ligny was even fiercer in the centre, with masses of men confronting one another at point blank range and pouring their musket fire directly into one another's ranks. The cobbled streets, alleys and doorways were choked up with the wounded, the dying and the dead. Houses were burned to the ground, or were still held as small forts. The entire village was wreathed in smoke which spread a misty black veil over the human turmoil. In the midst of the cries of the wounded, and the shouts of command, was the incessant death rattle of musket fire, the booming artillery salvoes, the crashing of burning timbers; the earth trembled with the thudding guns; at frequent intervals, houses exploded in flames and sparks and billowing black smoke; drums rapped out their staccato messages. "The Prussian bullets swept us away by the dozen," wrote Erckmann-Chatrain in Gérard's Corps. "Shot fell like hail, and the drums kept up their *pan-pan-pan*. It was a thousand times worse inside the houses, where the screams of rage mingled in the uproar. We rushed into a large room already packed with soldiers, on the first floor of a house. It was dark because they had covered the windows with sacks of earth, but we could see a steep wooden staircase at one end, down which the blood was running. We heard musket shots from above, and each moment the flashes showed us five or six of our men sunk in a heap . . . and the others scrambling over their bodies with bayonets fixed, trying to force their way up into the loft. The room was full of dead and wounded, the walls splashed with blood. Not one Prussian was left on his feet."[5]

Thielmann's Corps was reduced almost to quarter strength; few other reserves were left, and the Prussians were dropping from sheer exhaustion. Blücher and Gneisenau anxiously looked for help from Bülow or perhaps Wellington. But Bülow was still many miles away; and Wellington was himself occupied at Quatre Bras. Suddenly the attack by French troops began to slacken. Blücher and Gneisenau thought for a moment that the enemy was withdrawing. Then prisoners were brought in by the Prussian units on the extreme right, towards Mellet, and it was learned from them that a whole French Corps—d'Erlon's—was advancing towards the battle-field.

Yet to Blücher's astonishment, and great relief, this new French column abruptly halted and began once more to withdraw. D'Erlon, desperately needed by Marshal Ney at Quatre Bras, but told by Napoleon to advance towards Ligny to attack the Prussian right, finished by helping neither of them. His orders from one were confused and contradicted by orders sent by the other; and he did nothing but wander anxiously back and forth during that critical afternoon. When he had approached Ligny field at six o'clock, d'Erlon's movement had first been reported to Napoleon as that of the enemy. Napoleon at once suspended plans for an assault by the Guard; units from Girard's division were ordered to end their attack on the villages, in order to face an assault from a different direction. When the real identity of the newcomers was discovered, it was too late. By then, an order from Marshal Ney had sent d'Erlon hurrying back to Quatre Bras.

The details of this fiasco were revealed later. Meanwhile, during the slight lull in the fighting caused by d'Erlon's approach, Thielmann had ordered Clausewitz to prepare the troops for an assault. The Third Corps now emerged from its defensive position. Clausewitz hurriedly assembled the remaining cavalry brigade and a horse battery. The orders were shouted, and the Prussians moved out, down the slopes on to the Fleurus road. Advancing towards the bridge over Ligny brook, the Prussian detachments sent the French units scattering. Their comrades watching from the hill, Clausewitz among them, cheered as they watched the cavalry's progress. The attack was a brave, defiant gesture, but too slight to bring about a decision in Prussia's favour, even though other Prussian guns were rumbling forward, supported by dragoons. The French immediately reacted by dragging two heavy artillery pieces on to the high road, and two regiments of Exelmans' cavalry were lined up on the eastern side of the track. The French charged; the Prussians were forced back, one of the Prussian batteries was captured, and the French came on towards the Third Corps' slopes. For a moment this counter-attack looked as if it might cut through the Prussian left. Shouting out commands, Thielmann and Clausewitz hurriedly lined more infantrymen along the walls by the western side of the Fleurus road, while artillery opened fire upon the French from the Tongrinne heights and from positions near Tongrinelle. The rapid organization of reinforcements by Thielmann and his Chief of Staff was successful; menaced in front and on both flanks, the French withdrew from this part of the field.

But around the villages, the Prussian situation was becoming increasingly critical. A messenger came from La Haye to inform Blücher that the troops in the village had exhausted all ammunition, even the rounds in the pouches of the dead. The Field-Marshal insisted that the soldiers must keep on fighting with their bayonets, musket butts, and even their bare fists. Chief-of-Staff Gneisenau was told that Ligny could hold out no longer. He replied that it must, if only for another thirty minutes. Napoleon still had over 10,000 reserves uncommitted, including the *élite* Guard; and at eight-thirty, seeing a gap in the Prussian centre, he ordered the final French assault. Napoleon's troops flowed across the valley towards Ligny, and wave after wave of them over-ran the village. The Prussians, unable to halt the French advance, began to retreat, but still in reasonable order. On the slopes between Ligny and Bry, they formed squares supported by the *cuirassiers* and two squadrons of *Landwehr* cavalry. In the dwindling daylight, confusion increased, with horses and men crashing at one another then breaking apart before clashing again; Clausewitz, on the nearby hill, could see little of what was happening in the fading light; the din of battle was loud but he did not know who was gaining ground, nor whether the French would advance against the Third Corps' badly depleted lines.

Blücher furiously rode up to the fighting, and led a third cavalry charge against the French—and came the nearest yet to death. The Field-Marshal's horse, a fine grey stallion presented to him by the Prince Regent of Britain, was mortally wounded by a shot which struck its left flank, near the saddle-girth. Immediately, the horse faltered. Blücher desperately spurred the animal on to keep it moving; the stallion made one or two convulsive lurches forward, and began to stagger again. As the French cavalry galloped nearer, Blücher shouted to his *aide*: "Nestitz, I'm done for now!" Then his horse fell, rolled over and heavily pinned the Field-Marshal to the ground. Count Nestitz jumped down from his horse, Gneisenau told Clausewitz afterwards, and bravely held the bridle with one hand, his sword in the other, ready to die with the Field-Marshal. The French cavalry thundered past, so close that one of the enemy troopers collided with Count Nestitz's horse; but in the noise and darkness, the charge continued. Then the enemy was driven back again by the Prussians. Count Nestitz threw his cloak over Blücher, grabbed the bridle of a Prussian *Uhlan's* horse, and stopped others who were following. Half a dozen troopers raised the body of the dead stallion, dragged out the unconscious Blücher, and fled, just before the French rushed back again.[6]

With Blücher incapacitated, the command of the Prussian army fell to Gneisenau. Clausewitz's friend now had to decide what the Prussians should do. Clearly, they must withdraw; Clausewitz himself received orders that the retreat would be made towards Wavre.[7] Worked out some time before with Blücher, this choice of a withdrawal route had immense implications. The retreat was in no sense a rout. Broken divisions and battalions were assembled and moved back; a firm front was maintained at Bry and Sombreffe and along the road between them. On the extreme Prussian right, Clausewitz was again ordered by General von Thielmann to assemble troops for another assault. Even at this late stage, Thielmann and Clausewitz were determined to make one last attack. So, with the night air alive with the sounds of wounded men, small detachments from the Third Corps cautiously moved forward. This last action by Thielmann's troops was described by Clausewitz as "a very unhappy cavalry affair."[8] But the operation was nevertheless a brave one. With the remains of the first and second battalions of the Thirtieth Prussian Regiment, Major Dittfurth moved out from Potriaux, the village he had held throughout the afternoon, and advanced downwards to cross the Ligny stream. Despite the difficulty of distinguishing friend and enemy in the darkness, the Prussians opened fire on the French right in order to help the withdrawal of the battered Prussian centre. A French dragoon regiment from Exelmans' Corps charged the second battalion, but the Prussians ran to form a square and the attack was beaten off. Major Dittfurth pushed his men even further forward; the Prussians scrambled up a hill occupied by the French, and won possession at bayonet point. Two more French cavalry charges were driven at the Prussians; both were rebuffed. Then a division from Löbau's

Corps, which had been in the French reserve, was brought forward in heavy
column, and rushed at the small Prussian force. Major Dittfurth used his
second battalion to rake the French flank; the Prussian muskets flashed in
the darkness, and the French, confused and uncertain of the Prussians'
strength, retreated. But more French would return, and the Prussians would
inevitably be overwhelmed: Major Dittfurth sounded the recall, and his troops
hurried back to the Third Corps area.[9] Almost at once, a French cavalry
brigade came plunging after Dittfurth's men. The enemy horses clattered up
the Fleurus high road in an attempt to gain Sombreffe, and Clausewitz
himself was almost trapped as the French horses wheeled about him in the
night. "I had difficulty in fighting my way from the French *cuirassiers*," he
wrote later.[10] Then the Prussians of the Ninth Division grouped themselves,
Clausewitz among them, and the French were knocked back down the
slope. Men in the Third Corps collapsed exhausted on the hillside.

The fighting at last died down about an hour before midnight. The
Prussians continued to withdraw, covered by Thielmann's Corps which was
holding the line Sombreffe-Le Point du Jour. A pursuit was not attempted
by Napoleon and the Prussian units wearily moved along lines of retreat
specified by Gneisenau. General von Thielmann's Third Corps was the last
to leave the field of Ligny, and some hours would pass before the last of the
troops, including Clausewitz, departed. Thielmann's brigades and battalions
were so widely split, as reserves for the Prussian right and centre, that
Clausewitz had to work throughout the night to bring the survivors together
again. "All our troops were scattered and we could only find them again
with great difficulty," wrote Clausewitz. "The strongest brigade had been
sent to help the Second Corps and we had no single reserve left."[11] The
night was eerie and harrowing, spent among the debris and devastation of
the battle. "I believe my hair turned grey that night, and I only dismounted
my horse once, to write my report for the Field-Marshal," Clausewitz said.
Down the slope, on the other side of Ligny, were the camp fires of
Napoleon's army. All around Clausewitz in the darkness came the pathetic
moans of the wounded men, the whinnying of dying horses. To the right,
the villages still burned, a deep red glow piercing the darkness.

Then, as the Prussians tried to organize the retreat during the confusion,
the French launched one last attack against Thielmann's positions. A
cavalry detachment could be heard ominously drumming across the fields.
The horses galloped up the slope, over the bodies of the Prussians, through
the gaps in the walls, and fell thickly upon the Third Corps. The Prussians
ran to beat them off, cursing as they fumbled in the darkness for their
weapons, the men suddenly horribly frightened, having believed that the
fighting was all over. Lines were hastily formed, Prussian muskets blazed
out again, and the French reined back. "We only repulsed the enemy
cavalry through the excellent conduct of Pochammer's battalion,"
Clausewitz commented. The Prussian withdrawal continued.

Gneisenau had given General von Thielmann the choice of retreating either upon Tilly or Gembloux. Thielmann and Clausewitz studied the map by lantern-light: if Tilly were chosen, Thielmann's Corps would have to make a march along the Namur road to Marbais, risking a flank attack from the French. Once at Marbais, Thielmann would have to strike north, following the road taken by Pirch and Ziethen. The route would be littered with disabled waggons, broken-down guns, and hundreds of stragglers. The General and his Chief of Staff now studied the road to Gembloux: the road would be direct from Sombreffe; neither flank would be exposed; the road would be clear. Also, at Gembloux Thielmann could expect to meet Bülow, and if he did the two Corps could unite and take any of the four roads from Gembloux to Wavre. Either way, Thielmann and Clausewitz expected to be hotly pursued. They chose the Gembloux route.[12] Clausewitz supervised the final preparations for the departure. Already the road to Namur, upon which he stood, was jammed with the carts and wagons of other army units. Wounded men were being helped, or were being given rough road-side medical treatment. Soldiers lay in the ditches, or were propped up against the ditch banks. Some were slowly bleeding to death. Other men were wandering helplessly about, their eardrums shattered by artillery blast, their eyes blinded by the flashes.

A French officer in Napoleon's suite accompanied the Emperor round the battlefield the next morning, and described the carnage: "The dead in many places were piled two or three deep. The blood flowed from under them in streams. Through the principal street [of Ligny] the mud was red with blood, and the mud itself was composed of crushed bones and flesh."[13] Blücher had been carried six miles to the rear, still unconscious. His body was badly bruised; but a vigorous rubbing with brandy helped considerably, so much so that the Field-Marshal emerged from his concussion loudly demanding some of the medicine for internal use. The surgeon refused, but gave him a magnum of champagne.[14] Casualty estimates of the Battle of Ligny vary. But the Prussians probably lost about 16,000 killed, wounded and captured, almost one-fifth of their total force.[15] In addition, up to 10,000 Prussians deserted during the night. According to Gneisenau they were mainly troops from provinces which were once part of the French Empire. Some of them had even served with Napoleon in previous years.[16] Bonaparte's losses at Ligny amounted to about 12,000; Ligny was therefore another costly victory for him. If the battle could have been followed by a fast pursuit of the Prussians while they were still disorganized, the cost would have been worthwhile. But Napoleon and his generals were to make a serious mistake.

Meanwhile, Clausewitz heard reports of Wellington's engagement at Quatre Bras. As the battle of Ligny had started, the Anglo-Dutch force had found themselves in a critical position at the junction of the Nivelles-Namur and Charleroi-Brussels roads, six miles from where the Prussians were fighting

16—C

Napoleon. But Marshal Ney, hesitant and relying upon d'Erlon's arrival, had failed to take these important cross-roads. Wellington had managed to deploy his troops in time, and at nine o'clock in the evening, when fighting faded, both armies re-occupied the positions which they had held in the morning. The casualties were about equal, some 4,000 or 5,000 men being lost by either side. All armies felt satisfied with the results of the fighting of 16th June. Napoleon believed that he had gained his first objective, the defeat of the Prussians. Now he believed he could turn upon Wellington. Despite his failure to take Quatre Bras, Marshal Ney had at least stopped the Anglo-Dutch army from joining the Prussians. Wellington was undefeated, his army was now being concentrated, and he believed himself to be in a strong position. Blücher, although defeated, still considered his army to be in excellent order.

But from the allied point of view, closer co-operation between Wellington and Blücher was essential. For a few hours after Ligny, the British commander was even unaware of what had happened to his ally. In addition, many Prussians, with Gneisenau vocal among them, believed that Wellington had failed to honour a promise to help Blücher, a pledge given at the meeting at the Bussy windmill early in the morning of the battle. Yet Gneisenau overlooked the British commander's proviso that he would come, he said, if he were not attacked himself. With Blücher temporarily disabled, and with Gneisenau in virtual command, prospects for good relations between the two armies were faint. Matters were worsened by Wellington's lack of information from Ligny. Blücher had sent an *aide* just before his fatal charge. The *aide*, Major Winterfeldt, was to notify Wellington that Blücher was about to retreat. Major Winterfeldt rode as far as Piermont on his way to Quatre Bras, where he was shot by Ney's skirmishers. The Major lay wounded for some time before British troops found him. But he then refused to give his message to a subordinate. The Prussian officer Friedrich von Müffling, who was serving in Wellington's suite apparently disregarded the information that a wounded messenger was waiting outside the British headquarters.[17] So, for one reason or another, Wellington did not learn of the Prussian withdrawal until the next morning, when one of his own *aides*, Colonel Gordon, returned from a reconnaissance of Ligny. Wellington, who was waiting by the windy cross-roads at Quatre Bras, reacted calmly. "Old Blücher has had a damned good licking and gone to Wavre," Wellington said. "As he has gone back, we must go too."[18] So the decision was taken which would lead to the Battle of Waterloo and, for Clausewitz, the Battle of Wavre.

FOURTEEN

Waterloo and Wavre

"An army which preserves its usual
formations under the heaviest fire,
which is never shaken by imaginary
fears . . . is imbued with the true
military spirit."
(*On War*, bk. iii, ch. v.)

I

THE RETREAT TO Wavre meant that the Prussians must sacrifice their supply
base on the Rhine. But it also allowed the Prussian army to join first with
Bülow's Corps, and second with the Duke of Wellington's army, if the Duke
retired along his own line of operations between Quatre Bras and Brussels.
Gneisenau, distrusting Wellington, had at one point urged that the Prussians should move away from the Anglo-Dutch army, and fall back upon
Liege. But Blücher, supported by his Quartermaster-General, Grolman, had
disagreed.[1] On 17th June therefore, both the main armies were moving back
towards the same point. At the same time as he began his withdrawal,
Wellington told a messenger from Blücher's army that he would offer
Napoleon battle if one Prussian Corps were provided as support. Anxiously,
the British Commander awaited a reply. Meanwhile, Wellington was only
able to retire unmolested from Quatre Bras because of Marshal Ney's
inactivity. Despite an order from Napoleon to attack, Ney's men sat around
cooking a meal while the disorganized Anglo-Dutch army was making its
withdrawal. When Bonaparte arrived shortly after midday, he at once
ordered the troops to fall in. But the order was given too late; then came a
drenching thunderstorm which made the ground too sodden for the French
cavalry to outflank the British.

The last troops in Thielmann's Corps had been unable to leave Ligny
battlefield before sunrise. Throughout the early morning, Clausewitz feared
that the French would suddenly appear behind the retreating Third Corps
columns and fall upon the rearguard, provided by General Borcke's Ninth
Division and General Hube's cavalry. Despite the organization which
Clausewitz and the rest of Thielmann's staff had been able to carry
out, determined action by Napoleon could have been disastrous for the

Prussians. "But as in all such cases, the worst never really happened," Clausewitz wrote immediately afterwards.[2] Only later did he discover why the Third Corps was allowed to escape.

Napoleon was ill, and very tired. The Emperor had only managed to have just over twelve hours sleep in the fifty-one hours between three o'clock on the morning of 15th June and six-thirty on the morning of 17th June. The Emperor's body was frequently racked by severe pains; after the battle of Ligny he threw himself on a bed at Fleurus and fell asleep while the Prussians pulled back. Reports of the Prussian movement reached the French headquarters, but Napoleon was not woken. Durutte's division, for example, was positioned near St. Amand, and his patrols discovered Prussia's intentions. Jomini quotes Napoleon as saying: "I did not know that Durutte had passed the night on the flank of the Prussian line of retreat, so near that his advanced guards distinctly heard the noise caused by the march of their train and the confusion of their columns. Had I known this, I should have pushed these troops forward to harass the retreat, and, in spite of the darkness of the night and the failure of the intended co-operation [by Ney] I might have gained much."[3]

Marshal de Grouchy, who commanded the French Second and Fourth Corps, and who was soon to be Thielmann's main opponent, has received a good deal of blame for the Prussian escape. But this forty-eight year old Marshal, a brave and gallant soldier, fully realized the need for rapid pursuit. Grouchy was prepared for the chase; his cavalrymen had been ordered to wait by their horses and, learning to his surprise that Napoleon had left the field without issuing any instructions for the French right wing, Grouchy had followed the Emperor back to Fleurus. But by that time Napoleon was asleep, and no-one dared wake him. So Napoleon, a victim of enormous personal strain, and above all of his previous insistence that he alone should take the decisions, allowed both the Anglo-Dutch and the Prussian armies to slip away. Moreover, Napoleon underestimated Wellington time and again, and even more so Blücher. On 17th June when Napoleon received reports of Prussian columns moving towards Wavre, he refused to believe that Blücher would dare to move across the French front to try and join with Wellington.

So, although Clausewitz had good reason for his fears on the morning of 17th June, the Prussians were given an unexpected respite. Thielmann's leading troops began to arrive at the town of Gembloux two hours after the rearguard left Ligny battlefield. By that time Thielmann's scouts had also informed him that Bülow's Corps had reached Baudeset, on the old Roman road about three miles away. To give the rearguard a chance to draw closer, and to allow his troops some rest, Thielmann called a halt at Gembloux, despite the risk of a French attack. He and Clausewitz needed more time to organize the men and equipment, to estimate the remaining stocks of ammunition, to pull in the stragglers, and to decide what to do next. "We had been cut off from the Field-Marshal," said Clausewitz, "and had to find our own way."[4] There had been no confirmation that the Corps should head towards Wavre; the only instructions had been those hurriedly issued the previous evening when the battle was still in progress. Moreover, Thielmann and his Chief of Staff had no idea of the whereabouts of the First and Second Corps.[5] Unless contact could be made, the whole Prussian army would be extremely vulnerable to a French offensive. Thielmann therefore sent a messenger to Bülow to ask whether the other Corps commander had any information. But Bülow was unable to help.

For a time during the night of the battle even Blücher had been lost, when uncertainty had existed in the confusion about which field station he had been carried to. Gneisenau at last found the old Field-Marshal lying on the straw at the rough hospital at Mellery. Blücher smelled strongly of brandy, gin, rhubarb and garlic, these had been rubbed into his bruises to try to loosen his body sufficiently to help him back on a horse. And next morning back in the saddle he was, having embraced Wellington's liaison officer, General Hardinge, whose arm had recently been amputated. "*Ich stinke*," Blücher roared amiably, as he apologized for his spicy smell. The seventy-three year old Prussian Field-Marshal was fit to fight again.[6] Blücher and Gneisenau immediately dispatched *aides* to put some order into the scattered Prussian units. During the morning Bülow was instructed to march on Dion-le-Mont, a village three miles east of Wavre, *via* Walhain and Corbaix. Thielmann was told to continue the march on Wavre.

Thielmann ordered Clausewitz to prepare. The Third Corps started to march again at two o'clock in the afternoon. Passing through Ernage, Nil Perrieux, Corbaix and La Baraque, the main body of the Corps reached Wavre at eight o'clock having taken six hours to move eighteen miles. The roads were in terrible condition after heavy rain. The men had to tramp ankle-deep in the mud, wagons and guns had to be pushed and heaved, and the soldiers were exhausted. At La Bavette, a mile north of Wavre on the far side of the River Dyle, the Corps halted for the night. The rearguard reached the Dyle at about midnight, and bivouacked on the river bank. Other troops which had been detached to different units during the battle also continued to arrive. Only now could Clausewitz reliably estimate the casualties which the Corps had suffered at Ligny: about 1,000 men lost, and seven guns destroyed or captured.[7]

As the Third Corps had moved upon Wavre, Marshal Grouchy had at last begun his pursuit. The French commander was hampered by the jealousy between himself, and Vandamme and Gérard who served under him, and by his own lack of initiative. Grouchy had finally received orders from Napoleon at one o'clock to chase Blücher's army, but he did not set out until an hour later, and only reached Gembloux at nightfall, partly because of the bad state of the roads, partly through his personal lack of drive. At Gembloux, Grouchy only managed to capture a herd of 400 cattle, left behind by the Prussians. Marshal Grouchy was unequal to the task he had been given. He was an excellent soldier—if Napoleon were close at hand to give him orders and encouragement. In the Italian campaign Grouchy had fought with extreme courage, and had received fourteen wounds during the rearguard action after Novi; at Jena he had led a cavalry charge described by Lannes as "the most brilliant I have ever seen."[8] But Grouchy's efficiency deteriorated if he had to act on his own; and now he was at the head of a large force, separated not only from the main body of the French Army but—far worse—from Napoleon. Local inhabitants informed Grouchy that Thielmann's Corps had entered Gembloux at lunch-time; he then sent back a report to inform Napoleon that the Prussians seemed to be withdrawing in two columns, one on Wavre and the other on Perwez. Marshal Grouchy's evidence for this report, which reached Napoleon at two o'clock in the morning of 18th June, probably came from intelligence of Bülow's movement; Bülow was in fact moving upon Wavre *via* Walhain. "Perhaps it may be inferred that one portion is going to join Wellington," Grouchy wrote in his dispatch, "while the centre, under Blücher, retires on Liege . . . This evening General Exelmans is pushing six squadrons of cavalry towards Sart-à-Walhain, and three to Perwez. When their reports are at hand, then if I find the mass of the Prussians is retiring on Wavre I shall follow them . . ."[9] But Grouchy was still acting far too slowly. At the time that he wrote his report, the whole Prussian army had already concentrated at Wavre. Ziethen's Corps was on the left or western bank of the River Dyle; Pirch, Thielmann and Bülow were on the right. All were ready to resume offensive operations. Cavalry patrols were pushed out during the evening and night towards the Namur-Louvain road on the left, and on the right into the district between the Dyle and Lasne.

So well organized was Blücher that he could afford a very generous reply to Wellington's plea for help from the Prussians. Not only did the Prussian Field-Marshal agree to send one Corps, as the Duke had asked, but at daybreak on 18th June Bülow's Corps would march to help the Anglo-Dutch army, immediately followed by Pirch's troops. The First and Third Corps would hold themselves in readiness to follow. This very welcome news was received by Wellington at almost exactly the same time as Grouchy's report reached Napoleon. Blücher's message sealed the Duke's decision to accept battle with Bonaparte on 18th June. During the night Blücher sent out his orders to his Corps commanders. At daybreak General Bülow was to march from Dion-le-Mont, through Wavre, in the direction of Chapelle St. Lambert. If Wellington was engaged in battle with the French, Bülow was to attack the enemy flank. The Second Corps would follow in direct support. Bülow was chosen to lead the Prussian advance to link with Wellington because his men had not been at Ligny, but the choice could have been disastrous; his Corps lay farther from Wellington's army than any of the others, and Pirch could not move until Bülow's force had passed, which caused a further delay and endangered the Prussians. If Marshal Grouchy had been more active, Blücher's army might have been attacked while the delicate and complicated manoeuvre was being undertaken. But Grouchy, who had passed the night at Gembloux although nearly two hours of daylight had been left, delayed again on the morning of 18th June. Instead of marching off at dawn, the French Marshal ordered Vandamme to start out at six o'clock and Gérard at eight o'clock. In fact, they did not begin to move until eight and nine o'clock respectively. By ten o'clock Grouchy was at Walhain with Gérard, where they sat down for a breakfast of fresh ripe strawberries.

At half past eleven, the Marshal, still at Walhain, heard the distant roar of cannon. Gérard advised that the Corps should at once march in the direction of the artillery fire; but his commander refused to consider it. Grouchy insisted that his orders were to pursue the Prussians, as indeed he was: he dared not deviate from his instructions. The cannon fire was the opening bombardment of the Battle of Waterloo.

General Bülow had begun his march to meet Wellington at daybreak. Pirch and Ziethen followed at about noon, after the Fourth Corps had cleared out of their path. The roads were jammed with wagons, troops and baggage trains, and the track was again covered with thick mud. Field-Marshal Blücher was anxious to take his whole army to join Wellington, but he was apprehensive about his flank and rear. Marshal Grouchy was known to be near, and Blücher therefore decided to leave Thielmann's Third Corps at Wavre to block the French pursuit. If the French were not in strength, Thielmann was to march to join the main body, with only a small force left at Wavre as a rearguard. Leaving Gneisenau to carry out the final business with Clausewitz and Thielmann at Wavre, Blücher rode away from St. Lambert at eleven o'clock. Thielmann and Clausewitz were now faced with the threat of the full weight of Grouchy's superior force. Apart from preventing Grouchy falling upon the Prussian rear, the Third Corps were also to protect the road to Louvain in case the Prussians were forced to retreat. Moreover, Grouchy must be stopped from reaching Napoleon—and Bonaparte was to be in desperate need of his help. Much therefore depended upon the Third Corps left behind at Wavre. The troops were in good condition; morale was high, and the men were now more rested. But they were also cold, wet and hungry. "The troops had no food except meat, and they had had no time for slaughter and cooking," said Clausewitz.[10]

As Blücher and the main force left, Clausewitz hurriedly supervised the deployment of defensive positions in the sodden ditches and behind the hedges and walls around Wavre. But the only signs of French activity so far had been a few half-hearted attacks by General Exelmans' cavalry on the furthest outposts. Patrols had only seen part of Vandamme's corps. As yet the full strength of Grouchy's force was unknown. Thielmann therefore thought that his Corps would be better employed elsewhere. According to

Clausewitz: "In the beginning nothing much showed itself near Wavre, and we began the march towards the main army."[11] In the early afternoon it looked as if Thielmann and Clausewitz might yet take part in the battle with Napoleon at Waterloo. Soon after three-thirty, the Ninth, Tenth, Eleventh and Twelfth Divisions, with the reserve cavalry and artillery, were proceeding towards Frischermont and Chappelle St. Lambert. Clausewitz ordered a small detachment commanded by Colonel Zepplin to stay behind at Wavre.[12]

But Marshal Grouchy had at last received new orders. A dispatch from Napoleon commanded him to join the right flank of the main French army, and by doing so to strike at the Prussian main force which was moving to join Wellington. Napoleon urgently needed Grouchy's help. The Marshal was told: "Hurry, there isn't a moment to lose." Grouchy pressed on in a desperate attempt to reach Napoleon in time. But before he could join his Emperor, the Prussian rearguard at Wavre had to be shattered. Pajol was ordered to throw his troops over the River Dyle at Limale, Gérard at Bierges, Exelmans at Basse Wavre, Vandamme at Wavre itself.[13] At four o'clock the head of Vandamme's Corps appeared on the road from La Baraque leading towards the main bridge at Wavre. At the same time, General Exelmans' cavalry was seen massing in the fields at Dion-le-Mont.

A full-scale engagement was imminent. But the Prussian Third Corps was off-balance, organized as it was for the march towards Waterloo. General Borcke's Ninth Division, which had been positioned near the farm of La Huxelle, immediately fell back towards the town. Vandamme's troops were close behind him. But on reaching Wavre, General Borcke found that the bridges had already been barricaded by the rearguard from his own Corps: he was trapped on the wrong side of the river, which was swollen with the recent rain. Hurriedly, Borcke sent out scouts on horseback to find some other way across. General Exelmans' dragoons were only a mile and a half away at Dion-Le-Mont, and were likely to make a dash for Basse Wavre at any moment. Borcke's scouts returned: another bridge crossed the river half a mile downstream. Borcke's infantrymen ran along the bank and over the bridge, and immediately destroyed it behind them. The bank was lined with picked marksmen under the command of Major Dittfurth, and the men took cover behind the dripping willows and in the wet hedges. General Borcke himself pressed on for Wavre to reinforce Colonel Zepplin's rearguard detachment, which by this time had smashed loopholes in all the buildings which faced the river.

Thielmann and Clausewitz frantically organized the Prussian defence as Vandamme's Corps prepared for an assault. Fortunately the area had good defensive qualities. The River Dyle, normally shallow, was now running deep and swift, flowing in front of the Prussian positions to give good frontal cover. The town of Wavre on the left bank was connected with the few houses on the right by two stone bridges, the larger one built to carry the

FIELD MARSHAL VON BLUCHER, PRINCE OF WAGSTADT

Above *Field-Marshal Blücher, nicknamed* Vorwarts *and aptly caricatured here*

Overleaf *The grand entry of the Allied Sovereigns into defeated Paris on 31st March, 1814, after the flight of Napoleon*

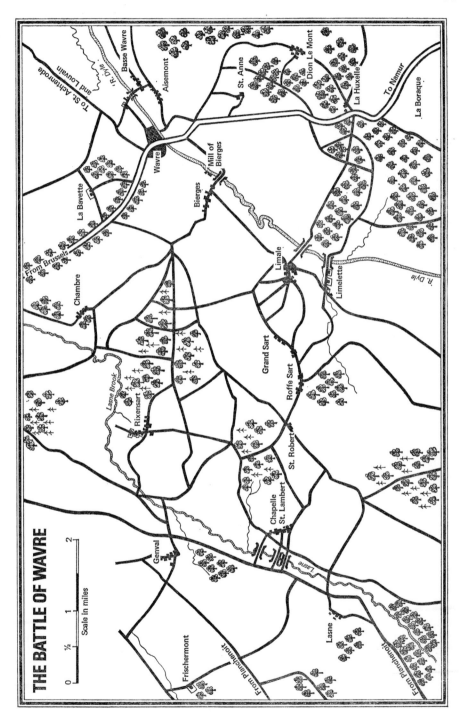

THE BATTLE OF WAVRE

Scale in miles

0   ½   1   2

Facing page: top *Field-Marshal Blücher trapped by his shot horse in the middle of the Battle of Ligny (16th June, 1815)*
Bottom *Receiving intelligence of the Battle of Ligny*

main Brussels-Namur road. Just under a mile upstream on the left bank
stood Bierges Mill, with a narrow wooden bridge linking it with the other
bank; further upstream still was the village of Limale. Here, and at the
hamlet of Limelette a mile further on, were more wooden bridges. On the
right bank of the Dyle a series of hills overlooked the town and the bridges,
and on the left bank lay another group of hills, although not as high. The
many hedges, lanes and hollows on the left bank compensated for the
greater command of the ground on the right. In these lanes, troops could be
deployed under cover, but the condition of the roads made movement slow,
tiring and difficult. General von Thielmann and Clausewitz mapped out the
defensive position: the General intended to hold the stream with a line of
skirmishers to prevent a surprise assault at any point; reserves would be kept
nearby, ready to be rushed to any threatened area. Clausewitz at once
ordered that the roads should be improved as much as possible, especially
those running parallel to the river. Kampfen's Tenth Division was placed
behind Wavre, based on a small wood near the Brussels road. The Twelfth
Division under Stülpnagel was brought back to Bierges and placed behind
the village. The bridge at this village was barricaded and the mill prepared
for defence, and one horse artillery battery was positioned nearby. The
Eleventh Division, commanded by Luck, was placed astride the Brussels
road, behind Wavre on the left of the Tenth Division.

The deployment went well. But one serious mishap occurred, described
by Clausewitz. "Through a completely inexplicable mistake, General
Borcke, with our strongest division amounting to a quarter of the troops,
had marched off towards the main army and we could not get him back."[14]
Borcke's division, which comprised six infantry battalions and an artillery
battery, did not return in time for the battle. After detaching troops to hold
Basse Wavre and to reinforce Zepplin, Borcke had apparently withdrawn in
the belief that the whole Corps was continuing the march to join the main
army, a mistake perhaps caused by his wide detour from Basse Wavre to La
Bavette, which had temporarily severed his contact with the rest of the
Corps.[15] Hube's cavalry division, which included Marwitz's and Lottum's
brigades, was posted with a battery of horse artillery near La Bavette, ready
to be sent where required, and the remainder of the artillery was spread
along the long front. Two more companies of infantry were sent to Basse
Wavre under Major Bernstaedt, to reinforce the detachment there. Three
battalions and three squadrons from Ziethen's Corps, commanded by
Stengel, were sent to guard the bridge at Limale.

Having seen to the dispositions, Clausewitz could only wait, impatient
and tense, for the French to begin the offensive. Fortunately, no-one in the
Third Corps knew that at Waterloo the French seemed about to destroy
Wellington. The situation was extremely critical for the Anglo-Dutch army;
Blücher, still on his way, was desperately needed. And Napoleon, if he was
finally to tip the scale in his favour, was in just as much need of Grouchy.

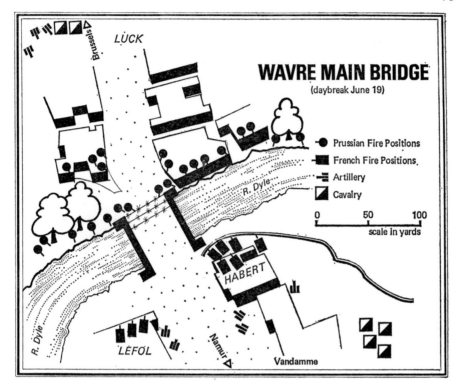

WAVRE MAIN BRIDGE
(daybreak June 19)

LÜCK

Brussels

R. Dyle

Prussian Fire Positions
French Fire Positions
Artillery
Cavalry

0   50   100
scale in yards

HABERT

R. Dyle

LEFOL

Namur

Vandamme

Clausewitz knew that at Wavre the Prussians would probably be outnumbered at least two to one. "It was evident that the coming fight was to be of
the fiercest description," he said.[16] Afraid the Prussians would retreat and
escape, Vandamme opened the attack for the French. He was impatient for
activity after the irritating delays on the march, and he was eager for his
Marshal's baton and jealous of Gérard and Grouchy. The time was half
past four. The French could expect just under another four hours of
daylight. The impetuous Vandamme was determined the Prussians should
be routed long before nightfall. Only a handful of Prussian sharpshooters
were posted in the house opposite Wavre. All were killed in the first French
rush. Vandamme's men pressed on to the main bridge over the Dyle. But to
reach the bridge the French had to advance into the open for the last few
yards, and as soon as they did so, they were met with terrible fire from their
front and from their flanks, as the Prussians opened up from behind the
hedges and buildings on the opposite bank. After only five minutes, General
Habert and six hundred Frenchmen lay dead, their bodies heaped upon the
wet cobbles. Vandamme's division was now in a desperate position. If an
attempt was made to retreat, the men would come under devastating fire

from the Prussian artillery batteries sited on the opposite slopes. The French were pinned down, and could only crawl to shelter behind the walls.

Marshal Grouchy galloped forward. He now knew that he was faced with a strong Prussian opposition; yet he had to reach Napoleon. If Vandamme had not thrown in his men, Grouchy might have been able to join his Emperor by making a detour around the area held by the Third Corps. But through Vandamme's precipitate action, Marshal Grouchy was committed. He was unable to disengage, because Vandamme was tied down; he had no choice but to press forward in an attempt to take Wavre and eliminate the stubborn Prussians. Grouchy ordered two attacks to be made on either flank, to support the initial assault. General Exelmans' cavalry was to push forward at Basse Wavre, while a battalion under Lefel was to attempt a crossing at Bierges mill. Clausewitz and General von Thielmann anxiously watched the French movements. The Prussians were thinly spread: a French assault at any one point had to be identified just before it was launched, so that reserves could be rushed to bolster the slender Prussian line. Several attempts by Lefel's battalion to force a crossing at Bierges mill were beaten back. French guns fired in support of Lefel's assault; Prussian artillery replied and silenced them. Another French battalion was sent to help Lefel, but this reinforcement was seen struggling slowly through the muddy fields towards the mill, and the Prussian batteries were ordered to concentrate upon it. The first shells exploded very near the Frenchmen, range was improved, and the next salvo shattered the French column completely.

All reports reaching Clausewitz indicated that so far the Prussian line was holding well. "Our position was so strong that the enemy was unable to force our ranks."[17] Repeatedly the French advanced at Bierges mill and at the main Wavre bridge. Each time they were repulsed, and the piles of French dead steadily mounted. One attack was led by Marshal Grouchy himself, almost besides himself with frustration and desperation at being unable to force his way through the Prussians. In another French assault, Gérard was leading a battalion across the open marshland to the mill bridge when he suddenly slumped with a Prussian bullet in his chest. As the infantrymen behind the tree trunks and banks continued to fire across the swirling water, Gérard was carried back to Walhain, to the same house where he had eaten strawberries for breakfast and had quarrelled with Grouchy about marching to the guns of Waterloo.

By now Grouchy was far too late to help Napoleon. Waterloo was over. "At eight o'clock the great battle was decided, but we did not know it," said Clausewitz. "With us the fight went on right into the middle of the night."[18] At about ten o'clock the French managed to gain a foothold on the Prussian bank. According to Clausewitz, the French success was due to the decision of Stengel, who was defending the Limale bridge, to leave the field and rejoin his own Corps, Ziethen's. This view does not accord with that put forward by other historians, who affirm that Stengel left much later, at daybreak on 19th June.[19] Pajol's hussars thundered across the wooden planks of the bridge, four abreast, and burst through the barricades. Teste's division followed with his men streaming across to the other bank. The Prussian right flank was seriously threatened. General von Thielmann himself was wounded at about this time, and although he remained in action, more work was thrown upon Clausewitz's shoulders. To plug the hole at Limale, Stülpnagel's Twelfth Division was rushed to the heights above the village to grapple with the French. Hube's cavalry followed. But the reinforcements were insufficient, and the Prussians had few other reserves.

"We fell back in disorder," wrote Clausewitz, "and had nothing but trouble in re-forming again." The light was fading fast, and confusion was made far worse by the choking black cannon smoke and the thick muddy quagmires. Stülpnagel was ordered to regain Limale and drive the French back and down across the River Dyle. He formed his men for the attack, with two battalions in the first line and three in support. Cavalry were positioned in the rear, ready to make a flank movement or to exploit a breakthrough. The order to advance was shouted; the drums began to beat and the men moved forward. But by now it was night, and in the darkness cohesion between units was virtually impossible; the formation of the ground and its folds and hollows was completely strange to the troops. As the front line was advancing, still in reasonable order, the Prussians suddenly stumbled into a sunken road, and as they did so French muskets flashed and roared at point blank range from the opposite side of the narrow track. Volley after volley poured into the disordered Prussians, who were blinded by the flashes, deafened by the noise. In the confusion and shock, men stood bewildered and rooted by fear before seeking cover. Scores of them were slaughtered. The Prussian second line, which was to have supported the first, had moved too far to the left in the dark, and had become itself a front line and suffered the same fate as the first. Stülpnagel desperately shouted for the bugles to sound the retreat, and the Prussian survivors came stumbling back, raggedly firing as they ran.

On the Prussian left, before Wavre and Bierges mill, the struggle continued despite the dark. Night made the battle more terrible: the flashes of the guns, the vivid explosions, the screams out of the blackness, the shapes silhouetted for a moment against the blazing houses, the Prussians shivering with cold and fear as they waited for the next assault. Thirteen separate charges by Vandamme's men were beaten back by the Prussians, with only four Prussian battalions left to defend Wavre against the whole of Vandamme's Corps. Three factors in this left sector helped the Prussians to keep back the French: the ability of the troops, the excellent defensive positions, and the skilful use of the slender reserves, organized by Thielmann and Clausewitz. At Basse Wavre, further downstream, the initial French assault had not been continued. The area around Limale therefore remained the

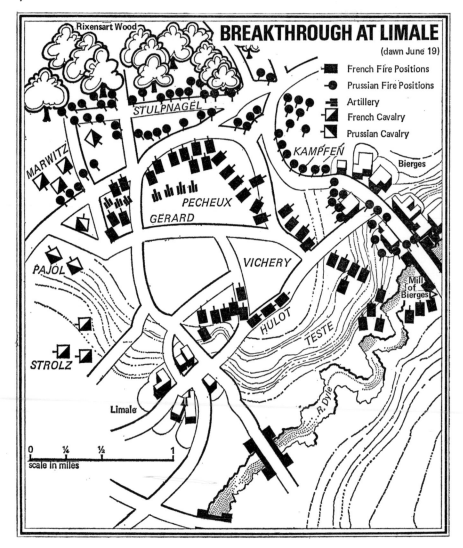

greatest threat to the Prussians, and even at midnight fierce fighting still
raged at the village. A lull followed as both sides regrouped their weary
troops. Clausewitz deployed the depleted Prussian units as best he could,
and two hours after midnight the battle flared up again with a new French
offensive against Stülpnagel's extended positions. "I hurried over there
collecting as many troops as possible from elsewhere," said Clausewitz.[20] He
added: "We still had no certain intelligence about the victory at Waterloo."
Above Limale, the Prussians were hard pressed for hour after hour. "From
two o'clock in the morning of the 19th until the first break of day,

Stülpnagel was attacked by the Corps which had crossed over," Clausewitz reported. But still the Prussians refused to give ground.

Soon after dawn the fighting around Limale grew even more intense; during the final hours of night, Grouchy had shifted more men over the bridge. The French Marshal believed that Napoleon must have been victorious at the other battle, and would soon arrive to give him help; Grouchy failed to send scouts to gain accurate information of the outcome at Waterloo. General von Thielmann and Clausewitz had suffered another setback: not only had Stengel's force marched off to join Ziethen during the night, but Colonel Ledebur and his detachment of five cavalry squadrons and two guns also slipped away, just before dawn. Thielmann had no idea how long his Corps would have to cling to Wavre. According to Clausewitz news of the Waterloo victory did not reach the Third Corps until mid-morning. "At ten o'clock we had a dispatch from General Pirch which gave us intelligence of the glorious victory. The General also said that he was now engaged in cutting off the Corps that was fighting against us."[21] As a result of this news, and as he believed that Grouchy would soon retreat when he heard of Napoleon's defeat, General von Thielmann now decided to switch to the offensive: Colonel Marwitz was ordered to strike at Grouchy's left flank above Limale, but only the Eighth *Uhlans* and two squadrons of the Kurmark *Landwehr* cavalry could be spared for this attack. To provide cover, two Prussian batteries opened fire on the French columns massed above Limale.

But Marshal Grouchy was himself preparing for one final massive French assault. His artillery, superior in number, disabled five of the Prussian guns. Grouchy then formed three divisions for the attack, divided into three columns; Teste was to strike at Bierges and the mill, Vichery at the Prussian centre, and Pecheaux was to move against Stülpnagel's weakened force. Hulot was to remain in reserve, and Pajol's cavalry was to turn the Prussian right flank at Rixensart wood. Twenty-eight French battalions would be opposed by no more than ten Prussian. As they watched the French massing for the attack Thielmann and Clausewitz knew that they could expect no help from elsewhere, despite the promise of support from General Pirch. "The point at which he [Pirch] wanted to cut the corps fighting us was so distant that it would have done us no good," said Clausewitz. "Once more isolated from the main army, because the enemy had outflanked us, we were left on our own, and we still had 45,000 men under Vandamme and Grouchy against us. We could only hold out for one more hour."[22] Only one battalion could be sent to reinforce the front line. The men were so tired after almost fifteen hours of battle that many had fainted, and some never recovered consciousness.

Against a rising din of artillery and snapping musket fire, the French came forward; file after file of them moved across the fields towards the river; they advanced despite the Prussian cannon fire which blazed into their ranks, spurting mud and bodies into the air. The front line of Prussian infantrymen opened fire with repeated, rolling volleys; still the French came on. They swarmed on to the bridges over the hissing, gurgling river; the Prussians held on to the last moment and fought with bayonets and knives and bloody bare hands. But the French pressed on. Outnumbered and overwhelmed, part of the Prussian line sagged. The Twelfth Division gave way. Rixensart wood was lost. Stülpnagel's brave men were finally forced back to new positions. The French advanced from ditch to ditch, and only Teste's attack on Bierges was checked.

Desperately, Thielmann and Clausewitz gave orders for as many troops as possible to be told of the victory at Waterloo. The message jumped from ditch to ditch, wall to wall: "Old Blücher has won . . .! Napoleon is in retreat . . .! *Vorwarts* is chasing the French back to Paris . . .!" Men were told the news even as they lay dying. Men were shouted it as they slumped wearily over their muskets, almost beyond hearing, too tired to lift their weapons. Men were whispered it as they lay wounded, and immediately tried to struggle to their feet. The news had an incredible effect. Running from their defensive positions, firing as they went, cheering and shouting, the Prussians advanced. Rixensart wood was re-taken with so vigorous an assault that for a moment Grouchy thought that the enemy had been reinforced.

But the Prussians had neither the strength nor the support to push forward. They were driven back from Bierges by Teste, whose men broke into the Prussian centre; Rixensart was re-taken; Thielmann's Corps was in danger of being sliced in two. The Prussian General still believed Grouchy would have to retreat when the news of Waterloo reached him. Indeed, it seemed incredible that the news had not already arrived. But Thielmann and Clausewitz knew that the Third Corps could not keep possession of the battlefield any longer. To do so would be to risk complete destruction. "At eleven o'clock we started our retreat," Clausewitz wrote. By withdrawing, Thielmann and Clausewitz hoped to gain time, and to keep the Corps intact. Thielmann could then turn and strike when Grouchy heard of Napoleon's retreat and himself began to withdraw.

Under cover of Marwitz's cavalry, the Prussian infantry retired. Colonel Zepplin evacuated Wavre, and a rearguard was positioned upon the Brussels road. The Prussians made an exhausted but fighting withdrawal. As soon as Colonel Zepplin left Wavre, Vandamme's men ran across the battered bridges at the town and at Bierges, over the mounds of dead, and forced two battalions of the Prussian Kurmark *Landwehr* regiment from their positions in a hollow behind Wavre. One of these battalions re-formed at a small wood near La Bavette, and attacked the approaching French, driving back a cavalry squadron. The other battalion checked a French detachment before continuing the retreat. Marwitz's cavalry clashed with the squadrons leading Vandamme's columns on the main road towards La Bavette and in

Facing page *Field-Marshal Grouchy* (*Marquis Emmanuel de Grouchy*)

a parallel lane to the left. The main body of Thielmann's Corps was given time to pull back through the village of Ottenburg. The Prussians then moved through St. Achtenrode, farther down the route towards Louvain.

Meanwhile, the French had halted at La Bavette. Here, Grouchy had at last heard the terrible news of Waterloo; the French Marshal was about to begin his own retreat. The roles of pursued and pursuer were to be reversed.

II

But the Prussians made a serious mistake. Clausewitz was blamed for this by his commander, General von Thielmann, and by historians like Heinrich von Treitschke. Marshal Grouchy was allowed to escape. During the night of 18th June, the main French army had already been harried by the victors of Waterloo, Wellington having agreed to leave the pursuit primarily to the Prussians. Gneisenau had organized what he termed a "hunt by moon-light," and the French had been driven and cut down without mercy. "It was the best night of my life," said the gleeful Gneisenau. But Grouchy was allowed to start his retreat at midday on 19th June unmarked by Thiel-mann's Corps. Not until the morning of 20th June did the Prussian chase begin. Thielmann declared that the mistake stemmed from Clausewitz's attitude during their own retreat from Wavre: Clausewitz, Thielmann complained, "had always seen everything very black, and in this particular case had not rested before he had found a position where we could wait for the continued march of the enemy."[23] Clausewitz had been dissatisfied with all the possible defensive positions until the Third Corps had passed through St. Achtenrode. There, on the other side of the village, the order to halt had finally been given. But by that time Grouchy had already stopped his pursuit; and before the Prussians turned to follow him, it was too late. The Prussians had gone too far. Clausewitz apparently fell victim to his typical over-caution, to his pessimism, and to his anxiety for everything to be exactly correct. But this is not quite true; Clausewitz could not be held entirely, or even mainly, to blame.

Grouchy had first heard of Napoleon's defeat at ten-thirty on the 19th, just as he was about to pursue Thielmann's battered Corps.[24] The French Marshal was given the news by a weeping messenger, Captain Dumonceau. "I thought he was mad," Grouchy said later.[25] Appalled and close to tears himself, Grouchy had been undecided what to do. He might make a flanking movement and attack Blücher's army from the rear, but then Grouchy himself would be threatened by Thielmann. He might retreat on Namur, or he might even, as Vandamme demanded, make a futile advance on Brussels. Meanwhile, Grouchy's troops had gone forward after Thiel-mann, and not until the French advance units reached La Bavette did Grouchy decide to commence the withdrawal on Namur. Nor was Thiel-mann the only threat which Grouchy had to face. At that time, Pirch was at

Facing page; top *Napoleon on the field of Waterloo*
Bottom *The Duke of Wellington* (left) *unites with Field-Marshal Blücher*
(right) *at "La Belle Alliance," Waterloo*
17—C * *

Mellery, on the Tilly-Mont St. Guibert road eight miles to Grouchy's rear; and the fly-away General Borcke who had left Thielmann the previous afternoon to join the main army, had since realized his mistake, and had been ordered by Blücher to remain at Couture. Part of Borcke's force stood between St. Robert and Rixensart; and while he had too few men to do Grouchy much damage, Borcke could at least have undertaken a major diversion.

Thielmann's Corps could not therefore be held solely responsible for Grouchy's escape; nor could Clausewitz personally. Among the main reasons given by Pirch for the late start of his pursuit was the exhausted condition of his troops. But Thielmann's were certainly in no better shape, and were probably even more tired and decimated. They needed time to rest, eat, for supplies to be issued, for depleted stocks of ammunition to be redistributed. In any case General von Thielmann only heard of Grouchy's retreat at about six o'clock on the evening of the 19th, about twelve hours after it had started. Thielmann and Clausewitz were unaware that Grouchy's withdrawal had begun until they received information from Borcke's scouts.[26] Neither the Corps commander nor his Chief of Staff had suspected that the French were no longer just behind, because Grouchy's strong rearguard was hovering nearby. Thielmann and Clausewitz believed that this force, commanded by Pajol, was not a rearguard, but the advance guard, thrown out by their pursuer. Pajol's men therefore provided a cloak for Grouchy's withdrawal. When Clausewitz wrote a letter a fortnight later, he still did not realize that Grouchy had started his retreat at midday on the 19th; Clausewitz still believed that the French "left in the evening."[27]

Clausewitz and Thielmann must have still been convinced at nightfall on 19th June that Grouchy's main force was still on their rear, and that only then did the French retreat start. Moreover, the Prussians were in no condition to attack the strong French rearguard. The Third Corps survivors were falling with exhaustion; they were outnumbered by Grouchy; the roads were in a terrible state; and many of the Prussians including Clausewitz had hardly slept for the past four nights. On the night of 15th–16th June the Corps had been force-marched to Namur and then on to Sombreffe, to fight at Ligny. On the night of 16th–17th June it had covered the withdrawal from Ligny. The night of 17th–18th June had been less strenuous for most of the troops, but Clausewitz, as chief of staff, must have been busy for most of his time putting the chaotic affairs of the Corps in order. The night of the 18th–19th had been spent fighting. Indeed, the Third Corps had fought brilliantly. Over 2,500 men from the Corps had been killed in preventing Grouchy from moving towards Waterloo; and now, during the night of 19th June, the Corps was temporarily no longer fit to fight. The failure to launch an offensive against Pajol's detachment is hardly surprising. More remarkable was the renewed vigour which the Corps displayed once the pursuit had started. At daybreak on 20th June,

Thielmann's troops finally attacked Pajol's force. The French fell back. At that time Grouchy's main units were leaving Gembloux, nearly seventeen miles away. The race to Paris had begun. For both defeated and victors, the next few days were filled with a special kind of horror. Men on both sides were pushed to the very limits of endurance; no mercy was shown; and a dark trail of destruction and death was spread across the Belgian and French countryside.

Despite the late start, a cavalry detachment from the Third Corps pushed on fast enough to overtake one of Grouchy's columns beyond Temploux on 20th June. The Prussian horses were too exhausted for the troopers to attack the French in any strength, but the Prussians still managed to drive back the enemy cavalry and capture four guns.[28] The rest of the Corps force-marched during 20th June, and reached a point beyond Gembloux by nightfall. But the head of the Prussian pursuit was taken by General Pirch's Corps, which attacked a heroic force of 2,000 French left by Grouchy at Namur. Grouchy himself pushed on, desperately hoping that he would reach Paris before the allied armies; and on the way he collected as many men as possible in order to defend the capital.

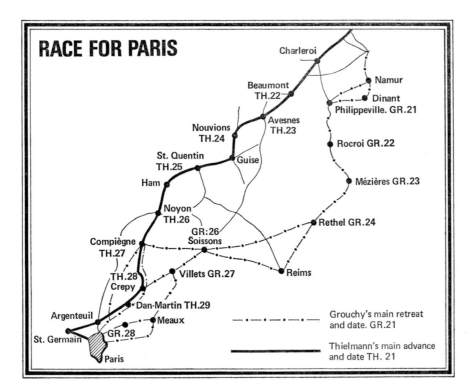

On 21st June, Napoleon reached Paris. Next day the Emperor abdicated in favour of his son, the King of Rome, and on 25th June Napoleon himself withdrew to Malmaison. But the war was still unfinished. Drawing his forces together, Blücher had continued to press on after Grouchy. Thielmann's Third Corps reached Beaumont on 22nd June, Avesnes on the 23rd, and St. Quentin two days later. "We went incessantly by forced marches by way of Ham, Compiègne, Danmartin, Argenteuil, St. Germain, to Paris, day and night," said Clausewitz. "The effort we had to make was such that some people shot themselves in despair. Others fell dead."[29] But at Compiègne, despite his weariness, Clausewitz found time to visit the imperial Château, which now stood empty. He wandered through the tall, elegant rooms where Bonaparte had lived, and loved; Clausewitz told Marie: "Napoleon celebrated his nuptial with Marie Louisa here. The bedroom and the bathroom are surrounded by mirrored walls and show that Marie Louisa does not belong to those of pure and noble nature. Everything breathes sensuality . . ."[30]

After conducting himself brilliantly on the retreat, Marshal Grouchy at last entered Paris. He had lost 4,000 men and sixteen guns in skirmishes during the previous few days along the River Oise. He had beaten the allies to the French capital. But Field-Marshal Blücher was driving his men remorselessly on, and was close on his path. Napoleon had fled, and Grouchy had no time to prepare the city's defences. Nevertheless, he and his troops frenziedly made all preparations they could. Clausewitz was engaged in one last clash, "two days of fairly hard fighting for the possession of the village of Iffy." Struggling continued bitterly around the outskirts of Paris and then, on 3rd July, the capital surrendered, just as Blücher was about to storm the city.

Napoleon was finished. The great Napoleonic struggle was ended. Many Prussians were now determined that the hated French should pay dearly for it all. They included Blücher and Gneisenau; but this time, unlike in 1814, Clausewitz disagreed. He believed that everything was over, and should be treated as such. The capitulation terms specified that the French troops should retire behind the River Loire and that the allies should make a formal, triumphant entry into Paris. Wellington objected strongly to the last provision; but Blücher was adamant. Repeating the words which Gneisenau had written to Stein the previous year, Blücher declared that it was a matter of honour to "enjoy the same distinction that the French had enjoyed in Berlin, in Vienna, and in Moscow."[31] For the next few days, Blücher himself virtually ruled Paris. He demanded that the city should pay a tribute of a hundred million francs, and pay for the complete re-equipment of his troops. In addition, each of his soldiers should be paid a bounty equal to two months' pay. Again echoing Gneisenau, Blücher was determined to blow up the Pont de Jena, which he considered to be a shameful monument to Prussia's 1806 humiliation. On 10th July, the day after Clausewitz and his corps marched into the city, some blasting was done on the bridge before it was agreed that it would be enough to change its name.

The aged Blücher's severity towards the French found a warm response among the Prussian army as a whole. A strong spirit of revenge was displayed in many different ways and varying degrees, which had begun with the barbarity practised by some of the soldiers during the race for Paris. Gneisenau, who was now proudly wearing Napoleon's seal ring, demanded with Blücher that the former Emperor should be arrested and shot. "Should we not regard ourselves as the instruments of Providence, which gave us such a victory so that we should exercise eternal justice?" he said. "Shall we not expose ourselves to the reproaches of the Prussian, Russian, Spanish and Portuguese peoples if we fail to do justice?"[32] Significantly, Gneisenau made no mention of the Austrians. Again, as in 1814, the statesmen in Vienna called for leniency and care over the handling of the French and their fallen leader. And Gneisenau was once more overstepping his military role, as the Duke of Wellington realized. Wellington declared that it was not for the generals, but for the sovereigns, to deal with Napoleon. His view prevailed, and Napoleon went to his second exile, on St. Helena, on 15th July.

Field-Marshal Blücher's period of power in Paris ended after the first week in July, when King Louis XVIII entered the city. Blücher's demand for an indemnity from the capital was refused. "Such an opportunity will not recur," the Field-Marshal pleaded. "Our finances need some such penalty, and we must not leave France again under the reproach of being tricked by this corrupt people."[33] Clausewitz had had a complete reversal of opinion since 1814. Now, he was thoroughly opposed to the demands for harsh revenge: he disagreed with Blücher that the "quilldrivers" would lose what the sword had won; he disagreed, too, with Gneisenau, perhaps for the first time and certainly the most vehemently. Conscious that war should have a constructive political end, Clausewitz was alarmed by the behaviour at the allied army headquarters. Too many Prussian officers were displaying "a frequent spirit of greed."[34] "My dearest wish now is that this aftermath should soon be finished," Clausewitz wrote to Marie on 12th July. "I dislike this position of having my foot upon someone's neck, and the endless conflicts of interests and parties are something I do not understand. Historically, the English will play the better role in this catastrophe, because they do not seem to have come here with a passion for revenge and for settling old scores, but rather like a master who wishes to discipline with proud coldness and immaculate purity; in brief, with greater distinction than ourselves."[35] The conduct of the Prussian high command, Clausewitz added, was "not of noble character."[36] This change of opinion was of immense importance for On War. In his book, Clausewitz was to stress, in a way that had never been done before, that political control over a war was absolutely necessary. He firmly refuted suggestions that the politicians should stand down when hostilities began, and leave the conduct of war to the generals. Military leaders who wanted too much power were dangerously at fault, Clausewitz believed. Without this change of heart between 1814 and 1815, and perhaps without his experiences of the aftermath of war in 1815, Clausewitz might never have developed these views in *On War*.

Thielmann's Corps moved to Loire on 10th July, having spent only one day in Paris. Later, the Corps headquarters was sited at Fontainebleau, and afterwards at Le Mans. Clausewitz suffered an acute feeling of anti-climax. A war which he had been fighting, or fiercely advocating, was now over. It had lasted twenty-two years. Clausewitz continued to attack those who sought revenge. While he certainly felt no liking for the French, his respect for them grew, as it did for their stubbornness to admit final defeat. Clausewitz wrote to his friend Gneisenau from Etampes on 24th July: "No disaster can make the French give in completely, not even humiliation. They regard us with a fierce, cold arrogance, with a scarcely concealed air of wickedness."[37] In another letter to Gneisenau from Le Mans on 18th August, Clausewitz scolded him for his policy of vengeance: "It is unwise to demand French disarmament, since it would push to the limit the exasperation of these people, who took up arms for the same cause as we did, only with more enthusiasm and greater daring."[38]

This belief, which echoed statements made by Metternich in 1814, was to be developed in *On War*, when Clausewitz described how an army could pass beyond the "culminating point of victory." The further a conquering force advanced, wrote Clausewitz, the more troops would be needed to maintain garrisons, and the longer would be communication lines. The territory was hostile, and there were "greater efforts by the enemy because of the increased danger."[39] It was disadvantageous and even dangerous to proceed beyond the "culminating point," Clausewitz continued. "Beyond that point the scale turns, there is a reaction; the violence of such a reaction is commonly much greater than the force of the blow."[40] Once again, there was a direct link between Clausewitz's experiences in 1815 and his observations in *On War*. Life in the army of occupation disagreed with Clausewitz. As he recovered from the physical ordeals of the campaign, and as boredom set in, he took up opium again. He wanted to go home to Germany, and the summer was only brightened by Marie's journey to stay with him. They visited Paris together.

Meanwhile, peace terms were being drafted. The treaty was provisionally agreed upon in October, to a renewed outburst of indignation from Blücher. The old warrior refused a fresh invitation from the Prince Regent to visit Britain. "Gracious Sir," Blücher wrote in his reply, "I regret that such unity is never to be found among ministers as has existed so usefully in these last wars among companions in arms. When I learned of the divergence of views among the diplomats I left Paris in order not to witness how the French, who had so grievously sinned against God and man, were openly protected by some of the allies. Although I had sacrificed 26,000 brave Prussians, no regard was paid to that at all, and everything that I had ordered for the general good was reversed because, according to the bookworms it had not been done according to the rules." Blücher concluded: "Herr Talleyrand and Fouché [the French representatives] more readily obtained a hearing, and on this occasion, too, have preserved the French from that castigation which they well deserve."[41]

Clausewitz was anxious to leave this atmosphere of bitterness, in which the Prussians were seeking to pick at the spoils. Now he was informed of his next appointment. On 3rd October he was nominated Chief of Staff for the Army of the Rhine. Koblenz would be his residence; and his superior was to be the man Clausewitz would have chosen above all others, Gneisenau. Soon after the signing of the Second Treaty of Paris on 20th November, Clausewitz and Marie rode away for their new home.

FIFTEEN

Clausewitz in Berlin

"There are field-marshals who would
not have shone at the head of cavalry
regiments, and *vice versa*."
(*On War*, bk. ii, ch. ii.)

I

GNEISENAU'S APPOINTMENT AS Commander-in-Chief of the Rhine army
resulted from the recent division of Prussia into seven military districts, one
of which covered the newly annexed areas along the Rhine. The first
months of Clausewitz's posting were among the happiest of his life: he was
Gneisenau's assistant, and their friendship had in no way been affected by
Clausewitz's disagreement with his attitude in Paris: Marie was with him:
Clausewitz even managed to enjoy the dinners, discussions and entertain-
ment which life at Koblenz offered. Clausewitz joined the city's social circle,
and he was influenced by the poet and writer Max von Schenkendorff,
among others. He became a closer friend of Stein, who was now living
nearby at Nassau. Clausewitz's work interested Stein, especially the plans
which had to be drawn up for the defence of Germany's western frontier.

Then, after far too short a time, Gneisenau was replaced and went into
semi-retirement. Clausewitz felt a severe sense of loss. The two men had
grown very close to one another. With Scharnhorst the friendship had been
one of leader and disciple, master and favourite pupil; with Gneisenau,
Clausewitz was more an equal. As Gneisenau wrote to Marie on 15th
August, 1816, soon after his departure from Koblenz: "I have had two lively
letters from Clausewitz, which pleased me very much. I am indebted to him
for many fine hours, a great deal of pleasure, much instruction, and much
comfort. Had it not been for him, when I was in terrible circumstances and
was introduced to him by General Scharnhorst, and so was helped by the
State, I should have been in desperate trouble. I shall always realize this
with a grateful heart."[1]

Clausewitz was saddened not only by Gneisenau's departure, but by the
choice of his successor. General von Hake came to Koblenz to be Clausewitz's superior, and a mutual dislike was felt between them. Hake was
meticulous, pedantic, and expected to be obeyed "like a tame spaniel,"

complained Clausewitz.[2] The General left his Chief of Staff no independent initiative, and disagreed with most of what Clausewitz said. "The smiles are taken from our faces," wrote Clausewitz to Gneisenau on 30th July 1816.[3] He added on 14th November: "It is an unpleasant feeling to be among unfamiliar opinions and ideas: I am a fish out of water."[4] Clausewitz's gout and depression returned, and as often as he could he went with Marie to take the waters and to find peace and quiet. During these excursions Clausewitz added to his swelling files of notes.

In 1816, Clausewitz's papers and notes were more and more taking on the form of a book. But for the moment, he was still busy evaluating his own ideas about the changes that must come about in modern warfare. He wrote: "These materials have been amassed without any real preconceived plan. At first my aim, without worrying about system and logic, was to put down the results of my reflections upon the most important points [of strategy] in quite short, precise and compact essays. The way in which Montesquieu has treated the subject appealed to me . . ."[5] At first Clause-witz intended his book for "intelligent readers already acquainted with the subject." Later he changed his mind and wrote for a wider readership.

Clausewitz undertook another project while stationed at Koblenz. He was annoyed and disappointed by what he felt to be the lack of official appreciation for Scharnhorst. "I cannot calmly accept that the State should do nothing for our late friend Scharnhorst," Clausewitz wrote to Gneisenau on 4th March, 1817. "I have accordingly written to General Boyen asking whether there is the least hope of something. He has replied politely, though it seems to me coolly and with indifference, that he has already made two futile attempts. What these are, he does not say."[6] Clausewitz wished Scharnhorst's memory to be honoured, and wanted the state to assist Scharnhorst's children. But Clausewitz believed that the War Minister, Boyen, stood little chance of achieving anything by appealing to the King or Chancellor. He turned to another idea instead, which he outlined to Gneisenau in a letter of 18th March. "Frau von Berg, who, as you know is in England again, has given me the idea of putting a piece in the English newspapers about the late Scharnhorst, since people in England do not even know him. She will take care of the translation and everything, and just wants me to write the article. I think it is an excellent idea, because our duty is to see that Scharnhorst takes his place in history." Clausewitz believed that the article might recreate interest in Scharnhorst, even though "the English do not have as much interest in German affairs and people as we do in theirs." This could perhaps be overcome by the fact that Scharnhorst was a Hanoverian, and from the same race as the King of England. As for the article itself, Clausewitz continued, he would be careful to write in such a way that the result was not offensive, embarrassing or too obscure, and would try to avoid controversy. The article "must avoid the appearance of putting him first in history . . . My feeling towards

Scharnhorst must never become the subject of a newspaper controversy, which would be unworthy of his memory." Finally, Clausewitz asked for Gneisenau's help with information.[7]

But Gneisenau disagreed with the idea. The time was not right, he said, and the article might pass unnoticed, or alternatively create hostility through giving the wrong impression. In a letter of 28th April, Clausewitz reluctantly agreed. But as the article was already written, he asked Gneisenau if he would read it. At the same time, Clausewitz renewed his complaint over the lack of support for Scharnhorst's family. "Had the Chancellor and Boyen originally urged this matter to be rapidly dealt with, they would have been congratulated." But Clausewitz told Gneisenau that the delay had made success unlikely.[8]

Clausewitz's *Über das Leben und den Charackter von Scharnhorst*[9] was for many years the most skilful appreciation of the General. Clausewitz's description of Scharnhorst was in some ways unconsciously one of himself, or at least the type of person he would like to have been. Scharnhorst, he wrote, had been clear-headed, with a keen and penetrating intellect. He had subjected his thoughts to a severe discipline. He had preferred to study war itself, rather than to read about it at second-hand in the books of writers like Jomini. He had had the rare ability to penetrate through the violence and confusion of war to identify the principles lying behind this fog. After collecting a multitude of facts, Scharnhorst had examined them like a high court judge, and had always substantiated his conclusions with historical proof. As a person, Scharnhorst had been incorruptible, Clausewitz continued. He had been kind, sensitive, and on rare occasions, emotional. Staid in appearance, although sometimes rather impressionable, he had been devoted to honour, courage and impartiality. He had distinguished himself as a soldier at Menin, Auerstädt and Eylau, Clausewitz wrote. In battle he had been calm, wise and confident—the qualities of a great commander—even though his voice had not been imperious nor his manner outwardly striking.

Clausewitz's description of Scharnhorst revealed the deep respect and feeling he had for his former tutor. Scharnhorst was still very much missed, and not only by Clausewitz. The reforms he had brought into the Prussian army were now being increasingly threatened. With peace came the problem of deciding which military reforms to consider as permanent, and which to abandon since the army was no longer on a wartime footing.

The War of Liberation had vindicated the efforts of the reformers, and they themselves had served well: Blücher, Gneisenau, Boyen and Grolman received honours and adulation. Blücher welcomed guests royally at his Silesian Estates, where he died in 1819; Gneisenau became a Field Marshal. But relations with King Friedrich Wilhelm were still strained. Blücher and Gneisenau had caused a good deal of ill-feeling, insisting as they had upon fighting the conflict their own way. Their conduct during the peace negotiations had caused the King embarrassment, as had their disturbing proposal for an integrated German *bloc*, led by Prussia: at one time in late 1814 Boyen and Grolman had even championed the idea of a war against Austria to secure Prussian leadership.[10] When Prussia's military leaders were attracting attention during their occupation of Paris, the Czar was reported to have said: "It is possible that sooner or later we shall have to defend the King of Prussia against his own army." Britain's negotiator at the peace talks, Lord Castlereagh, wrote in December, 1815: "I fairly own that I look with considerable anxiety to the tendency of their [the Prussians'] politics . . . the army is by no means subordinate to the civil authorities."[11] The unseemly and dangerous conduct of the Generals included a foolish duel fought in Vienna between General Boyen and the Prussian Minister Wilhelm von Humboldt; and they included Blücher's refusal of orders to evacuate France in November, 1815, unless certain fortresses were first surrendered to Prussia as pledges.

The King was bound to react to this infringement of his authority. Although the process was not sudden, the reformers experienced greater opposition from the conservatives, who were supported by the King, and who believed that Stein and Scharnhorst had "brought revolution into the country." According to the conservatives, the civil and military reforms would destroy the monarchy, and lead to war between those with and those without property; the *Landwehr* and *Landsturm* had provided the means for the liberals and those without property to undertake this struggle.[12] While the conflict with Napoleon had been in progress, the military reforms were generally accepted, if sometimes with great reluctance. Now, the conservatives believed, the process could be reversed.

This group of powerful Prussians was led by Prince Wittgenstein, the Minister of Police and a friend of the Austrian statesman, Metternich. Stein said that Prince Wittgenstein had "all the qualifications for securing a high position in life without accomplishments, real worth, or merit": He was "crafty, cold, calculating, persistent, supple to sycophancy . . . He aimed at money and secret bed-chamber influence."[13] Members of Wittgenstein's group included Duke Karl von Mecklenburg, Minister of Justice Schwarnweber, and the politician von Kircheisen. For a while the process of reversing the reforms was not apparent. In June, 1814, King Friedrich Wilhelm had agreed to merge the two parts of the War Ministry, and at first Gneisenau was expected to become War Minister; but he had preferred a field command. The eventual choice of Hermann von Boyen had still seemed a happy one: apart from Clausewitz, General Boyen had been closest of all the reformers to Scharnhorst, and he now intended to make the General's work permanent.

Boyen tried to establish a firm framework for universal conscription. Prince Wittgenstein argued that "to arm a nation will simply organize and facilitate opposition and disaffection."[14] To forestall this opposition, Boyen worked rapidly with Grolman, the chief of the General Staff and head of the second division of the War Ministry, on the *Wehrgesetz* law. This law, published in September, 1814, made all males aged twenty years and above liable for military service. The conscripts would be enrolled for three years in the standing army, two years in the active reserve, seven years in the first *Landwehr* levy, seven years in the second levy, and even after then they would still be liable for service in the *Landsturm*.[15] In November, 1815, another law followed, dealing specifically with the *Landwehr*. Although in wartime this force would unite with the standing army at brigade level, in peacetime it would constitute a national militia and be closely related to its local recruiting area.

In principle, Boyen's efforts were supported by Gneisenau and Clausewitz. Indeed, Prince Wittgenstein's reactionary group was continually suspicious of the small group at Koblenz when Gneisenau was still there, especially as Stein lived nearby. Nevertheless, Clausewitz strongly disagreed with some aspects of Boyen's programme. The two men, although both disciples of Scharnhorst, disliked one another: Boyen was cool towards Clausewitz, if polite. "Boyen," Clausewitz wrote to Gneisenau on 12th October, "has very different ideas to me on most issues, and finds me arrogant and of incompatible temperament."[16] Boyen was less dogmatic than Clausewitz, less rigid in his ideas, and less resolute; he considered Clausewitz to be brusque and stand-offish, as did many other people. For all his high principles, Clausewitz was still more of a realist than idealist; Boyen was often the reverse. For example, Clausewitz told Gneisenau on 14th November that he considered the War Minister's proposal for recruitment to be "a hotch-potch of liberalism and arbitrariness."[17] He believed that Boyen's proposal would lead to difficulties as to who would escape conscription; the rich would probably be favoured. In another letter to Gneisenau, of 28th April, Clausewitz attacked Boyen's system of selecting recruits according to their date of birth. This idea, he said, provoked a great deal of jealousy, and even those exempted at first could not be sure that during the next twenty-four years they might not at some time be enlisted. It would have been better to draw lots, he added.[18]

Clausewitz also criticized General Boyen's ideas for manning and training the *Landwehr*. Surely the War Minister flattered himself if he considered that the new *Landwehr* would excite the same patriotism as regiments of this force had done during the war? Boyen was certainly relying on this enthusiasm to persuade men to join. Clausewitz held that this was too optimistic: man-power would be scarce, and there would be too few capable instructors; standards of training and discipline would drop.[19] Arguments over the *Landwehr*, and over the larger questions of constitutional reform, were growing heated when Clausewitz took up his next appointment in 1818. Following another recommendation by Gneisenau, he was nominated Director of the General War School at Berlin by a Cabinet Order of 9th May. Clausewitz did not move to Berlin until the end of the year. In the autumn he acted as Commander at Aachen while the King attended a congress at the city. A Cabinet Order from Friedrich Wilhelm, of 17th August, read: "Since during the time a sovereign is in Aachen the presence of a Commander is necessary, I have chosen you for this post; and in giving it to you for this period, I am confident that you will fill it capably and to my entire satisfaction."[20]

As a result of the Aachen and Berlin appointments, Colonel Clausewitz was promoted Major-General on 19th September, 1818. But his departure from Koblenz was an unhappy one. Before sanctioning Clausewitz's appointment as Director of the War School, Friedrich Wilhelm had asked General Hake to provide a reference. "It was humiliating," Clausewitz complained to Gneisenau on 3rd February, 1818, "to be so little recognized by the King that the opinion of General Hake had to be requested, and after twenty-six years of competing with hundreds of others to have obtained at the end of it all nothing more than the frugal and certainly very qualified praise of this man."[21] Clausewitz believed this to be a further example of the King's injustice towards him; a feeling which was to deepen during the next few years.

The General War School, the *Allgemeine Kriegsschule*, was in much the same state as when it had opened in 1810 (on the same day as Berlin University), and when Clausewitz had taught there before leaving for Russia. The annual admission of students was fixed at fifty, and the three-year course was intended only for those officers who, "having acquired elementary knowledge in other establishments, desire to increase and perfect the same in every aspect of the art of war, in order to acquire the necessary skill for the higher and special demands of the service."[22] Later, on 5th October, 1859, the War School was to be renamed the War Academy, *Kriegs Akademie*, and to become famous as an integral part of the powerful German officer corps.

The War School Directorship might have seemed an ideal appointment for a man like Clausewitz. In recommending him, Gneisenau had believed that the position would open a wide range of opportunities for his friend.[23] This soon proved to be untrue. Clausewitz knew exactly what he wished to do, and on the face of it he now had the means to do it; but he found his power restricted and his frustration was only increased. Clausewitz discovered that his duties were purely administrative, and that the actual teaching at the school was controlled by a Committee of Studies. Clausewitz, as Director, had less power to teach his knowledge of strategy than he had had in 1811 as a junior lecturer. He found much to criticize in the curriculum and in the actual running of the school. He found it too much like a university, the officers who attended it behaving like university students—too easy-going. With his preference for military orderliness and strictness, Clausewitz believed that the students' books should be more closely examined, and that the place should be treated more as an army academy, or at least as a disciplined high school.[24]

The new Director drafted proposals for a stricter discipline and a more academic curriculum; the curriculum, for example, was to include a course in logic. The school's teaching, Clausewitz believed, should reflect the higher and broader educational requirements of the Prussian officers who had to fight war along new strategical and tactical lines; if warfare had changed, then so too must the educational qualifications needed for the officer corps. Clausewitz's proposals were set down in a memorandum to General Boyen on 21st March, 1819.[25] But Boyen was unenthusiastic. In any case, he was too involved in other matters, which would soon lead to his departure from the War Ministry.

Chances of further military reforms were fading rapidly, much to Clausewitz's anger and disappointment. By 1819 a number of defects were visible in the *Landwehr* some of which Clausewitz had prophesied, and some of which resulted from a shortage of funds, especially after a Prussian budget crisis in 1817. Military standards had declined. Lack of money for the line army had imposed restrictions upon its size, and recruits who could not be accommodated into the line were commonly placed in the *Landwehr* reserves, after a very meagre training. Again, owing to money difficulties, annual exercises for the first *Landwehr* levy had been reduced from two fortnights to one, and exercises for the second levy had been abolished completely. Inefficiency was revealed in the military manoeuvres of the autumn of 1818; and more support was therefore given to Prince Wittgenstein and his conservatives. Before, the conservatives had argued that the *Landwehr* was politically dangerous; now they could also say that the *Landwehr* was militarily useless.

Prince Wittgenstein and his followers concentrated their attack upon General Boyen. The *Landwehr* was a refuge for revolutionaries, they claimed, and the force could involve Prussia in war with other German states. This reserve army, Wittgenstein added, could complicate the successful operation of the "Carlsbad Decrees" which had been agreed between Austria and Prussia in the autumn of 1819, to try to curtail political revolutionaries inside Germany. General Boyen made his own position worse, and that of the military reformers, by attacking the Carlsbad Decrees. He declared that they constituted a wrongful intrusion into Prussia's domestic affairs, and that the Austrian-Prussian alliance which the Decrees implied was unrealistic.[26] Boyen's foolish indiscretion delighted Wittgenstein's group. The reactionaries were gaining ground on all fronts, and Wittgenstein managed to increase the King's suspicions of the reformers, including Gneisenau. Clausewitz had written to Marie in January, 1818: "The confidence which the King placed in him [Gneisenau] seems to have been weakened by insinuations," and Clausewitz had added that although Gneisenau had recently returned to Berlin, three weeks had been allowed to go by without Friedrich

Wilhelm inviting him to dine.[27] Wittgenstein also meddled in the conflict between Wilhelm von Humboldt, who led the fight for more constitutional reform after Baron von Stein had retired after the first Treaty of Paris, and Chancellor Hardenberg, who was more cautious.

Finally in December, 1819, Friedrich Wilhelm took action. He demanded a closer merging of the *Landwehr* with the line army, a reorganization of the *Landwehr* which would mean disbanding thirty-four battalions, and even in peacetime the incorporation of sixteen *Landwehr* brigades into line divisions. The *Landwehr's* separate inspection system was also to be abolished. In protest, Boyen and Grolman resigned. Clausewitz strongly criticized the defeatist attitude of the War Minister and the Chief of the General Staff: "I do not think it right to yield the battlefield so completely to the men of 1806."[28] At the same time, Chancellor Hardenberg managed to force Humboldt's dismissal. The reactionaries had won a complete victory. Although Clausewitz himself had little time for major constitutional reform, the ending of hopes for more military innovations was a bitter blow. The danger of a possible reversion to the pre-Jena attitude had been increased, and all that Scharnhorst and the other reformers had fought so hard for was now at risk.

Clausewitz felt that he had witnessed the end of an era, as indeed he had. "For twelve years my whole strength was devoted to Scharnhorst. He is no more," wrote Clausewitz to Gneisenau on 21st August, 1820. "And now his personal influence is rapidly fading away . . . I have served under so many men who are no longer here."[29] Clausewitz, as so often in his life, found himself in a middle position during the struggle with the reactionaries after 1815. He was by no means a revolutionary, and had strong doubts about liberalism, convinced that a strong government was necessary. But he believed in the *Landwehr*; a force seen by the reactionaries as a revolutionary weapon. Clausewitz wanted to bridge the gap between the professional standing army and the Prussian people, a gap which he believed had been one of the basic weaknesses in Prussia's defensive posture before 1806. He believed that the *Landwehr* would help form a bridge, as would the admission of more *bourgeoisie* into the officer corps. This had been Scharnhorst's aim when first advocating reforms; but now, with the reactionaries in power, the breach was in danger of reappearing.

Clausewitz's fears were to prove justified. The army was indeed to grow apart from the people again; it was to be looked upon as anti-liberal, and the personal instrument of the King. Ironically, with his belief in the regular army's need for true professionalism, and imbued as he was with the military values of honour and dignity, Clausewitz himself was not unlike those inside the army who helped to bring about this isolation; they believed that the army stood above ordinary, everyday, attitudes, and should conduct itself in quite a different manner from the civilians. So the army was to become separated, the movement accelerated by officers themselves. The reforms would be very largely reversed. On the other hand, these reforms were always ready to be put into use once again: As Clausewitz said, once the barriers had been torn down, they could not be entirely rebuilt. When the country was threatened, or felt itself threatened, reforms similar to those Scharnhorst, Clausewitz and the others had pushed into practice were re-introduced. In 1870 and again in 1914, the German Fatherland became once more a "nation-in-arms." In the meantime, during the years of peace, the army was to be considered anti-liberal by the liberals, and the idea of a militia, or *Landwehr* was to be considered revolutionary by the reactionaries.

Clausewitz expressed his ideas on the related subjects of *Landwehr* and liberalism in papers drafted after 1816. In 1819, before General Boyen had resigned as Minister of War, Clausewitz wrote *Über unsere Kriegsverfassung*, in which he compared the Prussian forces with those at the time of the 1806 disasters. The reforms, said Clausewitz, had certainly been expensive, but the critics should not forget that the country's very existence was at stake. The Fatherland was threatened by powerful neighbours, and should not hesitate to sacrifice half of its budget in order to guarantee the safety of its people, and to uphold the nation's dignity. Clausewitz reminded his readers that Frederick II—Frederick the Great—had dedicated two-thirds of his country's income to maintaining the army. Moreover, Clausewitz continued, Prussia urgently needed the *Landwehr*, especially in a defensive war, when the whole weight of the people must be thrown against the enemy. While admitting that many *Landwehr* officers lacked wartime experience, he declared that the way was now open for all men of energy and enthusiasm to join: the examples of Spain, of France, and of Germany during the War of Liberation, had shown the value of such officers, who were "sprung from the people."

Clausewitz admitted that to arm the people did create certain dangers: The *Landwehr* was given a feeling of strength which could result in "presumptuous rudeness and insubordination." But the danger of revolution inside the state was less than that of foreign invasion. "Prussia needs to arm all its people in order to resist the two giants who constantly menace her to the east and to the west. Does she then fear her own children more than these formidable enemies?"[30] This paper, which was a defence of General Boyen, despite Clausewitz's criticisms of some of the War Minister's proposals, remained unpublished: the document was probably intended for private circulation and did not appear in print until 1858.[31]

Clausewitz developed his ideas in a second memoir written at the end of the same year, 1819, when Boyen and Grolman were vainly protesting against the King's plans to re-shape the *Landwehr*. This document was entitled *Über die politischen Vorteile und Nachteile der preussischen Landwehr*. Clausewitz argued that the Goverment's true safeguard was not to disarm the people, but to conduct a wise and honest policy, in which the line army,

Facing page *Field-Marshal Blücher shortly before his death*

Published and Sold July 1, 1814, by EDW^d ORME, Bond St. (corner of Brook St) London.

PRINCE BLUCHER,

Field Marshal of the Prussian For...

the *Landwehr*, and the nation, could all show their loyalty to the monarch. Even if a revolution was feared, no advantage would be gained from suppressing the *Landwehr*: on the contrary, the line army might still be influenced by the revolutionary spirit, as had been the case in France when the regular army had "floated away" upon the wind of revolution in 1789. Another paper, *Einige Bermerkungen über die Ausführung der preussischen Landwehr*, was written in 1820; the last section not in Clausewitz's handwriting. This went into even greater detail about military reforms. And in *Über die Errichtung des deutschen Militärsystems*, drafted at about the same time, Clausewitz dealt with the recruitment and organization of forces in the various German states.

In outlook, Clausewitz was a conservative. His ideas for the *Landwehr* were far from sweeping and were always qualified. He was fully convinced that a professional soldier possessed special skills which set him apart from the civilian, and even from the civilian in the *Landwehr*. This distinction was one reason why Clausewitz believed that an effective *Landwehr* cavalry force was unattainable: an even greater degree of speciality was required, as he had written to Gneisenau on 28th April, 1817. Clausewitz admitted that the reliance which could be placed upon men in the *Landwehr* was always uncertain.

Clausewitz was even less of a revolutionary in political terms, although he was never hostile to liberalism, and indeed was attracted to its energy and broad view of life: on 23rd October, 1820, he suggested to Gneisenau that the French Revolution had brought much good, and had forced existing institutions to improve themselves. Nor could matters be put back to the situation before 1789; in their attempt to restore the old system, the reactionaries would merely create greater disorder. In addition, Clausewitz felt a good deal of sympathy for the suffering of the people affected by war: at Koblenz, for example, Clausewitz had been considerably distressed by the misery of life in the area after the fighting. On the other hand, Clausewitz had believed that these unfortunate people in the Rhineland should be strictly controlled, for their own good because only firm government could give efficiency. On 11th December, 1817, he wrote to Gneisenau that he found Joseph Görres, the editor of the intensely nationalistic journal *Rheinische Merkur* at Koblenz, to be generous and honest. But he was dangerous, too. "Görres has extreme democratic principles which are improper in a great monarchy," Clausewitz commented.[32] In another letter, on 25th October, 1818, he criticized the "Jacobinism" of the German patriot and poet Ernst Arndt, and of the scholar Johann Jahn. Clausewitz would probably have agreed with Goethe's lines: "Freedom is truly a glorious ornament, fairest of jewels; nevertheless it is not suited to all, as we know."[33]

The fullest and clearest expression of Clausewitz's political beliefs was presented in his *Meine Umtriebe*, written soon after the Carlsbad Decrees.

Facing page *Marshal Davout of France*

Clausewitz opened with a critique of the French Revolution. He condemned
the idleness and luxury which characterized the way of life of the French
nobility before 1789, when this favoured class had lived on endowments and
extravagant pensions. In France, the profession of arms had no longer been
warlike, but had become instead a sinecure and a privilege. While the
nobility had led their parasitic life, and so disgraced themselves, Clausewitz
claimed that the *bourgeoisie* had steadily become more powerful and enlight-
ened, spurred on by the oppression of the peasants. Another cause of the
French revolution had been the outmoded, inefficient and over-complicated
central administration.

In Germany, Clausewitz continued, the people had had less reason to
complain of the aristocracy and the administration. But the country had still
been borne along by the Revolutionary wave. Friedrich Wilhelm II had
alienated public opinion and had given the fanatics a pretext for action by
his extravagance, and by his mistresses; at the same time the intellectuals,
with their heads stuffed full of Greek and Latin and the ideals of Liberty,
had believed that the Revolution would recreate a Golden Age. Germany
had therefore greeted the Revolution with enthusiasm, Clausewitz continued. But the horrors, the evils of unbridled democracy, the attitudes and
actions of the Directory, all these things had restored the Germans to good
sense. Now the war with France was finished. But liberals were still foolishly
demanding the unity of all Germany, and the introduction of liberal
constitutional reform. The notion of German unity, Clausewitz maintained,
was based upon a dream, for only the sword could bring about German
political unity: one state would have to subjugate all others, and the time
for this had not yet come. The demand for constitutional reform was also
impractical. Clausewitz said that one must consider the lessons of history.
England, for example, had played her greatest role in the world when there
was the least political freedom, at the times of Queen Elizabeth and
Cromwell. Parliamentary debates could lead to strong resolutions, but they
could also paralyze Governments because they wasted time. In Germany,
with its many small, weak states, surrounded as they were by enemies,
Clausewitz believed that such time-wasting could be disastrous. It was vital
that the country should be able to act with secrecy and speed: a Parliament
such as that dreamed of by German democrats would surely have a
dangerous effect, people would be made restless, and convinced that they,
and they alone, were right.

Clausewitz stressed that Republican France was no model of serious and
orderly political life. Nor was Prussia like a dying man who urgently needed
to be revived with drastic stimulants. Was the situation really so bad,
Clausewitz asked? People dreamed of a German union, of German liberty,
German regeneration, but had no idea how to achieve them. They spoke as
if everything could be accomplished overnight by an explosion of democratic enthusiasm. Yet was any German state guilty of abusing personal

liberty? Were the Princes debauched? Were Art and Science in chains? Were people shot down in the streets or guillotined? Admittedly there were faults, Clausewitz continued. Taxes were heavy as a result of the war, and commerce had suffered. A dreadful famine had followed the bad harvest of 1816, during which the Prussian Government had failed to give aid and had shown an appalling lack of conscience. But while granting all this, Clausewitz maintained that Prussia was already liberal enough. Indeed, Austria had accused her of being too much so; and her leaders had been accused by Vienna of allowing the Prussian army to be animated by a troublesome spirit of independence.[34]

Abruptly, Clausewitz's *Meines Umtriebe* ended. The paper was probably not intended for immediate publication, since it contained harsh personal criticisms of Bülow, the Minister of Commerce, and Chancellor Hardenberg, as well as Chancellor Metternich of Austria. In the extract, Clausewitz emerges as a strong supporter of monarchical Government, legislating without the people, if always in their interests. This view could hardly be challenged by the ruling circle in Berlin. This only made King Friedrich Wilhelm's later treatment of Clausewitz doubly unfortunate or at least the treatment as Clausewitz saw it.

Clausewitz now had no hope of seeing even his qualified ideas for military reform being accepted; nor was his effort to revise the War Academy curriculum likely to succeed, despite the many heated arguments which took place. General Boyen's successor at the War Ministry was the man who had been Clausewitz's superior at Koblenz, General von Hake. Hake, who was to remain as War Minister until 1833, believed that an officer was perfectly well educated if he could read, write and do a little arithmetic. "Just show me anyone who afterwards needed much more," he said.[35]

The reaction against the reformers continued, even though the army's general efficiency steadily improved in such matters as training, equipment, staff work and administration.[36] The attempts to link the army with the people through the *Landwehr* had already been largely nullified; now the other two methods, higher education and the admission of the *bourgeoisie* into the officer corps, were also undermined. A Commission chaired by Clausewitz's former pupil, the Crown Prince, was set up in 1825 to study the question of army education. The Commission was to study the feasibility of schooling the *bourgeois* officers to compensate for their supposed lack of education: it was arrogantly assumed that for the aristocracy noble birth was education enough. The Commission reported: "To be sure, the road to the highest military goal should not be closed, or obstructed, to any man who by his talent and hard work overcomes the handicaps of his origins. Nevertheless, the true interest of the Army cannot be served if mediocre and uncultured men are at the State's expense merely trained to claim higher rewards before they make themselves fit to give greater service."[37]

This attitude, which was a complete reversal of Scharnhorst's policy of wider and better basic education, reduced the chances of the *bourgeoisie* of qualifying for the officer corps. The situation was exacerbated by the conduct of the non-noble entrants, who soon adopted the haughty manner of their high-born companions. They became more proud, more arrogant, and more aloof from the civilian world, than the military noblemen themselves.

By January, 1823, Clausewitz was thoroughly depressed and disillusioned, and wished to give up his military career altogether. He tried to become Prussian Ambassador to London. Indeed, the post was provisionally offered to him, and he needed only the King's final consent. Once more Clausewitz was supported by Gneisenau; the amiable Chancellor Hardenberg expected him to be successful; and he was also given strong help by Count Bernstorff, the Foreign Minister, who had become a close friend. But as soon as Clausewitz's name went forward, opposition to his appointment grew from those near Friedrich Wilhelm. The King himself had strong reservations, possibly because of the lingering memory of Clausewitz's "desertion" to Russia in 1812, but more probably because he distrusted Clausewitz as a member of the old reformer group, and disliked the irritating and persistent manner in which Clausewitz pressed for changes, for example to the War Academy curriculum. Clausewitz had never tried to ingratiate himself into the court circle; and his attempts to bring improvements at the War Academy had quickly brought him into conflict with members of the Government and Court. He was unpopular, too, with the civil servants. As Clausewitz later wrote to Gneisenau, on 9th September, 1824: "I have never been their enemy, but as I grow older I feel that I am becoming one."[38]

By the autumn of 1823, Clausewitz knew that his appointment as London Ambassador was too strongly opposed to leave any chance of his selection. Also against him was Sir George Rose, the British Ambassador to Berlin, probably because he had someone else he preferred.[39] Clausewitz was made even more miserable by the fact that he had never asked for the post in the first place, and had only agreed when the appointment had been provisionally offered to him; and now he was being attacked for that. "Unquestionably, the fact that I was offered the post at the London Embassy gave rise to many reservations," Clausewitz told Count Bernstorff in November. "I would have acted earlier and done away with these reservations by withdrawing my declaration to General Gneisenau. But such a step seemed a difficult one to take, since the matter had already been placed before the King, and I was prevented from withdrawing by the feeling of gratitude I had towards General Gneisenau, whose very friendly words I would have rendered useless."[40]

Typically, Clausewitz preferred to bow out quietly and avoid the humiliation of a struggle. He told Count Bernstorff: "Without wishing to ask what the position now is, as Your Excellency knows, I do know enough to realize that these reservations have increased rather than diminished. I must therefore urgently inform Your Excellency that it would be quite impossible, because of my feelings, even to wish for this post. I do not know the reservations to which my person gives rise; perhaps they are of the kind I could counter with pride. But I am very aware of how many qualities I lack which one has the right to ask for." In the next passage, Clausewitz gave an excellent self-portrait. His modesty sometimes amounts to total self-effacement. "It is not my nature to set myself up as a figure of doubt. I must confess to you, Count, that it offends my self-respect and my feeling of honour, which for whatever reason happens to be my heritage and forms a substantial part of my character. I have never, in my long period of service, begged the slightest favour; I have never looked for a position. Yet I see my pride being sacrificed for the first time, without really knowing myself how all this came about. I trust that Your Excellency will forgive this expression of my feelings, but it forms the basis of my request." Clausewitz asked that he should no longer be considered for the post. "Some people navigate their way through difficulties such as now confront me with tenacity, and a total absence of sentiment. But this is not for me. My character is simple and open, as my conduct must be, too . . . The minor humiliation which I would suffer from my rejection would be easy to overcome, since my resolve is stronger."[41]

To this disappointment was added another. A project that he should fill a diplomatic post in Munich also came to nothing. Count Bernstorff wrote to Clausewitz on 21st November: "It is very painful for me to have to tell you, my dear General, that the King has accepted neither my first nor my second proposal, with regard to the post in Munich, but has given it to Herr von Küster following an earlier plan of mine which amalgamated various Embassy posts in Germany. I too find this a very painful disappointment of my hopes, the fulfilment of which I would have valued greatly, for my interest in you and your happiness is as strong as is my respect and devotion."[42] Clausewitz had to remain as Director of the War Academy, frustrated and disappointed. His character, temperament, outlook—all were affected, or rather, traits which had always been there became far more pronounced. Outwardly, Clausewitz had good reason to be content with his career and achievements. He was with Marie, and although their marriage was childless, their letters never suggest any distress at the fact. Materially, Clausewitz was better off than ever before; his friends, if few in number, were close and loyal to him. His small circle included Prince Anton Radzivill and his wife, the Princess Louise, Gneisenau, and Count Bernstorff. For many years after Clausewitz's death Count Bernstorff's family carefully preserved an album. Beneath a portrait of Clausewitz was a verse written by the Count:

That which moves a tender woman's mind;
Which stimulates man to heroic struggle;
A pure mind's deepest undertaking;
Man's warmest heart, his most intense existence—
All these were united in him to perfection.[43]

Clausewitz also had reason to be proud of his military distinctions. Medals were still following him. The first award for his service in Russia, the Knight of the Order of the Holy Vladimir, fourth class with ribbon, was confirmed by the Czar on 3rd May, 1817, and was granted for Clausewitz's part in the fighting near Vitebsk on 15th July, 1812. He received the award in 1818. The following year came a golden sword of honour, inscribed "For Valour", presented by the Czar for Clausewitz's part at the Battle of Borodino. In 1821, Clausewitz was awarded the Order of the Knight of St. Annen, second class, formally confirmed in 1822. From Prussia, he received the Iron Cross, second class, for the 1815 campaign. He was also awarded the Red Eagle, the Swedish sword order, for his part at the engagement by the Gärda. Soon after his return to Berlin, Clausewitz was once more honoured by his appointment as military tutor to the Crown Prince, Friedrich Wilhelm, who was to succeed his father to the throne of Prussia in 1840. In May, 1821, Clausewitz was also privileged to be reaccredited to the General Staff, and on 30th January, 1827, his noble status was at last fully authorized. The King wrote identical letters to Carl, to his brother Gustav— now a Duisberg tax official, to Fritz, now Major-General and Commander of the Ninth *Landwehr* Brigade, and to Wilhelm, a Colonel and Commander of the Thirteenth *Landwehr* Brigade. In the letters Friedrich Wilhelm declared: "By this I hereby ratify your nobility and permit you to legalize the correct possession of the nobility."[44]

But neither friends nor distinctions were enough for Clausewitz: he was only in his forties; and felt he had a great deal to offer. But as always, he lacked the ability to push himself forward. As he had written to Gneisenau on 4th March, 1817: "For some time I have had the unfortunate habit of keeping everything to myself, and I should have been less reserved, less hidden away. One reason has been my fear of scorn, and the need to be sure of what I was doing. A superficial opinion which brought a rough reply would easily hurt me, and would be difficult to avoid as long as people are what they are."[45] On 3rd February, 1818, Clausewitz wrote: "I would be wise to make a secret vow—never to say a great deal."[46] He always feared having to give a spontaneous opinion: as Gneisenau told Hardenberg in a letter on 16th May, 1819, Clausewitz talked "in the language of modesty."[47] This modesty sometimes passed to embarrassing extremes. "With amazement, although at the same time with a warmer emotion," Clausewitz wrote to Gneisenau on 14th May, 1819, "have I noticed which of my proposals you consider to be the best, if I may be allowed to say so. Putting it this way will show how incapable I am myself of being so pretentious. Your Excellency will not take this as affected modesty, but rather the conviction, which public life soon gave me, that one must conform in rank and behaviour to the harmony of the prevailing balance."[48]

Disbelieving that one sometimes had to push forward in order to attract favourable attention Clausewitz thought it enough to be recognized by "the features of individual character, an unpretentious intellect, a modest disposition, a benevolent temper."[49] But of course these admirable features were not enough. Clausewitz himself exceeded them on occasions: sometimes, when roused, he could be extremely pressing and persistent if convinced he were correct, as he had been in 1812 before he went to Russia. This only made his personal situation worse. If he had been a Blücher or a Gneisenau, always ready to speak his mind loudly enough, or if he had been a Scharnhorst, with his quiet but dominant personality, Clausewitz's treatment by others would have been different. Instead, his sudden outbursts annoyed and angered those who disagreed with him, including the King; when Clausewitz withdrew into himself again, those same people found it easy to despise him. Not outspoken enough to be respected, Clausewitz became an irritant instead.

General von Brandt, a firm admirer of Clausewitz, wrote in his memoirs: "Nobody had to suffer such bitter experiences in his work as Clausewitz [when he was at the War Academy] who, with great urbanity, yes, even in the face of stupidity, never gave way to anything precipitate, harsh, or anything which displayed that kind of character." But the General added: "Nevertheless he caused all sorts of annoyances, which led to complaints with the General Inspection, with the War Ministry, and which probably played their part when he was later transferred to quite a different sphere."[50] A growing sadness filled the letters written by Clausewitz in the 1820s, typified by a note he sent to Marie while visiting Potsdam. "I am now well used to the fact that Potsdam always tends to remind me of many sad and serious things. It was always so, and it is natural enough, since I always feel strange and lonely here. I have returned to the house where I stayed with my father when he brought me to begin my twenty-nine years with the regiments. Not least, I have the deepest gratitude for all the happiness which Fate has given me since then, and which was first founded by that journey. But on the other hand I still have the same sadness which so filled my heart at that time, and which has really never left me. I admit that Fate so often smiled upon my life that I took it for granted. Yet, for all that, I have certainly never been quite free from that sadness."[51]

Another reason for Clausewitz's unhappiness and frustration at the War Academy was his belief that Scharnhorst was still too little recognized. Even his grave in Prague was atrociously neglected. "Not long ago old Major Meinert returned from Prague," Clausewitz told Gneisenau on 16th September, 1820. "He had visited Scharnhorst's grave, and learned from the grave-digger that the grave has almost been dug over and the remains almost removed, through the bad location of the site. If a monument is to be placed there, it had better be done quickly . . . I am writing to Your Excellency about this because you might be able to put the matter to General Knesebeck."[52] During the next few years, Clausewitz was constantly occupied with the attempt to bring back Scharnhorst's remains to Berlin, or at least to put up a decent monument. "It is said that flooding in the churchyard at Prague has caused a great deal of damage," Clausewitz wrote to Gneisenau in 1824, "and it is now difficult to discover exactly where Scharnhorst's grave is."[53] Not until 21st September, 1826, was Clausewitz able to tell Gneisenau that the remains had finally been brought to Berlin and re-buried on the 19th.[54]

By now Gneisenau had replaced Scharnhorst as the person to whom Clausewitz completely revealed himself. Only to his few close friends did Clausewitz display the full extent of his very real abilities: his clear, analytical thinking, his wide range of knowledge and perception, his firm commonsense. Only to his friends did Clausewitz reveal these qualities—and in his writing. And now, at the War Academy, feeling unrecognized and handicapped, feeling that everything he tried to do was liable to fail, and yet unable to press hard enough to bring success, Clausewitz began to concentrate upon setting down his military ideas on paper, and upon editing and polishing those notes he had already written. He withdrew further into himself, and into his documents. "Free as he was from all petty vanity," Marie wrote later, "from every feeling of restless, egotistical ambition, he still felt a desire to be really useful, and not to leave idle the abilities with which God had endowed him. In active life he was not in a position in which this longing could be satisfied."[55]

Students at the War Academy knew their Director as a rather severe, military figure, who was seldom seen. According to his one-time *aide-de-camp*, von Friedericki, the students "hardly got to know him since he lived in such a retiring fashion. Few knew anything of his earlier activities, which were so bound up with the fate of the Fatherland. Nobody dreamed that one day his name would be famous. Since we saw him so little, and then only when it was absolutely necessary, imagination was given free rein and rumours abounded. Yes, it was even believed that the General, whose facial colouring was, it must be admitted, ruddy, and whose nose was somewhat purple, that he was hunched over the wine-bottle from the early morning."[56] In fact, the red face and purple nose were caused by damage to the skin tissue during the terrible Russian winter of 1812. During those hidden hours at the War Academy, Clausewitz was busily writing, with Marie helping him sort the complicated scraps of notes. Working in his study or in the drawing room, Clausewitz either wrote or edited his previous papers dealing with the Italian campaign of 1796–97, the 1799 campaign in Switzerland and Italy, the operations in 1812, and from 1813 to the armistice, the 1814 campaign, and the final 1815 campaign. He wrote accounts of Frederick the Great, Gustavus Adolphus, Ferdinand of Brunswick, the seventeenth-century French general Henri de la Tour d'Auvergne Turenne, and many others. Above all he wrote the passages which were eventually to appear as the first three volumes of his collected works, entitled *Vom Kriege—On War*. Marie urged him to publish some of his work, but Clausewitz refused. He said that too much remained to be done, and to leave his documents unfinished would be to risk all he had written being misunderstood; there would be "endless misconceptions."

The author of *On War* may only have started writing as a last resort, having nothing else worthwhile to occupy his active mind. If he had been employed as he wished, he may never have taken up the pen to the same extent, may never have returned to the notes written while he was stationed at Koblenz. If Clausewitz—perhaps the greatest military teacher of his time—had been allowed to teach, or if he had been appointed Ambassador to London, his written work might never have been as prolific. But the very failures which so saddened Clausewitz helped to produce *On War*.

SIXTEEN

On War

"System in this treatise is not to be
found on the surface, and instead of a
finished building of theory there are
only the materials."
(*On War*, Introduction.)

I

On War is a potent blending of Clausewitz's experience, observation, study
and analysis. The book describes the dramatic transition of warfare which
had taken place during Clausewitz's lifetime. He examined the old and the
new forms of war, illustrated the differences between them, and exposed the
implications of the new developments.

Clausewitz's career had allowed him to be a unique witness of the
changes which had taken place. He had experienced the old forms of war in
1793 and 1806, and the new in 1812, 1813, 1814 and 1815; he had seen at
first hand how useless the old had been against the new; and had taken part
in Prussia's struggle to equip herself to combat France's modern and
massive armies. The three volumes of *On War* are studded with these
experiences: they are full of examples drawn from the campaigns in which
he had taken part, used both for detailed examinations of selected topics
and to illustrate basic principles. Throughout his life, Clausewitz projected
his own experiences into a wider context, as he had done in 1806 following
his capture after the battle of Auerstädt. *On War* is a similar kind of projection,
although on a massive scale, and integrated with detailed study of basic
theory. The 1806 campaign was used to provide examples of the retreat,
flank positions, defence of an area; 1812 for marches, subsistence, methods
of resistance, retreat into the interior, defensive war, the culminating point
of victory; 1813–15 for defensive war, the base of operations, relation of the
three arms ... But Clausewitz did not attempt to write a mere military
manual; and he realized the limitations of attempting to formulate a
general Theory of War. Instead, he devoted himself to the title of his work:
on war. He criticized the old, he introduced the new. "We shall take as
clear a view of the subject as we can without being tedious, and pass in
review the true and the false, reality and exaggeration," he wrote.[1] "We

have tried to emphasize the necessary and the general, and to leave a margin for the play of the particular and accidental; but to exclude all that is arbitrary, unfounded, trifling, fantastical, or sophistical. If we have succeeded in this object, we look upon our problem as solved."[2]

Clausewitz was determined that this work would be different to those textbooks of strategy which he criticized, which were so much a part of the old eighteenth-century era. "It has come to pass that our theoretical and critical books, instead of being straightforward, intelligible dissertations, in which the author always knows at least what he says and the reader what he reads, are brimful of these technical terms, which form dark points of interference where author and reader part company. But they are frequently worse, being nothing but hollow shells without any kernel."[3] He returned to this criticism in Volume III: "The expressions 'commanding ground,' 'sheltering position,' 'key of the country,' so far as they are founded on the nature of heights and descents, are hollow shells without any sound kernel. These imposing elements of theory have been chiefly resorted to in order to give apparent interest to the tactical commonplaces; they have become the darling themes of learned soldiers, the magical wands of adepts in Strategy . . ."[4]

This artificial attitude to strategy, Clausewitz claimed, was reflected in the military operations which made up the old form of war. "And on this field, where the conduct of War spins out the time with a number of small flourishes, with skirmishes at outposts, half in earnest and half in jest, with long dispositions which end in nothing, with positions and marches, which afterwards are designated as skilful only because their infinitesimal causes are lost, here on this very field many theorists find the real Art of War to exist; in these feints, parades, half and quarter thrusts of former Wars, they find the aim of all theory, the supremacy of mind over matter."[5] Combats had generally only been sham fights, Clausewitz continued. "In a word, hatred and enmity no longer roused a State to personal activity, but had become articles of trade. War lost a great part of its danger."[6] Campaigns became the personal plaything of monarchs, who used troops hired for the occasion. The result was a "restricted, shrivelled-up form of War." Sometimes, Clausewitz added, "neither battle nor siege took place, and the whole of the operations of the campaign pivoted on the maintenance of certain positions and magazines."[7]

This type of war, with its "algebraic actions," had come to an end. All the features which had characterized it were finished, including the formalistic angles and lines of operations, all summed up in the phrase "Methodicism." But the Germans took some time to appreciate this development, and had failed to do so by 1792, Clausewitz said. "It was then imagined possible to stem the tide in a national war by a moderately sized auxiliary army, which brought down on those who attempted it the great weight of the whole French people . . . the powerful nature of the enemy's system of attack was quite misunderstood, by opposing to it a pitiful system of extended positions and strategic manoeuvres."[8] The lesson was repeated in 1806 for Prussia, with the disastrous results of Jena and Auerstädt. "When in the year 1806 the Prussian Generals, Prince Louis at Saalfeld, Tauentzien on the Dornberg near Jena, Grawert before and Rüchel behind Cappellen-dorf, all threw themselves into the open jaws of destruction in the oblique order of Frederick the Great, and managed to ruin Hohenlohe's Army in a way that no Army was ever ruined, even on the field of battle, all this was done in a manner which had outlived its day, and with the most downright stupidity to which Methodicism ever led."[9]

"War," Clausewitz wrote, "had suddenly become an affair of the people once more, and that of a people numbering thirty millions, every one of whom regarded himself as a citizen of the State." He continued: "By this participation of the people in the war instead of a Cabinet and an Army, a whole Nation with its natural weight came into the scale. Henceforth, the means available—the efforts which might be called forth—no longer had any limits . . . By the extent of the means and the wide field of possible results, as well as by the powerful excitement of feeling which prevailed, the energy with which war was pursued was vastly increased. The object of its action was the downfall of the foe; and not until the enemy lay powerless on the ground was it imagined possible to stop . . . Hence the element of War, freed from all conventional restrictions, broke loose with all its natural force."[10]

The implications of unleashing this energy were immense, Clausewitz wrote. To begin with, old army rule books were swept away in the furious conflict which tore across Europe. This conflict was fired by hatred. No longer were campaigns to be conducted in a gentlemanly, chivalrous fashion: "Even the most civilized nations may burn with a passionate hatred of one another."[11] Rules and geometric calculations gave way to passion, massive friction and uncertainty. "So we see how, from the very outset, the absolute, the 'mathematical' as it is called, no longer has any firm place in military calculations; from the outset there is an interplay of possibilities, probabilities, good and bad luck, which . . . makes War of all branches of human activity the most like a gambling game."[12]

Throughout *On War*, Clausewitz repeatedly alludes to the uncertainties of modern war. "War is the province of uncertainty; three-quarters of those things upon which action in War must be calculated, are more or less hidden in the clouds of great uncertainty . . . War is the province of chance. In no sphere of human activity is such a wide margin left for this intruder . . ."[13] New strains were imposed upon the Commander-in-Chief. "The Commander of an immense whole finds himself in a maelstrom of false and true information, of mistakes made through fear, negligence, pre-occupation, contraventions of his authority, from either mistaken or correct motives, from ill will, true or false sense of duty, indolence or exhaustion, of accident which no man could have foreseen."[14]

If this was the case, what could be relied upon to increase the chances of victory? Battles had changed completely with the development of the new warfare, Clausewitz said. They were no longer half-hearted engagements in which one side touched the other for a short while then moved away again. Now, he continued, they were gigantic clashes in which two immense forces attempted to grind one another down. It was difficult for one to gain a decisive victory over the other; instead, the battle "burns slowly away like wet powder." Clausewitz continued: "But modern battles are not like this by accident; they are like this because the parties find themselves almost equally matched as regards military organization and the knowledge of the Art of War, and because the warlike element—inflamed by great national interests—has broken through artificial limits and now flows in its natural channel."

These massive armies now had to attempt to strangle one another slowly because each knew it was almost impossible to kill the enemy with one blow. Yet the aim, more than ever before, must be the complete overthrow of the enemy. Unlike the limited, artificial manoeuvres of earlier decades, "war is an act of violence intended to compel our opponent to fulfil our will." Clausewitz wrote: "What is 'overcoming' the enemy? Invariably the destruction of his military force, whether it be death, or wounds or any means." He added: "We assert that the direct destruction of the enemy's force is everywhere predominant; we advocate here the over-riding importance of this destructive principle, and nothing else."[15] But, if battles could only burn slowly away like damp powder, how could this complete destruction be accomplished? Clausewitz gave a clear answer: by more troops. These superior forces should be hurled at the decisive point. "The direct result of this is, that the greatest possible number of troops should be brought into action at the decisive point . . . We think, therefore, that . . . the superiority at the decisive point is a matter of capital importance, and that this subject, in most cases, is decidedly the most important of all. The strength at the decisive point depends upon the absolute strength of the Army, and upon skill in making use of it."[16] Clausewitz gave a lucid summary of his beliefs in Book IV, Chapter XI: "1. The destruction of the enemy's military force is the leading principle of War; 2. This destruction of the enemy's force must be principally effected by means of battle; 3. Only great and general battles can produce great results; 4. The results will be greatest when combats unite themselves into one great battle."

Inevitably, with both sides trying to bring the maximum number of forces into action, a colossal escalation of violence would occur. Both sides would be seeking to throw superior forces at the decisive point; both would be seeking great battles. Not only should this escalation be accepted, Clausewitz continued, but those who believed that bloodshed could—or even should—be avoided were making a foolish mistake. "Perhaps, by and by, Bonaparte's campaigns and battles will be looked upon as mere acts of barbarism and stupidity, and we shall once more turn with satisfaction and confidence to the dress-sword of obsolete and musty institutions and forms. If theory gives a caution against this, then it renders a real service to those who heed its warning voice." Clausewitz continued: "Let us not hear of Generals who conquer without bloodshed. If a bloody slaughter is a horrible sight, then that is a ground for paying more respect to War, but not for making the sword we wear blunter by degrees of humanity, until someone steps in with one that is sharp and cuts off the arm from our body."[17] The escalation of violence might spiral onward, Clausewitz said, forever reaching up to new levels of slaughter. "We therefore repeat our proposition, that war is an act of violence pushed to its utmost bounds. As one side dictates the law to the other, there arises a sort of reciprocal action, which logically must lead to an extreme."[18] This extreme, or total level of violence must be allowed to come, he added, because "superiority in numbers becomes every day more decisive."[19] Based upon these statements, Clausewitz's later titles the "Mahdi of Mass' and the "Apostle of Violence," would indeed seem correct.

But *On War* developed another theme, which was more sophisticated, and far more important. The theme was only half expressed probably because *On War* was unfinished. The only section which Clausewitz felt was in its final form was Book I, Chapter I, and it is in these passages that the underlying message of the book comes out most strongly. Clausewitz believed that one could write about war on two distinct levels: the abstract and the real. Considered abstractly, war would indeed reach extremes of violence. But Clausewitz added: "Everything takes a different shape when we pass from abstractions to reality." To the abstract belonged the attempt to disarm the enemy completely, to bring about his total overthrow. In reality, war should be very different. Great and bloody battles were essential in the abstract; in reality, they were not. "Destruction of the enemy's military force is in reality the object of all combats; but other objects may be joined thereto, and these other objects may be at the same time predominant."[20] Elsewhere in the book Clausewitz reiterates this: "We see then that there are many ways to one's object in War; that the complete subjugation of the enemy is not essential in every case."[21] "We look upon a great battle as a principal decision, but certainly not as the only one necessary for a War or a campaign. Instances of a great battle which have decided a whole campaign have been frequent only in modern times; those which have decided a whole War belong to the class of rare exceptions."[22] Battles need not in fact take place; the mere threat of them could achieve the same result. "The decision may be either a battle, or a series of great combats—but it may also consist of the results of mere relations, which arise from the situation of the opposing forces, that is possible combats."[23] Clausewitz stated: "Possible combats are on account of their results to be looked upon as real ones."[24] The situation might resemble that in trade: cash settlements (battles) sometimes took place, but more often credit was used (the threat of battles).

Moreover, Clausewitz wrote, everything depended upon a war's political objective. Indeed his assessment of the political role in war gave the book perhaps its greatest value. If the political objective were small, or limited, then the military effort could also be restricted. Military aims should always be shaped by political aims, and there could be many different degrees of the latter. "War does not, therefore, always require to be fought out until one party is overthrown; and we may suppose that, when the motives and passions are slight, a weak probability will suffice to move that side to which it is unfavourable to give way."

The matching of military to political aim marked the fundamental distinction between abstract and real war. Clausewitz stressed: "As war is no act of blind passion, but is dominated by the political object, the value of that object therefore determines the measure of the sacrifices by which it is to be purchased."[25] Once again, this point emerges most clearly in Book I, Chapter I. "The war of a community—of whole Nations, and particularly of civilized Nations—always starts from a political condition, and is called forth by a political motive. It is therefore a political act." Clausewitz continued: "Now if it was a perfect, unrestrained, and absolute expression of force . . . then the moment it is called forth by policy it would step into the place of policy, and as something quite independent of it would set it aside, and only follow its own laws, just as a mine at the moment of explosion cannot be guided into any other direction than that which has been given to it by preparatory arrangements. This is how the thing has really been viewed hitherto, whenever a want of harmony between policy and the conduct of a war had led to a theoretical distinction of the kind. But it is not so, and the idea is radically false. War in the real world, as we have already seen, is not an extreme thing which expends itself at one single discharge . . .

"Now, if we reflect that War has its root in a political object, then naturally this original motive which called it into existence should also continue the first and highest consideration in its conduct . . . Policy, therefore, is interwoven with the whole action of War, and must exercise a continuous influence upon it, as far as the nature of the forces liberated by it will permit." From this point, Clausewitz arrived at his most famous statement: "We see, therefore, that War is not merely a political act, but also a real political instrument, a continuation of political commerce, a carrying out of the same by other means."

The more violent the motives and the conduct of war, the nearer warfare will approach to its abstract form. But, Clausewitz added, "although it is true that in one kind of war the political elements seem almost to disappear, whilst in another kind it occupies a very prominent place, we may still affirm that the one is as political as the other." For: "Under all circumstances War is to be regarded not as an independent thing, but as a political instrument."[26] Clausewitz returned to this idea in Book VIII. "We know, certainly, that war is only called forth through the political intercourse of Governments and Nations, but in general it is supposed that such intercourse is broken off by war, and that a totally different state of things ensues, subject to no laws but its own. We maintain, on the contrary, that war is nothing but a continuation of political intercourse, with a mixture of other means." Normal political relations should therefore continue, as far as possible; and above all, political control of the state should be as strong in wartime as it is in peacetime. "War can never be separated from political intercourse, and if, in the consideration of the matter, this is done in any way, all the threads of the different relations are, to a certain extent, broken, and we have before us a senseless thing without an object."[27] Clausewitz warned, too, that "It is quite possible for such a state of feeling to exist between two States that a very trifling political motive for war may produce an effect quite disproportionate—in fact a perfect explosion."

Clausewitz was careful in making predictions for the future; but he did write: "Bounds, which to a certain extent existed only in an unconsciousness of what is possible, when once thrown down, are not easily built up again."[28] Apparently fearing that his description of abstract war might be mistaken for a description of real war, Clausewitz added a note of caution: "We must once more remind our readers that, for the sake of giving clearness, distinctness and force to our ideas, we have always taken as the subject of our consideration only the complete antithesis, that is the two extremes of the question, but that the concrete case in war generally lies between these two extremes." [29] He had developed his ideas of abstract war because, logically, this had seemed correct. But just as a distinction existed between the old and new forms of war, so differences existed between abstract and real war.

Marie later discovered a paper among Clausewitz's documents which described her husband's intention to re-edit his drafts for *On War*. Clausewitz had written: "My present view is to go through the whole thing once more, to establish by further explanation many of the earlier treatises, and perhaps to condense into results many analyses on the later ones, and so make a moderate whole out of it." Clausewitz had added: "My ambition was to write a book that would not be forgotten in two or three years, and which anyone interested in the subject would certainly take up more than once."[30]

Marie's brother, Heinrich von Brühl, came across another note, written by Clausewitz in 1827. "I look upon the first six books, of which a fair copy has now been made, as only a mass which still lacks a proper form, and which must still be revised once more." In this note Clausewitz underlined

GLORIOUS NEWS.

THE
ALLIED SOVEREIGNS

With their Armies of 150,000 Men,

ENTERED PARIS,

On the 31st Ult. after

HAVING TOTALLY DEFEATED
BUONAPARTE,

WITH THE LOSS OF

10,000 MEN and 100 PIECES of CANNON,

AMMUNITION, BAGGAGE, &c. &c. and

TEN GENERALS.

The EMPRESS and Her SON fled with Precipitation from

PARIS.

Poster announcing the destruction of Napoleon

*Heinrich Friedrich Karl Freiherr von Stein, from the portrait
by Heyne*

the importance he attached to the idea that "War is only a continuation of State policy by other means." He wrote: "Although the chief application of this point of view does not arise until we reach the eighth book, it must be still fully developed in the first book, and lend assistance throughout the revision of the first six books. Through this revision, the first six books will lose a good deal of dross, many cracks and holes will be filled up, and much that is of a general nature will be given distinct conception and forms."[31]

Clausewitz added: "Should the work be interrupted by my death, then what is found can only be called a mass of unformalized ideas. But as these are open to endless misconceptions, they will doubtless give rise to a number of crude criticisms."[32]

Disillusion and Death

"Standing still and doing nothing is
quite plainly the normal condition of
an army in the midst of war: acting,
the exception."
(*On War*, bk. iii, ch. xvi.)

I

DESPITE THE CONCENTRATED effort in the years between 1824 and 1830,
Clausewitz was never able to finish his revision. As he feared, there were
indeed to be "endless misconceptions." In 1830, he was called away from
his study and given other employment. He sorted his papers into as much
order as possible, sealed them in separate packets, labelled them, and "took
sorrowful leave of this employment which he loved so much."[1] Clausewitz
was never to open those packets again.

From mid-February, 1830, Major-General Clausewitz served in the
First Artillery Inspection Department, also retaining the Directorship of the
War Academy for a number of weeks. On 5th April he was also appointed
to the Supervising Commission for Military, Scientific and Technical Subjects, whose membership included Gneisenau and Müffling. The Commission's task was to check reports of manoeuvres and to give King Friedrich
Wilhelm its assessments of the efficiency of these exercises. Then, following a
proposal by his former superior officer and fellow prisoner-of-war, Prince
August, Clausewitz was sent to replace Major-General von Rühl as Inspector of the Second Artillery Inspection, based at Breslau. This appointment
was announced by a Cabinet Order of 19th August; and Clausewitz arrived
at Breslau in mid-September. At the end of the month he began an
inspection tour of East Prussia and Posen, the Prussian-controlled area of
Poland.

Meanwhile, international events were causing fresh anxiety. The second
half of 1830 saw the eruption of internal disorders which had been simmer-
ing in many European countries for over a decade. Nationalist and liberal
agitation had reached a climax. In the last weeks of 1830 revolutions broke
out in France, Belgium, parts of Germany, Italy, Switzerland and Poland.
Civil wars opened in Portugal and Spain, and the Spanish conflict con-

tinued until 1840. At root, the rebellions were a protest against the rigidity and failure of European conservative policies, aggravated as they had been by economic hardship. To Clausewitz, the unrest seemed to offer France a perfect opportunity to strike once more. The "unsettled, seething liberalism"[2] of Prussia's traditional enemy should once again be guarded against by firm military measures. France herself underwent the July Revolution, when, as a result of rising Liberal opposition in the Chamber of Deputies, Polignac's Ministry tried to strengthen the conservative hold by restrictive measures introduced on 25th July. The Liberals reacted violently, and managed to overthrow the *régime*. Revolution in Paris had strong repercussions in Belgium, where resentment against Dutch domination had been felt since Belgium had been forced into union with the Netherlands in 1815. On 15th August a revolt broke out and the insurgents gained control.

Before beginning his inspection tour in September, Clausewitz had hurried to see Gneisenau at Erdmannsdorf, to ask for a position under him should the Prussian forces be mobilized. The two friends had a long-standing agreement. Back in September, 1820, Gneisenau had asked Clausewitz whether, if another war should come about, he—Gneisenau—should apply for a post in the supreme command. "Your noble and strong character makes it impossible for you to speak anything but your frank opinion and the absolute truth," Gneisenau had written. Gneisenau had also asked his friend whether, if he did actually obtain command, Clausewitz would agree "at once, at the outbreak of hostilities, to be recalled in order to be Chief of Staff. So would we share friendship, fortune, fame—or Fate's disfavour."[3]

Clausewitz had replied: "Who, in the midst of the ruin of defeat, in the wreckage of our monarchy, defended Kolberg with cool and cheerful courage? Who sank Macdonald's army in the Katzbach and guided Prussia's army over the Elbe, Rhine and Marne, over all hostilities, quibbling and stupidity? In order to answer you—this spirit I trust and all will trust in it. This is my answer to the first query." Clausewitz continued: "With the second part, concerning myself, I confess I would rather have won fame at the point of a body of troops, with sword in hand. An honourable death would end a weary and paralyzed life. But I will gladly admit that even this wish would be silenced by the jealousy of seeing another standing by your side. Not because I understand you better than anyone else, but rather because I feel nobody would serve you with as much loyalty, sincerity and self-sacrifice as I."[4] Now, in 1830, this arrangement still held. Immediately, Clausewitz was livelier and happier than he had been for many years: once again active operations against the French seemed imminent, and Clausewitz would embark upon them at Gneisenau's side. Clausewitz's hostility toward the French returned, and he waited impatiently for hostilities and for a summons to take up his appointment with Gneisenau.

For the time being, Clausewitz remained based at Breslau, but his letters and conversation were animated as he watched the events. Friedrich Wilhelm von Brühl, Marie's cousin and Gneisenau's son-in-law, wrote: "We have seen Clausewitz every day. It was so kind and good of him to visit us often . . . It was a real delight for me to hear him speaking with such special clearness about great affairs, about how the world is once more reeling feverishly, and that it is likely to get worse." Clausewitz, wrote Friedrich to his father-in-law, was cheerful with the thought of war. "Clausewitz does not see it all black. On the contrary he is delighted with the turning point at which matters in France so plainly are."[5]

Marie had joined Clausewitz at Breslau, and she watched her husband become daily more excited at the prospect of doing battle with the French. Then, at the end of November, revolution broke out in the Russian-controlled area of Poland, adjacent to Posen. The Russian army commander Constantine panicked and fled the country. Warsaw was captured by the insurgents, who then set up a provisional government and tried to bargain with the Czar for reforms. The revolt might easily spread to Posen. On 11th December a personal messenger from the King knocked upon the door of Clausewitz's residence at Breslau: he was summoned to ride back to Berlin at once. He and Marie left directly and reached the capital the following day. At Berlin, Clausewitz was told that Gneisenau had indeed been given an army command, and that he was to be his Chief of Staff. But the area of operations was not to be in the West, as a precaution against French invasion, but in the East. Gneisenau had been ordered to take charge of the First, Second, Fifth and Sixth Army Corps, together named the Army of the East, and which was to act as an observation force in Posen. Clausewitz was bitterly disappointed; nor were the General and his Chief of Staff to leave at once. For two months they remained in Berlin, involved in conferences and administrative and political affairs. For Clausewitz, these activities ranged from drafting a paper for Prince August, connected with the work of the Military, Scientific and Technical Commission on the subject of the changed design of forage wagons, to highly controversial documents on international affairs.

Clausewitz advocated the centralization of the political-military intelligence services, which he maintained would give more up-to-the-minute reports on the situation. But Clausewitz found no success with his suggestion. Instead he himself wrote a number of papers, in which his opinions and assessments changed as the international events evolved. These memoirs, written while the conferences continued between Gneisenau, the Minister of War, Hake, and the Chief of the General Staff, von Krauseneck, were sometimes based upon views Clausewitz had expressed in his earlier documents. In August, 1830, for example, Clausewitz had drafted *Über einen Krieg mit Frankreich.*[6] This, a plan of war for operations against France, was not the first that Clausewitz had outlined since 1815; one had been written in about 1828.[7] But in the summer of 1830 Clausewitz had felt such a war to be more or less inevitable. If hostilities opened, he had written, Prussia should act without waiting for the Russians, and should immediately take the offensive, while remaining on the defensive in Italy and on the Upper Rhine. An Anglo-Dutch army should be launched from the Sambre, a Prussian army from the Moselle and Meuse, and an Austro-German army from Mannheim or Landau, with the three forces thrusting towards Paris. Since complete unity of command was impossible, Clausewitz had continued, each army should have its independent commander, as had been the case in 1815. In Belgium and Italy a strong defensive should be organized, for in these two areas the French could count upon the support of the local population. This memoir had been studied by Gneisenau in September, 1830, but the situation had been altered by the revolution in Belgium. The new *régime* had proclaimed independence on 4th October, and had persuaded the Dutch to sign an armistice on 28th October.

At the end of 1830, Clausewitz revised his ideas and formulated a new plan entitled *Betrachtungen über den Kriegsplan gegen Frankreich*.[8] He began by explaining the latest events: Poland was in revolt, Italy was unsettled and Austria was frightened of her, Belgium was in rebellion. If war were now to break out with France, Clausewitz said, a march from Germany upon Paris through Lorraine no longer stood any chance of success; an attack upon Lorraine would leave the Prussian frontier further north defenceless against a possible attack from Belgium. With the risk of a threat from Belgium, it would be better to remain on the defensive in the south, he continued, and make Belgium the target and the means for striking at France. In this way, Clausewitz maintained, north Germany could be protected, support would be offered by Holland and perhaps by England, and in Belgium itself the Prussians could rely upon help from the Orangists, the party which supported union with the Netherlands. Developments during the winter seemed to confirm Clausewitz's belief that Belgium was the real danger, or perhaps France working through Belgium. The Belgian National Congress declared members of the Dutch family of Orange-Nassau ineligible to hold office, and by February, 1831, the Congress had promulgated a new constitution, the most liberal in Europe.

In the same February, Clausewitz drafted a third memoir to substantiate his second. He was certain that war would break out with France sometime during the spring. At the same time he tried in Prussia to support the idea of a war against France, should hostilities be necessary. In a new memoir, *Die Verhältnisse Europa's seit der Theilung Polens*,[9] Clausewitz described France as still being a formidable adversary, unified, warlike, intelligent, and the master of rich resources. Clausewitz wrote another article in December, 1830, *Zurückfuhrung der vielen politischen Fragen, welche Deutschland beschäftigen, auf die unserer Gesammt-Existenz*,[10] which he sent anonymously to *L'Allgemeine Zeitung* for publication, but the article was not accepted. The article made a direct appeal to German patriotism. The Germans, said Clausewitz, were

not realistic enough. They followed ideas enthusiastically, but their enthusiasms were liable to be sentimental and vague. He warned that the Italian
and Polish rebels would seek—and obtain—French support. Germans
should not forget that France always favoured political unrest in Europe;
that she was the prime source of revolution; that she wished to use
revolution to meddle in the business of others. France would attempt to
avenge herself, reconquer previous French land, and recover Franch supremacy. Unless the national energy which had been generated in 1813 could
be re-discovered, Clausewitz added, Germany would be destroyed. When
sufficiently moved, Clausewitz could abandon his natural restraint and
become extremely emotional. These memoirs were certainly more highly
charged than any he had previously written. Clausewitz wanted his country
to take vigorous action, action in which he wished to be closely involved. All
Clausewitz's emotions, all his nervous, frustrated energies, were released. His
hatred of the French had been inflamed again; and he wanted war. At the
beginning of March, 1831, Clausewitz and Gneisenau travelled, not west-
ward as Clausewitz would still have preferred, but eastward to Posen. They
set out from Berlin in the evening of 7th March, and arrived at Poznan, the
principal city in the area, at five o'clock on the morning of the 9th.

Clausewitz disliked the Poles as much as he did the French. As far back as
May, 1812, when crossing the Grand Duchy of Warsaw on his way to
Russia, Clausewitz had shown his contempt of the Poles in letters to Marie.
He said that he had met with nothing but common impertinence, that he
despised the Polish nation, which was cowardly and cringing in adversity,
arrogant and insolent in better times. "I have found people here in
conditions which you cannot imagine," Clausewitz had written. "I am now
quite convinced that the partition of Poland was a great benefit, decided by
destiny, that this nation, which has been in these conditions for thousands of
years, should finally be released from them. The Polish enthusiasts, from
whom I cannot even except our friend Radzivill, are vain egotists. They
want to maintain the conditions under which Poland has lived until now.
Russia has shown the Poles a good example. In Russia the people are in a
far better condition." Clausewitz had added: "A thousand times I have
thought: if only a fire would consume them all, so that the purifying flames
would change this mound of dirt into clean ashes."[11]

Poland was an excellent example of the need for strong political control,
Clausewitz believed. Convinced that power was the essence of politics, and
concerned for political efficiency, he criticized those liberals who sympathized with the nationalistic movements in the country. In documents which
he wrote in December, 1830, Clausewitz made clear that he still considered
the Poles to be semi-barbarians. Politically, he said, the country was of no
more account than a desert steppe, open to all-comers.[12] Moreover, Clausewitz also believed that a unified and independent Poland would inevitably
join with France against Prussia.[13] He had welcomed the Czar's decision to

send a strong Russian army into Poland in February, 1831. But the anti-Russian insurrection was still in progress, and must not be allowed to spread into Posen; hence the organization of the four Prussian army corps in the area to establish a cordon at the frontier.

But while events on all sides moved rapidly, while the Russians began their harsh suppression of the Polish revolutionaries, Clausewitz was once again fretting at his inactivity. Gneisenau and his Chief of Staff shared a comfortable suite at the elegant Hotel de Vienne, Poznan. Clausewitz was bored. "We are involved in a remote kind of business," he wrote to Marie on 6th April. "To me it would be a thousand times better if we would get one of the enemy, whether Pole or French, by the ears."[14] The Prussian force remained as an observation army; there were no military operations. Clausewitz's depression returned far deeper than ever before.

His letters during the next few weeks showed a mounting impatience against those who sympathized with the liberals, and especially with the Poles. Revolutionaries in a host of different countries seemed to be gaining strength, and people refused to see the dangers. The weak opposition to the "rebel state" of Belgium "turns my stomach," he wrote on 9th June. Then he turned his anger against pro-liberal British journalists who had dared to criticize Prussian treatment of the Poles. "What does annoy me is that journalists are now speaking as if they were ministers and Cabinet, yet have only a half-knowledge," Clausewitz complained to Marie. "When one realizes that because of this, Britain, the old and natural ally of Prussia, now feels a mixture of hostility and disdain against Prussia, for which we have not given the slightest reason . . . one really must lament a state of affairs when things are given over to such elements."[15]

By the time that Clausewitz wrote this letter on 19th August, he was in a nervous and seriously disturbed condition. Moreover, his letters by now clearly indicated a premonition of death. This premonition was inevitably aggravated by an outbreak of cholera which swept from Russia through Poland to Posen. As the days passed, Clausewitz was obsessed with a death wish. "The beautiful days of our life have passed," Clausewitz had written to Marie on 28th May. "The supreme blessing would still to be to live with you far from this world. How little my position and my actual work pleases me. I am often obliged to be gay and to be pleased with small things in order to make my position bearable. But deep down in my soul I feel a profound melancholy."[16] Nine days later Clausewitz described his fear of disunity between the allies, prompted by Austrian jealousy of Prussia. "It makes me inexpressibly sad. I escape from all these calamities by telling myself that not much longer remains to us to live, and that we do not leave behind children."[17] Stein's death on 29th June deepened Clausewitz's melancholy. "So they die, one by one, those with whom we were familiar," he wrote on 9th July, "they remind us that the time is not far distant when we will vanish in our turn. I believe Stein died without regret because he saw many things from the same distressing aspect as I do, and felt that nothing could be done to avert the evil in the world."[18]

The factors which had made Clausewitz so unhappy throughout his life, especially in recent years, had had an accumulative and accelerating effect: the lack of appreciation from the King and his ministers; the belief that he could do far more if only he were given the chance, the conviction that war with France was inevitable, and that too few preparations were being undertaken for it. Perhaps there was disappointment, too, that hostilities with France had not already begun. Another source of unhappiness was Gneisenau's deterioration: his beloved friend was rapidly growing older and slower, both physically and mentally. The fire of Kolberg and the Katzbach was flickering lower. Sadly, Gneisenau realized this himself. "I will further put down how very dissatisfied I am with myself," he confessed to his son-in-law, Friedrich von Brühl. "The sovereigns are very unjust to place old generals at the head of their armies. I have experienced this with myself. First, through exertion, my eyes are weakened; then I have a dulled memory, and diminished physical strength. I am a nervy sieve. What service can I possibly carry out, with such infirmities? Daily, indeed hourly, I am reminded of this incongruity through my failure to attend to business which I forget to do. Clausewitz must have a great deal of patience with me." The sixty-one year old General concluded: "I do not want to frolic around the jewel on the King's crown any longer."[19]

Clausewitz desperately tried to hide his own depression and to interest the flagging Gneisenau in everyday matters. He discussed international affairs with him for many hours, in an attempt to keep his superior's mind alert. At the same time Clausewitz conducted himself as Chief of Staff with considerable skill. "With great application, Clausewitz followed the position and movements of the [Russian] army," commented General von Brandt, who visited Gneisenau's headquarters at the Hotel de Vienne. "The way Clausewitz judged matters, the way he formed conclusions from single movements and marches, the way he calculated the speed and duration of marches, the way he knew in advance where a decision would come—all were of the highest interest. What historians will only discover with laborious research, what critics will serve up later at the quintessence of military knowledge, he knew in one instant."[20]

But Clausewitz's intense misery continued, along with his gloomy preoccupation with death. Both are strongly apparent in another distressing, confused letter which he wrote to his anxious wife on 29th July. "Everywhere the French urged others to revolt and be disloyal, and proclaimed insurrection as the most sacred of rights. I believe that no-one will have the strength to resist this movement. Truly, in times such as these death is not to be feared." He continued: "If I die, dearest Marie, so it will be in my profession. Do not feel too sad about a life for which little could be done anyway. Stupidity is on the increase and is gaining ground every day. No man can defend himself against it, any more than he could against the cholera. It is at least a shorter suffering to die from the one as from the other. I cannot tell you how little I value human judgement, as I leave this world. This disease too must have its sway, and I would not have lived to see the day. So not much is lost.

"What makes me very sad is that I have not taken better care of you. The fault was mine. I want to thank you, dearest angel, for the help and for the support you have given me in my life. '*Oh, I have felt since I saw you, as if I stood before an angel's majesty. A pious feeling overcame me and made me shudder, and childlike my heart prayed—Please remain, beloved stranger, remain here, lead through the beautiful blessing in your eyes to the still peace of life, lead me back there from the storms of life. With a friendly spirit you have given me your hand. I am under the protection of an angel. Beautiful my path winds its way through life and bliss lives in the heavens.*' Do you remember these lines? They come from the beginning of our life together, and they shall be there at its end. I embrace you, my beloved angel, and hope to see you in better times."[21] On 13th August, Clausewitz wrote to Marie: "I am fully resigned that I can no longer expect this life to finish with an honourable decline. I am not lacking in courage and self-control, as I also realize I am outside the stupidity of mankind."[22]

During the evening of 22nd August, Gneisenau felt ill. Almost immediately, cholera was suspected. For the first hours Gneisenau was able to talk and even to joke. "This is a Field-Marshal's disease," he said. "I don't expect I shall recover from it."[23] Clausewitz, at his bedside throughout the night, left the sick room to scribble a note to Marie at ten o'clock in the morning of the 23rd. "The Field-Marshal is in danger of his life. He is so ill, and I need all the composure I can get to write these lines. He had diarrhoea last night, combined with fainting fits. At two o'clock he called the doctor, Gumpel, who recognized the danger that the disease might be cholera and they did everything they could to halt it." Clausewitz added: "They have stopped the diarrhoea, and the danger of cholera has receded slightly. But since then he has been very weak, and could suffer a stroke at any moment. The doctors have not abandoned all hope yet. But the danger is very great. You will have another message from me during the day."

At half-past six in the evening, Clausewitz wrote again. "There is no hope dearest Marie, and I shall probably finish this letter telling you of his death. Since two o'clock he has been in a complete coma. His death is not entirely to be assumed, for he still has some consciousness. But his spirit has completely gone. He does not recognize anyone any more. He spoke to me for the last time at three o'clock ... I am very well and try to keep composed by thinking of you, my dear beloved wife." Clausewitz scribbled at the end of the note: "The Field-Marshal is still alive. But I have no hope whatsoever. And the doctors have none despite the fact that he is still breathing."[24] Gneisenau died that night. Since he had been a cholera victim, his infected body was buried quietly. Clausewitz had to live in isolation for a while as a quarantine precaution. Alone, he continued to brood. Weakened by the death of "my beloved, cherished friend," Clausewitz was then dealt another blow by the treatment of Gneisenau's memory by the King. The official state journal, *Allgemeine preussische Staatszeitung*, announced the death of the Field-Marshal in a short notice extracted from the Posen Journal. Friedrich Wilhelm himself never made a formal announcement of regret over the death. "Not only had the King treated Gneisenau with disfavour right until the end, but he made no attempt to hide it," Clausewitz commented bitterly to Marie.[25] In a long, angry letter to Marie on 5th September, written from his place of quarantine at Kobylepole, near Poznan, Clausewitz revealed how personally he took this insult to Gneisenau, and how poorly he felt that he himself was regarded by the King. Clausewitz began on a note of brittle cheerfulness: "Now I sit here as a prisoner, in a derelict Polish house, and I do not know who has the more right to it, the army of mice that has grown up in it, or myself."

Clausewitz then deplored the silence of the *Staatszeitung* over Gneisenau's death, and the manner in which the journal had taken "a message of such importance from a miserable provincial newspaper." He feared that his own report to the King concerning Gneisenau's death might have offended Friedrich Wilhelm, though he could see no reason why it should. "I have long accepted that the King does not like me," Clausewitz continued. "And I know that with us a Chief of Staff can never reckon on thanks and recognition. But after so many words of satisfaction from others, I had believed I might be treated a little better, and that my position with regard to the King might not have deteriorated." Clausewitz said that he had written most of the official reports from Gneisenau to the King himself. If the King had known the true authorship, he might not have accepted them so well, he added. "The Field-Marshal has never added the slightest idea to them. I have always presented matters as I saw them . . . he has never made the slightest change. Even if the King does not know this, and even though I like the fact that the main credit is given to the Field-Marshal, I still believe that I could have expected the King to recognize that I too had something to do with them. And I will not deny that it is very painful for me. I seem to vanish completely . . . I confess that such a disgust has taken hold of my soul that I have lost all joy and all courage."[26]

Gneisenau was succeeded by General von Knesebeck, with whom Clausewitz had had a strained relationship. "I was stunned by the General's nomination," Clausewitz told Marie, "because you will remember I had hoped to have surmounted that obstacle. But at the same time, they have had the usual lack of consideration in the Cabinet—the Cabinet Order was on the 9th and I received it on the 15th, just as General Knesebeck came into the house." But this time all went well; the two men agreed to forget past differences, and Knesebeck, "very cordial and very sincere," praised Clausewitz's work. For a time, Clausewitz was more cheerful. "I feel very well," he reported, "and as you see from the newspapers, cholera is beginning to go from here. At least you do not have to fear anything as far as I am concerned from that quarter."

Russia at last stamped out the rebellion in Poland, when Field-Marshal Paskewitsch-Erivanski stormed Warsaw on 6th and 7th September. Now that the threat was ended of the revolt spreading into Posen, the Army of the East could cease its observation role. Clausewitz returned to Breslau on 7th November, 1831. Marie travelled from Berlin to be with him, worried about his state of mind after receiving his disturbing letters, but happy with the thought of seeing him again. Perhaps everything would now improve. "I felt such a delight from the thought of being with Clausewitz after this difficult separation," she wrote later to Countess Bernstorff, "and I dared to hope for at least a quiet winter, when all fears for the future, cholera, even the sadness of the loss of our dear friend, would fade. I travelled throughout one night, and thought the stars had never seemed so bright and so beautiful. I came here on a Wednesday, at lunch-time, some hours earlier than Clausewitz had expected me." Marie continued: "I was prepared to find him changed, because several times he had written telling me he would be. But he walked towards me looking younger, and radiant, looking very well indeed. The servants had decorated the entrance hall and staircase with flowers, and there was a small triumphal arch. He welcomed me among these flowers. It was the happiest of reunions, despite it being in the middle of mourning."[27]

Marie felt even more confident that everything would now be happy, and that Clausewitz could soon return to his writing. But she told Countess Bernstorff: "Later, to be sure, I noticed that his nerves were terribly shaken and frayed, and that inwardly he was really very sad. From his letters I was already well aware that in this last period of great sorrow, which God had sent him, he had received even more blows to hurt and sicken him, and perhaps he felt them harder since he was already in a weak state of health. Nevertheless, I hoped that the happiness of our life together, the peace which we had expected here, would make him well, and that little by little I would manage to soften and remove all these impressions. So we spent a week which, on the whole, was very happy, despite the fact that we were only together undisturbed for a little time; visitors, business, and household arrangements constantly interrupted us."[28]

On 16th November Clausewitz worked in his study until lunch-time. Then he felt unwell; he immediately went to bed and the doctors diagnosed a comparatively mild attack of cholera. Nine hours later, Carl von Clausewitz was dead.

Doctors testified that his death was more the result of his general condition, which had deteriorated through his pain and the shaken condition of his nerves, than from the disease.[29] Clausewitz had simply surrendered the will to live. A grief-stricken Marie wrote to Elise Bernstorff: "At least his last moments were peaceful and painless, and yet there was something heart-rending in the expression, the tone, with which he breathed his last sigh. It was as if he threw out life as a heavy burden from him. Soon after, his features became all peaceful and composed. But an hour later, when I saw him for the last time, they were contorted again with the most dreadful suffering."[30]

Clausewitz's grave was situated in the military cemetry at Breslau, a town which was eventually to be taken from his beloved Fatherland and given to the Poles, whom he hated so much. Since cholera had been the official cause of death, the funeral was unaccompanied by speeches. King Friedrich Wilhelm sent a message to General Ziethen, commanding general in Silesia. This, issued through a Cabinet Order on 20th November, stated :"Your report of the sudden death of Major-General von Clausewitz, Inspector of the Second Artillery Inspection, is as unexpected to me as it is painful. The army has suffered a loss which will be difficult to replace, which saddens me greatly."[31] These were the kindest words that Friedrich Wilhelm ever used with regard to Clausewitz; Gneisenau had not been honoured with any mention at all.

An obituary notice in the Silesian *Zeitung* on 22nd November, 1831, reported the cause of Clausewitz's death as "a nervous stroke." The article, signed by "The Officer Corps of the Second Artillery Inspection," stated: "Unfortunately it was only given for the undersigned officers to be able to respect the deceased as a leader for a short while. However, they have had sufficient opportunity to learn and to recognize his spiritual abilities as well as the high degree of humanity, justice and mercy owned by the deceased." Marie received an effusive letter from the Crown Prince, Friedrich Wilhelm. "My dearest, most respectful lady, I must be included in the ranks of the mourners who empty their hearts these days, who weep with you, who tell you that every noble heart in the army grieves with you. I follow the irresistible throng . . ."[32]

The most accurate and heartfelt lines to be published appeared in the *Staatszeitung*, another distinction Gneisenau had been refused. The notice was probably written by Clausewitz's admirer, Count Carl von der Gröben; and its contents reveal that the author had an intimate knowledge of Clausewitz. "Sadness gnawed at his heart, quietly, which beat with the most glowing love under an exterior which would sometimes seem cold. Therefore he became easily a victim of that disease . . . One would wish there were more like Clausewitz in the army. She had hardly ever had a more well-ordered mind in her ranks. His ideas of the art of war were forged from the deepest of research and burning experience. They were concerned with the highest policy, were comprehensive, and as simple as they were practicable. The writings which he has left us will also show him to those who did not know him personally . . . His noble bereaved widow will not keep them from those who follow him."[33]

Marie knew very well the real reason for her husband's death. "Life for him was a nearly uninterrupted succession of disappointments, of suffering, of mortification," she explained to Elise Bernstorff. "Oh yes, on the whole, he had achieved much more than he could expect when it started. He was well aware of that, and grateful. But nevertheless he never reached the summit. And every satisfaction always had a thorn in it, to add pain to the pleasure. He had friendship, to a rare degree, with the excellent men of his period. But not recognition . . . And how much he suffered for his happiness. What cares he shared with Scharnhorst. What pain he experienced with his death . . . And he was heartbroken with the way he believed the King, with indifference and disdain, treated the dear Field-Marshal's [Gneisenau's] memory. Perhaps he took this too sadly and too hard, more than was meant, because by this time his nerves were so affected." Marie concluded: "My most beloved friend, the whole happiness of my life has been so prematurely torn away from me. He was too deeply feeling, too fragile, too sensitive for this imperfect world, and had had perhaps still great suffering to go through. Now he has conquered all earthly pain."

Clausewitz's widow did not remain inactive in her grief. She was fully aware of what she must do, even though, as her friend Caroline von Rochow said, she had "lost everything when she lost him, because not for a moment has she lost her feelings that she felt for him as a fiancée."[35] Marie had the opportunity and the ability to make Clausewitz, who had considered himself a failure in life, a success in death.

EIGHTEEN

Epilogue

"Perhaps soon a greater brain may
give the whole work a casting of pure
metal instead of these single grains."
(*On War*, Introduction.)

I

LARGELY OWING TO Marie's efforts, Clausewitz became something more than a fine staff officer with wide experience of the campaigns in the Napoleonic Wars, someone who had played an important, but behind-the-scenes, part in the reorganization of the Prussian army, who was known to a small intimate group to have had an excellent grasp of strategy. Because of Marie the blood-red wine of Clausewitz's thoughts on war would intoxicate the generals in the coming decades.

The Franco-Prussian war which Clausewitz had considered inevitable was not to be fought for another thirty-nine years. But when this war came, in 1870, the generals were to be Clausewitz's disciples. He was to achieve far more for Prussia in 1870 than he ever could have done in 1831. Among the students attending the Berlin War Academy while Clausewitz was Director was a young officer in his early twenties. Like the others he probably considered Clausewitz to be undistinguished and unexceptional. But when Helmuth von Moltke had himself risen to the summit of the Prussian army, and, as Chief of the General Staff, directed the Prussian operations against the French in 1870, he was to be a more fervent student of Clausewitz than ever he could have been in the 1820s. As Michael Howard has written: "The Franco-German conflict was to be settled by the methods of Clausewitz."[1]

General Carl von der Gröben had noted in the *Staatszeitung* that "the writings which he has left us will also show him to those who did not know him personally . . . his noble bereaved widow will not keep them from those who follow him." Gröben himself was to help Marie with the task. Marie began the exhausting labour of sorting and publishing Clausewitz's manuscripts when she still lived at Breslau, helped by her brother Heinrich, at least until he fell ill. She continued after she had moved back to Berlin as lady-in-waiting to Princess Wilhelm. Assistance was given to Marie by

Gröben and by Major O'Etzel, who corrected proofs and researched the maps; after only six months on 30th June, 1832, the first works were ready for publication. "People will be justifiably surprised that a female hand dares to begin a work with contents such as these," Marie wrote in the Preface. "For my friends, no explanation is necessary. But for those we do not know, I hope a very simple explanation of why I was driven to it will remove any hint of conceit. The work which these lines precede had been the sole endeavour of my beloved husband, who has been taken too early from me and from his Fatherland. It has been his sole concern during the last twelve years. To complete it was his dearest wish. But it was not his desire to impart what he had written to the world during his lifetime; and when I tried to persuade him to change his mind he frequently told me, partly in jest, and partly perhaps from a premonition of his early death, 'You are to publish it.' These words, which in those happy days often brought tears to my eyes, however little I was inclined then to give them significance, now place a duty upon me."[2]

Marie prepared eight of the ten volumes of Clausewitz's collected works, *Hinterlassne Werke über Krieg und Kriegführung*, the first three of which contained his masterpiece *Vom Kriege*. Volume Four dealt with the Italian campaign of 1796–97, Volumes Five and Six with the campaign of 1799 in Switzerland and Italy, Volume Seven with the wars of 1812, 1813 up to the armistice and 1814, Volume Eight with the Waterloo campaign. Volumes Nine and Ten, which followed later, covered a variety of campaigns by leading generals and strategists.

Finding the documents in a muddled state, Marie used her own discretion in editing them and linking them together. Clausewitz's 1812 campaign, for example (Volume Seven) is split into three sections, and only the second, Marie believed, was intended as her husband's account of the campaign. The first and third were intended for another work, and displayed a marked contrast in style and content to the second. But Marie found the three sections in one bundle, with the dry, analytical second section sandwiched between the other two parts, which dealt with events in which he was personally involved. "They are left in the order in which I found them," Marie wrote in the Preface. "I did not feel justified in making any alterations." In the 1812 preface she mentioned the difficulties and defects of publishing material which had been left unfinished by its author. "We must always lament, that the premature stroke which deprived his country and his friends of one so dear to them prevented him also from completing his proposed task, and not only from adding the missing sections, but from revising what he had written, as he wished." Marie added: "Many a criticism, perhaps too harshly expressed in the first flush of feeling, would have been softened, many facts discovered later would have been used, and the present sketch would have been a finished work."[3] If the harsh criticisms had indeed been removed, Clausewitz's 1812 campaign would have been less vigorous and would have suffered as a result. But as Marie commented: "Those who knew his noble and gentle nature know how unwillingly he would have injured anyone's feelings."

Marie's health was seriously undermined by the strain of the work, by the unavoidable stirring of her own feelings in undertaking the task, by the effects of Clausewitz's death and by the stress of living with him in those last years and helplessly watching his decline. She struggled on with her massive task, desperately anxious to complete it. But in 1835, the year in which she authorized Volume Eight to be published, Marie was in a very frail condition. Her health deteriorated rapidly in January, 1836, and her cousin, Count Carl von Brühl took her to visit a specialist in nervous disorders at Dresden. There she died on 28th January. As she had wished, her body was taken to Breslau and buried beside the remains of Carl.

Already, Clausewitz's works were receiving acclaim, especially *On War*. His fame rapidly grew, and became linked with the rise of the great Prussian General Staff and the might of the Prussian army. After the latter's triumphs of 1866 and 1870, Clausewitz's renown became world-wide. He became a symbol, as important and as distinctive as the Prussian *Pickelhaube*. Clausewitz's message, presented in *On War*, was devoured throughout Europe and throughout the world. But the sadness and tragedy which had shadowed him throughout life continued. Clausewitz's message was only half-digested, and the result was disastrous. Clausewitz's military disciples only saw in *On War* those sections they wanted to see. They read of the logical necessity for great battles, of massive armies striking bloodily at the decisive points, of the natural escalation of violence. They cheered Clausewitz for his wisdom. Clausewitz had been careful with his forecasts of the future, and had written in the context of his own age; but the generals seemed to believe that he had written in a vacuum, and that his words were valid for all time. They overlooked Clausewitz's belief, so often repeated, that the defensive was the strongest form of strategy. They overlooked the fact that *On War* was unfinished; they believed that *On War* contained a blueprint for victory, even though Clausewitz had many times reiterated that his work could not be regarded as a military manual. In his introduction to the first British edition of *On War*, Colonel F. N. Maude said: "His work has been the ultimate foundation on which every drill regulation in Europe, except our own, has been reared."[4]

At the other extreme, with fatal consequences, Clausewitz's description of abstract war was taken as a description of real war—bloody slaughter, massive battles, utmost violence. Above all, the generals ignored Clausewitz's most important theme: that the ultimate control of war should be political. His dictum that "War is a continuation of policy by other means," was taken to mean that generals should supersede the politicians when war began, which was the very opposite of Clausewitz's belief. His stress upon the need for political control was deliberately obscured in German reprints

Facing page *King Friedrich Wilhelm III of Prussia*
(*from the painting by Wilhelm Herbig in Apsley House*)

of *On War* in the 1850s.[5] Field-Marshal Helmuth von Moltke declared: "The politician should fall silent the moment that mobilization begins."

The successes which Moltke won for Prussia in 1870-71 were the final vindication for Clausewitz's message—or the message as the Generals read it. *On War* was therefore championed by those who believed that all nations should have massive armies, ready to be thrown on to the offensive, aimed at totally annihilating the opposing force. Marshal Foch, who dominated French strategy before 1914 and who was fated to be supreme commander of the allied armies in France for the closing stages of the First World War, drew heavily upon Clausewitz—as he misinterpreted him—in his *Principles of War*, published in 1903. He quoted Clausewitz: "Blood is the price of victory. You must either resort to it or give up waging war," and wrote: "Modern war knows but one argument: the tactical fact, battle. In view of this it asks of strategy that it should both bring up all available forces together, and engage in battle all these forces by means of tactical impulsion in order to produce the shock."[6]

This was an adequate description of Clausewitz's thoughts on abstract, offensive war; but it ran totally opposite to his beliefs about real, defensive war. Generals like Foch overlooked his serious warnings, and vied with one another in increasing the offensive power of their armies. Yet Clausewitz had written: "Not only reason, but experience, in hundreds and thousands of instances, show that a well-traced, sufficiently manned, and well-defended entrenchment is, as a rule, to be looked upon as an impregnable point."[7] The Generals believed that they, and not the politicians, knew what real war was all about. Yet Clausewitz had written that if this belief was allowed to predominate, "we have before us a senseless thing without object." So, fed on their misinterpretations of *On War*, the Generals rode out with their massive armies in 1914. The barbed wire and machine guns made the positions they attacked "impregnable"; the result was senseless slaughter.

Clausewitz had been misunderstood and underestimated. The fault was partly his. In *On War*, as in life, he had been too logical, too anxious to debate rather than to declare, too anxious to consider the extremes before adopting a correct and sensible middle course.

Few of his nineteenth-century readers penetrated Clausewitz's logic in *On War* to evaluate his real meaning. When Clausewitz was alive, few men achieved a true understanding and appreciation of his personal worth. For much the same reasons, the best use was not made of *On War*, and the best use was not made of Carl von Clausewitz as a soldier and strategist. The man and the author were perhaps not so very different after all.

Facing page *The Prussian Minister of War, Leopold Hermann Ludwig von Boyen (1771–1848)*

References

CHAPTER ONE

1. Liddell-Hart, *The Ghost of Napoleon*, 21.
2. Pertz-Delbrück, *v*, 442.
3. Schwartz, *ii*, 253.
4. Demeter, 124.
5. *Cursory View*, 20.
6. *Ibid.*
7. *On War*, *i*, Chapter Three.
8. Carlyle, *French Revolution*, *iii*, 56.
9. Gooch, 359.
10. *Ibid*, 399.
11. Roques, 1.
12. Gooch, 189.
13. *On War*, *i*, Chapter Four.
14. Goethe, *Werke*, *xxx*, 278–334.
15. Schwartz, *i*, 240.
16. Seeley, *i*, 108.
17. Goethe, *Werke*, *xxx*, 315.
18. *On War*, *vi*, Chapter Fifteen.
19. *Ibid*, *viii*, Chapter Nine.
20. Roques, 2.
21. Schering, 35 *ff*.
22. Schwartz, *i*, 240.
23. Schering, 35 *ff*.
24. *Ibid.*
25. *Cursory View*, 18–23.
26. *Ibid*, 30–31.
27. Seeley, *i*, 197.
28. *Cursory View*, 31–32.
29. Paret, 14–15.
30. Jany, *ii*, 436.
31. Clausewitz, *Nachrichten*, 426.
32. Schwartz, *i*, 38.
33. *Ibid*, *i*, 242.
34. *Ibid*, *i*, 38.

CHAPTER TWO

1. Seeley, *i*, 303.
2. *Ibid*, *i*, 378.
3. Craig, *The Politics of the Prussian Army*, 25.
4. *Ibid.*
5. Schwartz, *i*, 38.
6. Roques, 6.

7. *Ibid*, 38.
8. Lehmann, *Scharnhorst*, *i*, 325.
9. *Ibid*, 319.
10. Schwartz, *i*, 266.
11. *On War*, *i*, Chapter One, Part One.
12. Maude, *1806*, 4.
13. Seeley, *i*, 248.
14. Paret, 43.
15. *Ibid*, 76–77.
16. Lehmann, *op. cit.*, *i*, 257, 299–300.
17. Paret, 80.
18. Clausewitz, *Nachrichten*, 428.
19. Paret, 101.

CHAPTER THREE

1. Herold, 263.
2. Schwartz, *i*, 176.
3. *Ibid*, 182.
4. *Ibid*, 186.
5. *Ibid*, 187.
6. *Ibid*, 191.
7. *Ibid*, 200.
8. Caroline von Rochow, 27 *ff*.
9. Roques, 21.
10. *Cursory View*, 43.
11. Seeley, *i*, 113.
12. Schwartz, *i*, 212.
13. Seeley, *i*, 247.
14. Roques, 12.
15. *Ibid.*
16. Seeley, *i*, 249–50.
17. Paret, 103.
18. *Ibid*, 104.
19. *Cursory View*, 34.
20. Seeley, *i*, 393.
21. *Ibid*, *i*, 368.
22. Jany, *iii*, 436.
23. Craig, *The Politics of the Prussian Army*, 24; Shanahan, 44.
24. Craig, *op. cit.*, 26.
25. *Ibid*, 26.
26. Maude, *1806*, 62.
27. Paret, 111.
28. Schwartz, *i*, 222.

CHAPTER FOUR
1. *On War, vi*, Chapter Thirty.
2. *Ibid, v*, Chapter Five.
3. Schering, 28.
4. *Ibid.*
5. Lettow-Vorbeck, 163.
6. Schering, 28.
7. Maude, *1806*, 76.
8. Schering, 28.
9. Schwartz, *i*, 45–48.
10. *Ibid*, 223.
11. *Cursory View*, 63.
12. *Ibid*, 60–63.
13. Schwartz, *i*, 45.
14. *Ibid, i*, 47.
15. Lettow-Vorbeck, 400.
16. Roques, 13.
17. Maude, *op. cit.*, 156.
18. Montbé, *ii*, 16.
19. *Cursory View*, 76.
20. Fuller, *Decisive Battles, ii*, 440.
21. *On War, iv*, Chapter Four.
22. Seeley, *i*, 263.
23. Schwartz, *i*, 54–62.
24. Roques, 13.
25. Vossler, 134, 137.
26. Seeley, *i*, 286.
27. *Ibid*, 287.
28. Henderson, 16.
29. *Cursory View*, 119.
30. Unger, *Blücher, i*, 301.
31. *Ibid*, 318.
32. Linnebach, *Scharnhorst's Briefe, i*, 296.
33. *Cursory View*, 121.
34. Seeley, *i*, 305.
35. *Cursory View*, 123.
36. Roques, 14, Schwartz, *i*, 62.
37. Schwartz, *i*, 461–87.
38. Roques, 17.
39. *On War, iv*, Chapter Seven.

CHAPTER FIVE
1. Schwartz, *i*, 67–72.
2. Herold, 345.
3. Schwartz, *i*, 342.
4. Schering, 33.
5. Schering, 33.
6. Schwartz, *i*, 280.
7. Schering, 35 *ff.*
8. Schering, 33.
9. *Ibid.*
10. Henderson, 20.

11. Seeley, *i*, 345.
12. Schwartz, *i*, 67.
13. Paret, 126.
14. *Ibid; Preussisches Archiv*, 8–15.
15. Paret, 127; *Preussisches Archiv*, 147–81.
16. Herold, 349.
17. Schering, 38.
18. Herold, 345.
19. *Ibid*, 265.
20. *Ibid*, 298.
21. Schering, 39.
22. Schering, 39.
23. Herold, 276.
24. *Ibid*, 277.
25. Schering, 38.
26. *Ibid*, 38–39.
27. Roques, 30.
28. Herold, 346.
29. Schwartz, *i*, 88 *ff.*
30. *Ibid*, 73–88.
31. Herold, 69.
32. Schwartz, *i*, 289.
33. Roques, 33–34.
34. Blaischke, 67.
35. Hahlweg, *i*, 91.
36. Ranke, 212.
37. Schwartz, *i*, 23.
38. Seeley, *i*, 480.

CHAPTER SIX
1. Schering, 62.
2. Hahlweg, *i*, 91.
3. Seeley, *i*, 393.
4. Henderson, 3.
5. Pertz-Delbrück, *i*, 667–71.
6. Seeley, *i*, 399.
7. Stein, *vi*, 167.
8. Ritter, *Stein*, 275.
9. Linnebach, *Scharnhorst, i*, 332; Paret, 119.
10. Seeley, *i*, 343.
11. Roques, 21–22.
12. Seeley, *i*, 443–45.
13. *Ibid*, 433.
14. Scholtz, *Boyen*, 107.
15. Shanahan, 105–09.
16. Henderson, 35.
17. *Preuss. Arch*, 101; Paret, 130.
18. Conrady, *Grolman, i*, 151.
19. Droysen, *i*, 209.
20. Roques, 34.
21. *Ibid.*

22. Schering, 64.
23. *Preuss. Arch.*, 533–36; Conrady, *op. cit.*, *i*, 159–62.
24. Shanahan, 137.
25. Roques, 41.
26. Seeley, *ii*, 50–53.
27. Hahlweg, *i*, 91.
28. Craig, *The Politics of the Prussian Army*, 46.
29. Shanahan, 109–14, 128–29.
30. Craig, *op. cit.*, 47; Vaupel, 67.
31. Roques, 42.
32. *Ibid.*
33. *Ibid.*
34. *Ibid*, 43.
35. Schering, 65 *ff.*
36. Schmidt-Bückeburg, 15 *ff.*
37. Roques, 37.
38. Schwartz, *i*, 313.
39. Schering, 67.
40. *Ibid*, 68.
41. Schwartz, *i*, 126–27.
42. Hahlweg, *i*, 92.
43. Roques, 37.
44. Schwartz, *i*, 130.
45. Roques, 35.

CHAPTER SEVEN
1. Lehmann, *Scharnhorst*, *ii*, 208–11.
2. Schering, 69 *ff.*
3. Craig, *The Politics of the Prussian Army*, 53.
4. Lehmann, *op. cit.*, *ii*, 263–67.
5. Schwartz, *i*, 349.
6. *Ibid*, *i*, 138.
7. *Ibid.*
8. Seeley, *ii*, 345.
9. Schwartz, *i*, 138.
10. Schwartz, *i*, 138.
11. Roques, 43.
12. *Ibid.*
13. Lehmann, *op. cit.*, *ii*, 268–70.
14. Henderson, 50.
15. Lehmann, *op. cit.*, *ii*, 268–70.
16. Seeley, *ii*, 48–49.
17. Henderson, 52.
18. Roques, 44; Schwartz, *i*, 140.
19. Roques, 44.
20. Lachouque, *Napoleon's Battles*, 253.
21. Roques, 45.
22. Schwartz, *i*, 361.
23. Lachouque, *op. cit*, 265.
24. Schwartz, *i*, 363.

25. Henderson, 58.
26. Boyen, *Erinnerungen*, *ii*, 106–08.
27. Seeley, *ii*, 132.
28. Schwartz, *i*, 139.
29. *Ibid*, 142.
30. *Ibid*, 145.
31. *Ibid*, 146.
32. Herold, 383.
33. Seeley, *ii*, 131.
34. Henderson, 62–63.
35. Schwartz, *i*, 149.
36. *Ibid*, 150.
37. Pertz-Delbrück, *i*, 608.
38. Gumtau, *iii*, appendix.
39. Paret, 158*n*; Klippel, *iii*, 523–44.
40. Paret, 164*n*.
41. Gumtau, *iii*, appendix.
42. Paret, 175, *Clausewitz Schriften*, note of 1811.
43. Clausewitz, *Meine Vorlesungen*, introduction.
44. *Ibid.*
45. *On War*, bk. *vi.*, ch. *xxvi.*
46. *Meine Vorlesungen*, introduction.
47. *Ibid.*
48. Caroline von Rochow, 40.
49. Schwartz, *i*, 194.
50. Paret, 182.
51. Pertz, *ii*, 191 *ff.*
52. Schwartz, *i*, 411–20.
53. Pertz, *ii*, 159 *ff.*
54. *Ibid*, ii, 161 *ff.*
55. Boyen, *op. cit.*, *ii*, 104.
56. Schwartz, *i*, 421–25.
57. Droysen, 323.
58. Treitschke, *i*, 458.
59. Roques, 46.
60. Treitschke, *i*, 460.
61. Pertz, *iii*, 621–76.
62. *Ibid*, *iii*, 623.
63. Lehmann, *Knesebeck und Schön*.
64. Roques, 55.

CHAPTER EIGHT
1. Schwartz, *i*, 505.
2. *Ibid*, *i*, 484.
3. *Ibid*, *i*, 516.
4. *Ibid*, *i*, 516.
5. *On War*, Editor's Preface.
6. *On War*, bk. *iii*, ch. *viii.*
7. Seeley, *ii*, 445.
8. Roques, 55.
9. Schwartz, *i*, 516.

10. Pertz, *ii*, 285.
11. Clausewitz, *1812*, 3.
12. *Ibid*, 5–6.
13. *Ibid*, 8–9.
14. *Ibid*, 11.
15. *Ibid*, 19.
16. *Ibid*, 26.
17. Tarle, 57.
18. Clausewitz, *1812*, 33.
19. *Ibid*, 25.
20. *Ibid*, 38.
21. Schering, 113.
22. Clausewitz, *1812*, 43.
23. *Ibid*, 44.
24. *Ibid*, 101.
25. Tarle, 63.
26. *Ibid*, 67.
27. Schwartz, *i*, 24.
28. Schering, 111.
29. *Ibid*, 112.
30. Clausewitz, *1812*, 106–07.
31. *Ibid*, 107.
32. *Ibid*, 108.
33. Schwartz, *ii*, 63.
34. Tarle, 75.
35. Clausewitz, *1812*, 110.
36. *Ibid*, 122.
37. Tarle, 106.
38. Lachouque, *Napoleon's Battles*, 296.
39. Clausewitz, *1812*, 128.
40. *Ibid*, 131.
41. *Ibid*, 132.
42. Schering, 116.
43. Clausewitz, *1812*, 134.
44. Tarle, 126.
45. Clausewitz, *1812*, 137.
46. Tarle, 109.
47. Clausewitz, *1812*, 139.
48. *Ibid*, 179.
49. Schering, 115.
50. Clausewitz, *1812*, 139.

CHAPTER NINE
1. Clausewitz, *1812*, 142.
2. *Ibid*, 151.
3. *Ibid*, 160.
4. *Ibid*, 159.
5. *Ibid*, 164.
6. *Ibid*, 166.
7. *Ibid*, translator's preface: *xiii–xiv*.
8. Lachouque, *Napoleon's Battles*, 304.
9. Clausewitz, *1812*, 168.
10. *Ibid*, 173.

11. Schwartz, *i*, 487.
12. Clausewitz, *1812*, 142.
13. Tarle, 152.
14. Clausewitz, *1812*, 182.
15. Herold, 414.
16. Clausewitz, *1812*, 189.
17. *Ibid*, 191.
18. *Ibid*, 192.
19. *Ibid*, 193.
20. Schering, 116.
21. Schwerin, Gräfin Sophie, 317–21.
22. Seeley, *ii*, 530.
23. Clausewitz, *1812*, 197.
24. Blaischke, 28*n*.
25. Schwartz, *i*, 538.
26. Schering, 116.
27. Seeley, *ii*, 530–33.
28. Clausewitz, *1812*, 199.
29. *On War*, bk. *iii*, ch. *v*.
30. Seeley, *ii*, 546.
31. Tarle, 180.
32. Seeley, *ii*, 546–47.
33. Schering, 117.
34. Clausewitz, *1812*, 199.
35. Schering, 117–18.
36. Clausewitz, *1812*, 38.
37. Schering, 119.
38. Schering, 118.
39. Clausewitz, *1812*, 202.
40. *Ibid*, 203.
41. *Ibid*, 204.
42. Tarle, 239.

CHAPTER TEN
1. Clausewitz, *1812*, 212.
2. *Ibid*, 204.
3. *Ibid*, 205.
4. *Ibid*, 205.
5. *On War*, bk. *i*, ch. *vii*.
6. *On War*, bk. *i*, ch. *vi*.
7. Clausewitz, *1812*, 207–08.
8. *Ibid*, 209.
9. *Ibid*, 210.
10. Vossler, 80.
11. Schwartz, *i*, 493.
12. Clausewitz, *1812*, 215–16.
13. Tarle, 277.
14. Clausewitz, *1812*, 211.
15. Tarle, 275.
16. Schwartz, *i*, 538.
17. Vossler, 92–93.
18. Clausewitz, *1812*, 216.
19. Vossler, introduction.

20. Seeley, *ii*, 530.
21. Clausewitz, *1812*, 220.
22. *Ibid*, 221.
23. *Ibid*, 222.
24. *Ibid*, 231.
25. *Ibid*, 225.
26. *Ibid*, 232.
27. *Ibid*, 233.
28. *Ibid*, 233.
29. *Ibid*, 237.
30. *Ibid*, 238.
31. Schwartz, *i*, 497.
32. *Ibid*, 496 *ff.*
33. Clausewitz, *1812*, 240.
34. Schwartz, *i*, 539.
35. Schering, 120.
36. Boyen, *Erinnerungen*, *ii*, 333.
37. Hintze, *Die Hohenzollern*, 468–69; Treitschke, *i*, 481.
38. Paret, 192.
39. Clausewitz, *1812*, 240–41.
40. *Ibid*, 248.
41. Droysen, *ii*, 41.

CHAPTER ELEVEN
1. Roques, 61.
2. Droysen, *i*, 503.
3. Paret, 194–95.
4. Henderson, 85–86.
5. Schwartz, *ii*, 68.
6. Ranke, 212.
7. Schwartz, *ii*, 73.
8. *Ibid*, 75.
9. *Ibid*.
10. *Ibid*.
11. *Ibid*.
12. *Ibid*, 76.
13. Shanahan, 206–07, 218–24.
14. Schwartz, *ii*, 75.
15. *Ibid*.
16. Schering, 123–24.
17. Henderson, 100.
18. Schering, 124.
19. Schwartz, *ii*, 17.
20. *Ibid*.
21. Henderson, 101.
22. Lachouque, *The Anatomy of Glory*, 294.
23. Henderson, 102.
24. *Ibid*, 103.
25. Schering, 124.
26. *Ibid*, 126.
27. Pertz, *ii*, 601.

28. *Scharnhorst's Briefe*, *i*, 480.
29. Henderson, 105.
30. *Ibid*, 108.
31. Ranke, 219.
32. Pertz-Delbrück, 594.
33. Clausewitz, *Werke*, *iii*, 315.
34. Clausewitz, *Über das Lebens und den Charakter von Scharnhorst*, 199.
35. Henderson, 109.
36. Shanahan, 218–24.
37. Clausewitz, *Über . . . von Scharnhorst*, 196–97.
38. *On War*, bk. *vi*,, ch. *xxx*.
39. Henderson, 116.
40. Ense, 270.

CHAPTER TWELVE
1. Schering, 126.
2. Schwartz, *ii*, 19.
3. Pertz *iii*, 16.
4. Schering, 127.
5. *Ibid*.
6. *Ibid*, 128.
7. Schwartz, *ii*, 31.
8. *On War*, *iii*, Chapter Sixteen.
9. Henderson, 130.
10. *Ibid*, 131.
11. Schwartz, *i*, 20.
12. *Ibid*, 100.
13. *Ibid*, 101.
14. *Ibid*, 101.
15. *Ibid*.
16. *Ibid*, 102.
17. *Ibid*.
18. *On War*, bk. *vi*, ch. *v*.
19. *Ibid*, Chapter Eight.
20. Fuller, *ii*, 482–83.
21. *On War*, bk. *vi*, ch. *viii*.
22. Pertz, *iii*, 520.
23. Henderson, 190.
24. *Ibid*, 192–93.
25. Roques, 65.
26. Ritter, *Staatskunst*, *i*, 110–11.
27. Müffling, 33.
29. Henderson, 206–07.
30. Schwartz, *ii*, 20, 25.
31. *On War*, bk. *ii*, ch. *v*.
32. Pertz, *iii*, 580.
32. Seeley, *ii*, 535.
34. Henderson, 254.
35. Schwartz, *ii*, 116.
36. *Ibid*, 118.
37. Roques, 65.

CHAPTER THIRTEEN

1. Schwartz, *ii*, 141.
2. Gardner 24, Kelly, 52–54.
3. Schwartz, *ii*, 148.
4. Erckmann-Chatrian, *Waterloo;* Gardner, 97–98.
5. Gardner, 107.
6. Sibourne, 110.
7. Schwartz, *ii*, 149.
8. *Ibid.*
9. Kelly, 56.
10. Schwartz, *ii*, 149.
11. *Ibid.*
12. Kelly, 68–69.
13. Gardner, 112.
14. *Ibid*, 113.
15. Fuller, *ii*, 509.
16. Gardner, 112.
17. *Ibid*, 109.
18. Malmesbury, *ii*, 447.

CHAPTER FOURTEEN

1. Stanhope, 108–10.
2. Schwartz, *ii*, 149.
3. Gardner, 115.
4. Schwartz, *ii*, 149.
5. Kelly, 70.
6. Brett-James, 86.
7. Kelly, 57.
8. Ratcliffe, 9.
9. Kelly, 90.
10. Schwartz, *ii*, 150.
11. *Ibid.*
12. Kelly, 109.
13. Ratcliffe, 38.
14. Schwartz, *ii*, 151.
15. Kelly, 113.
16. *Ibid*, 114.
17. Schwartz, *ii*, 151.
18. *Ibid.*
19. Kelly, 119, 124–25.
20. Schwartz, *ii*, 152.
21. *Ibid*, 151.
22. *Ibid.*
23. Schwartz, *ii*, 152.
24. Kelly, 133.
25. Ratcliffe, 43.
26. Kelly, 138.
27. Schwartz, *ii*, 152.
28. *Ibid.*
29. *Ibid.*
30. *Ibid*, 154.

31. Henderson, 317.
32. *Ibid*, 316
33. *Ibid*, 319.
34. Roques, 67.
35. Schwartz, *ii*, 164.
36. *Ibid*, 163.
37. Roques, 67.
38. *Ibid*, 67–68.
39. *On War*, bk. *vii*, ch. *xxi.*
40. *Ibid*, bk. *vii*, ch. *v.*
41. Henderson, 320–21.

CHAPTER FIFTEEN

1. Pertz-Delbrück, *v*, 139.
2. Roques, 69.
3. Pertz-Delbrück, *v*, 128
4. *Ibid*, 162.
5. *On War*, Preface.
6. Pertz-Delbrück, *v*, 192.
7. *Ibid*, 197.
8. *Ibid*, 213.
9. Schwartz, *ii*, 488–92.
10. Meinecke, *ii*, 13–22.
11. Craig, *Problems of Coalition Warfare*, 19.
12. Craig, *The Politics of the Prussian Army*, 68.
13. Seeley, *ii*, 144.
14. Meinecke, *ii*, 310.
15. Craig, *The Politics of the Prussian Army*, 69.
16. Roques, 71.
17. *Ibid.*
18. *Ibid.*
19. *Ibid*, 72.
20. Schwartz, *ii*, 198.
21. Pertz-Delbrück, *v*, 289.
22. Schellendorf, 48–49.
23. Roques, 72.
24. *Ibid.*
25. Meinecke, *ii*, ,111.
26. *Ibid*, 373; Craig, *The Politics of the Prussian Army*, 68.
27. Craig, *The Politics of the Prussian Army*, 68.
28. *Ibid*, 75.
29. Pertz-Delbrück, *v*, 439.
30. Schwartz, *ii*, 433 *ff.*
31. *Ibid.*
32. Roques, 79.
33. Goethe, *Xenien*, 678.
34. Schwartz, *ii*, 200–44, Roques, 79–80.

35. Höhn, 266.
36. Craig, *The Politics of the Prussian Army*, 77.
37. Demeter, 73–74.
38. Roques, 72.
39. Schwartz, *ii*, 255.
40. *Ibid*, 256.
41. *Ibid*.
42. *Ibid*, 258.
43. *Ibid*, 262.
44. *Ibid*, *i*, 4.
45. Pertz-Delbrück, *v*, 192.
46. *Ibid*, 289.
47. *Ibid*, 370.
48. *Ibid*, 371.
49. *Ibid*.
50. Schwartz, *ii*, 246.
51. *Ibid*, 253.
52. Pertz-Delbrück, *v*, 443.
53. Blaischke, 88.
54. Pertz-Delbrück, 527.
55. *On War*, Preface.
56. Schwartz, *ii*, 247.

CHAPTER SIXTEEN
1. *On War*, bk. *v*, ch. *xviii*.
2. *Ibid*, bk. *viii*, ch. *ix*.
3. *Ibid*, bk. *ii*, ch. *v*.
4. *Ibid*. bk. *v*. ch. *xviii*.
5. *Ibid*, bk. *iii*, ch. *xvi*.
6. *Ibid*, bk. *viii*, ch. *iii*.
7. *Ibid*, bk. *viii*, ch. *iii*.
8. *Ibid*, bk. *vi*., ch. *xxx*.
9. *Ibid*, bk. *ii*, ch. *iv*.
10. *Ibid*, bk. *viii*, ch. *iii*.
11. *Ibid*, bk. *i*, ch. *i*.
12. *Ibid*, bk. *i*, ch. *i*.
13. *Ibid*, bk. *i*, ch. *iii*.
14. *Ibid*, bk. *iii*, ch. *viii*.
15. *Ibid*, bk. *iv*, ch. *iii*.
16. *Ibid*, bk. *iii*, ch. *viii*.
17. *Ibid*, bk. *iv*, ch. *xi*.
18. *Ibid*, bk. *i*, ch. *i*.
19. *Ibid*, bk. *v*, ch. *iii*.
20. *Ibid*, bk. *iv*, ch. *v*.
21. *Ibid*, bk. *i*, ch. *ii*.
22. *Ibid*, bk. *iv*, ch. *xi*.
23. *Ibid*, bk. *vi*, ch. *xxviii*.
24. *Ibid*, bk. *iii*, ch. *i*.
25. *Ibid*, bk. *i*, ch. *ii*.
26. *Ibid*, bk. *i*, ch. *i*.
27. *Ibid*, kb. *viii*, ch. *vi*.
28. *Ibid*, bk. *viii*, ch. *iii*.

29. *Ibid*, bk. *vi*, ch. *xxx*.
30. *Ibid*, Preface.
31. *Ibid*.
32. *Ibid*.

CHAPTER SEVENTEEN
1. *On War*, Preface.
2. Schwartz, *ii*, 349.
3. Pertz-Delbrück, *v*, 440 *ff*.
4. *Ibid*, 442.
5. Sybel, 264.
6. Schwartz, *ii*, 418–39.
7. Roques, 143.
8. *Ibid*, 86–87.
9. Schwartz, *ii*, 401–08.
10. *Ibid*, 408–17.
11. Schering, 109.
12. Schwartz, *ii*, 302.
13. *Ibid*, 401 *ff*.
14. *Ibid*, 333.
15. *Ibid*, 382.
16. Roques, 92.
17. *Ibid*.
18. *Ibid*.
19. Sybel, 274 *ff*.
20. Schwartz, *ii*, 448–49.
21. *Ibid*, 374 *ff*.
22. *Ibid*, 380.
23. *Ibid*, 297.
24. *Ibid*, 385. *ff*.
25. Roques, 94.
26. Schwartz, *ii*, 389 *ff*.
27. Bernstorff, *ii*, 227.
28. *Ibid*.
29. Schwartz, *ii*, 440 *ff*.
30. Bernstorff, *ii*, 227.
31. Schwartz, *ii*, 441.
32. Schwartz, *ii*, 443.
33. *Ibid*.
34. Bernstorff, *ii*, 228 *ff*.

CHAPTER EIGHTEEN
1. Howard, *The Franco-Prussian War*, 76.
2. Schwartz, *ii*, 452.
3. Clausewitz, *1812*, Editor's Preface.
4. *On War*, Introduction.
5. *Theory and Practice of War*, ed. Howard; Paret, *Clausewitz and the Nineteenth Century*, 30.
6. Foch, Chapter Three.
7. *On War*, bk. *vii*, ch. *x*.

Bibliography

Basic information about Clausewitz's life is obtainable from his letters to Marie, and to a lesser extent from his letters to Gneisenau. Unfortunately few letters from Marie to her husband have survived. Nor have many from Scharnhorst to Clausewitz survived, probably because the former was such a notoriously bad letter-writer. Clausewitz's correspondence with his wife is contained in a number of works, all of which are either German or French publications. The latest and most detailed of these, although dealing more with Clausewitz's career than his private life, is Professor W. Hahlweg's *Carl von Clausewitz, Schriften, Aufsätze, Studien, Briefe* (Gottingen, 1957). All the German and French biographies of Clausewitz, including that by Professor Hahlweg, make use of Karl Schwartz's *Leben des Generals Carl von Clausewitz,* 2 vols (Berlin, 1878), and this has also been the work most frequently employed by myself. Other biographies of Clausewitz include: Heuschele, Otto, *Carl und Marie von Clausewitz* (Leipzig, 1935); Linnebach, K., *Karl und Marie von Clausewitz: Ein Lebensbild in Briefen und Tagebuchblättern* (Berlin, 1917); Camon, H., *Clausewitz* (Paris, 1911); Roques, P., *Le General de Clausewitz* (Paris, 1912); Schering, W., *Carl von Clausewitz, Geist und Tat* (Stuttgart, 1941); Caemmerer, R. von, *Clausewitz* (Berlin, 1905); Blaischke, R.,*Carl von Clausewitz, Ein Leben im Kampf* (Berlin, 1934); Meerheimb, *Karl von Clausewitz* (Berlin, 1875); Bernhardi, *Leben des Generals von Clausewitz* (Tenth supplement of *Militär Wochenblatt,* 1878); Rothfels, Hans, *Carl von Clausewitz, Politische, Schriften und Briefe* (Munich, 1922) and the same author's *Carl von Clausewitz, Politik und Krieg* (Berlin, 1920). German biographies published in the 1930s and early 1940s, notably those by Schering and Blaischke, tend to be slanted to present the National Socialist interpretation of Clausewitz, both as a man and author.

Among the biographies of Clausewitz's contemporaries, the following are specially useful and contain letters written either by or to Clausewitz, as well as a number of important documents: Pertz, G. H. and Delbrück, H., *Das Leben des Feldmarschalls Grafen Neithardt von Gneisenau* (Berlin, 1864-80); Pertz, G. H. *Gneisenau* (Leipzig, 1850); Seeley, I. R., *Life and Times of Stein,* 3 vols (Cambridge, 1878); and Boyen, H. von, *Erinnerungen aus dem Leben des Generalfeldmarschalls Hermann von Boyen,* 3 vols (Leipzig, 1889-90).

For Clausewitz's involvement with Prussian military reforms, I have mainly relied upon these three works: Craig, G. A., *The Politics of the Prussian Army,* 1640-1945 (Oxford, 1955); Paret, P., *Yorck and the era of Prussian Reform, 1807-1815* (Princeton, 1966); and Shanahan, W. O.,

Prussian Military Reform, 1786-1813 (New York, 1945). Valuable information is also to be found in Karl Linnebach's *Von Scharnhorst's Briefe* (Munich-Leipzig, 1914).

The standard translations of *Vom Krieg* are those by Colonel J. J. Graham (London, 1918) and O. I. Matthijs Jolles (New York, 1943). For Clausewitz's *Principles of War*, I have used the British edition translated by Hans Gatzke (London, 1943), and for his memoirs of the 1812 campaign the British edition (London, 1843) has again been adopted, although the passages quoted have been checked with the original.

Other works consulted or quoted include the following:

PRUSSIAN REFORM

Bülow, H. von, *Neue Taktik der Neuern wie sie seyn sollte* (Leipzig, 1805)

Clausewitz, C. von, *Meine Vorlesungen über den kleinen Krieg*, 1811 (deposited at Münster University)

——, *Nachrichten über Preussen in seiner grossen Katastrophe*, tenth volume of *Kriegsgeschichtliche Einzelschriften* (Berlin, 1888)

Decken, F. von der, *Betrachtungen über das Verhältnis des Kriegsstandes zu dem Zwecke der Staaten* (Hanover, 1800)

Delbrück, Hans *Geschichte der Kriegskunst im Rahmen der Politischen Geschichte*, 7 vols (Berlin, 1900–36)

Demeter, K., *The German Officer-Corps, 1650-1945*, translated by Angus Malcolm (London, 1965)

Denkwürdigkeiten der Militärischen Gesellschaft, 5 vols (Berlin, 1802–05)

Görlitz, W., *History of the German General Staff* (New York, 1953)

Gumtau, C. F., *Die Jäger und Schützen des Preuss. Heeres*, 3 vols (Berlin, 1834–38.)

Hintze, O., *Die Hohenzollern und ihr Werk* (Berlin, 1916)

Hohenlohe, Prince F. L., *Reglement für die Niederschlesische Inspection* (Breslau, 1803)

Huber, Ernst, R., *Heer und Staat in der deutschen Geschichte* (Hamburg, 1938)

Jany, Curt, *Geschichte der Königl. Preuss. Armee bis zum Jahre 1807*, 3 vols (Berlin, 1928–39)

Kessel, E., *Zu Boyen Entlassung* (Berlin, *Historische Zeitschrift* clxxv, 1953)

Ritter, G., *Stein: Eine politische Biographie* (Stuttgart, 1958)

——, *Staatskunst und Kriegshandwerk* (Munich, 1954)

Rosinski, H., *The German Army* (London, 1939)

Scharnhorst, G. von, *Handbuch der Artillerie*, 3 vols (Hanover, 1804–14)

——, *Militärische Schriften*, edited by von der Goltz (Dresden, 1891)

Schellendorf, Bronsart von, *The Duties of the General Staff*, translated by Lieut. W. A. H. Hare (London, 1908)

Schmidt-Bückeburg, R., *Das Militärkabinett der preuss. Könige und deutschen Kaiser* (Berlin, 1933)

Stein, Frieherr vom, *Briefwechsel, Denschriften und Aufzeichnungen*, 7 vols (Berlin, 1931)

Vaupel, R., *Die Reorganisation des Preuss. Staates unter Stein und Hardenberg* (Leipzig, 1938)

MILITARY CAMPAIGNS
Germany and Belgium
A Cursory View of Prussia from the Death of Frederick II to the Peace of Tilsit, anonymous (London, 1809)
Brett-James, A., *The Hundred Days: Napoleon's last campaign* (London, 1964)
Craig, G. A., *Problems of Coalition Warfare: the military alliance against Napoleon, 1813–1814* (USAF Academy, 1965)
Falls, C., editor, *Great Military Battles* (London-New York, 1964)
Fuller, J. F. C., *Decisive Battles of the Western World*, vol. ii (London, 1955)
Gardner, D., *Quatre Bras, Ligny and Waterloo* (London, 1882)
Houssaye, H., *Napoleon and the campaign of 1814*(London, 1915)
——, *Iéna et la Campaigne de 1908* (Paris, 1912)
Kelly, Hyde, W., *The Battle of Wavre and Grouchy's Retreat* (London, 1905)
Lachouque, H., *Napoleon's Battles*, translated by Roy Monkcom (London, 1966)
——, *The Anatomy of Glory—Napoleon and His Guard*, translated by A. S. K. Brown (London, 1961)
Lettow-Vorbeck, O. von, *Der Krieg von 1806–1807* (Berlin 1899)
Malmesbury, Lord, *Letters of the First Earl of Malmesbury, 1745–1820*, 2 vols (London, 1870)
Maude, F. N., *The Jena Campaign, 1806* (London, 1909)
——, *The Leipzig Campaign, 1813* (London, 1908)
Montbé, A. von, *Die Chursächsischen Truppen im Feldzuge 1806–1807* (Dresden, 1860)
Panckoucke, editor, *Victoires, Conquêtes, des Francais de 1792 a 1815*, 27 vols (Paris, 1818)
Petre, Floraine, *Napoleon's Last Campaign in Germany* (London, 1913)
Ratcliffe, B., *Marshal de Grouchy and the guns of Waterloo* (London, 1942)
Reboul, F., *Campagne de 1813* (Paris, 1910)
Siborne, Captain, *History of the War in France and Belgium* (London, 1844–52)
Stanhope, P. H. *Notes of Conversations with the Duke of Wellington, 1831–1851* (London, 1888)
Thiry, I., *Iéna* (Paris, 1964)

Russian campaign
Fabry, G., *Campagne de Russie*, 5 vols (Paris, 1903)
Marqueron, L., *Campagne de Russie*, 4 vols (Paris —)
Panckoucke, editor, *op. cit.*
Ségur, P. P. de, *History of the Expedition to Russia by Napoleon*, 2 vols (London, 1825)
Tarle, E., *Napoleon's Invasion of Russia, 1812* (London, 1942)
Vossler, H., *With Napoleon in Russia, 1812* (London, 1969)

OTHER BIOGRAPHIES AND AUTOBIOGRAPHIES
Bernstorff, E. von, *Ein Bild aus der Zeit 1789–1835*, 2 vols (Berlin, 1896)
Boyen, H. von, *Erinnerungen aus dem Leben des Generalsfeldmarschalls Hermann von Boyen*, 3 vols (Leipzig, 1889–90)
Brandt, H. von, *Aus der Leben des Generals Heinrich von Brandt* (Berlin, 1869)

Clausewitz, Carl von, *Über das Leben und den Charakter von Scharnhorst* (*Historische-Politische Zeitschrift, i*, Berlin, 1832)

Conrady, E. von, *Leben und Wirken des Generals Carl von Grolman*, 3 vols (Berlin, 1894–96)

Droysen, J. G., *Das Lebens des Feldmarschalls Grafen York und Wartenburg*, 3 vols (Berlin, 1851–52)

Ense, von Varnhagen, *Blücher* (Berlin, 1933)

Ergang, *The Potsdam Führer: Frederick William I, Father of Prussian Militarism* (New York, 1941)

Haggard, A. C. P., *Madame de Stäel* (London, 1922)

Henderson, E. F., *Blücher and the Uprising of Prussia against Napoleon, 1806–1815* (London, 1911)

Herold, J. C., *Mistress to an Age: A Life of Madame de Stäel* (London, 1959)

Klippel, G. H., *Das Leben des Generals von Scharnhorst* (Leipzig, 1869–70)

Lehmann, Max, *Freiherr vom Stein*, 3 vols (Leipzig, 1902–05)

Marwitz, F. von der, *Aus dem Nachlasse Friedrich August Ludwigs von der Marwitz*, 2 vols (Berlin, 1852)

Meinecke, F., *Das Lebens des Generalfeldmarschalls Hermann von Boyen*, 2 vols (Stuttgart, 1895–99)

Müffling, F. C., *Aus Meinem Leben* (Berlin, 1851)

Regele, O., *Feldmarschall Radetsky: Leben, Leistung, Erbe* (Vienna, 1957)

Rochow, Caroline, und Marie de la Motte-Fouque, *Vom Leben am preuss. Hofe, 1815–1852* (Berlin, 1908)

Scholtz, G., *Hermann von Boyen, ein Lebensbild* (Berlin, 1936)

Schwerin, Gräfin Sophie, *Eine Lebensbild* (Berlin, 1909)

Sybel, von, *Gneisenau und sein Schwiegersohn, Graf Frederick Wilhelm von Brühl* (Berlin, *Historische Zeitschrift*, Band 69)

Unger, W. von, *Blücher*, 2 vols (Berlin 1907–08)

——, *Gneisenau*, (Berlin, 1914)

GENERAL WORKS

Carlyle, Thomas, *The French Revolution* (London, 1889)

Earle, E. M., editor, *Makers of Modern Strategy* (Princeton, 1961)

Foch, Marshal, *The Principles of War*, translated by H. Belloc (London, 1918)

Gooch, G. P., *Germany and the French Revolution* (London, 1920)

Holborn-Hajo, *A History of Modern Germany, 1648–1840* (New York, 1964)

Howard, Michael, editor, *The Theory and Practice of War* (London, 1965)

——, *The Franco-Prussian War* (London, 1967)

Liddell-Hart, Basil, *The Ghost of Napoleon* (London, 1933)

Taylor, A. J. P., *The Course of German History* (New York, 1962)

Treitschke, Heinrich von, *Germany History in the Nineteenth Century*, 7 vols (New York, 1915–19)

Index